Early Modern History: Society and Culture

General Editors: **Rab Houston**, Professor of Early Modern History, University of St Andrews, Scotland and **Edward Muir**, Professor of History, Northwestern University, Illinois

This series encompasses all aspects of early modern international history from 1400 to *c.*1800. The editors seek fresh and adventurous monographs, especially those with a comparative and theoretical approach, from both new and established scholars.

Titles include:

Guido Alfani
CALAMITIES AND ECONOMY IN RENAISSANCE ITALY
The Grand Tour of the Horsemen of the Apocalypse

Caroline Castiglione
ACCOUNTING FOR AFFECTION
Mothering and Politics in Early Modern Rome

Robert C. Davis
CHRISTIAN SLAVES, MUSLIM MASTERS
White Slavery in the Mediterranean, the Barbary Coast, and Italy, 1500–1800

Rudolf Dekker
CHILDHOOD, MEMORY AND AUTOBIOGRAPHY IN HOLLAND
From the Golden Age to Romanticism

Caroline Dodds Pennock
BONDS OF BLOOD
Gender, Lifecycle and Sacrifice in Aztec Culture

Elizabeth Drayson
THE LEAD BOOKS OF GRANADA

Steve Hindle
THE STATE AND SOCIAL CHANGE IN EARLY MODERN ENGLAND, 1550–1640
Katharine Hodgkin
MADNESS IN SEVENTEENTH CENTURY AUTOBIOGRAPHY

Craig M. Koslofsky
THE REFORMATION OF THE DEAD
Death and Ritual in Early Modern Germany, 1450–1700

Beat Kümin
DRINKING MATTERS
Public Houses and Social Exchange in Early Modern Central Europe

John Jeffries Martin
MYTHS OF RENAISSANCE INDIVIDUALISM

A. Lynn Martin
ALCOHOL, SEX AND GENDER IN LATE MEDIEVAL AND EARLY MODERN EUROPE

Peter Mazur
THE NEW CHRISTIANS OF SPANISH NAPLES 1528–1671
A Fragile Elite

Laura J. McGough
GENDER, SEXUALITY AND SYPHILIS IN EARLY MODERN VENICE
The Disease that Came to Stay

Samantha A. Meigs
THE REFORMATIONS IN IRELAND
Tradition and Confessionalism, 1400–1690

Craig Muldrew
THE ECONOMY OF OBLIGATION
The Culture of Credit and Social Relations in Early Modern England

Niall Ó Ciosáin
PRINT AND POPULAR CULTURE IN IRELAND, 1750–1850

H. Eric R. Olsen
THE CALABRIAN CHARLATAN, 1598–1603
Messianic Nationalism in Early Modern Europe

Claudio Povolo
THE NOVELIST AND THE ARCHIVE IN 17TH CENTURY ITALY

Penny Roberts
PEACE AND AUTHORITY DURING THE FRENCH RELIGIOUS WARS C.1560–1600

Thomas Max Safley
MATHEUS MILLER'S MEMOIR
A Merchant's Life in the Seventeenth Century

Clodagh Tait
DEATH, BURIAL AND COMMEMORATION IN IRELAND, 1550–1650

B. Ann Tlusty
THE MARTIAL ETHIC IN EARLY MODERN GERMANY
Civic Duty and the Right of Arms

Richard W. Unger
SHIPS ON MAPS
Pictures of Power in Renaissance Europe

Johan Verberckmoes
LAUGHTER, JESTBOOKS AND SOCIETY IN THE SPANISH NETHERLANDS

Claire Walker
GENDER AND POLITICS IN EARLY MODERN EUROPE
English Convents in France and the Low Countries

Johannes. C. Wolfart
RELIGION, GOVERNMENT AND POLITICAL CULTURE IN EARLY MODERN GERMANY
Lindau, 1520–1628

Melinda Zook
PROTESTANTISM, POLITICS, AND WOMEN IN BRITAIN, 1660–1714

Early Modern History: Society and Culture
Series Standing Order ISBN 978–0–333–71194–1 (Hardback)
978–0–333–880320–2 (Paperback)
(outside North America only)

You can receive future titles in this series as they are published by placing a standing order. Please contact your bookseller or, in case of difficulty, write to us at the address below with your name and address, the title of the series and the ISBN quoted above.

Customer Services Department, Macmillan Distribution Ltd, Houndmills, Basingstoke, Hampshire RG21 6XS, England

---

Also by Caroline Castiglione

Patrons and Adversaries: Nobles and Villagers in Italian Politics, 1640–1760.

Accounting for Affection

Mothering and Politics in Early Modern Rome

Caroline Castiglione
Brown University, USA

First published 2015 by
PALGRAVE MACMILLAN

Palgrave Macmillan in the UK is an imprint of Macmillan Publishers Limited,
registered in England, company number 785998, of Houndmills, Basingstoke,
Hampshire RG21 6XS

Palgrave Macmillan in the US is a division of St Martin's Press LLC,
175 Fifth Avenue, New York, NY 10010.

Palgrave is the global academic imprint of the above companies
and has companies and representatives throughout the world.

Palgrave® and Macmillan® are registered trademarks in the United States,
the United Kingdom, Europe and other countries.

ISBN 978–0–230–20331–0

This book is printed on paper suitable for recycling and made from fully
managed and sustained forest sources. Logging, pulping and manufacturing
processes are expected to conform to the environmental regulations of the
country of origin.

A catalogue record for this book is available from the British Library.

Library of Congress Cataloging-in-Publication Data

Castiglione, Caroline.
Accounting for affection: mothers, families, and politics in early modern
Rome / Caroline Castiglione.
    pages cm.— (Early modern history : society and culture)
Includes bibliographical references and index.
ISBN 978–0–230–20331–0 (alk. paper)
    1. Families—Italy—Rome—History—17th century. 2. Mothers—Italy—
Rome—History—17th century.   3. Rome (Italy)—History—1420–1798.
I. Title.
HQ630.15.R66C37   2015
306.8509456'32—dc23   2014049656

Typeset by MPS Limited, Chennai, India.

For Marie Celeste, true to her name
neither this life nor death could hold her

Contents

List of Illustrations

Acknowledgments

Give me other mothers and I will give you another world.[1]

St. Augustine (354–430 CE)

A mother's love is instinctive, natural love, while a woman's love for her father contains an element of duty, that for her husband, an element of principle. And, by as much as love outweighs duty and principle, so the bond of maternity outweighs those of marriage or filial obligation.[2]

Moderata Fonte (1555–92)

Most mothers just try to figure out what they're supposed to do – and how they can do it in public.[3]

Erma Bombeck (1927–96)

From the ruminations of a medieval theologian to the musings of a late twentieth-century comic, motherhood has preoccupied its critics and its participants for centuries. So many aspects of it remain controversial, including the one raised by Moderata Fonte in the Renaissance: Does maternal affection constitute a unique expression of human relations, and if so, of what sort? Why motherhood came to have a political valence in the seventeenth century was the question with which I began my own research, for the implications of that shift have haunted the experience of the maternal ever since. Immersion in archival sources convinced me that the intersection of the maternal and the political in the seventeenth century (while significant) was but one of the nexus points where women crafted their ideas on mothering. Their disputes over family history, their participation in medical conflicts, and their struggles over the religious debates of their day also influenced their vision of the maternal. This book maps the contradictions at these interstices in the city of Rome – it traces the navigation by specific women through the dilemmas that constituted family life. During such familial controversies, women insisted on the validity of a mother's role as familial advocate (or *mater litigans*) in what contemporaries called the "theater" of Rome. It was an activity as necessary as a mother's attention to her children's physical survival. Women articulated the maternal as central to patrilinear dynasties. They praised the merits of love (downplaying its dangers) and raised maternal affection to the standard for all family members' behavior. They advanced the idea in the judicial arena that children's wishes should not be ignored in dynastic politics. A modern configuration of maternity would elide these seventeenth-century combinations and instead confine the maternal to a sphere separate from the political. It is to the complexities of early modern motherhood that this book returns. It illuminates how women shaped the familial and the political in their times, with words and ideas that transcended these two categories, and without understanding (of course), the long-term implications that their celebration of the maternal would hold for their descendants.

Any work that has traversed so many unforeseen excursions in primary sources and historiographical fields inevitably has done so with the generosity of institutional support and good-natured comrades. Early inspiration and essential advice for my interests in maternal matters came from the series editor, Edward Muir. For his continued editorial input and thoughtful mentoring, I am especially grateful. Sincere thanks belong also to the anonymous readers of the book manuscript, as well as to Holly Tyler and Jenny McCall at Palgrave Macmillan for their suggestions in producing the book. Critical to the illustrations and genealogical information included here have been the contributions of Suzanne Scanlan, Lisa Tom, Mona Delgado, and Alessandra Franco. Irina Missiuro's editorial expertise helped tremendously to bring the volume to its final form.

This book would not have been completed without fellowships from the American Council of Learned Societies; the Howard Foundation; and research support from Brown University, especially the Cogut Humanities Center Faculty Fellowship, the Wendy J. Strothman Faculty Research Award in the Humanities, and the Salomon Award. I am also happily indebted to dear colleagues at Brown University in the departments of Italian Studies and History, whose warm welcome some years ago made all the difference to what this work and its author became. I thank them individually for their interventions in the pages that follow, along with the archivists, and Italian and American colleagues who shared their knowledge as this project evolved. I extend similar thanks in specific chapters to conference audiences for their stimulating questions and suggestions.

Without the wise insights of John Marino (patiently repeated as necessary over the years), I would have lost rather than found my way to closure here. To Giovanna Benadusi and Beth Hyde, I owe the double debt of scholarly know-how and engaged friendship that inspired me to live and to write better. For loving kindnesses amidst losses and occasional triumphs, I thank the global Castiglione–Martinez–Clemente network in all its memberships and nomenclatures, but especially Bob and Sam for their treks through Italy and my mother, Joyce, and late father, Paul, whose encouragement underwrote all my journeys.

This book is dedicated in loving memory to Marie, a beloved sister who was parted too young from those who loved her. Her expansive mind and lively spirit took in everything while she tended to the detailed practicalities of protecting her corner of the earth and its inhabitants. A more fitting monument to her would be for us to do the same.

Introduction

Figure 0.1 Antonio Tempesta, *Plan of the City of Rome*, 1645. Detail with Campo de' Fiori. Courtesy of www.metmuseum.org.

Rome, January 1646. In the darkness of a winter evening, a mother and a boy moved toward the sounds of soldiers and the flickering lights in piazza Campo de' Fiori (Figure 0.1) – a lively market square by day, a convenient meeting point at night – for it was near the home the two had just abandoned. Either the cold or the weight of the secret the boy carried must have overwhelmed him, because although already 11 years old, he arrived in the piazza in the arms of his mother. His two older brothers and older sister trailed alongside their father, who was disguised in hunter's dress. All the children wore the garments of pages, but if the mother also wore a costume, no one has recorded it. Perhaps the bulk of a child long past the age to be carried was enough to mask that she was Anna Colonna (1601–58), descendant of one of Italy's oldest noble families, wife of the former pope's nephew (now disguised beside her as a lowly hunter), and mother of the four children making their way toward the carriages waiting for them in the piazza.

Her husband Taddeo Barberini and his brothers had reaped the benefits of their uncle Maffeo's long papacy as Urban VIII (r.1623–44). The greatest artists and architects of the age had celebrated the Barberini in gargantuan ceiling paintings, controversial expressions of religious piety, and unique palace architecture that dazzled Rome and served as model for ambitious monarchs elsewhere. The Barberini had temporarily been the equivalent of royalty, simultaneously divinely sanctioned and unabashedly worldly. Nothing escaped their purview, not even the most renowned scientist of the age. Galileo endured condemnation by the Church orchestrated by the anger and the insecurity of Urban VIII. The restless territorial and dynastic ambitions of the Barberini led them to war with the rival Farnese family over an extensive holding in the papal realm, the Duchy of Castro. The Farnese successfully converted the local conflict into a war with European implications and with European powers in battle against Barberini hubris. After the disastrous conflict, the death of Urban VIII placed them under intense and perhaps life-threatening scrutiny by the succeeding pope, who exploited popular animosity over Barberini taxation to raise charges of war profiteering. Slipping out of Rome in disguise appeared to be the surest way to safety.

As wife of the nephew of the pope, Anna had had a recognized public and diplomatic role that positioned her, with her husband's family, at the height of the political and social power structure of seventeenth-century Rome. In 1646, her future and that of the Barberini was far from clear in the hazardous aftermath of Urban VIII's papacy. The best place to wait out this political storm was one of the Barberini properties in the countryside. Anna put down her son, Nicolò, with the promise that she too would join them soon in their rural refuge. But the boy set her straight: "It is night now, Signora Madre, we're not going to the country, we're running away."[1] Since her brother-in-law Cardinal Antonio Barberini had already fled for Paris, her son's comment probably made it clear to Anna that her departing family were abandoning Rome not for one of their nearby country estates, but for the French capital.

What was Anna thinking as she watched the carriages transporting her children fade from view? A few years before, alone in Rome waiting for her husband to return from the war that the Barberini could neither win nor end, she had dreamed of a day in the country, sitting in the sunlight while the children played, and Taddeo benevolently surveyed the scene.[2] Her letters to him had emphasized her loving attention to her children, although they also reveal a worry about her own death and a recognition that her time as mother was drawing to a close. Others had now to mentor the children, especially the boys, who stood on the threshold of adult life in Rome. But it was unlikely that she had imagined that her years of intimate mothering would end in the Campo de' Fiori standing with the armed vassals of the Colonna, watching the Barberini family, to which she thought she had also belonged, leave her behind. Later, Anna and the Barberini would all reunite again briefly, in Paris, but her life as mother, as she had known it, ended that night.

This book analyzes the complexities of bearing, tending, putting down, and walking away from children that constituted mothering in early modern Rome. It begins with Anna's maternal dilemmas and concludes with those of her great-granddaughter. Aristocratic mothers were at the mercy of a dynastic system not of their own making, but all families, even lower-class ones, could have their patrilinear elements and painful rifts. Yet, aristocratic women played specific and somewhat unusual roles within their social context. In the volatile politics of the Roman scene, a woman served as an ambassador for her families' interests; as an intermediary between her powerful clerical brother-in-law and her husband; as an advocate in the judicial arena, for her own interests or those of her children.[3] The step from her expected diplomatic duties to protest was a short one, and the trip entirely justified if a child was involved. These aspects of a mother's labor had profound legal, cultural, and political import, although we have only recently begun to explore motherhood beyond its biological implications in the early modern world.[4] Matriarchy clearly has a history at least as complex as patriarchy, and it was as mothers that many women gained a political voice in the past.[5]

By the time of Anna's shocked goodbye, paternal authority and the patrilinear family were enshrined in European society, reinforced by legal, literary, artistic, and religious signposts. Beginning in the fifteenth century, Renaissance humanists had solidified its relevance in treatises on the family that packaged ancient arguments for merchant households. Such texts stressed the subordination of the wife and mother to paternal authority, assumed to be the ultimate guide to familial prosperity and longevity. Chastity and obedience, thrift and patience, were the paragon virtues for female family members.[6] Baldassare Castiglione's oft-reprinted dialogue on court society seemed to broaden the range of acceptable female behavior.[7] Women at European courts did craft wider roles for themselves than those of their peers in republican regimes. Simultaneously, however, among noble families emerged stricter systems of inheritance that designated much of the family patrimony as belonging to a single male heir and confined most of his sisters and brothers willingly or unwillingly to religious life. The paterfamilias in such a domestic enterprise was likened to a monarch and vice versa.[8] The submission of individual and especially female desire to larger dynastic plans was an assumed feature in the emergence of primogeniture.

Roman mothers offered correctives to the culture of this male-controlled patrilinear family, defined genealogically by men and by the relatively new legal strictures of primogeniture. They insisted on the mother's prerogatives in rearing her children, the centrality of maternal love to the dynastic enterprise, and the value of the mother's contribution to the governing of a successful aristocratic family. Alongside the patriarchal family emerged calls for its reform: for the view of the family as a consortium of interests, rather than the domain of an absolute monarch; for the psychological and physical extrication of the family from issues of inheritance; for the consideration of a child's wishes for her future, rather than the confinement of most of the children to the convent or the monastery; for the elevation of maternal love to the standard by which the affection of all family members would be measured. In Rome, these maternal critiques of the patrilinear family became highly developed by the early eighteenth century, when maternal love won a place alongside dynastic ambitions as a paradigm of family life. This book examines how Roman women elaborated such maternal arguments, appropriating the vocabularies of politics, religion, family history or medicine to advance their claims for the significance of the mother's role. In the eyes of their critics, their success rendered Rome a city in which matrifocal politics had won the day. And although a lively scholarly tradition has debated the extent to which the Papal States were governed by a centralizing monarchy or whether they remained an incoherent patchwork of territories and interests,[9] little attention has been paid to how the judiciary gendered the politics of Rome, causing men who faced litigating mothers to seek political patronage in Naples, Milan, or Vienna rather than in their native city.

Roman aristocratic mothers were not alone in their attempts to elaborate alternative family practices and an expanded role for mothers within the family.[10] Those who praised motherhood in the seventeenth century imagined it as a resolution of the contradictions of female identity:

daughter, wife, mother, Christian, legal advocate, financial counselor, mediating figure at the nexus of two families. That any relationship could resolve this constellation of social roles was impossible, of course, but the increasing number of sources that lauded maternal feeling suggests a heightened engagement with its potential to clarify women's lives – to offer women who became mothers a well-defined identity that could serve as a moral fulcrum in a world that imposed so many conflicting expectations upon them. Ruminations on the significance of maternity to the lives of women surfaced in the early modern debate on the place of women in society, in which literate women (including some married women) defended their sex against misogynist critiques, old and new.[11] Known by its French appellation, the *querelle des femmes* was a literary debate whose published works encompassed more than two thousand titles, a disproportionate share of which were written by Italian women.[12] Even the female founder of the genre, Christine de Pizan, although she wrote in French, was Italian in origin.

Authors who gained popularity in the seventeenth-century *querelle des femmes* brought a new inflection to the deliberations, adding observations from contemporary life to the display of literary virtuosity that was by then characteristic of the *querelle des femmes*.[13] Such texts captured the shift in attitudes toward the patrilinear family with which Roman mothers were also engaged. The Venetian author Moderata Fonte (1555–92) compared the relative weight of a mother's burdens within such a system in her dialogue *The Worth of Women* (published posthumously in 1600). The triumph of maternal love was celebrated in her clear manifesto: "A mother's love is instinctive, natural love, while a woman's love for her father contains an element of duty, that for her husband, an element of principle. And, by as much as love outweighs duty and principle, so the bond of maternity outweighs those of marriage or filial obligation."[14] Fonte reversed the earlier Renaissance notion that maternal love, which originated in a woman's body, was inferior to the love of the father, which was supposed to begin in his mind.[15] She elevated love as superior to duty and praised maternal love above all, the latter revisions, as we shall see, critical to remaking the maternal and familial in seventeenth-century Rome. Both the dramatic dialogue of the *querelle des femmes* and the quotidian discussions among Roman family members undermined the terms of the patrilinear, and suggested possibilities for change.

Roman women operated in a political and social context that was particular to them – an elective monarchy in a city that was more open than most to the influx of new noble blood and to cash infusions of any variety. Their struggles paralleled, nonetheless, those of women elsewhere, wherever states gained political leverage by aligning their interests with those of female subjects. The emergence of new ideas of mothering and the family intertwine the development of the state, especially its judicial expansion.[16] Controversies in religion, changes in medical care, and disputes in politics also intersected the history of motherhood in Rome. The activities, letters, petitions, and testimony of Roman aristocratic mothers open a window on the role women played in the evolution of the maternal. Familial disputes could be propitious moments for challenging family practice. Such familial disputes, beginning with the struggles of Anna Colonna and ending with the generation of her great-granddaughter, illuminate the politicization of the family in Rome and its shift toward its modern maternal orientation.[17]

Roman Aristocrats in a Resurgent Monarchy

Motherhood was but one of the many aspects of aristocratic life influenced by the presence of an elective monarchy in Rome. When the papacy returned in the early fifteenth century to Rome from exile in Avignon, the papal capital was not an impressive town in comparison with the sparkling Renaissance cities of Florence or Venice, sophisticated centers of banking, trade, and manufacturing. Rome's economy was largely pastoral and agricultural, its densest population huddled along the bend of the Tiber, its streets narrow and frequently clogged with pilgrims or gorged with livestock that grazed with abandon on the ruins of ancient Rome and in the shadow of the city's rock quarry, the Roman Colosseum. Rome's nobility was venerable and competitive. Its greatest families, such as the Colonna and the Orsini, vied to control the city as if it were a disputed rural fief. The popes reconquered the city by force, remade it in relatively short order by a combination of aggressive city-planning and vast architectural enterprises such as the rebuilding of the basilica of Saint Peter. The old local aristocratic rivals to the medieval popes were coopted into the Renaissance papal monarchy: Pope Martin V (r.1417–31) was Otto Colonna, an election that initiated a productive fusion between old dynasties and the new papal ambitions. The papacy had come back to Rome to stay.[18]

Rome drew to it the greatest Italian families that quickly saw the merits in advancing one of their sons in this resurgent monarchy with its escalating need for financiers, learned men, artists, and architects. Their influx rendered Rome a new kind of city: by the sixteenth century it was the closest approximation in Italy to the center of a national elite. Such connections were forged between the highest-ranking clerics of the Roman Catholic Church, the College of Cardinals, whose relations married and intermarried each other.[19] A family whose most promising son had risen to this elite level of the church hierarchy had hopes of the papacy, an office that offered even greater possibilities of familial enrichment through its control of benefices and offices of lucrative import for their holders. Winning the papacy pulled a man's relations to Rome, where they Romanized themselves by purchasing territories, buying or building urban palaces, and making great marriages for their children. They aimed high and grabbed what they could: who knew when the papal throne might come their way again?

Because of the elective nature of the papal monarchy, alongside the papal court there emerged a constellation of highly competitive aristocratic courts that rivaled one another in the pursuit of worldly magnificence and the race for the papal tiara. By the mid-seventeenth century, the families competing at such levels were hybrids of old aristocratic families of medieval origin (like Anna Colonna's family) and outsider families who had migrated to Rome (like the Barberini who were originally from Florence). Relative to other Italian cities, sixteenth- and seventeenth-century Rome became – and remained – open to newcomers who were drawn to the money and the possibilities the papacy could offer. Capturing the papacy (or a cardinal's hat) necessitated the appearance of high social standing and the commitment of at least one son in every generation to the church. Successful aristocratic families thus replicated the dynamic at the top of the theocratic state: a powerful cleric, his brother, his brother's wife and his brother's children attempted to advance the interests of the larger lineage through ecclesiastical, marital, and financial strategies.[20]

Guiding an aristocratic family through the political upheavals of Rome necessitated the participation of all family members, female and male. It has rightly been called a "team sport," and aristocratic women played a vital role in such a familial system.[21] Like men, women relied on networks of relatives, friends, and associates to promote family interests. The mother's contacts could be as important in the advancement of the children as the father's relatives.[22] In certain activities, aristocratic women could move with more freedom than aristocratic men. Women received visitors to their family palaces, initiated and solidified alliances through an exchange of visits and through arrangements of marriages. Maternal activity was a necessity to the flourishing of their dynasties. One explanation for the centrality of female activity to Roman dynastic politics was the fragility of male honor in early modern Rome. The rules of decorum surrounding male encounters had become so complex that it was nearly impossible for men to meet each other without some damage to their honor. It was problematic for men's carriages to pass each other on the street without incident, much less for men to speak to each other in the same room. Since women, according to this theory, lacked the characteristics of male honor, they could, therefore, serve their families in such activities with less risk.[23]

But what was the aristocratic family to which women and men pledged their service? Contemporaries and later historians relied on the nominal shorthand, "the aristocratic *casa*." The *casa*, however, was simultaneously a lineage, a historical legacy, a living family, and a financial enterprise. An individual *casa* was often symbolized by a particular and costly palace in Rome. Nothing came closer to encapsulating the family's identity on the Roman scene than its prestigious home. For the very oldest families who had vied for power in the chaotic Rome of the Middle Ages, the family palace doubled as fortress, sometimes a fortress that grew organically out of the ruins of the ancient city, such as the Theater of Marcellus, first an ancient amphitheater, then a thirteenth-century fortress for the Savelli, and finally, in the sixteenth century, the palace of the formidable Orsini family (Figure 0.2). Aristocratic families used such structures to forge ties to their neighborhoods and solidify connections between them and the tenants of their palatial enclaves.[24] By the next century, new social and familial configurations required that the aristocratic *casa* reflected the changing times. The Barberini palace, built between 1628 and 1637 in the newly developing northwestern neighborhood on the Quirinal hill, uniquely inscribed in architecture the bifurcated family strategy by which one brother in each generation carried on the family lineage, and at least one other brother took clerical vows and attempted to rise through the church (Figure 0.3). The palace thus designated a wing for the clerical brother(s) (on the right) and a wing for the brother who was chosen to carry on the lineage (on the left). Into its design were also incorporated the apartments for Anna Colonna, whose rooms were more attractive and better situated than those of her husband.[25]

The *casa* also implied beloved landed estates in the countryside because, for all the urbanization and sophistication of the new Rome, it had not shaken off its country roots. The fiefs partially defined the family's identity and were the source for its aristocratic titles and income. A *casa* required the preservation of properties held in *fedecommesso* or entail. Entail placed properties in a trust, and required heirs to withhold them from sale. In Rome, wills were the documents

166   **ROMA**

Figure 0.2 *Teatro di Marcello*. From Lodovico Totti, *Ritratto di Roma Moderna*. Rome, 1638. Courtesy of Houghton Library, Harvard University (IC6.T6412.638r).

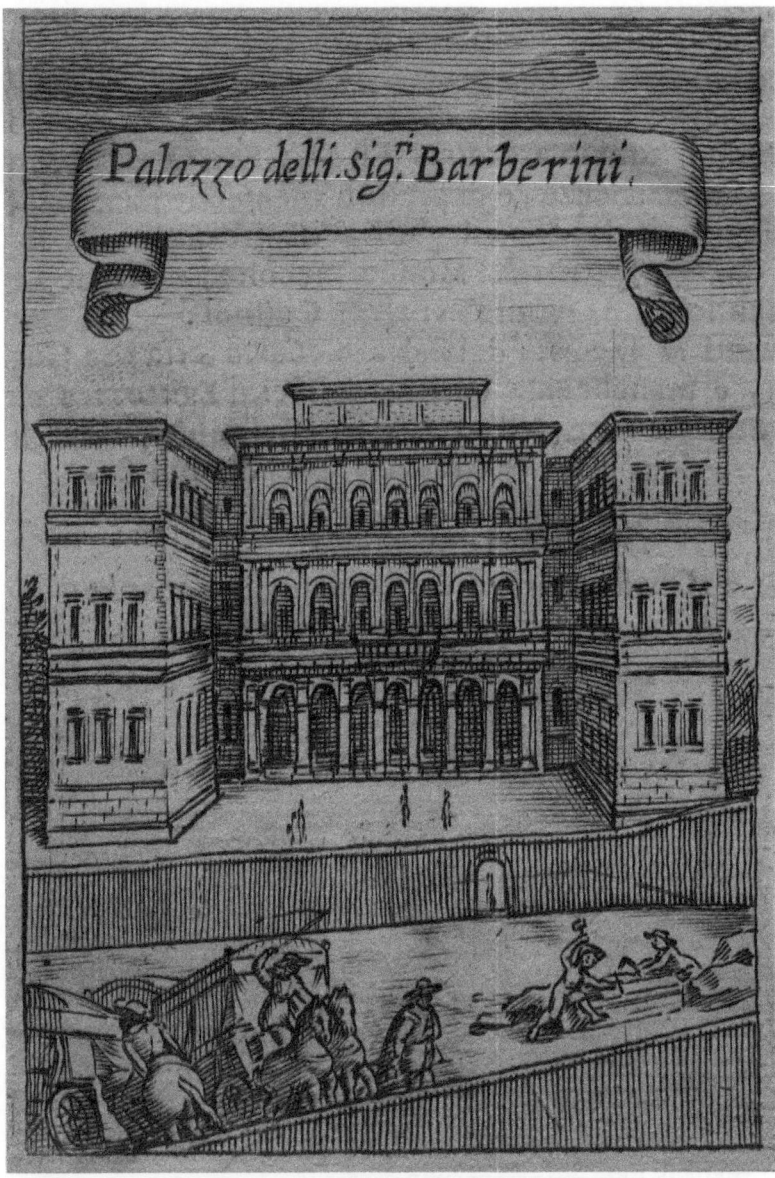

Figure 0.3 View of the Palazzo Barberini. Courtesy of Museo di Roma, Gabinetto Comunale delle Stampe.

that most frequently established *fedecommessi*.[26] During the seventeenth century, an increasing number of families converted property held in *fedecommesso* to primogeniture, an even more restrictive form of entail, which designated a single male in each generation as the universal heir.[27] Simultaneously, more of the family's assets were designated as entailed holdings than ever had been before.[28] In dire economic circumstances, the temptation to reduce the complexity of the aristocratic *casa* to its assets held in primogeniture was very great. But such a limited definition scarcely captured the complex meaning the *casa* held for Roman aristocrats.[29]

While aristocrats continued to derive their identity from their illustrious past, the nature of competition in Rome also demanded destabilizing expenditures, to make sure that one's family remained among Rome's relatively open ruling class. Sometimes, cash-strapped families could be forced to make tough choices about which of their properties to sell and which to hold onto, as the inflation of the sixteenth century and the costs of a sufficiently grand life in Rome continued to rise. The alienation of prestigious territories was scarcely a desirable outcome, and the increasing recourse to primogeniture in the seventeenth century was at least, in part, an attempt to arrest the financial free fall of some dynasties. Other measures included rationalizing and reducing expenditure and drastically reducing the number of daughters and sons who could marry. None of these potential solutions was implemented without controversy, and disgruntled family members, including and especially women, were active in determining the strategy to rescue a family in trouble.

The Making of the *Mater Litigans* in Rome

In Rome's complex familial system, a woman acted as an informal ambassador for her families' interests through her visits with other aristocratic families. She kept open the critical lines of communication between her natal and marital families and between her brother-in-law the cleric (sometimes considered to be the head of the family) and her husband. She wrote letters to her clerical brother-in-law to keep him informed about events in Rome, since missions for the church took him on the road as part of his expected activity if he wished to advance in its hierarchy. A Roman mother was involved in the arrangement of the marriages of her offspring, especially her daughters. She continued such activities across the phases of her lifetime, including during pregnancy, unless nausea or other complications curtailed her public appearances.[30]

Roman mothers thus acquired a certain diplomatic deftness that was increasingly expressed (with their rising literacy) in writing.

Yet, writing remained a specialized trade, requiring five years to learn to do well. It was typically the purview of men. It emerged only gradually as an acceptable female activity as women's literacy moved from focusing exclusively on reading to the practice of rudimentary writing.[31] As relative newcomers to writing, women's models for female literacy were few, especially in Italy, where women and writing were still considered an unusual enough combination that they were rarely captured together in painting.[32] Representations of learned women were typically those of another time and place, such as the Sibyls, figures from Greek antiquity who could also foretell the future. The Cumaean Sibyl was sometimes depicted with the symbols of music because she was supposed to have sung her prophecies, a detail included by Domenichino in his sumptuous rendering of this ancient icon (Figure 0.4). Italian women were inspired by Saint Teresa of Avila (1515–82), whose status as religious writer made her literacy more acceptable in the early modern context.[33] Teresa helped bridge the gap between women and script, as a comment by Anna Colonna in her last will and testament reveals. The noblewoman described a painting of Saint Teresa (likely an image by Romanelli) as part of the altar decoration of a chapel convent of which she was the chief patron. The popular and better known moment associated with Saint Teresa was her religious ecstasy, which was also the subject of Romanelli's painting (Figure 0.5). Anna's reference to it in her will was "Saint Teresa is there writing," indicating that, for the noblewoman, writing was the noteworthy activity that memorialized the saint on canvas.[34]

Neither the Sibyl nor the saint capture what must have been the ordinary experience of writing in the lives of most aristocratic women, who wrote under the demands of family politics (only their autographic letters were considered acceptable), amidst the exigencies of the domestic (sometimes with a large number of children in tow), or while on far-flung travels that set a few women in motion along with their husbands across the Mediterranean. As Costanza Pamphilj, writing from Sardinia, explained to her niece: "Please excuse the bad handwriting, but I am writing you while sitting on the floor." Living conditions were crude. Trailing along with her were at least two young children.[35] Although writing was required of Roman aristocratic women, their formal training with a pen remained limited. It was typically so minimal that they wrote with an improvised handwriting and an inventive orthography that make some of their letters a challenge to decipher. An aristocratic

Figure 0.4 Domenichino, *Cumaean Sibyl*, 1610. Courtesy of Galleria Borghese, Rome.

woman was still expected to write on her family's behalf, even if her male relatives then later complained about the mediocre results.[36] Letters crafted in the beautiful hands of secretaries were amended with an apology in the noblewoman's hand, to explain why he, rather than she, had written the letter.[37]

Figure 0.5 Giovanni Francesco Romanelli, *Ecstasy of Saint Teresa*. Convent of the Discalced Carmelites of Regina Coeli (since destroyed). Courtesy of Istituto Centrale per la Documentazione, Rome.

The proliferation of women's letters and other informal writings indicates the growth of their audiences, both enthusiastic and adversarial. Writing by women found its place in the rising sea of litigation that washed over Rome in the seventeenth century.[38] Mothers employed their literacy to navigate these treacherous waters, for the same skills employed in service to the dynasty might be used against it.[39] The explosion of lawsuits in the seventeenth century had its origins in early Renaissance Italy, when the peninsula's burgeoning economy, expanding political regimes, and diverse legal traditions fueled an increasing demand for lawyers and notaries. By the eighteenth century, Italy had a very large number of lawyers.[40] In Rome, with a population of approximately 160,000, there was one lawyer for about every 140 people in the city.[41] Access to notaries was even easier than contact with lawyers. Notaries recorded routine transactions, business deals, marriage agreements, and last wills and testaments for clients who ranged from the highest to the humblest echelons of society.[42] Across the social spectrum, urban residents acquired familiarity with the intricacies of the law and law courts. Legal literacy was high in Italian cities; it extended to women who, with some provisos, could dispose of and receive property, and with the sanction of male kin, act as the guardian for their children during widowhood.[43] Aristocratic women sharpened their legal understanding in consultation with specialists, but as one litigating mother reminded her critics, though she sought the advice of legal counselors, they did not control her.[44] Legal maneuvers were also much the talk of aristocratic family meetings or *congregazioni*, which many women attended, especially in periods of familial crisis.

The figure of the *mater litigans* (the litigating or advocating mother) became a fixture on the Roman scene. It was a short step from women's required diplomatic functions to the contentious activity of legal protest. I have invented the term *mater litigans* as a way to describe the legal acumen and tenacity shared among Roman noblewomen.[45] She is everywhere in the Roman archives and merits fuller recognition in the politics of the seventeenth-century city. From a mother's point of view, advocacy might be entirely justified if a child was involved or if she thought she might save the family from further harm. Such activities bridged the distance between marriage, widowhood, and even religious life. From her deathbed, the noble widow-turned-nun Camilla Orsini Borghese/Suor Maria Vittoria simultaneously tended to her soul and assessed potential marriage partners for her granddaughter. Not even death would free her of her such earthly obligations – she would continue to be, her daughter-in-law predicted, "a good advocate before

God" for the causes dearest to the family members she left behind.[46] The *mater litigans* was a secular inflection of older medieval beliefs about the Virgin Mary: the Mother of God who out-argued the devil for souls stranded at the border between salvation and damnation. Largely pushed aside by official church doctrine of the Catholic Reformation (which favored the deferent and obedient Mary),[47] she lived on in the practice of maternal advocacy in the eternal city.

To challenge the status quo, litigating mothers navigated a labyrinth of judicial avenues, at times as confusing to contemporaries as they are to twenty-first-century readers today. After the return of the popes to Rome, the city's population quintupled in size, adding to the strain on the two judicial systems that adjudicated conflict in the growing city.[48] Both papal law courts and the law courts of Rome's city government had their roles in the seventeenth century. Roman aristocrats preferred to avoid the city government courts when possible. The most prestigious papal court in Rome was the Sacra Rota, but lawsuits were expensive and exposed the problems of the family to many eyes. Litigants could approach the Rota obliquely, asking a magistrate to provide an opinion in the matter, using the opinion to discourage a familial rival from a full-blown lawsuit. The Cardinal Vicar was another possibility, a key figure on the Roman scene, who tended to issues related to morality and familial disputes in and around Rome.[49] Approaching him might keep a family matter a bit more private than the courts could be expected to do. Alternatively, Roman aristocrats appealed to the pope himself, beginning with a plea in writing to the papal *auditore*, a key official of the Apostolic Chamber. By the seventeenth century, the *auditore*'s role was primarily judicial, and he could find himself on the front line of complex familial disputes.[50] The financial and legal difficulties of aristocrats were so numerous that an entire papal bureaucracy had to be created to handle them. The Congregation of the Barons heard petitions from creditors seeking recourse for the unpaid loans of noble families, but it could be consulted on a variety of disputes regarding inheritance, succession, dowries, and the problems of general indebtedness among Rome's nobility.[51]

With its overlapping tribunals and myriad means of protest, Rome was, as Hanns Gross has aptly called it, "a many-headed hydra," where power was dispersed in many places, where one might slay a judicial adversary only to see her rise to fight again.[52] Disputes could be complex, pitting some children's interests against others, since mothers showed a proclivity for sticking up for their girls, especially concerning their marriage prospects. Relations with family members could sour, and a litigating mother might not shirk from fighting her own children or from taking on her husband's relatives, if the situation required it. The *mater litigans'* vision of what was best for the family could be controversial, questioning clear legal precedents and undermining longstanding dynastic practices.

One litigating woman in the seventeenth century incited outrage among her foes and still strikes terror among Roman aristocrats today. She was Marie-Anne de la Trémoille (1642?–1722), called Marianna while in Rome. Born in France, bad luck and her husband's early death in exile brought her to Rome, where she married the last Duke of Bracciano, Flavio Orsini (1620–98) in 1675.[53] The Orsini were already in financial trouble, without a male heir, and faced a number of formidable legal entanglements. Flavio lacked direction and liked to hide out in the family castle in Bracciano; his brother Lelio lived as something of a recluse in the Orsini palace; his cardinal brother Virginio passed away in 1676.[54] Marianna, however, brought litigious energy and an encouraging enthusiasm toward any financial efforts of the part of Flavio.[55] She also supplied a convenient dowry in which to conceal some Orsini assets from creditors and international connections who helped secure pensions from the French King to Flavio.[56] While Flavio was alive, she acted as co-litigant with him, meeting with lawyers and keeping track of the cases, and after his death, she continued his legal battles.[57] Marianna was certainly the greatest female litigant of the seventeenth century, with 12 cases before the Congregation of the Barons alone. Though the couple remained childless, Flavio ultimately chose Marianna as his universal heir, leaving her to battle on without him and not specifying who should inherit beyond her.[58] Whereas the Orsini brothers – Flavio and Livio – were hesitant, Marianna was decisive. Her legal acumen served the Orsini well. Marianna arranged the marriage of her sister, Louise-Angélique, to a Roman aristocrat, and she successfully advanced the career of her brother, Joseph Emmanuel de la Trémoille, in the church. She repeated the efforts of many fortune seekers to the papal city before her: she Romanized the La Trémoille and attempted to fortify the Orsini of Bracciano with this infusion of French relatives.[59] To the chagrin of the Gravina branch of the Orsini family, Marianna remained in control of the Orsini Palazzo di Pasquino. The Orsini of Gravina were eventually able to wrest the family archive from her, but not until the ascension to the papal throne of one of their relatives (Benedict XIII, r.1724–30).[60] Otherwise, things remained as Marianna had devised them: with her sister's husband as heir to the disputed Orsini palace, with her clerical brother successfully established as member of the Rota court, and with the possibility of re-founding the Orsini through an offspring of her sister and brother-in-law. If her sister had not died young from cancer in 1698 (the year Flavio also died) or if Marianna had not become distracted by larger diplomatic missions in service in Spain on behalf of the French king, she might have succeeded.[61]

What Marianna laid bare was the female contribution to Roman aristocratic life – the way in which, as the noblewoman Eleonora Boncompagni put it, a formidable aristocratic woman might be "the backbone of the *casa*."[62] Although not a mother, Marianna behaved like a Roman matriarch, and her persistence counterbalanced Flavio's confused dynastic loyalties and ambiguity about deciding the future of the Orsini family. Marianna was not, however, an exception among aristocratic women, but rather an extreme version of a larger pattern in Roman society. Women appeared frequently among the cases heard by the Congregation of the Barons, whose archives illuminate the financial and familial dilemmas of Rome's great and powerful. Women were a sizable group in the throng of petitioners and litigants to the Congregation, present in about 24 percent of all the cases the tribunal adjudicated in the early modern period.[63] For scores of women, involvement with the judgment of the Congregation was a once-in-a-lifetime event. Such women could be found among the creditors clamoring for the settlement of the debts owed to them by noble families. While such litigants could be of modest background, they included Roman noblewomen as well as the Queen of England, who, in 1696, sought payment on her loan to the Ludovisi family. Most Roman families whose entangled affairs were aired before the tribunal had one of their women actively involved in staring down the demands of the dynasty's creditors. More than 40 women in Rome dealt with the tribunal two or more times in their lifetimes, in order to settle disputes over property or inheritance. The Congregation of the Barons was but one such avenue for such concerns – a single outlet in a city of many judicial venues. The strong presence of women in its adjudications underscores the widespread presence of women in the courts of Rome.

The activities of Roman mothers were part of a larger pattern of female advocacy in the Italian peninsula, where widows sought custody of their children from Florentine magistrates, female servants used wills to redress financial delinquencies on the part of their Tuscan masters, and unhappily married women sought exits from their marriage through Venice's Patriarchal Court.[64] As law courts became more central to state power, women became stronger advocates for themselves and their families and learned how to navigate expanding judicial and bureaucratic systems. I have called the constellation of such practices among peasants in early modern Italian states "adversarial literacy," and this term also clearly applies to the strategies of aristocratic women and to the emergence of the *mater litigans* as an integral aspect of Roman mothering.[65] Its potent combination of legal tenacity and emotional tenderness reached its fullest elaboration in the seventeenth century.

The extent to which such activities constitute political behavior in the early modern world is now easier to recognize since historians have come to understand politics as "an ongoing bargaining process" between rulers and their subjects.[66] Historians of Italy have extended the argument even further, identifying law courts as the critical vehicles for cultivating allegiance between rulers and subjects. Law courts were the site for politics and political change to the extent that such courts allowed marginal members of society to bargain for their rights. The impact of this kind of state-building had European-wide repercussions, but it had a particularly profound impact on the history of the peninsula.[67] Italy's legal culture fueled its public debates, defining their terminology and contributing to a variety of political and potentially conflicting responses to them.[68] A careful examination of the *mater litigans* reveals both the possibilities and the limitations of the law for remaking the domestic and the political.

Domestic Affairs and the Theater of Rome: Hidden and Public Transcripts of Family Life[69]

The model of the *mater litigans* extended beyond the confines of Rome and can be linked to the shifting attitudes toward motherhood emerging elsewhere in seventeenth-century Italy. It is but one of the veins to emerge from the excavations in the massive archives generated by judicial institutions. Scholarly exploration in such materials has undermined longstanding interpretations of popular belief, state development, and the history of the family, among other fields. The past that has emerged in light of these discoveries has forced historians to tell a more complex story about society and the historical actors who shaped in it. Debates still rage over the extent to which judicial sources in particular provide us access to lived experience or to unmediated beliefs on the part of those who testified or who litigated. The inequities of power between judges and the interrogated, between lawyers and litigants shaped the testimonies that emerged in the legal arena. Trial evidence, some scholars believe, may best reveal the performance required by its setting – a carefully rehearsed script by which a person hoped to achieve his or her legal aims – winning a case, escaping punishment, or settling a score.[70] Seventeenth-century Romans were well aware of this aspect of law courts. They considered them an integral part of what they referred to as the "theater" of Rome, or more simply *"il mondo romano"* [the world of Rome].[71] To take a familial dispute into a tribunal or before a papal official was to expose what they called their "domestic affairs" [*affari domestici*] to the scrutiny of outsiders. The audience and the performance aspects of legal disputes were well understood by contemporaries. Within judicial documents, however were places where the testimony coached by lawyers broke down or where the differences between magistrates and litigants reached an impasse. Such "ruptures" provided opportunities for employing trial evidence to understand people in the past.[72]

In the case of the Roman *mater litigans*, her fledgling literacy fueled both legal interventions and informal epistolary sources. Both are useful for reconstructing the maternal dialectic that allowed mothers to recognize and sometimes praise social rules, but neither to internalize them without question nor to practice them in every circumstance. The proliferation of such writing by mothers allows us to compare both the "public" and "hidden" transcripts of family conflict.[73] Letter writers clearly recognized the extent to which their epistolary experiments would circulate far beyond their intended recipients, blurring the distinction between public and hidden testimony.[74] But, because of the deficiencies in their training as writers, noblewomen's letters often have an informal and improvised aspect. Artifice was difficult for such writers to come by, although it was at times attempted. Many women's letters instead have a conversational and rambling quality that leaves the reader with the impression of eavesdropping or gaining access to thoughts the writer had not mastered the art of censoring or fashioning. Their letters are closer to oral culture, rather than to the literary style of their époque, and capture the words uttered within the palace walls and the practices of everyday life that constituted mothering in the seventeenth century.[75]

While typically scholars have focused their efforts in either judicial or epistolary sources, this book grapples with conflicts that were neither exclusively in the domestic sphere nor entirely in the theater of Rome, but which unfolded in the overlapping territory between these spaces of aristocratic life. Such a focus limits the number of examples one historian can pursue, but it allows for a more nuanced interrogation of the problem of mothering and family life in early modern Rome. A study based exclusively on legal records would highlight the adversarial aspect of family life, which was certainly present. However, a close scrutiny of the evidence in family archives reveals that judicial interventions influenced but did not define familial dynamics and connections. Some Roman men, for instance, who were the beneficiaries of the patrilinear system, were increasingly ill at ease with its demands by the late seventeenth century.[76] A full understanding of Roman family life has to account for this ambiguity, which presents itself in a variety of ways behind the scenes of litigation – the half-hearted pursuit of lawsuits, the appropriation of the language of maternal love to describe an uncle's or a father's affection, the refusal to make out a will that would have obliterated many aristocratic mothers' possibilities for litigation. The unwillingness of men to specify a daughter's dowry or to exclude a wife's future role in the family suggests the ambiguous relationship of men to the demands of patrilinear dynastic politics. Flavio Orsini was not by any means the only Roman aristocratic man who had difficulty performing his expected gender role.[77] Male ambivalence created a void into which women spoke the alternatives for the family, including the triumph of maternal love as the standard of familial affection and the relaxation of the rules of patrilinear inheritance. Mothers were frequently at the fraying edges of family politics and family practices, improvising loopholes, importing the language of religion and of politics because legal precedent was quite solidly against them, extrapolating from the medical and the domestic in order to sketch a larger role for women and for the familial improvements they espoused. Their linguistic appropriations and conceptual bricolages were not all successes – chronicled here are also their failures, the conflicts in which they were defeated in the short term because there were no extant words or legal frameworks that existed to support the alternatives of which they dreamed.

Aristocratic mothers beckoned their male relatives to the ill-defined territory of emotion, typically expressed around their oft-mentioned word, affection [*affetto*], but also in the terms of passion [*passione*] or love [*amore*]. These contrasted with the more measured language of *caritas* [the love required of a Christian], duty [*dovere*], or service [*servizio*], the latter two defining the appropriate relationship of the individual to the *casa*. Such terms had established pedigrees and reinforced familial hierarchies. Love, on the other hand, conjured danger and inspired erroneous behavior. It was evoked to explain why an individual would do something that was socially or politically illogical, such as loving a person below his or her social rank[78] or insisting that the wishes of a child for her future should be considered. Religious belief counseled specific limits on the place of love in family life.[79] Love for children was considered necessary, although too much parental love was viewed as a sin. In popular sayings of the day, the death of a child could be attributed to the mother's excessive love for her or him. A parent's wish to allow a child to marry as s/he wished was tempered by the fact that such a marriage might threaten the financial ruin of the family. Parental love had its virtues and its perils.

The mothers in this study found the rhetoric of danger increasingly less meaningful than the positive benefits of affection in family life. This detail is significant and underscores the fallacious and unfortunate path of twentieth-century scholarship that recounted the history of the family in terms of simplistic progress: the notion that people in the past did not love their children, and familial relations lacked an affective element until the coming of the modern family. The modern family's arrival was postulated anywhere from the Renaissance to the eighteenth century.[80] What changed in the seventeenth century was not the arrival of affection, but rather the erosion of belief in the risks associated with it, and a more secure place for emotional connections amidst dynastic considerations. This was the shift the mothers in this study attempted to bring about.

It is also easier to capture what the Roman aristocratic mothers meant by maternal love if we set aside rigid dichotomies between emotion and reason. The philosopher Martha Nussbaum has suggested that emotions are "judgments" and are best considered as part of "intellectual activity."[81] Because emotions are concerned with external objects that mean a great deal to us – but which we cannot control – emotions can generate a sense of "neediness and lack of self-sufficiency."[82] Although they have strong physiological components, emotions are not merely physiological reactions.[83] As Nussbaum shows in persuasive detail, emotions have been (and continue to be) viewed with some suspicion in the West, yet without taking emotions into account, systems of ethics remain inadequate and too remote from human experience. While Nussbaum argued for the fuller incorporation of emotions into ethics, historians too have begun to consider the impact that emotions and shifts in perceptions of emotions have had on social, legal, and political change.[84]

Maternal love certainly presents its own particular interpretive problems, since from the seventeenth century forward, there was a tendency to locate it in positive opposition to the defects of the social order. In light of this idea's long and far-reaching influence in modern Europe, it can be challenging to analyze maternal practices and feelings that could (and later did) all too easily become caricatures, inescapable traits inherent in the female sex, localized in the home, and contrasted with reason and the public world of men.[85] Our preconceptions thus make it especially difficult to uncover maternal affect in its premodern form. The dual goal here is to understand what contributed to its triumph – what problems did it resolve? – and also to analyze the complexities of mother love between the seventeenth and the early eighteenth centuries without assuming that its future stereotypes defined its past manifestations.

This book illuminates these nuances by analyzing specific controversies in which beliefs in love's pitfalls, the demands of dynastic politics, and the claims of maternal affection came into conflict with one other. For instance, one Roman aristocratic mother, Ippolita Ludovisi, argued in favor of allowing all of her many daughters to marry if they wished, rather than placing most of them into the convent, as had been the family practice. Ippolita's affection for her daughters triggered a crisis of religious meaning regarding the highest ethical choices possible in family life. Her defense of her daughters' free will became for her a matter of conscience that she also believed was in the best interests of the dynasty. In the increasingly medicalized world of childrearing, close attention to the daily ills of children was proscribed as the work of mothers, but as the aristocrat Eleonora Boncompagni observed, such intense attention could lead the mother to fall into the sin of excessive love. Understanding the history of medicine from the point of view of parents (still a vastly understudied topic in medical history) allows us to map what I call the nexus of impossibility at the core of the domestic and familial in Rome. Mothers were frequently at this boundary, where all that they were required to do could not be successfully reconciled. Their attempts to resolve the contradictions among the medical, the spiritual, and the maternal can tell us a great deal about the process by which familial love, and especially parental love, emerged as the paramount considerations in domestic life, triumphing over the venerable discourse on its perils.[86]

The predicaments of Roman mothers came to my attention during my search for archival materials related to village politics. By chance, I came across one of the mothers in this study, Olimpia Giustiniani, in conflict with her two sons, one of whom mistakenly wished to rule the family to its detriment as "absolute Padrone" and one of whom thought that the master ledger must be master of familial relations. In the course of trying to reconstruct the political culture of villagers, I found that Olimpia also came into focus, for she reminded me of the villagers, with her scratchy makeshift literacy and a language of protest improvised from words typically employed for the purpose of her subjugation. Though it would have pained her to hear such a comparison, she intrigued me enough to see whether there were other women like her. One of her seventeenth-century rivals, her son Cardinal Francesco Barberini Junior, unwittingly provided me with some of the best evidence for the kinds of resistance women who married into his family could be capable of, even if it was much to his own regret. In another case examined here, he battled his sister-in-law Teresa Boncompagni in the 1720s for custody of her only child. Teresa was unlike any Roman mother I had yet encountered: she wore the mantle of affectionate motherhood without apology; she elided the language of service and duty; and she defended the rights of her daughter to have a childhood, rather than to be married without knowing her mind at the "tender age" of 12. Teresa wrote as though the audience that would accept her views already existed. Although it was Cardinal Francesco who won the case, he insisted that his victory was limited because both the magistrates and the "world" of Rome actually sided with her – they acknowledged that her emotional tie to her daughter was more significant than the legal and dynastic preoccupations that motivated the cardinal.

Though I recognized (as did Cardinal Francesco) that the times in Rome had indeed changed, supporting Teresa's arguments if not securing her a victory, I became curious about the kind of mother who had raised such a daughter. Did protest travel along matrilines the way inheritance passed through men? Teresa's easy confidence sent me in search of her mother, Ippolita Ludovisi, who, I discovered, had successfully argued for all of her daughters to marry if they wished, rather than be forced into the convent against their will. Ippolita herself was so astonishing that she too implied some preceding influence – and the search for her mother led me to look for Costanza Pamphilj, whom I found sitting on the floor in Sardinia, a few years before she gave birth to Ippolita. She was dead not two years later, and the possibility for maternal influence seemed to die with her. Ippolita, however, later found a formidable substitute mother in the form of her much older sister-in-law, Eleonora Boncompagni, who loved her as a daughter and who taught her, through some 800 pages of correspondence, what it meant to meet the other challenges of motherhood in the nursery, where death and illness were the adversaries, and a new professionalization of the medical profession challenged the place of mothers in the care of their children. Eleonora Boncompagni suggested the ways in which the independent advocacy of mothers in the theater of Rome echoed their autonomy in the domestic affairs of the nursery, where they were just as engaged as they were in their diplomatic duties.

These women's lives reveal the multifaceted dilemmas of mothering in Rome that have given shape to this volume. Though they were not monolithic in their thinking about maternal affection, they all argued that their maternity offered them insights and skills that had validity alongside social norms, legal precedents, and dynastic considerations. The women read their own social milieu as potentially receptive to their claims and so their aspirations are intriguing maps of what was plausible in their social contexts.[87] By the end of seventeenth century, they found a political outlet and a social milieu more supportive of their ideas, underscoring the importance of the intersection of their lives as mothers with the political culture of Rome. Anna Colonna, who inspired the first chapter, introduces the reader to the seventeenth-century difficulties for women who wished to delineate a greater space for the maternal in the dynastic organization of Rome. Anna attempted to describe the possibilities of a new configuration of the family, centered on father-mother-children, or what we would call the nuclear family, an entity for which she had no word, since *casa* referred to the dynasty in its multifaceted complexity and *famiglia* referred not only to blood and marital relations under the same roof, but also to the servants who co-resided with them. Olimpia Giustiniani's mothering dilemmas provide the focus for Chapter 2, which analyzes a maternal perspective on the governing of the aristocratic *casa*. Olimpia accepted the outlines of the dynastic as constitutive of Roman family life, but she rejected any son's claim to rule it absolutely or regulate it exclusively by the account book. She offered maternal insights on the family as best governed by the calculation of "the interests common to us all," as she defined its politics. In the midst of their political and diplomatic roles, women were also charged with reproducing the family and keeping their offspring alive, activities that they associated with their "domestic affairs," but about which we still know relatively little. The voluminous correspondence of Eleonora Boncompagni, explored in Chapter 3, sheds light on the practices and the hierarchies of this domestic space in which aristocratic mothers claimed the autonomy that allowed them to reject the views of men (including those of their husbands and physicians) if they thought it in the best interest of their children. Yet, the nursery was also a solitary space in which the mother had to make decisions that might mean life or death for her offspring, a place in which it was difficult to reconcile the medical, the maternal, the familial, and the spiritual. If women successfully reared their children to adulthood, they were then considerably involved in the transition of those children to adult life. Ippolita Ludovisi's determination to allow all six of her daughters to marry if they wished forms the centerpiece of Chapter 4. In order to create such possibilities for her girls, Ippolita had to challenge her in-laws' management of familial finances and reject their view of free will that had confined extra girls to convents. By Ippolita's theological reckoning, she reoriented the patrilinear toward a truer theological interpretation of free will and expanded the successful future of the *casa* to include the well-being of all of its heirs, regardless of gender.

Throughout the conflicts at the center of these chapters, Roman aristocratic women employed the language of service and affection and wrestled with the relationship of emotion to duty. They took the dynastic family for granted, though they argued for a larger place within it for mothers and for the wishes of children. In the last chapter, Teresa Boncompagni illuminates a late expression of such female advocacy in Rome and outlines the contours of mothering in a new century. Her struggle was a familiar one: holding on to her child during her widowhood, a moment when children (who legally belonged to their father's families) typically were raised by their uncles. To the dismay of her adversary brother-in-law, it was matrifocal politics that had triumphed in Rome – mother love and affective familial connections had won recognition alongside dynastic politics, the deeds of venerable ancestors, social norms, and legal frameworks. Her view of the centrality of maternal affect to the well-being of the child and the family certainly had a long future ahead of it, eventually becoming the enduring configuration of womanhood embedded in European modernity. Perhaps the model of the future-seeing Sibyl is not a bad allegory after all for the efforts of Roman aristocratic women, who anticipated the triumph of affection in the family alongside its dynastic goals and business enterprises. It is unlikely that they could have imagined the enduring problematic of equating the family with the maternal against which modern feminism would continuously struggle.[88] Nor could have they anticipated a world where the political arena would exclude the participation of women. Unwittingly, they also played a role in such changes, but they did so in order to defeat the limitations on their own lives, employing the failing categories at hand to challenge the status quo of their times.

1
Practicing Motherhood When the Definition of "Family" Is Ambiguous

Anna Colonna and the Barberini Dynasty, 1627–47

Even in a city where exemplars of maternal virtue were abundant, Anna Colonna Barberini (1601–58) stands apart from her peers.[1] Her heroic attention to dynastic interests and her devotion to her husband and her children were intertwined with her enthusiasms for Catholic Reformation piety, a tangle of commitments that she reinvented throughout her life. As the wife of Taddeo Barberini (1603–47), nephew of Pope Urban VIII (Maffeo Barberini, r.1623–44), her experiences incorporated all the intense demands that could be brought to bear upon a mother of her stature (Figures 1.1 and 1.2). She served brilliantly as the nexus between the Colonna and Barberini dynasties, expanding the connections between them for the benefit of both. Since she was the wife of the pope's nephew, she played an important public role in Rome, receiving dignitaries on behalf of the pontiff, writing letters, and reciprocating visits to other aristocratic families.[2] From the late 1620s through the 1640s, she also faced the burdens of childbearing and the rearing of her four children who survived the perils of infancy. Mothering consumed her days, caused her anxiety and simultaneously inspired her affections. When the Barberini fell under intense scrutiny after the death of Urban VIII in 1644, Anna remained in Rome as the beleaguered family's staunch defender while the Barberini men sought safety by fleeing to Paris. She was the *mater litigans* par excellence, left to save what the men of the Barberini dynasty were in no position to defend.

The origins of Anna's heroic Roman motherhood are sometimes linked to the failure of the Barberini to support her. Greatness in this equation was thus a compensatory strategy for the defects of marital kin. Yet Anna's maternal dilemmas were by no means unique to her. Divided and complex loyalties characterized the allegiances of Roman

Figure 1.1 Attributed to Gabriele Renzi, *Princess Anna Colonna Barberini.*
Courtesy of Albright-Knox Art Gallery, Buffalo, NY.

aristocratic mothers. There was no single entity called the family to
which such women belonged.[3] In medieval and early modern Europe,
as in antiquity, the family (*familia, famiglia*) included not only the
kin group but the servants as well. This was the sense in which Anna
still used the word *famiglia*, although increasingly in the seventeenth
century more of the male servants were lodged in a dwelling separate
from the family palace.[4] Anna referred to the Colonna as "*la mia casa
paterna*" [my paternal house]. In her letters to Taddeo she referred to
the Barberini as "*la vostra casa*" [your House]. Aristocratic *case* [houses]
in Rome were typically ruled by their high-ranking clerical members,[5]

Figure 1.2   Bernardino Cametti, *Prefect Taddeo Barberini*, 1704. Courtesy of Museo di Roma.

and included a far-flung set of relations linked through a venerable male ancestor. In Anna's lifetime, the Barberini family had no fewer than three high-ranking clerics – Pope Urban VIII, Taddeo's older brother Cardinal Francesco Barberini (1597–1679), and his younger brother Cardinal Antonio Barberini (1608–71).

Most dear to Anna was the nameless unit of herself, the children, and Taddeo. Although she hoped to promote good will among all these familial enterprises, she clearly favored the unit of *madre-figli*-Taddeo and tried to argue for its interests first, while never completely dismissing the other dynastic undertaking.[6] Anna's concept of the family is best glimpsed in her correspondence with Taddeo, which reveals how she acknowledged the multifaceted dimensions of the dynastic, but still insisted upon the preeminence of an entity for which she had no specific name. Anna operated on its behalf in a world where there was a highly evolved iconography of aristocratic identity and discourse of dynastic loyalty, both richly elaborated first in the Renaissance and re-elaborated in Italy often thereafter. Against this venerable historical framework, Anna had to improvise without vocabulary and with little precedent for prioritizing the *madre-figli*-Taddeo unit. There were many nuances in her improvisation, a complexity borne from witnessing the grave difficulties of her natal and marital families. There was danger in her solutions as well, since the noblewoman insisted on prioritizing the nuclear family, but this fragile configuration would not survive the near annihilation of the Barberini dynasty in the 1640s. Anna's struggle to reorient the dynastic enterprise to the nuclear family brings into view both her improvised alternatives and the complex web of obligations, loyalties, and interests in which Roman aristocratic mothers operated in the seventeenth century.[7] Its patterns were intricate but its threads could easily fray, as the life of Anna Colonna underscores.

The Future of Two Dynasties: The Union of Anna and Taddeo

At the relatively late age of 26, Anna Colonna was married to Taddeo Barberini, a man two years her junior. Like her sisters, she was religiously devout and dreamed of becoming a nun. Her family decided otherwise.[8] Taddeo was so deferent to his father and his uncle, Pope Urban VIII, that he allowed them to pick his bride.[9] The marriage in 1627 was decidedly one of dynastic strategy. The ceremony sanctifying the political union was celebrated by the pope himself in Castel Gandolfo.[10] During the 1620s, the destiny of the Barberini soared in Rome: two of Urban VIII's nephews had already been made cardinals, and Taddeo secured a prestigious alliance for the family with his marriage to Anna, daughter of the Conestabile of Naples, Filippo Colonna.[11] Such an alliance accomplished key goals for each side. It united the Neapolitan branch of the Colonna family with the rulers of one of the most prestigious states in Italy. All great aristocratic families throughout the peninsula sought such ties to the papacy. The marriage also allowed the Barberini, a relatively modest family of newcomers to Rome, to make an alliance with a dynasty far more ancient and prestigious than they.

The rightfulness of the union was incorporated into the design of the Barberini's innovative family palace on the Quirinal hill. Begun during the late 1620s and unique in its design, the Palazzo Barberini alle Quattro Fontane enshrined in architecture and celebrated in its ceiling paintings the significant place of the family in Rome.[12] Its design embodied the bifurcated strategy of Roman aristocratic families: the north wing was intended for Taddeo, the brother who was designated to carry on the lineage, and the south wing was planned for the clerical brother, Cardinal Francesco[13] (see Figure 0.3 in the Introduction). The wing of each brother, though joined by a connective loggia, was conceived as a separate palace.[14] Because of her significant diplomatic role, Anna's apartments – in the wing of the palace designated for Taddeo – were more impressive than those of her husband.[15] It was she, more than he, who would play a critical ceremonial function in the city. She received important visitors after they had made their official visit to the pope.[16] Taddeo's mother, Costanza, had formerly and unhappily played such a role, and she gladly relinquished it to Anna after her marriage to Taddeo. Thereafter, Costanza required no more of the palace space than simple rooms for her religiously austere lifestyle and an attic room for her chickens.[17]

Anna's role was significant in helping the Barberini avoid the controversies over precedence that frequently occurred in the encounters between aristocratic men in Rome, where tempers and titles were inflated during the reign of Urban VIII.[18] For the Barberini, such conflicts had intensified after Taddeo was awarded the ceremonial title of Prefect of Rome in 1631.[19] He assumed that he had preeminence in all encounters, including in meetings with visiting dignitaries, who preferred to avoid meeting with Taddeo altogether in order to avoid insults to their honor or potential challenges to the honor of the pope's nephew.[20] Taddeo sought to avoid similar encounters, so great was the intensity of such controversies.[21] By contrast, men tended to accord precedence to women, simplifying the encounter between Anna and visiting dignitaries and other well-born Roman aristocrats.[22]

Anna Colonna's apartments in the family palace were, therefore, designed with great care in light of her ceremonial activities. In her apartments, architecture and painting did much of the boasting about the rightfulness of Barberini rule. Visiting dignitaries such as Cardinal Richelieu of France could observe in Anna's apartments on the *piano nobile* a complex iconographical program, which legitimated Barberini power and illustrated the intertwined destiny of the two families joined by the marriage of Anna and Taddeo.[23] The ceiling painting in her *salotto*, *Divine Wisdom* by Andrea Sacchi, for instance, allegorized wisdom as woman whom the worthy ruler must pursue and love[24] (Figure 1.3). The complex scriptural allegory announced the union of the two families in its details. Barberini bees, lions, and suns furthered the allegorical argument that the Barberini were indeed "lovers of

Figure 1.3 Andrea Sacchi, *Allegory of Divine Wisdom*, 1629–33. Courtesy of Galleria Nazionale D'Arte Antica in Palazzo Barberini.

wisdom" and that their rule was thereby divinely sanctioned.[25] Subtle details incorporated symbols of the Colonna family, including the family emblem of the column, depicted as the cloud upon which Wisdom dwells.[26] Sirens, which had appeared in Colonna family crests since the mid-sixteenth century, materialized in the paint and in the plaster in the corner of the ceiling cornice.[27] With arms raised, the sea creatures hoisted Barberini suns into the celestial realm in which Divine Wisdom ruled.

From the *salotto*, visitors could enter the family chapel, where depictions of the Holy Family sanctified the procreative future of the family.[28] A critical role for Anna was to bear the next generation of the Barberini, and this aspect of the marriage found its allocation in palace architecture in a private stairway that connected the noble couple's two apartments.[29] During the planning of the *salotto* and chapel Anna was pregnant with her son Carlo, born in early 1630.[30] One of the earliest public events in the chapel was the baptism of Anna's daughter, Lucrezia, in September of 1632.[31] The Palazzo Barberini alle Quattro Fontane not only incorporated the glories of Urban VIII's papal rule, but also illustrated the future of the dynasty that would continue beyond his papacy, a future that began with Taddeo's marriage to Anna.

Anna was the critical nexus in the collaboration between these two dynasties, old and new. She had to balance her activities on the part of natal and marital kin alongside the considerable physical and psychological demands of raising the Barberini heirs amidst the reality of high childhood mortality. She attended to this latter task with the utmost seriousness and anxiety. Her activities were multivalent, consuming her days; as she summarized life during her children's early years, "I don't have time to eat."[32] Anna's difficulties in her life with the Barberini are well known, better known than her successes. Her adversities have been traced to her marriage to the pope's nephew, a union which supposedly doomed her to difficulty and betrayal. Taddeo was considered by some a proud and difficult man.[33] In this context, it might be assumed that Anna's attitude toward him remained in the realm of "dutiful respect required of a woman in seventeenth-century society."[34] The whole of their marriage has sometimes been extrapolated from the events following the death of Urban VIII, when Taddeo and his brothers found themselves under intense and perhaps life-threatening scrutiny by the succeeding pope, Innocent X (Pamphilj, r.1644–55). In fear for their lives, they fled for Paris, taking Anna's children with them, but leaving Anna behind, against her wishes, without letting her know their plans, and without the financial means to sustain herself.

In an emotional letter to her son, Carlo, in 1646, Anna complained that Taddeo had abandoned her in Rome and that he would not allow her to join her children in France.[35] The historian Pio Pecchiai compared her experience at this time to that of a guard dog abandoned at the family palace, the ultimate symbol of misplaced fidelity.[36] Anna nonetheless launched a counteroffensive against the deeds of the succeeding pope that contributed to the eventual rescue of the Barberini property from confiscation by the new pontiff. Then, during the last decade of her life, Anna, now widowed, hoped to recover her dowry from the Barberini to complete her building projects at a Roman convent. She was forced to sue the Barberini for the return of her dowry – scarcely a fitting compensation for the depth of loyalty she had shown them a decade earlier.[37] The dismal experiences of Anna with the Barberini even had their modern echoes, since the best known image of her, a seventeenth-century portrait bust attributed to Gabriele Renzi, was sold off by the Barberini and ended up in a North American museum during the twentieth century (Figure 1.1). The sculpture's peripatetic future seemed to repeat Anna's painful displacement from the dynasty that desperately needed and distanced her in the years following Urban VIII's papacy.

While the sequence of events can certainly be substantiated in the sources, the interpretation oversimplifies the long history of Anna in the Barberini family, and the extent to which she successfully generated a close rapport with Taddeo, even if that bond was more difficult to extend to his brothers and did not survive the grave difficulties of the Barberini family in the mid-1640s. Despite attempts by the architectural historian Patricia Waddy to reform our opinion of him, Taddeo may indeed have been a maddeningly difficult man, but that a woman could attempt a relationship of trust and affection with such a man is not only possible, it is scarcely an unusual scenario.[38] Yet, his rapport with relatives was less haughty than his behavior on the streets of Rome and with visiting dignitaries to the city.[39] Taddeo also seems to have valued Anna and her advice during the earlier decades of their marriage. That she alone was considered dependable enough to tend the Barberini affairs during their self-imposed exile is certainly an indication that he trusted her. She did, after all, eventually, join him in Paris. She left Paris, apparently to continue her religious patronage in Rome, although more likely because she thought she could be of greater service to the Barberini children in Rome rather than in the French capital.[40] There is little, in any case, in her letters of the 1630s and early 1640s that presages the couple's extreme difficulties of 1646, although there are hints of problems with his brothers. Finally, Anna's lawsuit, although outside the scope of this chapter, was scarcely a unique phenomenon, as widowed women were frequently at odds with their husband's family and their offspring for the return of their dowry.[41] The nature of dowries made such dilemmas exceedingly common. The earlier epistolary evidence suggests that Taddeo was in agreement with her wishes regarding the future use of her dowry for charitable purposes, even if their children and his brothers had difficulty later complying with his wishes.

Anna's earlier experiences in the Barberini family illustrate how she intertwined motherhood with her marital life, with her keen spiritual devotions as well as with her considerable attention to household management. Her use of the terms *affetto* and *amore* in terms of maternal activity echoed a refrain increasingly repeated on the peninsula in the seventeenth century. This chapter explores how Anna linked love, affection, and loyalty to a new vision of the family, which, in the mid-seventeenth century was fragile and destined for failure among the Barberini, but would continue to surface as a challenge to the dynastic and patrilinear version of the aristocratic *casa*.

Love and Trust in a Seventeenth-Century Family

As Anna balanced the myriad responsibilities incumbent upon the wife of the pope's nephew, she simultaneously bore the next generation of the Barberini family. Between 1628 and 1635 she gave birth to five children – two girls and three boys. Four of these children would live to adulthood; one, Camilla, died just before her second birthday.[42] Two would become clerics (Carlo and Nicolò) and one boy, Maffeo, and the surviving girl, Lucrezia, would marry. Anna fulfilled a critical obligation of bearing a sufficient number of children to carry on the lineage and to allow some children to enter clerical life and advance (as Carlo later did) at least to the cardinalate, a cherished goal on the Roman aristocratic scene.

Childbearing deepened her tie with the Barberini. Her love for Taddeo remained another link between Anna and the rest of the Barberini brothers. Anna sought to deepen her rapport with her marital kin as well as to forge a strong familial tie between husband, wife, and children. The letters of Anna to Taddeo provide clues as to the nature of this rapport and the success of her relationship with him, even if their affection and trust were extended with difficulty to his brothers.

The task of writing letters was among the many duties required of Roman aristocratic women of Anna's rank, although such women were rarely provided adequate instruction for their epistolary endeavors.[43] Anna's letters were thus orthographically inventive and sporadically punctuated. When Anna's handwriting was superseded in some letters by the elegant calligraphy and stiff formulas of the family secretary, the letter typically also included an apology for her not writing the letter herself.[44] Her grammatically suspect prose and scratchy handwriting was the trustworthy text desired by Taddeo, perhaps because her fluency more than compensated for the limitations of her penwomanship.

The first time Anna wrote extensively to Taddeo was when he traveled in service of the papacy in the early 1630s. It is clear from such writings that Anna assumed that Taddeo was a sympathetic reader who would be interested in her daily rounds of parenting alone three children under the age of four in the early 1630s – the endless search for wet nurses, the children's teething troubles, and their mysterious fevers. Her insights pour forth for pages: her organization of Taddeo's apartments and attention to his possessions and Barberini properties;[45] the recurring trouble with Taddeo's pages and other disrespectful servants;[46] the emotional cost of his absence to her and her fervent desire for his safe return;[47] minor thefts in the household; problems of her own health and excuses for delaying the medical remedy of purging;[48] and reports on the decisions made in meetings of the Barberini family, the *Congregazioni*, as such family meetings were called. In the second cache of letters from December 1641 to December 1643, written during the Barberini family's disastrous war against the Duke of Castro, the three children and a fourth child born in 1635 had all survived the perils of infancy and early childhood. Anna now faced the challenges of the moral and educational progress of the older children and the difficulties of situating in their careers her first two sons, who were on the edge of young adulthood.[49] A set of dangers mentioned in 1633 become more prominent in the 1640s: Anna felt the strains caused by difficulties across the generations of two aristocratic families, the Colonna and the Barberini.

If we assume that her letters in their meandering fluidity mimic her conversations with Taddeo, then they demonstrate a "subtle interplay" between the couple that psychoanalysts today associate with love.[50] At a minimum, Anna and Taddeo shared an intimate interest in the minutiae of the domestic and the dilemmas of the familial that suggests that their relationship was more than a dutiful exchange of ceremonial courtesies and conjugal duties. His absence left a gap in her life she attempted to fill by writing. He evidently expected the outpouring even if we lack the evidence that he responded in the same quantity.[51] If we take her at the words of the salutations and signatures of her correspondence, Taddeo was "her most beloved lord," and she was his "servant and consort" who "loved him as she loved herself." The latter is a tender closing, but its repetition might have inclined him to think it a formula. However, as she explained at great length in one of her letters, Taddeo could have married a woman "of a better family, with greater wealth, and more talents with which to serve him," but there was no woman who could have had more affection or a more sincere love for Taddeo. Nature or Fortune or God doled out the gifts of birth and wealth, so for them God was owed the praise. Taddeo, however, could never find a woman to match the love that "originated in her will."[52]

Tightly linked to her marital devotion was her maternal involvement with the Barberini children. In their very young years, their lives were precarious, as were those of all children in this period. The first Barberini offspring were received with jubilant attention by Taddeo's siblings. In Cardinal Francesco's account of Taddeo's life, he included a touching portrait of the antics of his little niece Camilla, who passed away very young.[53] Clearly, the Barberini brothers were devoted to the next generation of the family. Yet, the survival of the children rested squarely on Anna's shoulders, especially the selection of wet nurses, critical servants in an aristocratic household, since a woman of Anna's social status was unlikely to have breastfed her young children. Her letters from the early 1630s suggest that finding and retaining wet nurses for her children was a frequent activity for her, intertwined with dealing with the children's maladies. Since children were breastfed for as long as two to three years, Anna faced the difficulty of securing enough acceptable wet nurses for all three children. Breast milk was believed to have an impact on the moral as well as the physical development of the child, thus selecting the wet nurse was a particularly crucial choice.[54] Anna carried the responsibility of the choice of wet nurse, although she consulted with the Barberini physician, and she expected the long accounts of her wet-nursing dilemmas to be of interest to her husband. Anna interviewed and observed scores of women, eventually calling upon the niece of the wet nurse of Taddeo himself, a woman eliminated from consideration because she arrived at the Barberini *casa* with a seven-month-old baby girl who "looked like a cat."[55]

Given the death of her first child, Camilla, the physical ailments of her other children were particularly nerve-wracking. Anna juggled the inevitable dilemmas of the frequent childbearing practiced among the Roman aristocracy. In the early 1630s, Anna struggled actively to secure the survival of three children very close in age: Carlo (about three years old); Maffeo (about two years old); Lucrezia (about a year old or less). During their illnesses, she moved from her own apartments in the Palazzo Barberini alle Quattro Fontane to sleep on a makeshift bed in the children's room.[56] Anna related her everyday mothering dilemmas to Taddeo, describing the children's ordinary ailments, such as Maffeo's teething difficulties and his fever, as well as the physical demise of Carlo's wet nurse, whose ill health she described with emotion and as a divine punishment for Anna's sins. In the midst of the crisis over Carlo's wet nurse, Maffeo's fever continued, and the physician suggested that Anna secure a new nurse for him as well or "she could lose the child."[57] In the ups and downs of childrearing and through their ailments as toddlers and teenagers, Anna was always at her post, monitoring them at night, seeing to special dinners when they were ill, consulting with the doctors, soliciting Taddeo's advice about their future.[58]

Despite a variety of dilemmas, Anna expressed delight at her efforts on her children's behalf. To her great relief, by the early 1640s the Barberini children had passed the most dangerous years of childhood maladies, and her children's health was mostly good. Physically weakened by a mysterious ailment in her early forties, Anna shrugged off her miseries by noting she would rather be ill herself than have to witness the illness of her children, since she knew well the mortal peril that maladies could pose for them.[59]

While Anna sometimes referred to her attention to the children and the Barberini *casa* as an obligation, she more frequently framed her actions in terms of her *amore* and *affetto* for Taddeo and the children. She also acknowledged, however, that this love of hers could also be seen as a fault, but one that she hoped others would share: "I know that I am too fond of these children ... but I wish there were also others who were thinking about them."[60] Such feelings prompted her to disagree (or justified her disagreements) with some of the Barberini expenditures. "Motherly affection" inspired her to advance her opinion, and despite the shortcomings of the origins of her insights (they were rooted in her excess), she showed herself in no way willing to abandon them. Her love allowed her to frame her critique of the Barberini in terms of a higher good (the physical and financial survival of the children), revealed to her by the affection that she bore them.[61]

For Anna, Taddeo was an essential presence in their upbringing, the "absolute *padrone*" who completed the familial unit that occupied her days.[62] Through her letters, Anna attempted to deepen Taddeo's trust of her to an extent that would allow her greater autonomy in dealing with the affairs of the larger aristocratic household, or what she referred to simply as the "*negotij* [sic] *della Casa*."[63] Although she claimed ignorance in the management of certain undertakings, she argued that her love for him would teach her what she needed to know.[64] She requested more information from Taddeo about certain projects since "whoever walks blind falls down." She expressed dismay at the "disorders" of the *casa*, but trapped as she was, in the middle of "so many chiefs," she could scarcely list all of her concerns, suggesting instead that she would tell Taddeo everything "if I am still alive when you get back."[65]

Her position in the aristocratic household was certainly more powerful by the 1640s than it had been in the early 1630s. She tried to be transparent about her economic activities; to attend to specific financial transactions, including the purchase of a new fief; to offer financial advice, even condemning the behavior of the treasurer who failed to collect debts owed to the Barberini; or to take issue with the timing of liquidating certain Barberini investments.[66] Weeping, incompetent servants threw themselves at her mercy.[67] Anna was strict in her evaluations of employees, but capable of positive judgment and, in the right circumstances, advocated on their behalf.[68] In all things, she begged Taddeo's intervention, since she could not always make his employees obey her, but her advice was clear and it eventually won out. Documents that she requested, including summaries of investments and expenditures and other financial information, eventually passed through her hands to him. "The servants say that I am terrible," she admitted to Taddeo, but until he returned to manage the affairs of his household she would not have it otherwise.[69]

Anna's letters reveal the extent to which a highly motivated and active mother juggled conflicting obligations, but privileged the interests of the children over other interests. There was a tone of duty in Anna's account of her obligations to the Colonna family, and to the larger Barberini dynasty as well, whereas her love for her children is more closely intertwined with her love for Taddeo. Demarcating the "nuclear" from larger dynastic interests of the *casa* was difficult since Anna had no word for family in the nuclear sense we mean it today. For Anna, the *figli* could have a potential set of conflicting interests within the larger *casa*. She hoped this alternative nameless unit could be ruled by an "absolute padrone," Taddeo. He completed the unit she had in mind, which was not whole without him. She admitted that, in his absence in the 1640s, she sat down and wept with the children. This emotional revelation was embedded in a letter stuffed with concerns about the financial future of the children – economics and heightened emotions were frequently entangled in her mothering. She felt more acutely the need for Taddeo when the two boys (Carlo and Maffeo) were trying to sort out their futures – Maffeo was supposed to be the cleric, although as he reported to his mother, the idea repelled him if he wasn't going to be able to perfect his horseback riding, his true passion. During Taddeo's absence, Maffeo was named the abbot of Subiaco and should have been tonsured immediately, but Anna refused – she would not make such decision without her husband.[70]

Not even the Barberini brothers escaped Anna's scrutiny in her letters to Taddeo. Her surveillance of such matters probably cost her support from Cardinal Francesco who, along with his brothers, was more acquainted with the demure model of femininity represented by their mother.[71] Anna, by contrast, worried openly about whether Taddeo and his brothers, the Cardinals Francesco and Antonio, were sufficiently concerned with the financial future of the Barberini offspring. She reported with dismay how much she disagreed with the decisions of the family *Congregazioni*.[72] The decisions were only made to "spend more, no one ever talks about paying."[73] She knew the problem of increasing financial disarray of the Barberini firsthand – she reported that she was pressed by creditors of the family for payment as early as 1633, partly a problem caused by the shortcomings of the Barberini accountant, but a sign to her that the family spent more than it could reasonably expect to pay.[74] Although in this period Anna never sought a judicial solution to her differences with the Barberini, her letters outline the concerns that a *mater litigans* might well have with relations whom she judged lacking in sufficient foresight for offspring.

For though there was a social logic to the Barberini's costly magnificence, Anna regarded some expenditures as financial miscalculations that would be borne by the next generation: "These children," she wrote in 1642, "will not be as well-off as people think they will be."[75] The disparity between the present and future scenarios of the family would be exacerbated by the inevitable loss of the papacy, a day that Anna hinted at in her calculations of her children's future. Anna's oblique acknowledgment of this inevitable fact was dangerous territory, however, since speculations on the death of the pope were expressly forbidden by Pope Urban VIII, and he assiduously cultivated ties with astrologers such as Tommaso Campanella to ward off potential evil influences upon his destiny.[76]

Critiques of Barberini expenditures were exacerbated by the events of the early 1640s, when the papal family became bogged down in Urban VIII's disastrous war of Castro against Odoardo Farnese, lord of the Duchy of Castro. Farnese had failed to pay his debts to Roman creditors in 1640–41, an offense for which the pope was expected to respond to protect the creditors. He had also snubbed a marriage alliance with the Barberini in 1639.[77] An escalation of tension between Pope Urban VIII and his unruly subject eventually led to a costly and unpopular war, and Anna, who remained in Rome, was concerned about its financial impact on the Barberini.[78] Popular opinion, by contrast, emphasized that the Barberini family profited from their failed and expensive war.[79] Under the rule of the subsequent pope, the Barberini would be subject to investigation for charges of war profiteering.[80]

Anna, however, surveyed the situation in a very different light in the early 1640s. She emphasized that too many expenditures from the Barberini *casa* were required to sustain Taddeo's activities in the war. She argued that the expenditures related to Taddeo's service in the war (she included everything down to the sheets she sent to him) should be reimbursed to Taddeo's household. She acknowledged that Taddeo would probably not want to mention these things to his brothers due to his "modesty," but his attention to these matters was essential because "his absence meant that the eye of the father was not there" to look after the interests of the children (about whom "no one" was thinking) and, as a result, "others enrich themselves and don't spend from their own *casa*."[81] This stark division of the Barberini into clerical and lay *case* is intriguing. It reflects, in part, the shift in living arrangements, since Anna and Taddeo, after only two years of residence in the new palace, transferred from it to the older family place on the via dei Giubbonari. The reasons for such a move are obscure, ranging from the supposed dampness of the new palace, to Anna's dislike of the quality of air on the Quirinal hill, and to her beliefs that the old palace was luckier to produce male offspring.[82] The move underscored the further physical separation of the two wings of the family and corresponds to an argument for their clear division that Anna was making in her letters. It also reflects Anna's sense that the children's interests had to be kept first in mind, and that Taddeo and she must privilege the interests of the children over dynastic and papal interests. It seems that Anna won this argument because accountants were later asked to keep specific lists of Taddeo's expenses while he was on the road during the war.[83]

Probably due to her criticism of their behavior or for other inscrutable reasons, the Barberini brothers remained rather remote from her during Taddeo's absence, although she was still in communication with Cardinal Francesco, with whom she corresponded, and whom she petitioned frequently on behalf of a number of individuals who hoped to win his favor.[84] Yet, she also had to rely on Taddeo to communicate and negotiate with his family, especially Cardinal Francesco. This pattern was already expressed in the correspondence of the early 1630s, when (as a relative newcomer to the family), she wrote that, "she wasn't told much about the events of the *casa*."[85] In April of that year, she expressed dismay that Taddeo's other brother, Cardinal Antonio (whom she hadn't seen since Christmas) had been seriously ill and that she knew nothing about it. As a result, she did not help with his care. By the early 1640s, she was more philosophical about Barberini family values, acknowledging that Cardinal Francesco probably did not see her because "he had so much to do." Always quick to blame herself, she wondered if her own faults had anything to do with her brother-in-law's lack of interest in the children.[86] Anna wistfully expressed her increasing loneliness for Taddeo as the months turned into years of separation and she sustained herself on rumors of his return.[87] In 1643, as Christmas approached, she wished that Taddeo could overcome his "modesty" and ask his uncle, the pope, or Cardinal Francesco to let him return to Rome for a few days to be with his children.[88]

To justify her very decisive opinions about what the Barberini should not be spending, Anna had recourse to the language of maternal affection. We have no evidence for doubting the love she expressed for her offspring, but the word "love" does seem at times to serve as a compensatory rhetorical cover for the fact that Anna lacked humility and deference vis-à-vis the Barberini. A further bending of gender rules was in her insistence that maternal love – as she defined it – could be practiced by Taddeo and his brothers anytime they put the needs of the children before those of the dynasty. Maternal love was the standard by which the affection of other family members should be judged. Anna's alternative recourse to a political model of fathering by an "absolute padrone" did not actually capture the kind of family which she hoped to help bring into being. Her expressed hope that Taddeo would become the absolute padrone (as one must assume he was not, as she implied by her request) was perhaps to inspire him to behave with greater courage toward his brothers. But, if Taddeo were the absolute padrone, maternal love would also be his master. He was to rule so the children could come first.

Although Anna was steadfast in her critique of over-expenditure and associated this watchfulness with a trustworthy wife, she did also appreciate the other characteristics of the Barberini, especially their displays of affection. She noted Cardinal Francesco's accompaniment of his nephews to see the pope. She described emotional scenes unlikely to reach Taddeo otherwise. During her own visit to Pope Urban VIII, she noted that the pope's eyes filled with tears at the mention of Taddeo's name.[89] Similarly, she recounted the emotional displays by the children due to her husband's absence.[90] As the war dragged on, the situation was emotionally charged and financially fraught. The end was nowhere in sight. One rainy January, Anna dreamed of a day in the country, sitting in the sunlight while the children played and Taddeo benevolently surveyed his family.[91] But neither love nor trust nor Anna's will could bring the epistolary scene to life.

Competing Allegiances: Dutiful Daughter, Devoted Christian

Anna's independent ideas about the Barberini family challenged the assumption that the Roman aristocratic family was directed entirely by the clerical brother – a challenge to the status quo not likely to be well viewed by the multiple clerics of the Barberini family. Her improvised definition of the nuclear unit may not have been persuasive, but Anna did succeed in increasing the trust that Taddeo placed in her. She became the person upon whom he could most securely rely. Her fantasy of the kind of family day she wanted with him was expressed to him, perhaps only as an ideal but an ideal that had a place in their dialogue. Alongside the dream was a deep sense of foreboding about the Barberini children's future. Unfortunately, she had also to concern herself increasingly with her paternal family's calamities in the 1640s. Simultaneously, an intensifying religious fervor and fear about her own impending death (she had now reached about the age when her own mother died) inspired her to push forward with a promise she made to God to build a convent for the Order of Discalced Carmelites in Rome. At first glance, these two issues appear odd ones to insist upon during the complexities of an absent husband and a difficult war, but both suggest the extent to which, in the 1640s, good will and mutual respect continued to exist between the couple and between their respective families. This was certainly cultivated by Anna, who elaborated the bonds between the two families in words and attempted to strengthen them by action.

The death of Anna's father in 1639 was a loss also of a personal tie between the two families. Anna's father, Filippo (1578–1639), had cultivated his own shared interests with the Barberini – it may have been he who acquainted the rulers of Rome with Tommaso Campanella, who became an astrological advisor to Urban VIII and who seems to have devised the complex iconography of the ceiling painting *Divine Wisdom* in Anna's apartments.[92] The death of Filippo Colonna was further complicated by the subsequent loss of his son, Federico (1600–41).

The passing of the two men initiated a period of grave difficulty for the family. The Colonna had more need than ever of powerful allies like the Barberini, since they were in financial free fall. Anna's letters describe her goals for the Colonna, of securing valuable assistance for them from various members of the Barberini family.[93] Her motivating metaphors intertwined familial and religious iconographies of devotion. Anna's loyalty to her *casa paterna* is expressed in her metaphorical shorthand for it, "bones and blood." The potential alienation of Colonna fiefs, a financial loss as well as a public humiliation, struck her as particularly painful because it represented the loss of what was acquired by the "bones and blood" of the ancestors.[94] In the midst of her brothers' many difficulties, she confessed how much she would like to distance herself from the anxiety-provoking weight of their affairs, but she could not since (as she put it), "she had a great obligation to the bones of my Father ..."[95] Anna's sense of daughterhood was expressed as duty, inescapable duty.

Grudgingly but faithfully, Anna remained involved in her surviving siblings' attempts to save the situation, collaborating closely with her brother Cardinal Girolamo (1604–66) and her brother Marcantonio (d.1659), the heir-apparent to the Colonna's landed wealth.[96] The viceroy in Naples refused to allow Marcantonio to take possession of some fiefs due to the family's indebtedness, potentially endangering the family's ownership of valuable territories. The loss of fiefs was an affront to Marcantonio's honor. There were rumors that he would not, as his father had once done, receive the title of the *conestabile* of Naples. Ceremonial honors in Rome were threatened as well. Along with the Orsini of Bracciano, the Colonna family enjoyed the prestigious right to be present alongside the pope on ceremonial occasions, the right of the *soglio*. As the difficulties of the Colonna became public knowledge, the Duke of Bracciano, Paolo Giordano Orsini II (1591–1646), sought to deny Marcantonio the right of the *soglio*, questioning whether without the possession of the prestigious Duchy of Paliano, the new duke of the Colonna had the right to this ceremonial honor.[97]

Anna solicited the help of Taddeo and the Barberini with these problems. Taddeo wrote back with advice about what Marcantonio should do, and facilitated his appointment as Conestabile of Naples.[98] Unfortunately, Taddeo's brother, Cardinal Antonio, backed the Orsini Duke of Bracciano in the conflict.[99] Urban VIII, however, eventually confirmed Marcantonio's right to assist at the *soglio*.[100] Taddeo managed to remain good allies with his in-laws, even if such ties were complicated by Cardinal Antonio's loyalties. Anna reminded Taddeo that her brother would long be the faithful servant of Taddeo and his children.[101] Marcantonio and Cardinal Girolamo brought horses for Taddeo's use to Rome as demonstrations of their gratitude and loyalty.[102] Her two sisters, members of the Discalced Carmelite order, recited special prayers daily before a miraculous Madonna for Taddeo's safe return to Rome.[103] Anna freely admitted that the Colonna family chaos had taxed her beyond her energy, but loyalty to her father, specifically to "the bones" of her father, demanded her participation in their struggles, since she was the vital link to the resources of the Barberini family.[104]

Loyalty to ancestral bones was a particularly powerful metaphor for aristocrats, who, in the frenzy of land sales in seventeenth-century Rome, were sometimes forced to exhume ancestral bones from the churches of their alienated territories. The Roman branch of the Colonna family had had to do just this in 1629, after they sold their prized territory of Palestrina to the Barberini.[105] For Anna, the connection to ancestral bones was likely reinforced by the fervor of her spiritual devotion, which involved the veneration of relics, especially of bones. Like many of her contemporaries, clerical and lay people, she desired the most minute of physical connections to sacred bodies. A priest in Bologna, for instance, confessed his frustration in 1646 at being unable to extract surreptitiously a hair from the venerated blessed body of Catherine Vigri (later canonized in 1712).[106] In 1638, Anna hoped to secure part of the remains of Filippo Neri, founder of the Oratorians of Rome. Members of the order anxiously hid the body, eventually offering her "the heart, a nerve, a tooth, and some hair of the saint."[107] Later, while in exile with the Barberini in Paris, Anna concluded that the unexpected arrival from Spain of the finger of Saint Teresa, at a time when diplomatic relations between the two countries were severed, was a sign from God that she should return to Rome to continue her patronage of the convent of Discalced Carmelites.[108] The bones of the ancestors, like the finger of the saint, pointed out the rightful direction for aristocratic behavior. Religious and familial devotions are conflated in the noblewoman's letters and for her these were inspiring rather than conflicting appropriations.

It was through a series of financial rewards which had come to her as wife and mother in the Barberini family that she hoped to fulfill her religious obligations. She had made a vow to build a convent for the Discalced Carmelites, the order to which her sisters belonged. Anna's extensive involvement and patronage of the convent that became Santa Maria Regina Coeli has been told as a narrative of Anna's struggle against the Barberini in order to fulfill the goals of her religious patronage.[109]

Yet, there is little in Anna's letters to suggest that she was expecting Taddeo to be an adversary to her wishes. By the time she wrote to Taddeo in October of 1643, her vow was seven years in the past – made at the time of the birth of her last child, Nicolò.[110] Urban VIII had already given his approval for the project in early 1643. She hoped that the pope would grant her an indulgence for her act of piety.[111] Even Cardinal Francesco already had knowledge of her intentions, approved of her undertaking, and had previously paid visits to her sisters in the convent.[112] She also clearly wanted Taddeo's approval. From him, she hoped to have the promise that he would finish the project in the event of her death, and so she communicated specific details of the enterprise to prepare him for this possible eventuality.[113]

Her letter to Taddeo regarding the convent underscores the reliable frugality she had esteemed in previous letters. She had carefully invested the gift of 4,000 scudi that Urban VIII had given her on the birth of her son, Carlo. She had also saved and then invested all she could of her monthly income allotted to her as wife of Taddeo (100 scudi per month for the 16 years that she was "in the house of Your Excellency"). Her financial diligence had paid off, and she had nearly the 20,000 scudi necessary to begin the project.[114] This meticulous accounting mirrors the way she detailed her previous financial concerns over the collection of loans to the Barberini; the most advantageous time for the Barberini to cash in investments; and the appropriateness of Barberini expenditures. She remained the financially savvy wife throughout her correspondence, including in her plans to build her convent. (It should be noted that the convent ultimately cost Anna about twice her original estimate, which suggests perhaps how the Barberini also found themselves in financial difficulty after their ambitious building projects.)[115]

The letter provided Taddeo an overview of the location of the convent and its basic design. Anna had given similarly elaborate insight into Barberini properties, and as we have seen, detail was a crucial part of the way she related to Taddeo. The letter communicated the legal issues surrounding the completion of the convent in the event of her death. If she predeceased him she asked that the portion of her dowry that belonged to her by law (10 percent is what she claimed) should be given for the completion of the convent.[116] Her epistolary wishes were to be followed by a formal drawing up of her will. The letter has clear notarial and legal influences. It constituted notice to him about what she was already doing. It makes clear reference to her legal and financial ties to the Barberini and asks him to sanction legal steps she is about to take. The mere mention of these things, however, is not an indication of a failed union. Financial technicalities were the stuff of their correspondence. Anna merely called to mind for her husband the documents drawn up at the forming of their marital bond and the relevant legal statutes of Rome. She had wanted to do so in person, but his sporadic presence in Rome gave her no possibility. When in Rome, Taddeo was obviously "worried and weighed down by his serious assignments in the service of His Holiness."[117] In addition to trying by epistolary means to involve Taddeo in finishing the convent in case she did not live to do so, she also hoped that he would assist her in the short term by allowing one of the Barberini architects, Francesco Contini, to work on the project.[118]

Subsequent correspondence shows that Taddeo approved of the plan and willingly allowed her the services of Contini, the architect.[119] In December 1643, she sent Taddeo one of the medals cast in honor of the laying of the convent's foundation stone.[120] Probably her greatest obstacle after Taddeo's death turned out to be the Barberini nemesis, the successive Pope Innocent X, who for four years blocked the movement of the nuns into the convent, but from whom Anna eventually extracted permission.[121] But the building of Santa Maria Regina Coeli, in the years while Taddeo was alive at least, advanced with Barberini support. It was an exciting and heartfelt project for Anna, certainly less troubling for her than the financial difficulties of the Colonna. Despite the financial difficulties of her Colonna brothers, Anna's money went to Regina Coeli, the future residence of the Colonna sisters. The convent also received the Colonna's blessings, however, since her brother Cardinal Girolamo was present at the convent's foundation ceremony along with Cardinal Francesco Barberini. Emissaries of each family extended their good will.[122] The Colonna and the convent may have been obligations dearer to Anna than to Taddeo, but the evidence suggests that he supported her undertaking and complied with her requests. She petitioned him as her lord, but a lord from whom she expected to receive a yes.

Holding Up the Sky: The Colonna Siren in Service to the Barberini

Despite a difficult war, Anna motivated both families to participate in the fulfillment of her religious promise. She also helped to sustain her paternal family with the help of her marital one. These were significant achievements for an aristocratic mother, who served as intermediary between the two dynasties. To express her gratitude to Taddeo for the support he and the Barberini had offered the Colonna, Anna reminded him of the enduring loyalty the Colonna would show Taddeo and his family. Her brother Marcantonio would be his loyal servant. Her pious sisters prayed for his safe return from war. Despite her sense of foreboding in the early 1640s, Anna probably had not imagined the magnitude and the rapidity with which she would have to return the Barberini's assistance. Such future (and vague) possibilities were only hinted in her letters. After the death of Urban VIII in the summer of 1644, the possibility rapidly became reality. As seems to have been foretold in Andrea Sacchi's ceiling painting in the Palazzo Barberini alle Quattro Fontane, it was now time for the Colonna to raise the Barberini sun and sons back into the aristocratic orbit of Rome (Figure 1.4). In the 1640s, such lifting would be left to Anna, who would act like an aquatic Atlas and raise the Barberini above the turbulence rising against them in Rome.

The Barberini difficulties of 1645–46 had some parallels with the ones suffered by the Colonna earlier in the decade. They faced potential financial obliteration and irreparable damage to their honor. While all papal families were forced to endure reprisals at the end of their rule,

Figure 1.4   Andrea Sacchi, "Emblem of the Colonna and Barberini families," detail from the ceiling painting, *Allegory of Divine Wisdom*, 1629–33. Courtesy of Galleria Nazionale D'Arte Antica in Palazzo Barberini.

the backlash against the Barberini pope's long reign was especially intense. Under suspicion for having made money out of their disastrous War of Castro, they fled while under investigation, prompting the civic officials of the communal government, the Roman Senate, to call for the confiscation of their properties to cover revenues lost after the hated taxes imposed by Urban VIII were abolished.[123] Everything the family had built for itself in Rome and in the countryside was now in jeopardy. According to the letter of Anna to her son Carlo in 1646, in the face of difficulty the family had closed ranks against her. Taddeo and his brothers took the Barberini children to Paris.[124] They would not (according to her letter) allow her to travel to Paris to take her rightful place at the side of her offspring because they wished to keep them from her influence.[125] Without her dowry, she was unable to make a new life for herself in Rome. Pride prohibited her from returning to the Colonna, since she did not have her dowry that had been allotted to her as her inheritance.[126] In a very short period of time, her life had collapsed: she had lost her children, her husband, and her future.

Taddeo's behavior toward Anna seems less than honorable and certainly not what she expected. What could possibly explain it? Anna's letter to her son clearly states that Taddeo's behavior was part of a larger pattern of his failure to recognize the love that she had shown them throughout their marriage, regardless of his behavior toward her. Their father had never appreciated her, nor had he reciprocated her love for him.[127] Her earlier scattered skepticism about her Barberini brothers-in-law became a full-blown critique by the crisis of 1646, at which time her criticism of Taddeo was conflated with those of his brother, Cardinal Francesco, who – she had long complained – left her out of family decision-making. While it is certainly possible that Taddeo never experienced for her the depth of emotion she expressed for him, it is important to recognize the peculiar situation in which the Barberini found themselves. In a brief comment to her son Carlo, Anna noted "that there is nothing left to save or to defend," all the major landed assets of the family had been seized.[128] The pope, as she put it, "threw *fedecommesso* to the ground."[129] The word "defense" implies (and most historians would agree) that Anna was specifically left behind in order to defend Barberini interests and property. Anna's anger about the magnitude of the task is certainly understandable, but her responsibility at this disastrous juncture is also in some sense the logical outcome of the earlier arguments she made to Taddeo in her letters. She was the best servant in his household, the most active wife he could have asked for. He trusted her. Upon whom else could the Barberini possibly rely?

If the Barberini indeed feared for their lives, Anna's status as Colonna would have given her a modicum of protection that they did not have. The Barberini's other allies had to abandon them in the hostile environment of the new papacy. This left the Barberini with only Anna and the Colonna dynasty. The Colonna, unfortunately, were problematic allies since, due to their landed holdings in the south of Italy, they were obviously pro-Spanish, whereas the Barberini had thrown themselves into the arms of the French.[130] Anna was clearly a Colonna, but she had also spent almost 20 years in the public eye as mother in the Barberini family. She was (and she remained until the end of her life) a hybrid figure, a loyal member of the Colonna dynasty whose identity as Barberini was also paramount. She signed her letters with both names (Colonna and Barberini). She was a passionate mother, intensely interested in her children's future, but she was also the wife of the former pope's nephew, a public position she had occupied in the city for two decades. That she knew how to formulate arguments and work through challenges rationally and thoroughly was evident in her letters. The trust she had hoped to build with Taddeo inclined itself in 1646 toward her utility as a servant, rather than toward the emotion he might feel for her as a wife. If Taddeo Barberini was cruel to leave her, he would have been insane to take her. There was simply no one better. She had won this argument, with all its terrifying consequences for her.

Her famous defense of the Barberini before the Roman Senate brought into public view her role as *mater litigans* that had hitherto remained in the familial realm. In the statement (read by her cousin, Cesare Colonna), Anna reminded her audience of the illustrious achievements of Urban VIII and of her great-grandfather, Marcantonio Colonna II (1535–85), the commander of the Christian fleet at the victory against the Turks at Lepanto (1571).[131] She noted that Urban VIII's supposedly inappropriate deeds and taxes were much in keeping with the politics of the papal city, and that he had protected it from invasion, plague, and heresy. To sustain the city against such threats required the building of fortifications and other structures to protect it. Not surprisingly, he raised taxes to do so. Her great-grandfather's victory and military success neatly served to deflect listeners' attention from the Barberini's recently disastrous war. The defense combined the achievements of the two families to defend the Barberini from extinction. It was also good rhetoric to remind Barberini critics that it was the Colonna–Barberini alliance that was under attack, and that for her, an attack on the Barberini was an attack on the achievements of the Colonna family. Although the Colonna brothers distanced themselves from Anna's attempts to rescue the Barberini, and the Roman Senate expressed its doubts over her conflation of the two dynasties, Anna stood firm at the nexus of the two families.[132]

Thus, it is difficult to interpret the events of 1646, which – on one level – demonstrate a spectacular failure between the couple; between Anna and the Barberini in general; between the preeminence of the dynastic and the noblewoman's hope for the nuclear. Yet, on another level, they illustrate that Anna was viewed as an extremely trustworthy ally, albeit an ally with her own ideas and a willingness to complain. Anna did indeed eventually travel to Paris after her defense of the Barberini in Rome, but she returned again to the papal capital in June 1647 to "be of some service to the *casa* and to ... my children."[133] It was she who oversaw the management of Barberini territories and acted as a guardian for her son Carlo's interests in Rome, when Taddeo died in November 1647.[134] Upon Cardinal Francesco's return to Rome in February 1648, he assumed preeminent control of the Barberini family.[135]

Even prior to the disasters of 1645–47, Anna did not experience dynastic allegiance as a given in aristocratic families or even in herself, so she struggled to strengthen it by recourse to metaphors beyond the family, including religious symbols. They helped steady her through crises, especially those in her paternal family. She revived her familial loyalty through its parallels to her religious devotion to relics: "the great obligation to the bones of my Father ..."[136] She sought to populate the abstraction of dynastic loyalty with human forms with which it might be easier for her to experience solidarity. As the mother in the aristocratic *casa*, she had the task of physically reproducing it, and so it is not surprising that, as she peopled the present *casa*, she peopled the past *casa* with tangible lives – the bones and blood of ancestors. Religious practices thus revived her faltering aristocratic loyalties to the Colonna in the 1640s.

The living proved more problematic for Anna than the dead. Her insistence that the "nuclear" family could have a separate identity from the *casa* was more difficult, since Anna lacked a word for the specific family enterprise she was discussing. Hence, she relied simply on the word *figli*, whose needs were understood by an excessively affectionate mother. It was an improvised argument with far fewer precedents than the metaphors of religious devotion that she employed to describe her allegiance to the family. It arose as it did for Italian mothers elsewhere, out of her peculiar status as a mother in the aristocratic household, with all the conflicting loyalties such allegiance implied. Although this nameless proto-nuclear Barberini family could not survive the extraordinary external pressure of the mid-1640s, it was scarcely the only ideal that buckled under the strains of the seventeenth century. Aristocracy, monarchy, and religion cracked under commensurately terrible blows. Anna attempted to call her version of the family into being with her writing and very likely talked it to her difficult spouse Taddeo, whom she imagined as critical a player as herself in this improvised familial unit. Her cobbling together of quotidian domestic care and epistolary fantasies of sun-kissed unity, her simultaneous role as loyal servant of the Barberini and angry critic of some of the family's choices suggest the extent to which she experimented with alternative authority in the family which would include the input of the mother and be centered in the couple, rather than in the high-ranking cleric of the family.

Although Anna's improvisation on the family failed, Anna proved herself worthy of the trust she insisted she deserved. Her aspirations for the family contained novel definitions and controversial adjustments to the hierarchy of the Roman aristocratic family, which was supposed to emanate from the authority of the clerical brother.[137] After Cardinal Francesco returned from Paris in 1647 and the Barberini were successfully reintegrated in Roman society, he would reject Anna's participation in the family, writing of her with bitter criticism and cutting her out of negotiations for her daughter Lucrezia's marital future.[138] Anna would remain in Rome, but she would eventually live apart from the Barberini, in her own house, near her Colonna relatives.[139] Her attempt to elevate the significance of the bond between husband and wife – and, by extension, between parents and children – did not survive the crisis of 1646, the death of Taddeo in Paris in 1647, and the Barberini's successful separation of Anna from three of her four children after the family returned from Paris.[140] But it certainly gained adherents in Rome and elsewhere, however, suggesting that Anna's ideas about the marital bond and the nuclear family enterprise were not as odd as they might have first appeared to her detractors in the 1640s.[141] Having supported the Barberini through their troubles, Anna devotedly finished her convent and constructed a residence of her own, worthy of her status and near to her Colonna kin.[142] She was far from the last mother in Rome to question dynastic practice, rewrite its configuration of power, and fail in the bargain. To another of these alternatives we now turn.

2
"The Interests Common to Us All"
Olimpia Giustiniani on the Governing of the Roman Aristocratic Family

As the trials of Anna Colonna suggested, life in a Roman aristocratic family could pose dilemmas for its women and men. While ostensibly under the direction of the highest-ranking cleric of their families, such dynasties were also (by necessity) populated by brothers who married and generated the continuation of the lineage. Relations between brothers could be tense, exacerbated in the seventeenth century by the pressures of economic difficulty and the necessity of conspicuous consumption in a society crowded with many micro-courts of power, with ancient families anxious to bolster their prestige, and with newcomers bent on advancing their fledgling status. In a city run by a theocracy and open to newcomers, the bifurcated structure of Roman families promoted dynastic success but family members could not escape the dilemmas of such arrangements. Who had the final say in a family organized along these lines? And what were the other family members to do with their resentments toward those who governed the bifurcated Roman aristocratic dynasty?

Aristocratic families maneuvered amidst divergent ideas about rule and the appropriate exercise of power in the seventeenth century. One paradigm that gained adherence was absolutism, referred to in family sources as the *"padrone assoluto"* or absolute *padrone* of the family. It implied that the male head of the dynasty was ultimately responsible for the family's decision-making and direction. Concomitant with the political spread of absolutism was the practice of primogeniture, the legal restriction that concentrated most of the inheritance in the hands of one son. The pattern had come late to Rome, firmly established among the Barberini only in 1685. Alongside primogeniture emerged the emphasis on restricted marriage – the practice of allowing only one or two children in each generation to wed. The rest typically professed religious vows. Such practices could potentially reinforce the absolute *padrone* as the head of the *casa*, except that the Roman aristocratic family had two de facto *padroni* – its ecclesiastical and its married brother, a fact that complicated how the model worked in Rome. Primogeniture placed much of the family's property off limits from sale, if an ancestor had successfully legally entailed it. The same legal maneuver that ostensibly increased the prestige of the recipient simultaneously imposed further restrictions on his freedom to do with his inheritance as he would like.[1] In the face of financial doom, the activities of the absolute *padrone* had to run in the direction of careful accounting and more judicious expenditure, if the family were to survive precarious times. Another master of the family was the master ledger, and by law, the man who exercised primogeniture was subject to its reckoning. By the terms of primogeniture, he was to leave the family fortune improved, not diminished at the time of his passing. Accountants busied themselves with such tallies as Roman men passed from this life to the next.[2]

One woman who ruminated upon these paradoxical terms of family governance was Olimpia Giustiniani Barberini (1641–1729).[3] Olimpia faced similar dilemmas to those of her predecessor (and mother-in-law), Anna Colonna Barberini (1601–58), when it came to the governing of the aristocratic *casa*. Olimpia had ample time in which to think about such issues. Her marriage in 1653 to Maffeo Barberini (1631–85) had occurred when she was only 12 years old; her spouse was about 12 years her senior (see Figures 2.1 and 2.2). Some 75 years later, when Olimpia was in her eighties, she was still involved in family controversies, namely, the dispute over the custody of the Barberini granddaughter, Cornelia.[4] Olimpia had begun bearing children in her mid-teens – first two girls, Costanza (b.1657) and Camilla (b.1660), and then three boys, Francesco (b.1662), Urbano (b.1664), and Taddeo (b.1666). Olimpia's greatest challenges can only be glimpsed here and there in fragmentary correspondence that survives her. Since for much of her life she was not physically separated from those closest to her, she left a faint epistolary record compared to that of Anna Colonna. Olimpia expressed in writing her feelings of isolation during her early years as a mother. Then 16 years old, Olimpia longed for childcare advice from her grandmother, Olimpia Maidalchini.[5] Olimpia went on to successfully navigate many such pitfalls, raising five children to adulthood. By the time Olimpia reached her early forties she was engaged in the task of making marriages for her offspring, a key role for women of her caste. That same decade saw the loss of her husband, Maffeo, who died in 1685 when he was only in his early fifties, throwing Olimpia into widowhood with only one of their

Figure 2.1 Jacob Ferdinand Voet, *Portrait of Olimpia Giustiniani Barberini.* Courtesy of Istituto Centrale per la Documentazione [E42861] Rome.

daughters married and none of the boys having begun the clerical career so essential to the family's future success in Rome.

Yet, the Barberini were scarcely leaderless, for still very much alive was Cardinal Carlo Barberini (1630–1706), who, though one year older than Olimpia's husband, would outlive him by more than 20 years. Cardinal Carlo's tutelage repeated the pattern of the previous generation. Taddeo Barberini, Maffeo's father, had also died relatively young, at the age of 44. What had remained strong and continuous in the Barberini family was the presence of its clerics, who included two cardinals in the generation of Taddeo – Cardinal Francesco Senior (1597–1679) and Cardinal Antonio (1608–71). Given the continuity of clerical brothers in the Barberini family, the transitions between the generations of men who would procreate must have been heavily influenced by these cardinal patriarchs, who had longevity on their side. It may have been the clerical brothers who

Figure 2.2 Copy of portrait by Carlo Maratta, *Maffeo Barberini*. Courtesy of Galleria Nazionale D'Arte Antica in Palazzo Barberini, Galleria dei Ritratti.

were more understanding of their relatives than their married brother.[6] But as we shall see, such men could also exhibit their own intransigence to those who would challenge their authority.

So Olimpia grew to motherhood and to adulthood in a clerically dominated Barberini dynasty, where the clerical brother had one side of the family palace, and the married brother, the other half (see Figure 0.3 in the Introduction). Residing side by side did not eliminate the potential tensions in such arrangements. Olimpia's insights open a window on how aristocratic mothers saw the complexity of the two-brother rule. In her later years, the delineation of the boundaries between the dynastic enterprise and herself became more critical, as her seven-decade role in her marital family changed, and the Barberini financial dilemmas continued into a new century. The aristocratic family was neither a straightforward institution nor exclusively (in the case of aristocrats) a triumphantly successful financial enterprise,[7] although such success was critical to their survival. Rather, it was a negotiated set of relationships that changed over the life cycle of its members.[8] Family dynamics could be supportive and adversarial, driven by economic interests and simultaneously inspired by strong emotional bonds.[9] Their multifaceted nature complicates early modern and modern theories about its governing. Olimpia and one of her sons, Cardinal Francesco (1662–1738), were fascinated with the problem of governing the *casa*, especially with women's place in the political order of the household. Cardinal Francesco dreamed of a private and mercantile solution, while his mother turned to what he regarded as the dangerous public world of Rome. By the time Olimpia took up such issues with her son in the late seventeenth century, she was an old hand at familial controversies, with clear ideas about gender and power as they were theorized and practiced in seventeenth-century Rome.[10]

Little Pouty Faces and Wounded Pride: Tensions and Transitions among the Rulers of a Dynasty

A love letter from Olimpia to her husband in 1678 suggests the problems of two-brother rule of the Barberini and provides a woman's perspective on their resolution. A dispute between Olimpia's husband, Maffeo, and her brother-in-law, Carlo, resembled the kind of disputes over male honor that took place outside aristocratic households. This was the gray and potentially violent area of who had precedent over whom when men encountered men in early modern Rome.[11] Although they did not result in violence, issues of precedence were at stake between the two rulers of the Barberini *casa*. Olimpia's husband, Maffeo, resisted the pretensions of his brother, Cardinal Carlo, who was assuming the mantle of familial control from his aging uncle Cardinal Francesco Senior, who died the next year (in 1679). At issue was Maffeo's ill health, which his brother took upon himself to manage. An incident in the spring of 1678 inspired Olimpia to write a missive to her husband that echoes the advice-giving orientation of Anna Colonna's letters to her husband Taddeo. It reveals the same mix of deference, criticism, and support for the nameless marital unit, as well as allegiance to the dynastic one.[12] Thus, the agenda of Anna, while a failure, found an echo in a new generation of the Barberini *casa*. Although Olimpia signed the letter "Your wife and servant," to underscore the lowliness of her status, the content and the tone of the advice suggest a rough equality between the two spouses. Olimpia wrote didactically about how, in service to Christianity and the Barberini *casa*, one might agree to endure some mistreatment from the clerical brother in the family. Olimpia enjoined Maffeo to see the family from the broader perspective of the patrilinear, but reiterating (as Anna had done) the significance of the marital unit represented by herself and Maffeo.

Issues of precedence produced controversies over the respect brothers owed to each other.[13] Olimpia wrote what at first glance appears to be an apologetic love letter to her husband, expressing regret that she had doubtless earned her husband's "disgust" for her role in the incident, but reminding him that she had on many other occasions expressed "her affection" and "her passion" for him. Maffeo had evidently been ailing, and, against his wishes, Olimpia had agreed to keep her distance from her sick husband, perhaps to avoid her own infection or putting his weakened health in jeopardy. She had further agreed with Maffeo's brother Cardinal Carlo that Maffeo should be treated by Carlo's personal physician, rather than by the physician whom Maffeo preferred. Olimpia's letter expressed a number of criticisms of that doctor in particular, and doctors in general. Yet, she evidently cooperated with Carlo, agreeing not to visit Maffeo and consenting to bring the physician in for her husband's treatment, hence Maffeo's disgust with her – and her reason for writing him to make amends. Although Maffeo was supposedly much improved physically, he was now suffering from a wound to his stature in the household. Olimpia reiterated her devotion to him, since her cooperation with Cardinal Carlo was interpreted as a sign of spousal disloyalty and a further source of ill will between the brothers. Despite recent events, she hoped, in the close of her letter, that, in the future, she would have no other thought than to obey him and to follow him, as she declared herself forever his "wife and servant."[14]

Her analysis reveals the tensions between brothers, strains that were especially acute at the transition between generations. Up until 1679, the year in which Maffeo and Carlo's uncle, Cardinal Francesco Senior, died, the Barberini family would have been under the tutelage of the 82 year-old cardinal.[15] The disagreement over Maffeo's treatment took place in a transitional period between Cardinal Francesco Senior's rule and Cardinal Carlo's stewardship of the Barberini. Although Cardinal Francesco Senior was still living, in 1678 his advanced age probably prevented him from fulfilling the demands of ruling the family. Cardinal Carlo had probably begun to assume this role, since Olimpia refers to Cardinal Carlo as "uncle" in her letter to her husband, while in a letter written three years earlier she still referred to him as "brother."[16] The purpose of her letter to Maffeo is in part to beg her husband to acknowledge Cardinal Carlo's emerging position in the family, albeit in intriguing terms defined by Olimpia herself. She explained that she had obeyed Carlo's advice about the doctor in order to avoid his "little pouty faces," an observation that captures how she was caught between the men's conflicting demands. If Cardinal Carlo was now to govern, then Olimpia could not risk disobeying him. However, this was clearly a new dynamic for all of them, since she also felt keenly that what she did could be misconstrued as disloyalty by her husband.[17]

Olimpia offered her husband the following observations that suggest the extent to which either she or Maffeo should accept the model of the clerically governed aristocratic family, and what set of priorities should determine how they see the situation. She counseled "her Prince" that the two of them give the

> closest attention first to the glory of God and the good of our own souls, and then to the well-being of their *casa*, and their children, and that for them they search every advantage for their souls and for their bodies, and that in all the rest they follow the inclinations of our uncle [Carlo] so that he might do in this world as God will do in the next.[18]

Her advice to accept the tutelage of Cardinal Carlo suggests that Olimpia and Maffeo were scarcely renouncing the governing of the family to him. Indeed, if it is the couple that tends to the *casa* and children, then it is not clear what the cardinal brother's domain is, although managing the family's ailments would be one such area, and supervision of the servants, including the doctors, another. She counseled, in other words, some deference to Cardinal Carlo's wishes, to which they should reconcile themselves as they would to the governing of God in the hereafter. One wonders if, in Olimpia's theology, even God would be allowed to tend to the *casa* in the heavenly realm. The roles of Carlo and God are vague in the noblewoman's analogy.

She urged the two brothers instead to recognize the "many interests that are common to all of us," and "to put aside so much intensity of feeling about the servants (namely the doctor, in this case)." She reiterated that the basis of their rapport was their allegiance to this larger dynastic project. In this scenario, it was a woman who articulated the shared interests of the patrilinear as one man made the transition from brother to "ruling" uncle. As both wife and sister-in-law Olimpia had long been in the position of conflicting loyalties, simultaneously assuring her husband of his preeminence while urging him to bow (as she did) a little to his brother/uncle's whims in service of the common interests of the dynasty.

The tone of her advice suggests the joint purpose of husband and wife. Olimpia may have called herself a servant, but she wrote more as her husband's partner in shaping the Barberini family destiny. During the 1670s, Olimpia would have been fully immersed in raising her children by Maffeo, although as her observation of Cardinal Carlo's pouty face attests, she would have also been frequently involved with her cardinal uncle-in-law and her cardinal brother-in-law. Olimpia's letter downplays her compromised loyalty by reclaiming the task of situating the children in their adult lives as the married couple's shared activity, the same goals that Anna had defined for Taddeo and herself. However, we cannot be certain whether Maffeo accepted her assessment of this compensatory scheme, her apology, or her expression of passionate loyalty. His extant writings of a personal nature are also very few, but the preservation of her letter suggests that Olimpia's expression of her affection and of "the interests common to us all" had some meaning for him. It was not the last time Olimpia would deliver a lesson in what it meant to serve the patrilinear, but it was the last time she would so from a position of relative safety.

In the waning years of the seventeenth century and through the first years of the eighteenth century, Olimpia found herself in the most difficult years of her widowhood, in conflict with one and then another of her sons. Urbano (1664–1722), who was to carry on the family lineage, was a spendthrift ne'er-do-well who (in her view) was misguided in his belief that the family was best ruled by an absolute *padrone*. Her other son, Francesco (1662–1738), rose to became a cardinal in the church and a rigorous accountant of the family riches that his brother consumed at an alarming rate. After the death of her husband in 1685, Olimpia was left to negotiate with these two men, one of whom claimed everything and spent all within his reach, and the other of whom counted everything and saved all he could. Despite the continuity of leadership by clerical brothers and uncles, the Barberini were evidently failing in the transition of the tutelage of a new generation in the early eighteenth century.

Olimpia took issue with the views of both of her sons. Although she would avoid the costly judicial routes that many a *mater litigans* sought out if necessary, she acted with the initiative of a *mater litigans* in the Barberini drift downward, here lending support and at other times refusing to cooperate if she disagreed with her sons' plans. She drafted petitions to the pope and courted allies to help her navigate the demands of two adult sons, each of whom became impossible, in her view. Olimpia challenged their assumptions about the rule of the family and questioned the place of accounting in the relations among family members. Neither the ideology of the absolute *padrone* nor master ledgers could supersede the place of affection in the aristocratic *casa*. Neither could negate the contributions of aristocratic mothers, nor appropriate their possessions, nor dismiss their input on the governing of the household. Their pattern of sacrifice and generosity, affection and initiative necessitated recognition. Mothers offered alternatives to those promoted by men as families sputtered and some failed in the late seventeenth century. Olimpia's insights suggest the contours of this alternative vision.

The Barberini family member of the late seventeenth century who has left the most complete record of his insights and his struggles on the family front was Olimpia's son Cardinal Francesco, sometimes referred to as Cardinal Francesco Junior (1662–1738) to distinguish him from his great-uncle Cardinal Francesco Senior (1597–1679). His ruminations linked together the multifaceted aspects of the aristocratic family under his proud allegiance to "the Barberini *casa*," an enterprise that probably only looked coherent at specific junctures: on his brother's wedding day(s), for instance, or later, at his own funeral.[19] At other times, the busy cardinal was left with the difficulty of cobbling together the decorous presentation of the dynasty to the rest of the "world," sustained by his increasing devotion to the bookkeeping which would make such a presentation possible. Cardinal Francesco reiterated these themes in a number of hybrid texts – writings that were simultaneously narratives of the Barberini family history; musings on the emotional and financial ties between individuals (especially women) and the *casa*; diatribes against those who could govern neither themselves nor the *casa* in the proper manner (among whose number was his own mother, Olimpia).

Olimpia and Cardinal Francesco debated three distinct but intertwined concerns related to the governing of the *casa*. Both (but Olimpia in particular) worried about the power that belonged to the universal heir Urbano, since he tended to ignore all limitations placed on that authority. Both were concerned with the financial fate of the family since the Barberini were experiencing financial disaster. Cardinal Francesco (more than Olimpia) expressed concern about the "public" nature of their demise and hoped to limit the damage to the reputation of the family. Finally, each offered reflections on the emotional ties between the individual and the *casa*, specifically, the role affection was supposed to play in a set of relationships so obviously shaped by power, money, and concern for appearances. Although the European aristocracy has been described as cold in its familial relations and draconian in its demands on its offspring,[20] the interactions between Cardinal Francesco and Olimpia at the turn of the eighteenth century suggest that affection was an expected part of Roman aristocratic family life. It was embedded in other themes of interest to both mother and son, specifically authority and property. These influenced, but did not eliminate the affective ties between members of one aristocratic dynasty (once again) at the end of its run on the Roman scene. Cardinal Francesco and Olimpia knew they would die, but like all aristocrats, they dreamed the family would endure. This chapter looks comparatively at how one mother and her son reckoned with the demands that dream made upon the living.

(Again) at the Edge of the Precipice: The Barberini in the Late Seventeenth Century

The Barberini's financial misery was acute at the end of the seventeenth century, but it certainly had illustrious company in Rome. Economic, social, and cultural factors shaped a pattern of noble indebtedness that had emerged a century before, in the late sixteenth century. Runaway inflation at the end of that century certainly did much to erode the yields from land, where revenues from agriculture were fixed by law and custom. Other types of noble investments also deteriorated due to the impact of inflation, and inflation itself tended to encourage indebtedness.[21] Roman nobles continued to seek monetary remuneration for their military services, as did Francesco Colonna, who proved himself a valuable soldier in the armies of the King of Spain. Unfortunately, he (and many others) waited in vain for significant financial rewards from distant warring monarchs. In the meanwhile, they parted with prestigious fiefs in order to pay their debts.[22]

According to Pio Pecchiai, a mid-twentieth-century biographer of the Barberini, Urbano Barberini was emblematic of the failings of the entire Roman aristocracy. His image, in the Gallery of Portraits in the Palazzo Barberini alle Quattro Fontane, depicts him later in life, when his expansive lifestyle began to take its toll (Figure 2.3). His spendthrift ways may have been due to a passion for gambling, a passion shared by many among his caste. Pecchiai makes much of other extravagances, such as a costly pair of celebrations sponsored by Urbano in honor of the monarchies of France and Spain in August 1704.[23] For Pecchiai, Urbano was symptomatic of what went wrong when a former Florentine family forgot the virtues of its mercantile ancestors and embraced the decadent Roman aristocratic life.

Figure 2.3   Anonymous artist, *Urbano Barberini*. Courtesy of Galleria Nazionale D'Arte Antica in Palazzo Barberini, Galleria dei Ritratti.

Yet the expansive need for great expenditure was related, in part, to the demands of living splendidly in a spiritual and political capital. By the sixteenth century, Rome had become increasingly important as a destination for Italian aristocrats because the pope had become the most powerful bishop in Italy. He controlled a vast number of benefices, offices, and the financing of the papal debt.[24] Capturing the papacy or the cardinalate for a son necessitated the appearance of high social standing. "Making oneself greater," as a contemporary put it,[25] involved a number of potentially expensive undertakings, including the building of a family palace; increasing landed patrimony; becoming the patron of artists and architects, sponsoring magnificent spectacles and festivities, to name only a few of the activities engaged in by those wishing to be considered among the Roman aristocracy. "Making oneself greater" could (and did, to some) appear to be superfluous expenditure; it could also be viewed as an investment in the possibility of raising one son to the ranks of *papabili*, making better marriages for other children, or convincing potential creditors that the *casa* in question was worth a loan risk. Investment and superfluous expenditure were curiously intertwined in early modern Rome.

Expenditure leading to the alienation of fiefs, however, was scarcely a desirable goal. The purpose of placing properties in entail, or *fedecommesso*, was to force family members to restrict prestigious properties from sale. Heirs were to live from the income of their lands and were charged with improving rather than dissipating assets. More families in the seventeenth-century modified the *fedecommesso* to restrict its inheritance to a single boy in each generation as the universal heir.[26] Alongside the emergence of this more restricted form of inheritance – primogeniture – was the allocation of even more of the family's wealth to this form of entail, leaving even fewer resources for the remaining children.[27] Since, in theory, primogeniture was supposed to eliminate from possible sale the most prestigious assets, how was it even possible for Urbano Barberini and many of his peers to liquidate such holdings?

The risk for noble alienation of fiefs had its origins in the late sixteenth century, during the papacy of Sixtus V (Peretti, r.1585–90). In light of the great indebtedness of many older aristocratic families, in 1585, Sixtus V offered the possibility of securing loans or *monti*, guaranteed by the Apostolic Chamber, using the families' properties as collateral.[28] Many newer noble families also quickly fell into the pattern of borrowing through such loans. By the seventeenth century, even the Farnese family, perhaps the greatest of the sixteenth-century papal families, had to borrow more than 900,000 scudi in just five years.[29] Similarly, the family of Sixtus V, who had created the system of loans to save the nobility, was in financial trouble within a decade of their papacy.[30] The loans themselves proved insufficient, however, to rescue the most financially unstable families, and in 1595, Clement VIII (Aldobrandini, r.1592–1605) was pressed by creditors to take stiffer action against nobles who defaulted on their loans. Delinquent families would now be forced to sell their estates to pay their debts.[31] A new papal bureaucracy, the Congregation of the Barons, was created to process such transactions. Staffed by clerics and lawyers, the Congregation became the vehicle through which noble fiefs were alienated. Its inventories of adjudications read as a "who's who" of Roman greats. Among that number were many women – about one out of four of all the matters brought to the Congregation in the early modern period involved a woman.[32] Aristocratic family crises drew both women and men into the legal wrangling over how to save the family from ruin, or how to secure the debts that another family owed, and might have owed for decades, to their creditors.

Though the papal loans may have brought some short-term stability to noble family finances, it is clear that landed estates remained the key to re-establishing and maintaining a family's economic well-being. The amount of the *monte* the Cesarini family received in 1585, for instance, was determined by the amount of revenues from the Cesarini lands, which would be used to pay the interest on the loan, and eventually (hopefully) the principal.[33] Subsequent *monti* offered similar terms to noble families.

Like nobles across Europe, Roman nobles reorganized their finances and their families to survive this period of crisis. They restructured their financial portfolios, restricted their expenditures, and survived the economic crisis of the late sixteenth and seventeenth centuries. They were not, as one biographer of the Barberini has suggested, blinded by the "inexorable gilded decadence" of Rome.[34] Their financial rescue is instead all too familiar: the reason of accounting and the association of superfluous expenditure with the sin of vanity, the worthy quest for the financial grace promised by devotion to the master ledger, the praiseworthy Roman echo of what aristocrats elsewhere in Europe also achieved. It had been the refrain of Anna Colonna in the 1640s to the Barberini as she anticipated the end of the Barberini papacy. Purse strings would have to be tightened if the family future was to be secured.

Aristocratic families were certainly assisted in their efforts by the credit innovations of the popes, although for some families (including the Barberini), the arrival of loan money did not always yield immediate stability in their financial situation. Indebtedness inspired controversy among members of noble families. The relatively new papal bureaucracy of the Congregation of the Barons rose up amidst already existing institutions and other channels of grievance.[35] If petitions to the Congregation of the Barons were unsuccessful, one could appeal to the pope himself, beginning with a plea to the papal *auditore*, an official of the Apostolic Chamber whose role by the seventeenth-century was primarily judicial and included family disputes.[36] The papal bureaucracy was a "web of jurisdictions," as one historian has aptly termed it, and there were numerous paths and counter-paths through that labyrinth when relatives remained uncooperative or the first opinion was not to one's liking.[37]

Cardinal Francesco feared that any recourse within such a system could make more public the embarrassing struggles of a family in fiscal dissolution. This was certainly the inspiration for Cardinal Francesco's impressive literary output – his need to write and rewrite the family history in a way that made sense of his desired method for saving the family from financial ruin. From the late seventeenth to the early eighteenth century, family concerns consumed Cardinal Francesco's attention and income to an unusual degree, even for a cardinal with his roots in Rome. Urbano (the designated universal heir of the family's properties held in primogeniture) should have been managing the landed wealth. Instead, he spent his time dissipating the family fortune and attempting to sell valuable Barberini estates. On several occasions, Cardinal Francesco prevented the alienation of a fief, only to discover that Urbano had found a way to undo all of his efforts. "No one knows," Urbano's mother lamented in 1697, "what could have become of so much money; the interest on the debts, already so far behind, isn't being paid, he doesn't pay for his own household, or that [of his wife], or that of his Mother."[38]

Ultimately, the Barberini staved off their financial ruin, retained some of their significant holdings, and miraculously, considering Urbano's propensity for botching almost everything, even continued the lineage with a legitimate heir, Cornelia, born in 1716.[39] After Urbano's death in 1722 and the successful arrangement of the marriage of Urbano's daughter Cornelia in 1728, Cardinal Francesco was able to withdraw from his de facto management of Barberini affairs, beginning around 1731. But in the late 1690s and early 1700s, such success seemed very far from becoming a reality, and Cardinal Francesco and his mother Olimpia attempted to plot a course through the financial storms that threatened to overturn all that the Barberini had constructed and reconstructed in the seventeenth century.

Absolutism from a Woman's Point of View

As the Barberini financial difficulties increased, Olimpia Giustiniani penned occasional statements and provided accounts of her financial situation in the Barberini household.[40] Her most systematic critique of the behavior of her wayward son Urbano emerged in a text she wrote between the fall of 1697 and January of 1698. A nineteenth-century archivist summarized its contents with the following description: "Papers in which Signora Donna Olimpia describes in her own hand the good-for-nothing conduct of Signore Principe Urbano her son in the governing of the *casa*, and demonstrates the incivilities she receives from him."[41] Considering the details of the story she tells, the term "incivilities" puts it mildly. Also inaccurate appears to be the claim that the account was in her handwriting – while an annotating hand appears to be hers, the two types of handwriting in the document are the elegant cursive of secretaries. This is further confirmed in the text, in a reference to the original copy held by someone else, perhaps for safekeeping. The annotations in her own handwriting suggest, however, that she reviewed what the account contained.[42] The text begins in the third person, but switches to the first person by the second page. It has repetitions and some garbled expressions, which suggest that, however beautiful the hands that copied it, there was an earlier draft written by someone in haste and anxiety. Although not addressed to anyone in particular, her story is likely a plea for intervention either by the papal auditor or the pope himself. Even if such a critique did not lead directly to a formal lawsuit, it sheds light on the noblewoman's opposition to the way her son governed the Barberini in the last years of the seventeenth century.

Olimpia's text has two distinct but related sections: a five-page history of the Barberini *casa* and her role in service to it, and a three-page list that documents the most irresponsible financial actions of her son Urbano. Her story and her list of Urbano's improprieties communicate her disgust with his misbehavior, especially given how starkly it contrasts with her own scrupulous sacrifices for the Barberini *casa*. Olimpia begins her story in 1653 with her wedding, an event that rescued the Barberini from a recently marginalized status in Rome, and concludes the story in the last years of the seventeenth century with the frightening conduct of her son Urbano and the "rabble" with whom he associates. In her history, Olimpia is both the spouse destined to "re-establish" the Barberini *casa* in 1653 and (later in the narrative) the widow struggling valiantly to stave off its demise. Olimpia chronicles the Barberini's new downfall ostensibly from the margins of the patrilinear family and from the perspective of someone who, hypothetically, was only to be commanded, but not to command. Her husband was dead, her children were already adults, and the mantle of governing the *casa* had already passed to a younger but problematic generation. What role could Olimpia Giustiniani legitimately play in such a scenario?

Olimpia legitimates her insights into the good governing of the Barberini by presenting her motives and her actions in the best possible light and by illustrating their efficacy in helping the family during its financial demise. She contrasts her scrupulous behavior with that of her son Urbano's fundamental misunderstanding of his role as *padrone* of the Barberini *casa*. His error in thinking that he was an absolute *padrone* caused her personal suffering and the downfall of the *casa* itself. Olimpia did not choose the word "absolute" haphazardly – she chose it in order to critique her son, to help define more clearly not only what he did wrong, but also what she thought were the limits of her own obligation to the *casa*. Political language became the realm where destiny met daily life.

Olimpia saw the history of the Barberini family in the latter part of the seventeenth century as a story of miraculous survival, rather than as a glorious succession of generational triumphs. Her marriage in 1653 to Maffeo Barberini, "as is known to all the World ... re-established the *casa* Barberini."[43] She had subsequently "suffered with great emotion ... [the] downfall of her house (meaning that of the Barberini), since she was destined by her ancestors to re-establish it."[44] The recklessness of her son was particularly disconcerting because it ignored the labors of previous generations to restore the family after its serious difficulties at the end of Urban VIII's papacy (r.1623–44).

Destiny (even destiny constructed by one's ancestors) enhanced the drama of what she had to say. Her importance to the family is not exaggerated, in light of all that befell the Barberini in the 1640s, as her great-uncle Pope Innocent X (Pamphilj, r.1644–55) threatened the Barberini family, who fled to exile in France. Through the efforts of Taddeo's wife, Anna Colonna, and the pressure of the French monarchy, the Barberini were allowed to return to Rome and to their aristocratic landowning status, beginning in January of 1648.[45] Taddeo died in the French capital, but his sons returned to Roman aristocratic society. His oldest son, Carlo (1630–1704), renounced any claim to becoming the Barberini "universal heir" in order to pursue an ecclesiastical career, and Pope Innocent X made him a cardinal in 1653.[46] Maffeo, the second son, became the heir to most of the family's fortune and was married to the pope's great-niece, Olimpia Giustiniani, that same year.[47] Olimpia was the daughter of Maria Flaminia Maidalchini and Andrea Giustiniani. She was the granddaughter of Olimpia Maidalchini, as powerful an aristocratic mother as any who had emerged on the Roman scene. As the sister-in-law of Pope Innocent X, Olimpia Maidalchini wielded power in Rome – to some critics, an inappropriate level of power.[48] Olimpia Maidalchini could not bear to part with her granddaughter, although she had arranged her marriage. So, early in their marriage, the couple evidently resided with her in the family palace in Piazza Navona.[49] The marriage of Maffeo and Olimpia had indeed rehabilitated the formerly ignominious Barberini, whose demise had been brought about by the very family to which they subsequently allied themselves in matrimony. Appropriately, an opera celebrated this symbolic uniting of old adversaries. *Dal male, il bene (From Evil, Comes Good)* was performed in 1654 in the Palazzo Barberini alle Quattro Fontane to honor the newlyweds.[50]

Olimpia's marriage was one of the critical elements in the ceremonial, social, and financial reintegration of the Barberini into Roman aristocratic society from which they had been briefly cast out. Although she did not recount in detail the family's stormy history in the 1640s, she expressed pride in what her marriage to Maffeo had meant for the Barberini. She noted the amount of her dowry (60,000 scudi) and the fact that Cardinal Francesco Senior had sent jewels to her.[51] Olimpia viewed her marriage as a significant new beginning for the Barberini *casa*, but she clearly feared that, given the behavior of her son Urbano, she might now be witnessing its end.

Despite all that Olimpia suffered because of her son, she claimed that it was her affection *(affetto)* that kept her from ignoring the Barberini's financial ruin.[52] When Urbano tried to orchestrate the sale of Monte Rotondo, one of the Barberini fiefs that she regarded as a significant part of the family patrimony, Olimpia surrendered her dowry to the family in July of 1697 in the hopes that she could save Monte Rotondo from alienation. In such circumstances, Roman aristocratic widows were then supposed to seek their sole financial support from their sons.[53] She did this "to make it known more with works, than with words, the affection she bore the *casa*, and [her] *figli* [sons or children]."[54] Olimpia's affection is a refrain which opens and closes her history of the family and surfaces whenever she expresses the willingness with which she worked for the *casa*. As Anna had done before her, Olimpia amalgamated the terms of religion to describe her devotion to the aristocratic *casa*. In this case, her affection motivated her to action in the same way her religious faith motivated her to charity. "Whoever is moved by zeal has to put her hand to it," she had observed some years before, in a letter to nuns who requested her help.[55] Olimpia's affection necessitated a similar commitment to action on her part if it were to have any meaning.

Olimpia took special interest in preventing the sale of Monte Rotondo because it had been purchased early in the papacy of Urban VIII, and it had given the Barberini their first noble title. It represented the beginning of the Barberini ascent to the status of titled aristocracy, heirs to the great but financially embattled families like the Orsini (from whom they bought Monte Rotondo) and the Colonna (from whom they would later buy Palestrina). Olimpia emphasized that her attempt to save Monte Rotondo from alienation was done with the knowledge and the cooperation of other responsible family members, such as her brother-in-law Cardinal Carlo and her son Cardinal Francesco. Olimpia's first successful efforts to thwart the sale of Monte Rotondo to Marchese Litta were done, as she notes, "with the complete satisfaction of her brother-in-law because her son the Cardinal was in the Romagna."[56] When she mentions the donation of her dowry to the *casa* she notes that the legal document describing her donation had to be done "according to the wishes of her brother-in-law Cardinal Carlo." Both comments emphasize that, for Olimpia, working for the *casa* meant working in conjunction with a number of other male family members, especially her clerical ones, a primary responsibility to her marital family.

Olimpia also notes that she shared a vision of the importance of certain properties with her son Cardinal Francesco, especially Monte Rotondo, purchased by the Barberini in 1624. Olimpia claimed to be repeating his description of the meaning it had for him. She noted that he had written to his brother, Urbano, begging him not to sell the fief, since it was the "first Title of their *casa*, and the location of the bones of the Prince Prefect their Grandfather."[57] The location of ancestral remains became an especially sensitive subject for Roman aristocrats in the seventeenth century, when rising families like the Barberini bumped the older families from their ancestral fiefs, forcing living and dead family members alike to abandon prestigious holdings. Now it would be the Barberini's turn to exhume their dead and forsake a territory, a painful ritual that underscored the failure of one generation to live up to the expectations of its ancestors.

Urbano, however, was not a man persuaded by ancestral bones. Unfortunately for Olimpia, he was instead moved by her actions to "compensate" her for her efforts. The bitter "recompense" for her sacrifices was that he personally attacked properties and possessions that were dear to her.[58] Urbano treated the *casa* Barberini as though it "belonged to His Enemies," she wrote, rather than to members of his own family.[59] At the time she wrote this account, she found herself isolated in the Barberini household, without the use of carriages or horses, terrorized by a son who had dared say that she should leave the doors unlocked or "he would have them opened with violence by his guards [*sbirri*]."[60] Olimpia argued that the source of his villainy toward her was anger over her surrender of her dowry to save Monte Rotondo from sale:

The day after [I surrendered my dowry] the Prince my son angered by that Donation went with many men from his Court to extract from me a little vineyard [*vigna*], that I had for my amusement, and [since] I had the keys, he broke all the doors, and put in other locks, fired the *vignarolo* that I had there, and chased away the man who had already paid to collect the fruit ...[61]

At this point, Olimpia said, her brother-in-law, Cardinal Carlo, with the assistance of other cardinals, sought the intervention of the papal auditor, who ordered the prince to stop. The prince, however, continued, and a few days after his first attack he did the same thing to a little garden and its caretaker, and "at the end of many weeks he did the same thing to another little *vigna* that she enjoyed in Palestrina," sending away the sharecropper and keeping his share of the harvest.[62]

Olimpia claims that the cause of Urbano's anger was her role in saving Monte Rotondo, a property Urbano clearly wanted to sell. But how could such a responsible and affectionate mother face such a contrary and violent son? Olimpia argued that, after the death of her husband in 1685, Urbano (then 21 years old) was corrupted by others, who

for their own particular aims gave the child the idea that he was the absolute *Padrone* and that he could do what he wanted: So he began to sell the valuables of the Barberini family with no gain whatsoever for the *casa*, and then the estates, part sold outright and part pawned, without ever having to explain to anyone what he was doing.[63]

Urbano (according to his mother) had confused his status as *padrone* (universal heir of the lands held in primogeniture) with the idea that he was an "absolute *padrone*." The word "absolute" is the most intriguing term that Olimpia introduces. It is at the center of her conceptualization of how her son Urbano lost his way.

With increasing frequency in the late seventeenth century, "absolute" became associated with the French court. No two capitals in Europe had more ties in the seventeenth century than Paris and Rome, though not all their ties were amicable ones. Absolutism was a type of political power exercised by a monarch (an emerging model was the French King Louis XIV) who claimed to rule alone (in the sense that he did not have to account to anyone) and who acknowledged fewer legal restrictions on his authority than his predecessors had done. And while historians no longer think that absolutism really existed in practice, either in France or in the Papal States (or anywhere else for that matter), in the late seventeenth century, this style of rule (if not its actual power) was vivid in the minds of many elites. Olimpia's choice of a word that was both a political and a familial term helped her critique Urbano's behavior as illegitimate. In Rome, the adjective "absolute" would have been associated with Louis XIV's usurpation of property.[64] Relations between Louis XIV and the Holy See were particularly tense in the late seventeenth century. Louis offered proof of his Catholic piety by revoking the Edict of Nantes in France and by making war on "heretics" like the Dutch Calvinists, but he had a tendency to make war on Catholic powers too when it suited his purposes. He fought for decades to expand his control of the French Catholic Church's revenues and highest ecclesiastical offices. In the 1670s, Cardinal Francesco Senior, who had warmly welcomed Olimpia to the Barberini family, was charged with evaluating Louis's right to control certain ecclesiastical revenues. All matters related to France were likely widely discussed among the Barberini, whose fortunes had been so dependent on that court in the 1640s. After 1680, the existence of antagonisms between the French monarch and Pope Innocent XI (r.1676–89) worsened and became even more widely known in Rome.[65] Olimpia would certainly have been aware of the intensity and the acrimony imbedded in the choice of the word "absolute."

Since Olimpia's petition was probably directed to a papal official in Rome, her choice of the adjective "absolute" was likely intended to suggest arbitrary power that reaches beyond legitimate boundaries. As Louis had tried to do in expanding his control over the church in France, so her son tried to do in controlling all the properties in the family. While Urbano was obviously the *padrone*, like Louis XIV he was not in practice an absolute one: there were many restrictions on what the universal heir might do. It was the purpose of the mother's narrative to explain how Urbano's behavior violated those standards. Her account shifts the family into a political framework that helps to delegitimate Urbano's activites. Her choice of what was becoming increasingly a negative political term helped to cast Urbano's behavior as illegitimate.

Urbano mistakenly believed (according to Olimpia) that all of the properties and all of the income associated with the Barberini *casa* belonged to "him." This is what made him a misguided absolutist in her eyes. Threatened by his actions, she noted, "I have nothing of his,"[66] demarcating what belonged to her from the properties held in entail, or *fedecommesso*, which were his insofar as he was their designated custodian. Regarding the rural properties he confiscated from her, Olimpia emphasized that since he had no part in their purchase or their maintenance, they were not his for the taking. The first *vigna* attacked by Urbano she had had cultivated "for her amusement," helped with expenses by her uncle Innocent X and her uncle (by marriage to the

Barberini) Cardinal Francesco Senior. The second property in Palestrina had been given to her by her husband. Urbano picked off the profits of the latter, chasing off her sharecropper from his share of the produce. The third property, near San Pietro in Montorio (on the Janiculum hill) she had bought herself after her husband's death in order to raise citrus fruits and flowers, a cultivated pursuit shared by many of her well-born peers, as much for its pleasure as for its produce.[67] Sadly, she added that "[because of] the recent and continuously distasteful events I haven't drawn any satisfaction from it."

Urbano demonstrated a similar misunderstanding about his rights to other possessions. After his attempt to confiscate his mother's vineyards, "searching always for new ways to precipitate the *casa* and alarm everyone," Urbano had duplicates made of the receipts for the Barberini jewels and valuables deposited in the Monte di Pietà, a respectable pawn shop that provided ready cash for valuables. Some of the items had been deposited by his father Maffeo and some by Olimpia, "to live on," as she put it, and to raise money to marry her daughter Camilla in 1688. She had even paid the interest on the pawned jewels, further substantiating her individual ownership of such items.[68] With his fake receipts Urbano attempted to keep his mother from being able either to claim the jewels or pay the interest necessary to keep her from losing them. In her opinion, this was "a great damage to the *casa*, since such things were part of the *casa fedecommessa* that I had always endeavored to preserve as best I could."[69] Due to her efforts, she was able to rectify the situation and stop his use of the fake receipts.[70]

Urbano not only went after the moveable wealth deposited in the Monte di Pietà, but also threatened other belongings Olimpia described as hers. He wanted to force her to have drawn up an inventory of all of the possessions in her apartment (meaning in the Palazzo Barberini alle Quattro Fontane), or, as she put it, "to describe everything that is in my power."[71] She showed resistance to including in the inventory anything she considered her own.[72] Olimpia's power evidently included her ability to control certain possessions belonging to the *casa* itself. Her admission that she had pawned jewels to secure the marriage of her daughter, Camilla, was an example of her own intrusion into the technical holdings of the *fedecommesso*. Although broadly defined, the nature of the *fedecommesso* was that it could be divided among heirs, each of whom would be charged with preserving their portion of it. Olimpia continued to operate from this older definition, ignoring the new terms of primogeniture, which located nearly all the entailed property in the hands of one son, with very limited inheritance and marriage possibilities for the rest.

Olimpia's control of specific goods within "her power" and her refusal to surrender the receipts enraged Urbano and slowed down the possibility of getting his hands on these items, which, according to Olimpia, she employed for better and more legitimate purposes. Urbano responded violently to Olimpia's resistance. In Rome, Urbano and men of his court attacked her rooms in the Palazzo Barberini alle Quattro Fontane, "breaking doors, walls, and windows," taking the contents that belonged to her. They then did the same with her wardrobes in the villa at Palestrina, to which she held the keys, breaking down the doors and taking the contents – wall hangings, silver, sheets and "things of her own ... made by her ... for her own use."[73] Also from Palestrina, in the rooms where her female servants lived, he took two trunks containing linens and articles of Olimpia's clothing. Such items would be easy for Urbano to pawn or sell for ready cash. They could have had little meaning to him otherwise.

Olimpia distinguished between Urbano's careless *personal* claim to objects from his tutelage of the *fedecommesso* that was entrusted to his management in his lifetime. To underscore this distinction, she argued that of her possessions that were within the *fedecommesso* (the jewels and the objects in her apartment), nothing she had was from Urbano personally, but rather was from the *casa*, "which she preserved the best she could." While the immediate cause of his hostility may have been the donation of her dowry, there is a part of the Barberini family history that Olimpia chose not to tell, and that seems related to her son's demands. In 1685, her husband Maffeo drew up a final will, which required that the most valuable parts of the Barberini patrimony be inventoried and placed under entail; these items included "real estate ... annuities, government bonds and movables."[74] Inventories of this wealth "were to be drawn up within two months of [Maffeo's] death; in case of non-compliance, the heir could not take control or enjoy any fruits of the estate."[75]

Stealing Olimpia's clothes and handmade linens was probably not what her departed husband had in mind when he called for the survey and sequestering of the disparate parts of Barberini wealth. Cardinal Carlo's attempt to intervene on behalf of Olimpia and stop Urbano from "confiscating" his mother's vineyards suggests that the rather draconian inclusion of much of the property of the *casa* under the terms of entail did not signify that it would all be under the control of Urbano's whims. Urbano's demand for the receipts of jewelry and the "inventory" of the possessions in her apartments were probably closer to his father's intentions. Olimpia resisted this as well, asserting "her power" over certain possessions and referring (tellingly) to her loyalty to the *casa fedecommessa* rather than to the son whom primogeniture made the most privileged person of his generation. Olimpia's ownership of her properties is substantiated in the account both by their origins from outside the *fedecommesso* and by the fact that she managed them or that she brought them (in the case of the agrarian properties) or that she also made them (in the case of her handiwork). Such activities marked such things as separate from the patrilinear.[76]

Olimpia had corrected what she perceived as the failings of such a system by unilaterally providing for her second daughter, Camilla (1660–1740). In 1688, Olimpia deposited some of the family jewels in the Monte di Pietà to raise money for Camilla, "who remained in her hands after the death of her father." Since Olimpia believed that her daughter was insufficiently provided for, she made a secret deal to have additional funds paid to this daughter and her son-in-law after her own death. Such funds originated in the allowance for her expenses promised to her by the Barberini at her marriage – it amounted to 20,000 scudi, or her monthly unpaid allowances for her "32 years, five months, and 11 days" in the Barberini family.[77] It was a good gamble – she lived 40 years after the matrimony. She pointed out that Urbano, by contrast, did nothing to provide for his second sister, although he had taken all the money collected as seignorial dues on Barberini properties in the Stato di Regno on the occasion of the marriage of his older sister, Costanza. Urbano, in Olimpia's eyes, reaped all the benefits of the patrimony without carrying out any of his obligations to the *casa*.[78] Olimpia overstepped the boundaries of the system of primogeniture when she thought she had a higher obligation to one of her offspring. She rejected Urbano's indifference to his sister, whom he might have planned to dispense to a convent for a dowry that amounted to much less than what her marriage would require.

Thus, although she refers to herself as the poor and miserable mother, her account records the extent to which Olimpia was an able woman who knew how to use her status to negotiate a marriage for a second daughter (thus diluting the practice of restricted marriage). She also navigated well the papal bureaucracy to curtail the bad behaviors of her absolute *padrone* son. She certainly believed that, by comparison, she was the responsible member of the *casa*, and she ignored the possibility that Urbano may have learned some of his independent ways from her. Urbano sold movables and landed properties "for no gain for the *casa* whatsoever" – a major failing on the part of the universal heir who was charged with increasing, rather than decreasing, the financial worth of the family. Olimpia's actions were the productive ones, inspired by her sense of having been destined to rescue the *casa* and motivated by her affection for it and her other offspring, including her daughter, Camilla.

Preserving the *casa* "as best one could" did not mean, however, being subsumed by it. She clearly valued her autonomy, even as she worked with like-minded family members to try to rescue it from ruin. Olimpia clung to her "power" over some Barberini goods, which limited the absolute *padrone*'s "right" to take everything. Even if such a right had been the intent of her husband's will, it did not mean (in Olimpia's view of the family) that Urbano could dispose of property without having to answer to the living and the dead family members. Her cardinal brother-in-law evidently agreed with her. "Ruling alone," in the manner claimed by Louis XIV, was unimaginable in the Roman aristocratic *casa*, at least as understood by Olimpia, who proved to be a better adversary of absolutism than the French aristocrats lured to Versailles by Louis XIV.

As a member of the Barberini *casa*, Olimpia expected to remain free to tend to her vineyards, to enjoy her own handicrafts and personal possessions, and to look out for her daughter if she perceived she was unjustly provided for. This was probably the status in the family she expected when she married Maffeo Barberini in 1653. She had been reared, after all, in the shadow of her formidable grandmother, Olimpia Maidalchini, whose activities in the papacy of her brother-in-law, Innocent X, had inspired scandal in Rome during the late 1640s and early 1650s. Yet, the everyday lives of Roman women were not the opposite of such behaviors, but rather a more moderated set of practices that still pointed the way toward some independence within the patrilinear. Olimpia justified her willingness to interpret freely the parameters of her husband's intentions in establishing primogeniture because she believed she understood correctly and behaved properly toward the aristocratic *casa*. One honored the destiny provided by the ancestors. One generated yields, rather than debts. One cooperated (as she mostly did) rather than acted without consulting family members. Although these ideals are clear in Olimpia's history of the Barberini, the mother never successfully communicated these caveats to the wayward son, who may have been inspired by her independence but missed her emphasis on serving the *casa fedecommessa*.

Mothers versus Master Ledgers

The decade subsequent to Olimpia's rejection of her son Urbano's behavior proved to be fraught with further difficulties for the family. Her other son, Cardinal Francesco, wrote several accounts chronicling the unnecessary financial free fall suffered by the Barberini. As he waged legal battles to block his brother's alienation of family property, he (and his legal advisors) were forced to tell and retell how the good cardinal had managed to "dress the wounds" of his *casa*.[79] At the end of the first decade of the eighteenth century, things were scarcely better for the beleaguered cardinal, who argued that, in addition to the problem of the reckless Urbano, he had also to battle his mother. Through his vitriolic history of the family, written in 1710, it is possible to glimpse the disputes he had with Olimpia, who evidently sidestepped her cardinal son during the preceding year in order to make her own successful plea to the papal auditor to amend her situation in the Barberini *casa*. Olimpia's problems were evidently no longer with the wayward son, but had shifted to the son who had been her ally the decade before. Directly petitioning the papal auditor had secured Olimpia a consistent annual income of 2,000 scudi, to be paid to her by Cardinal Francesco (Figure 2.4). This would help codify the amount she could expect from him, rather than negotiate with him (or his staff) for the payment of her daily expenses. It was a sum from an old agreement, stipulated in a document of 1698, to clarify what her sons owed her, since the Barberini had never repaid her dowry.[80] Ideally, we would have more details of the story from her perspective. However, Cardinal Francesco's detailed account chronicles her activities and suggests her attitudes, so different from an overbearing child (in this case, Cardinal Francesco), rather than her wayward son Urbano.

Olimpia's earlier account in 1697/98 depicted her as an ally of her son Cardinal Francesco. In his version of the Barberini family history she was an embarrassing and uncontrollable liability. The lengthy title of his 1710 text highlights the cardinal's opinion: "A Historical Report on the motives and reasons that Her Excellency goes on foot, and lives otherwise inappropriately to the station which God has granted her, and of the longstanding desire of *Signore Cardinale* Francesco to see that she be served with all the decorum befitting a son of his birth and dignity."[81] Cardinal Francesco's account is written in the third person, and his motives are clearly stated – he hoped to undo the decision by a papal *auditore*, made in October of 1709, that required him to make cash payments to his mother for the interest on her dowry, rather than provide her with goods and small amounts of cash as he had been previously doing, under the terms of her donation of her dowry to the Barberini *casa* in 1697.[82] While we cannot be sure that Cardinal Francesco was the sole author of this history, it shares many characteristics with other accounts written about his activities. It was surely written with his approval, and

Figure 2.4   Copy of portrait by Carlo Maratta, *Cardinal Francesco Barberini Junior*. Courtesy of Galleria Nazionale D'Arte Antica in Palazzo Barberini, Galleria dei Ritratti.

most likely with his direct input. It is an opinionated vision of how the *casa* should function, and of the proper role of mothers and sons within it. Longer and more complicated than Olimpia's seventeenth-century account, there are hints in it of how the clarity of Cardinal Francesco's calculations could become convoluted in the realities of life in the Palazzo Barberini alle Quattro Fontane, especially in the context of dealing with a widowed mother with ideas of her own.

Cardinal Francesco's history chronicles the years between 1685 and 1710. His own contribution to rescuing the *casa* dominates this very difficult period that he organizes into three distinct conflicts. In the first part of his account, he tears down his mother as an important and responsible family member and stresses how he supported her financially despite her behavior. In the second part, he emphasizes how valiantly he struggled against his brother Urbano's proclivity for generating debt, especially the debts that threatened the sale of one of the territories connected with Palestrina, the Barberini's most prestigious fief. The third part recounts the crisis with his mother that prompted the writing of the history in 1709–10. It contains a transcription of a letter to Cardinal Paolucci, whom Cardinal Francesco asked to speak to the pope on his behalf.[83] In this last section, the Barberini cardinal stresses how the recent success of his mother in securing a papal order for the payment of the 2,000 scudi for her yearly support was both unreasonable and impractical for her own well-being and for the reputation of the *casa*.

Rhetorically, Cardinal Francesco's account is less consistent than the one his mother wrote. Considered individually, the pieces of his argument sound persuasive, but reviewed together, they can be difficult to reconcile. Cardinal Francesco opens his story in a nonchalant way, claiming that he would be glad to pay a bit more for his mother's "maintenance" but he would like his audience to consider (in light of the story he has to tell) that it may not be the most prudent course of action. The nonchalant Francesco (and, later in the account, the melodramatic Francesco) only wanted what was best for Olimpia and what was best for the *casa*. The recent decision by the papal auditor requiring Cardinal Francesco to pay his mother 2,000 scudi per year would only lead the family into further financial difficulty. In Cardinal Francesco's eyes, the Barberini were felled by an internal power struggle and by the negligence of their own recordkeeping. The result of the Barberini's accounting failures was that they were the object of ridicule before "the World," as Cardinal Francesco put it. His mother's behavior served only to subject the family to further negative public scrutiny.

Cardinal Francesco's version of the Barberini story brings together a number of emotional and ethical dilemmas facing the cardinal. It combines his opening dispassionate commitment to accounting with a dramatic intensity that plays itself out in the physical person of the cardinal: his "back is to the wall"[84] or he "is throwing himself into the arms of Monsignori" who could intervene for him.[85] He describes his difficulty in holding back tears when he considers "the fatality of his disgrace."[86] Like his mother, he claimed that Christianity helped guide his actions and gave his suffering some meaning, although the contradictions of being both a Christian and a Barberini probably must have occurred even to the cardinal.[87] Cardinal Francesco represented himself as a talented manager of the Barberini finances but he also had to answer the charge leveled by the pope himself that he had been an insufficiently devoted son, that he hadn't tended to his mother's need as "divine reason" required.[88] The pope's response suggested the extent to which Cardinal Francesco was considered out of step with his times, elevating the rule of the master ledgers over the demands of filial devotion. Cardinal Francesco's response reveals the underlying struggle between these two orientations in the aristocratic family *casa*. He claimed that he wanted to protect his mother from her creditors, her own bad habits, and the inevitable loss of status her financial choices would require her to make.[89] But the pope's critique suggested that some of Cardinal Francesco's contemporaries wondered whether he had crossed the line between preserving the patrimony and alienating the relatives. Any history written to answer so many questions had to lose in consistency to gain in comprehensiveness, and the cardinal tended to be catholic when constructing his own defense.

Cardinal Francesco (like his mother) emphasized his contribution to rescuing the family finances from his brother's spendthrift ways. He contrasted his behavior with the missteps of his nemesis – considered, in this case, to be the mother rather than the wayward brother Urbano. The best example of the purity of his efforts is in his struggle to save the territory of Corcolle, a significant agricultural holding attached to their prestigious villa of Palestrina. How he characterizes this dilemma reveals that damage to Barberini honor was central to the core of his critique of his mother's activities as well. Her financial and familial errors damaged the Barberini family reputation as much as the loss of prestigious territories.

The Barberini struggle to save Corcolle reminds us that the Barberini were dying financially by the same mechanisms by which they had stepped over the older noble families: when debts rose high enough and creditors clamored to be paid, the noble family could be allowed (i.e., forced) to sell a property to make good on those debts. Clearly, Urbano's special talent for expenditure contributed to this situation. However, Cardinal Francesco's only criticism in this account of his brother was the acknowledgment that Urbano had generated a large number of debts (as much as 50,000 scudi) to a merchant named Gherardini "who said he gave ribbons, gold trims, laces, and precious cloth to lackeys and to prostitutes at the request of the *Signore Principe*."[90] When Gherardini petitioned the Congregation of the Barons for the payment of his debts, Cardinal Francesco attempted to intervene, requesting that the creditors had to be satisfied with the yields from the prince's patrimony, rather than cannibalize the patrimony itself. At a minimum, the cardinal believed that the Congregation should consider off-limits from alienation the family's most prestigious fiefs.[91]

Under consideration for alienation was Corcolle, a holding attached to the villa of Palestrina. Palestrina was probably the most renowned rural property of the Barberini family. Purchased in 1630 from the Colonna, one of the great Roman aristocratic families, Palestrina conferred the title of prince on the Barberini. It was also formerly the ancient setting for a Roman temple, and its ruins and astonishing mosaic extended its historical significance to the classical world. The fief provided the Barberini a magnificent setting for their seasonal *villeggiatura* to the Roman countryside during the hottest months of the year.

Alienating Corcolle was a serious mistake, according to Cardinal Francesco. It was the body (*corpo*) of Palestrina and, if it were dismembered, the territory of the city would have been left a "skeleton" in comparison to its former grandeur.[92] His struggle to save Corcolle in the Congregation of the Barons underscored the helplessness of the cardinal. Initially, it seemed that nothing could be done to counteract the mounting claims of creditors:

> Every account, every supposition, every petition that was made by the Prince Cardinal Francesco was not only not rejected, but served as a resolution ... for the Congregation of the Barons ... printed edicts were ordered affixed throughout Rome, in such a way that everywhere it was known that they were selling Corcolle, the jurisdictional tenuta of Palestrina belonging to the *casa* Barberini in order to pay Gherardini, the creditor of His Excellency Prince Urbano, [to pay] Butchers, Grocers and fruitsellers ... [93]

In the face of such ignoble and demanding foes, Cardinal Francesco described himself, "as they say, with his back to the wall," and looked first to "the infinite mercy and Omnipotent Divinity so that he might be granted assistance and strength, and the means to save his *casa* from total extermination."[94] He found practical help by taking his case to three *monsignori* who doubtless had some important connections and whose intervention he especially needed after the death of his uncle Cardinal Carlo in 1704. They agreed to look after his interests and, through them, Cardinal Francesco assumed a staggering burden of debt payment in order to rescue Corcolle.[95]

The story of the near loss of the prestigious territory of Corcolle brought together the cardinal's greatest fears about the "extermination" of his *casa*. The Barberini were risking extinction because they were squandering the income from their lands on useless trifles. They could be forced to sell Corcolle to pay for the finery of his brother's prostitutes.

Cardinal Francesco also implied that, once the Congregation of the Barons started to move against a property, the creditors came out in large numbers, and without accurate recordkeeping, the Barberini could fall victim to specious claims on their property.

For Cardinal Francesco, the posting of the edicts announcing the sale of Corcolle was especially humiliating. In many parts of Rome (from the Quirinal hill to the altar of Saint Peter) were scattered architectural and emblematic reminders of the lofty status of the Barberini family in the seventeenth century. Cardinal Francesco's text leaves the reader with the impression that they were practically pasting the edicts over the family emblem, the Barberini bees. For him the edicts were an agonizing reminder of how far the Barberini could fall if something could not be done to shore up the crumbling *casa*. In his eyes the Barberini's "familial," or "private," dilemma was amplified by the announcement of the lowly social standing of the creditors: "Butchers, Grocers and Fruitsellers." He thought these small claims could have been settled by papal chirograph, a considerably less humiliating way of resolving the issue.[96] These tiny creditors of the Barberini were socially insignificant individuals, hardly worthy adversaries of the great Barberini *casa*.

But the edicts related to the sale of Corcolle in the archive of the Congregation of the Barons don't mention Gherardini, butchers, grocers, or fruitsellers.[97] So Cardinal Francesco's version of how much the edicts themselves communicated to the "public" is somewhat exaggerated, although their juxtaposition with the former symbols of Barberini greatness would certainly have been jarring. Documents in the Barberini archive do suggest that Cardinal Francesco was correct in assessing the risk tiny creditors in great number could pose to the *casa*. A folio-size sheet of paper listed 97 creditors to whom the Barberini owed more than 50,000 scudi around 1711. The amounts ranged from nine scudi owed to a tailor to 5,200 scudi owed to a druggist at the Trevi fountain.[98] Noble indebtedness was common, but nobles were more frequently indebted to other nobles – they were the primary (although not the only) creditors of the *censi* (loans) taken out by other noble families with their estates as collateral.[99] While Cardinal Francesco may have accepted that pattern of noble indebtedness, he rankled at the threat posed by the "rabble" of tiny creditors, who, together, could threaten the noble *casa*.

The story of Cardinal Francesco's rescue of Corcolle showed him in the best possible light: the diligent Barberini son forced to humble himself to save his *casa* from common creditors. It was the same presentation Olimpia had used for herself in chronicling her efforts to save

Monte Rotondo from sale, suggesting a shared set of aims between mother and son. But his account introduced another theme that was paramount in his struggle with his mother: failures in bookkeeping led to the disgrace of the family before "the World."[100] Cardinal Francesco built such an argument after he systematically destroyed his mother's reputation as a valuable member of the Barberini *casa*. In support of this interpretation, he recasts almost everything in her account as negatively as possible. Although he never cites her earlier petition, he responds specifically to the version of the family history that it represents. He downplays the importance of her marriage to his father by noting that the dowry she brought to the marriage was, in fact, less than what was testified in the notarial documents for the marriage.[101] He makes no mention of the larger symbolic or social significance of the alliance with the Pamphilj, which – as Olimpia was right to note – had a prestige value for the Barberini that would not have been easily translated into monetary terms. He reduced her to an account-book entry.[102]

In contrast to Olimpia's claim that she worked in conjunction with her brother-in-law and her son, Cardinal Francesco critiqued her more independent actions, such as providing for her daughter "secretly" by promising her more money after her death.[103] In light of his father's stated wishes in his last will, Cardinal Francesco claimed to be shocked at her attempt to control the receipts for the jewels and other Barberini valuables. He recounted the controversy over the jewels at some length, noting the difficulty his brother Urbano had with his mother on this issue. He neglected, however, to tell the part about the duplicated receipts, emphasizing instead that his brother had tried unsuccessfully to get various tribunals to force his mother to surrender whatever jewels or receipts for jewels were in her possession. The controversy over the jewels between Olimpia and Urbano inspired Innocent XII (Pignatelli, r.1691–1700) to appoint a special commission of three cardinals to investigate the controversy. They concluded that Urbano should pay 3,000 scudi to his mother's creditors who were clamoring for restitution and, in exchange, she should offer him the receipts for the jewels and the furnishings. Although Urbano put up the money, Olimpia refused to surrender the receipts and, consequently, Urbano cut off her support (which he technically owed to her, as long as he had her dowry).[104]

Even Olimpia's seemingly admirable sacrifice of formally surrendering the dowry in order to save Monte Rotondo becomes suspect in Cardinal Francesco's account. It was his mother, he argued, who desired to save the fief.[105] He did what he did to please her – at great personal sacrifice – because he had to assume many loans at high interest to try to meet the demands placed by the Congregation of the Barons on the Barberini if they wanted to retain Monte Rotondo. Cardinal Francesco argued that he was forced to sell Monte Rotondo, "a jewel so beautiful," because his mother refused to surrender the receipts and the inventory of the Barberini jewels.[106] Such paperwork could have been used as collateral for better credit, "but there was never any ... reason sufficient to move her, and she consistently refused to give any receipt."[107] Instead, he had to take loans at high interest to try to rescue Monte Rotondo. Since he failed to meet the financial demands of the loans, he was forced to sell the fief in 1699 to the marquis Francesco Grillo of Genoa.[108] At the same time, he had to "give up the support of his mother in order not to remain suffocated by the weight of so many debts and interest that had accumulated."[109] Like his brother Urbano, he cut her off, gambling that she would do nothing or that she would not find a higher authority responsive to her plight. He was wrong on both counts.

Clement XI (Albani, r.1700–21) was unsympathetic to the Barberini brothers' legalistic wrangling with their mother: "expressing himself more in terms of a father, than a prince he ordered Cardinal Francesco ... to pay [his mother's] creditors who ran continually to his holiness."[110] After the death of Cardinal Carlo in 1704, Clement XI had a *monsignore* speak to Cardinal Francesco to encourage him "to aid his mother without conducting research into so many legal articles, but with the unique natural law [*ragione*] and Divine precept that does not allow his mother to lack for her necessities and her past maintenance."[111] The cardinal agreed, since he wanted "to honor the most supremely clement suggestions of his holiness." He willingly "paid for her household, provided her with her own carriages, had her accompanied on *Villeggiatura* to Castello [Gandolfo], Palestrina, and San Vittoriano, where he put everything at her disposition."[112] He paid her substantial debtors. When the items that mattered most to her in the Monte di Pietà were in danger of being lost, Cardinal Francesco, "enduring any inconvenience," paid the money necessary to recover them.[113] Olimpia was thus compelled to surrender the receipts "by necessity," and this was "advantageous for her and one of the things that only a son could do for his mother."[114] In this way, the jewels "were not lost to the descendants of Urban VIII, and his mother did not have the distasteful experience of seeing them lost to the *casa*."[115] Both of these statements emphasize that Cardinal Francesco was the only person behaving responsibly in the family crisis – a consistent narrative, although a suspect one.

He claimed that he then returned to the support of Olimpia throughout his struggle to save Corcolle without any help from his brother, and still found the money, as he put it, "to meet the obligation he owed to God to give to the poor their portion of his ecclesiastical income."[116] Her request for the yearly payment of 2,000 scudi mystified Cardinal Francesco. When he heard the news, "he thought he was dreaming since he had daily demonstrated the deference a son was required to show his mother and she had never said anything to him directly nor through the means of others, and so he had supposed that she was serene and content."[117] Cardinal Francesco claimed he did whatever he could to understand "the motives that could move the soul of the Signora Principessa to act in this way." He decided that the source of her unhappiness had been an indiscretion on the part of one of his household staff. When Olimpia had requested some bread, the household steward (*dispensiere*) responded that he couldn't supply it without a request from the *Maestro di Casa* or the accountant. He recognized the pettiness of his servant's remarks (referring to them as "some such trifles," [*bagatelle*]) but he also criticized his mother's method of making her complaints known.[118] If she was short of money, she should have come to him directly. Even after she had made her wishes known "publicly," Cardinal Francesco continued to try to dissuade her, visiting her daily (one can only guess at the level of tension in those meetings) or sending mutual friends, relatives, and even his mother's confessor to try to get her to reconsider.[119] He expressed disgust at her complaints before the papal auditor, which "didn't serve to do anything but create a ridiculous scene before the whole world."[120]

As was the case with the posting of the notices of the sale of Corcolle, it was the excruciatingly public part of the affair with his mother that bothered Cardinal Francesco. The "world" knew about the Barberini difficulties once their disagreement came before the papal auditor. Using privately chosen intermediaries would have been more appropriate, in Cardinal Francesco's opinion, and would have helped the family avoid the "scene" the cardinal found so shameful. Cardinal Francesco suggested that, even after she had succeeded in securing the decree from the papal auditor, "you will (eventually) see her wandering through Rome on foot, crying at every street corner about how she is treated by the Barberini *casa*, reduced to such a state by her sons, which she used to do before Francesco assumed her maintenance."[121] It is nearly impossible to imagine the proud niece of Innocent X, traveling on foot in Rome, much less shouting on street corners (a not-so-subtle comparison of her to a prostitute). Her cardinal son's considerable gift for dramatic exaggeration reached new depths where his mother was concerned. His overemphasis suggests how great a violation he considered his mother's attempt to regain partial control of her dowry and to speak about her concerns with those outside the *casa*. Yet, she found a willing audience in the pope and the officials who served him, including the papal auditor.

Cardinal Francesco tried to convince papal officials that his mother had seriously misrepresented her treatment in the *casa*. He sent his own auditor, his secretary, his *maestro di casa*, and his accountant, in order to convince the papal auditor that

> she was *Padrona* of the whole stable, of the whole Guardarobba, of all the villas, the gardens, and the palaces in the countryside as well as in Rome, of all the servants of the Signore Cardinale, and that she could dispose freely of the cellars and the pantry, being only obliged to have a receipt made for whatever she took ...[122]

In Cardinal Francesco's familial calculus, Olimpia was the *padrona* of the family, but she (like everyone else) had to answer to the account books. Such a request was part of a necessary reform of her behavior, since

> She didn't make use of accountants nor *maestri di casa*; Signor Cardinal Francesco her son knows the carelessness that she uses in governing herself, since she puts money in her purse and she spends without keeping an account book with debit and credit or any notation and a footman or a waiter governs her whole enterprise, only God knows how badly she is served.[123]

Only the cardinal and God himself were wise enough to recognize Olimpia's household sins. A truly responsible Barberini family member had to be diligent about receipts for the tiniest of household exchanges. Dishonest creditors waited at every door of every Barberini property, and they were doubtless aided by underhanded servants within the *casa*. To avoid sinking to the status of merchants, the successful noble family had to match (and, if necessary, outdo) the mercantile practice of its creditors. The facade of aristocratic display needed the structure of clear accounting.

Consensus and Calculation in Governing the Aristocratic Household

Cardinal Francesco's choice of the word *padrona* underscores that the dispute between Olimpia and her sons revolved around the ambiguity about who governed the aristocratic *casa*. The problem was intensified during transitions, when clerical brothers became clerical uncles, or sons became *padroni*, sometimes before they were ready. The rigorous demands of travel placed upon the son in the church could also contribute to a situation in which critical family members could be frequently absent from Rome. By necessity, clerical sons had to travel if they wished to advance their careers, and such efforts competed with attention to familial affairs. Such circumstances heightened the importance of female members of the *casa*. Such requirements, combined with the early death of one or both parents, could sometimes leave the universal heir without any older family members to guide his actions or limit his missteps. Olimpia, a capable and energetic woman, by her own estimation lost her son to the influence of "others," and the would-be absolutist dragged the family finances and dynamics into dangerous dissolution. Some sons, evidently, would never be ready to govern.

Mounting debts and the failure of designated heirs to recognize that responsibilities, along with property, were entailed in *fedecommesso* could further complicate family governing. But Urbano may have felt that the perks of his rule were over before they started: at his father's death, the debts of the Barberini family outweighed their financial assets by more than 600,000 scudi.[124] From the perspective of a 21-year-old heir, he had gained more limitations than possibilities upon his inheritance to the family fortune, such as it was at that time. Perhaps the irresponsible behavior on his part was encouraged by the Barberini's embrace of primogeniture just as he assumed the mantle of the family's future. Combined with the requirement of "spending to make oneself greater," as Amayden observed, Urbano could easily have been enticed to spend magnificently, by the nefarious "others," Olimpia mentioned. Both Olimpia and Cardinal Francesco used his behavior to underscore one of the fundamental weaknesses in the system of primogeniture in such situations: a family might gain prestige in the assembling and retaining of impressive holdings, but a family could potentially lose it all when the absolute *padrone* of such wealth was irresponsible. The risk of an absolutist was real: the wild Urbano had demonstrated that. The resolutions of his errors could be the lengthy process through the Congregation of the Barons or through petitioning and winning the sympathy of the pope. But papal institutions created to save Roman nobles from financial ruin could also exacerbate it by facilitating the alienation of fiefs. Legal jurisdictions of magistrates overlapped, and when one found a decision not to one's liking, one could carry the problem somewhere else, all the way to the pope himself, if one were as bold and as savvy as Cardinal Francesco or his mother Olimpia, who avoided law courts but not the papal court.

Who was in charge once the designated universal heir so profoundly misunderstood his role? At his best, Urbano was absent from Rome, living at least remotely within his means, and indifferent to the larger concerns of the *casa*. At his worst, he "acted as an enemy," as his mother put it, and if necessary had to be treated as one. His absence or his malicious presence left a void in the Barberini *casa*, and it is in this void that the power struggle between Olimpia and Cardinal Francesco began, into which the contribution of the noble mother was as critical as that of the cardinal son, as the dispute over her dowry and her jewelry reveals. Disputes between the cardinal son and his mother seem to have been restrained up to the death of Cardinal Carlo in 1704, but with the passing of this older member of the Barberini family, the tension between Francesco and his mother became more pronounced, as her legal pursuit of regular payments after the surrender of her dowry and his vitriolic text in response make clear. The patrimony of an aristocratic family was composed of many different properties, accounts, and valuables, and in times of crisis, some of these would be sacrificed so that the rest could be saved.[125] There was an increasing disparity between Olimpia's and the cardinal's vision of how that might be done. The future of her daughter Camilla was not open to negotiation, in her view.

Cardinal Francesco's articulation of the merits of good management is not unique; they exist in other Roman sources as well, such as books on household management, which were printed in Rome during the seventeenth century.[126] Antonio Adami, one of the self-appointed experts on noble (and non-noble) households, pointed out the folly of profligacy and poor accounting, and argued that even illiterate peasants made marks on the wall with a piece of charcoal to keep records.[127] In *Il Perfetto Maestro di Casa* (a copy of which was in the Barberini Library), Francesco Liberati argued that the wise padrone relied on a *maestro di casa*, who was bound to know (and be able to monitor) the habits of the servants better than the *padrone* ever could.[128] Cardinal Francesco seems to have shared the underlying principles of these books – with their faith in accounting rigor and obsessive distrust of most servants. His struggle to bend his mother to this creed suggests that devotion to the judicious governing of worldly goods was an ideal among the Roman nobles, even if practiced with difficulty within one's own household.

Ironically, Cardinal Francesco (the self-anointed savior of the family from financial ruin) contributed to the public scandal by turning the noble palace into a counting house. Historians have come to recognize this choice as the inevitable trajectory of the aristocratic *casa* if it was to survive. Attention to careful management of properties was not the invention of Cardinal Francesco's generation. His grandfather, Taddeo Barberini, was an effective manager of the Barberini's patrimony,[129] and such stewardship was not uncommon among the Roman nobility.[130] Olimpia herself could clearly be shrewd about the value of the paper trail (as the incident with the receipt for the jewels shows), and she certainly took personal interest in the management of her properties, hiring the *vignarolo* (sharecropper), and demonstrating an interest in the lands' produce. One can imagine that she also knew the members of her urban household well and, in that daily face-to-face world of servants and fellow family members, the level of accounting rigor demanded by her cardinal son must have looked excessive. Did one surrender (as Olimpia apparently was asked to do) the future independence promised by a dowry only to be required to get receipts for bread? What did it mean to be the *padrona* of such an enterprise? Olimpia might also have viewed Cardinal Francesco's "rescue" of the Barberini jewels from the Monte di Pietà very differently. From her vantage point, the receipts secured a modicum of independence in a state of Barberini financial dissolution, when neither she nor her daughter were receiving adequate support.

Since, by Cardinal Francesco's account, Olimpia resisted his repeated attempts to negotiate a different settlement regarding her dowry, it is safe to assume that she had decided that she should opt for some independence from her sons, the one who had insisted on ruling as a tyrant and the other who insisted on the rule of the master ledgers. Neither of these must have struck Olimpia as particularly appealing modes of governing the *casa*. Olimpia's account makes clear that part of the pleasure in belonging to the Barberini *casa* went beyond playing what she called her "destined" role; if she belonged to the family then she had to have the freedom to pursue the things that interested her: cultivating some rural property; looking after her daughters' well-being; enjoying her apartments in the Palazzo Barberini alle Quattro Fontane. Pleasure was an essential component in the aristocratic *casa*, and if denied, then some distance (for Olimpia, financial distance) was probably necessary to restore it.

Olimpia and Cardinal Francesco both agreed that there should be limitations on the power of the individual entrusted with the stewardship of the Barberini property held in entail. Their clashing perspectives show us how difficult such parameters could be to draw to the general agreement of all concerned. "All the world," it seemed to the Barberini cardinal, watched his family's humiliating slip down the Roman social ladder. But as the disagreement with his mother showed, ascending the ladder was fraught with as much public scrutiny as the fall when there was little agreement about which part of the patrimony was most critical to save or when family members found that such rescue missions required too great a personal cost. Anyone who has ever gazed in wonder upon the mighty monument to recordkeeping built by the early modern nobility must remember that its massiveness conceals the dissent of those who, like Olimpia, seem to have wondered what was being lost when that level of accounting complexity crossed the threshold of the noble *casa*. The *casa* was more than a business; it was also a dynasty – a monument in land, in genealogy, in buildings as well as a complicated set of human relationships between noble family members and the people who served them. Even in times of crisis, it was risky to emphasize one aspect of the *casa* to the exclusion of the rest. In the face of criticism by two sons, Olimpia articulated a boundary between herself and the aristocratic enterprise, positing that a successful aristocratic *casa* had to be mindful of such separations, carved in her narrative by "things of her own ... made by her ... for her use."[131]

Both Olimpia and Cardinal Francesco promoted the idea that an emotional bond connects the individual to the noble family. Beyond the evenhandedness of its opening, Cardinal Francesco's is the more emotionally charged of the two accounts. The tragedy of the *casa* manifests itself psychologically and physically with his "crying" and "throwing" himself physically into the arms of his potential benefactors. However, his passionate sentiments clearly run in the direction of the *casa* in the abstract rather than toward any individual family member in particular. The individuals he most praises in his account are the "good friends" who help him work his financial miracles.[132] His account also had to answer the charge that he had not been a good son in the eyes of Pope Clement XI himself: Cardinal Francesco was overly legalistic with his mother and failed to do what a son should, that is, support his mother no matter what the legal particulars of her dowry or her debts might be. The cardinal answered this charge by enumerating his acts of filial devotion (cash payments and debt settlements) and suggesting by his extremely negative portrait of his mother that she probably received more of his filial dedication than she deserved.

Olimpia's affection for the *casa* and her *figli* was one of the most significant reasons she gave for the personal sacrifices she made on their behalf. Her written account and her deeds simultaneously underscored her emotional ties to the *casa*, while marking out her separateness from it. Olimpia navigated a world of economic and cultural upheaval where a mother's affection assumed a greater valence, however vague its definition and unprecedented its legal status.[133] She ruminated as much on the complexities of power in the family as she did on the place of affection within it, but she never abandoned one for the other. She rejected both a familial political order in which one son might rule alone and the mercantile model in which all had to answer to the master ledger, personified (I suspect) in her mind by Cardinal Francesco. Her rejection of his overtures to negotiate her dowry suggests that, for Olimpia, affection (like accounting and power) had to have its limits within the aristocratic *casa*.

3

At the Nexus of Impossibility

The Medical and the Maternal
in Seventeenth-Century Rome

The activities of a *mater litigans* advanced family interests and were an integral part of the lives of Roman aristocratic women, although such deeds could disturb seventeenth-century observers, especially if they crossed the boundaries between service to the *casa* and freewheeling independence.[1] While advocating for her natal and marital families was critical, it was scarcely a woman's sole obligation, although it has proven easier to capture than the details of women's domestic affairs, such as childbearing and childrearing. We know far more about aristocratic women's public functions than we do about their maternal role in the nursery. The latter is a shadowy domain, where mothers encountered different but no less formidable adversaries – illness and death, the latter sometimes inexplicable, dreadful in its mystery and frequency. These two realms of female activity, the domestic and the political, figured prominently in the lives of aristocratic women, as the long days of Anna Colonna among the Barberini illuminated. A comparison of Roman women's reproductive and public functions reveals that there was a domestic iteration of the *mater litigans*, an obscure twin of its conflicting obligations and conflicts. In neither realm was the outcome entirely within the mother's control. In both domains, she was considered subordinate to the *padrone* of the dynasty. For aristocratic families perilously close to genealogical disaster, the procreation and survival of offspring was suffused with anxiety. The pressure upon the mother to bring about its resolution became commensurately greater than in a family bountiful in progeny. For if there could be no survival for an aristocratic family without its prestigious territories, nor could there be any future without the physical replication of the dynasty in a new generation. An exploration of medical matters is especially instructive for understanding mothering and conflict, since illness itself was a moment for anxiety and frequent disagreement among family members about the best course of action.[2] Medical conflicts also reveal the emotional distress of mothers in times of intense maternal care, a moment in which, it was believed, such emotions could both facilitate but also potentially compromise the health of mother and offspring.

The intricacies of maternal maneuvers through such situations have been hard to grasp, since childcare in sickness and in health was done more in person than in writing, leaving us in ignorance about the domestic realm of Roman mothers. The separation of mothers from daughters could create contexts in which women wrote rather than talked about the difficulties of post-partum recovery and the stopping of the flow of breast milk.[3] Inexperienced and isolated mothers also sought long-distance counsel through letter writing. Olimpia Giustiniani wrote a disconsolate missive to her grandmother, Olimpia Maidalchini, longing for advice about her firstborn's difficulties. She eventually turned to her midwife for much-needed insight about her newborn.[4] Anna Colonna, who knew well the pain of losing a child, poured out her mothering troubles in letters to her husband, Taddeo Barberini, whose military duties in the 1640s kept him from Rome. Circumstances of distance, the remoteness of family members, or life-threatening situations prompted written communiqués by women who were unable to see those whom they most trusted.

These glimpses of the domestic side of the *mater litigans* swell to a flood of information, rumination, and protest in the letters of Eleonora Boncompagni Borghese (1642–95). In a rare compendium of medical wisdom and insights on childrearing, she contemplated the problems of the aristocratic mother in over 800 pages of letters that range widely over the medical and the familial, the domestic and the political as they intersected in the world of aristocratic women.[5] They were motivated by the miles between Eleonora and her much younger and beloved sister-in-law, Ippolita Ludovisi Boncompagni (1663–1733). Since Ippolita was in the most intense period of childbearing and childrearing, Eleonora focused frequently on the difficulties of the nursery and of the survival of young children. Especially critical in the mid-1680s was the survival of Ippolita's son Ugo, the long-awaited heir of the Boncompagni family, who was born healthy but subsequently suffered from a "labyrinth of maladies" that were both inexplicable and fatal.[6]

By the seventeenth century, Roman mothers faced such situations in a shifting medical context, where physicians encroached upon the (mostly) female sphere of the nursery. Physicians were relative newcomers to such settings; they arrived there during the same period in which the respective roles of physicians, barbers, barber-surgeons, and midwives came under increasing scrutiny.[7] Their attention to very young children had been scant between antiquity and the Renaissance, but in the seventeenth century they would bring the young under their consideration.[8] Romans sought them out especially in the desperate case where the sole heir of a dynasty might be seriously ill or in danger of dying. Typically, the care of infants and toddlers was the domain of mothers, midwives, wet nurses, and – when called in by the mother – surgeons. Husbands and fathers also participated in decisions about childcare, as Anna Colonna's detailed communiqués to her husband Taddeo illustrated. Physicians suggested, but Anna directed, with input from Taddeo, what needed to be done.[9] The increasing recourse to the physicians challenged the way aristocratic women envisaged their activities as caregivers and resulted in an additional obligation for such women – the monitoring of the professionalized medical care of their children. The input of medical professionals necessitated more complex decisions regarding children's care in the event of illness, which was frequent, and in a setting in which a wide range of medical, religious, and popular interventions had long been available but where no clear set of priorities applied. Mothers needed to develop special expertise in assessing relatively new choices alongside older practices, advocating for some procedures and opposing others, even if male family members and medical experts disagreed with their views.

Women were close to the porous boundaries between cookery, medicine, and quackery.[10] They were intimately tied to the practice of healing and the physical tending of the sick, although midwives were the only legally licensed female professional healers.[11] Like many of her female Roman peers, health was a key topic of Eleonora's epistolary output.[12] Her knowledge likely raised her to the status of familial expert in matters of health. Eleonora emphasized women's roles in the acquisition and assessment of professionalized medical knowledge, as well as the coordinating of family medical care among practitioners.[13] It was a common feature of everyday life to request, without the consultation of a physician, the intervention of a barber-surgeon for bleeding, as Eleonora frequently did.[14] Eleonora prescribed medical remedies, at least to family members, including remedies that might be taken orally, as well as those spread over the skin. She linked successful mothering to a mastery of syrups, waters, and poultices, products applied to and ingested in the body. She elided the emerging hierarchical distinction made between surgeons, who used their hands, and physicians, who used their intellect to determine medical treatment and were the only healers allowed to prescribe oral medications.[15] Good mothering required knowledge of the external treatment of the body as well as the swallowing of certain cures. Eleonora didn't disagree with all physicians' judgments, and she held some of them in high regard. A good physician and surgeon were invaluable in times of illness.[16] She claimed, however, that she "had considerably more experience than they did" in the treatment of childhood illnesses, and that the acquisition of that expertise was critical to successful mothering.[17]

Such knowledge was scarcely sufficient, since successful mothering without the appropriate demonstration of affection was impossible. She underscored that a mother's emotion also held risks because it could undermine her ability to observe and diagnose. All the mother's efforts could prove insufficient to save a gravely ill child, an agonizing dilemma once as ubiquitous as it is now obscured from our view. Eleonora's goal was to guide her young protégé to success, but her letters reveal the nexus of impossibility at the core of the maternal and the medical in seventeenth-century Rome. Her attempt to make Ippolita a medically savvy mother was fraught with perils and contradictions. Performing the very duties Eleonora counseled eventually jeopardized Ippolita's ability to do other, critical tasks, including expressing maternal emotion but not being ruled by it. The dynamic exchange between Eleonora and Ippolita pinpoints such dilemmas and reveals the contradictions that the younger mother found especially troubling. Eleonora had hoped to teach Ippolita how to meet the adversaries of the nursery, including frequent illness, meddling physicians, misinformed fathers, and "ignorant" wet nurses. Yet, performing the intimate monitoring of a child's health undermined Ippolita's ability to perform other maternal duties, including the acceptance of the loss of the child Eleonora had so meticulously advised her on how to save. Eleonora charted the territory that Ippolita had to face, but ultimately, her maternal map failed the younger mother. These two mothers, separated by a generation, by the Roman countryside, and by medical differences, illuminate a clash of perspectives that unsettled mothering in the seventeenth century and extended the negotiations of the *mater litigans* from tribunal to cradle, from negotiating with male relatives to bartering with the Almighty over the life and death of a child.

The View of Motherhood from Midlife

Eleonora wrote to bridge the distance between herself and her admired sister-in-law Ippolita Ludovisi, who had married Eleonora's twin brother,

Gregorio (1643–1707) in 1681. Eleonora resided in Rome, where in her youth she had married into one of the wealthiest and most prominent families, the Borghese. Her brother and his new wife Ippolita lived 70 miles from the papal capital, in the Duchy of Sora, the Boncompagni's most prestigious territory at the boundary between the Papal States and the Kingdom of Naples. Ippolita had grown up a city girl and once declared to her uncle that she never wished to leave Rome.[18] But her marriage to Gregorio had led her to the Boncompagni's castle, where snow could stay on the mountains until late April, and the gentle waterfall of the Liri River was the auditory backdrop of their country lives[19] (Figure 3.1). The marriage of Ippolita and Gregorio was considered a great match in Rome. Gregorio wrote her ardent love letters, vaunting her future place among the Boncompagni: "My house is your house and in it you are the Absolute Padrona."[20] Gregorio's mother was similarly enthusiastic, rejoicing that Ippolita would govern the Boncompagni and her husband, Gregorio, who needed her guidance.[21] Ippolita linked an impressive Roman dynasty to the Boncompagni, a family whose

Figure 3.1   After Ernst Fries, *View of the Waterfalls near Isola di Sora with Peasants in the Foreground*; after Ernst Fries, Lithograph, 1849–51. Courtesy of the British Museum.

most prestigious territory, Sora, pulled them toward the Kingdom of Naples. The tie to the Ludovisi reinforced the Boncompagni connection to the papal city. While Ippolita's brother appeared to be nothing but trouble, her uncle, Cardinal Niccolò Albergati Ludovisi (1608–87), was a potentially valuable Boncompagni ally, who could assist them in papal politics. He could be courted through Ippolita, who was very attached to the cardinal.[22]

Gregorio was much taken with Ippolita's affection and refinement.[23] Eleonora was also extremely fond of her sister-in-law, and she communicated the respect and admiration of her siblings as well, underscoring that "the greatest fortune of our *casa* is you."[24] Eleonora considered it a dream to spend hours in conversation with Ippolita.[25] She professed to love Ippolita as a daughter, as "mothers truly love when it is merited and not as merely required as with my daughter for whom I have only the *caritas* required by God for one's neighbor, and nothing more."[26] With her own daughter she kept up the communications required by decorum,[27] whereas with Ippolita she maintained a steady stream of gifts and good wishes.[28] She confessed that she loved her more than her own daughter, and Ippolita's offspring more than her grandchildren by her daughter.[29] Eleonora was genuinely moved by Ippolita's outpourings of warm feelings, her generous deliveries of fish and fruit, and her expressions of concern for the older mother.[30] Eleonora's illnesses and personal circumstances made it difficult for her to respond in kind, which embarrassed her, though she forwarded exemplars of the latest French fashion, gifts for Ippolita's daughters, and her recommended cures, sometimes at the request of Ippolita.[31] She considered Ippolita an exceptional daughter: "Another like you would be hard to find," although by her own admission, she, "bad" mother that she was, did not deserve "a daughter as good as Ippolita."[32] A love this intense bordered on selfishness on her own part, since Eleonora "for her own interest," wanted Ippolita to live nearer to her.[33] But in her despondent moments, proximity seemed more of a necessity than an indulgence, as Eleonora considered the sight of Ippolita, Gregorio, and their children one of her few consolations, "the only medication for her soul."[34] But such a consoling vista was rare, since her maladies left her as motionless as "a log," as wide as an Alpine cow, unable to travel to those whose presence would have brought such comfort to her.[35] She had to settle for a painting of her favorite family.[36]

Despite the distance, Eleonora expressed her desire to serve Ippolita, Gregorio, and their offspring, especially during the illness of their eldest child, Ugo (1684–86).[37] Eleonora, ever more anxious for news of the ailing boy, pledged her devotion with increasing fervor, avowing that she would send her own blood, if it could aid him.[38] At Ugo's death, she reminded the young mother that she was with her "in her heart and in her thoughts."[39] Although distance and Eleonora's health problems prohibited her from seeing Ippolita and her children as often as she would have liked,[40] she wrote continuously, sought out medical opinions, and sent them the medications that she thought most efficacious, as demonstrations of her affection and her devotion.[41]

Eleonora's letters mitigated Ippolita's isolation during difficult years. Ippolita could not rely upon the advice of her mother, who had died when Ippolita was two years old. Ippolita did have the assistance of her experienced mother-in-law, who resided in Sora, but she actively sought out the long-distance exchange with her older sister-in-law, Eleonora, with whom she shared her troubles in writing, between their visits with each other. Sadly, Ippolita's frequent and copious correspondence to Eleonora is now lost. To Ippolita's frequent missives, Eleonora responded in kind, offering her varied medical and maternal experiences in a correspondence that stretched across more than a decade.

Eleonora viewed domestic matters from the perspective of midlife and from the success of having raised her own children to adulthood. She looked back in hindsight, prompted to such reflections by the difficulties of Ippolita, the "young thing" then fully immersed in the demands of frequent childbearing, childrearing, and the seemingly endless round of maladies that constituted daily life.[42] Eleonora pondered the meaning of illness and of medical care, and was especially attentive to discrepancies in interpretation between Eleonora and her younger sister-in-law, between Eleonora and medical professionals, and between Eleonora and other family members. Eleonora attempted to describe a coherent set of practices that would allow the younger Ippolita to navigate the conflicting medical advice and services at her disposal, and to care effectively for her young offspring in a way that promised the greatest chance for their survival.

Aristocratic family practices had profoundly shaped such domestic affairs. Excessive limitations on how many children could marry meant that some women's task of childbearing could be particularly highly pressured. This was certainly the case with Ippolita because the fecundity of her husband's mother, Maria Ruffo Boncompagni (1620–1705), had been squandered by the limitations on marriage to only two of the thirteen children, Gregorio (the spouse of Ippolita) and his sister, Eleonora.[43] Gregorio had fathered only one illegitimate daughter during his first marriage of 12 years and his sexual liaisons on the side.[44]

Of Gregorio's ten siblings who lived until the 1680s, seven were girls (and six of these were in convents), one of his brothers had taken clerical vows (Francesco) but this brother was of frail health and not expected to live long and died in 1690. At his death, the next brother (Giacomo) then entered the church (and eventually became a cardinal), while a third, much younger Boncompagni brother, waited in the wings (Antonio). Gregorio was the heir-apparent, determined to have a son, and obsessed with worry about the boy, Ugo, whom Ippolita bore him on May 6, 1684.[45] A significant portion of Eleonora's early correspondence was devoted to Ugo's health problems, which emerged gradually and worsened as he approached his first birthday. They would continue intermittently until his untimely death in December 1686.[46]

The Boncompagni were not alone in their dilemmas. Death and tight restrictions on the number of children of each generation who could marry had decimated the Ludovisi as well. Tragedy and youthful mortality further weakened their family tree. One unfortunate loss early in the seventeenth century had been that of Cardinal Ludovico Ludovisi (1595–1632), who died at the age of 37. Ippolita's father had sought to address their dwindling numbers by including an adopted family member, a cousin, Cardinal Niccolò Albergati (1608–87), who adjoined Ludovisi to his name. Cardinal Niccolò was considered by Ippolita to be very much a part of her family. She assiduously followed news of his health, and his passing caused her considerable grief.[47] Ippolita had been without her parents from the age of two, and by the 1680s, Ippolita's much older spendthrift brother had yet to produce an heir (and would later die the same year as his infant son, 1699). One of Ippolita's sisters (Olimpia, or Suor Anna) was in a Roman convent, an unhappy and unpredictable nun.[48] Lavinia, her remaining sister, had died shortly after giving birth to her son (who also died) in 1681.

Eleonora sought to mentor her motherless and nearly sisterless younger sister-in-law from a more settled phase of the maternal timeline, after her three sons and one daughter had survived to adulthood. Her aches and pains and bedridden Sundays unfolded in a life emptying of children, an absence that left her, therefore, time to reflect upon her own struggles as a mother, and upon the hereafter, to which she conceded she had devoted little effort in the hustle and bustle of Roman life.[49] While Eleonora's stated aim was to serve Ippolita, her effusive comments capture the multifaceted nature of long epistolary exchanges. Eleonora's pensive ruminations were sometimes words written as much to herself as to her beloved Ippolita, though advice specifically for the younger mother flowed freely from the pen of Eleonora.[50] For Ippolita's sake, Eleonora tried to be of general good cheer. Sometimes, a healing remedy had good effect, as in the case of a special potion from Sicily or Eleonora's successful recourse to donkey milk.[51] The ensuing truce with her maladies gave her a needed reprieve after months of difficulty.[52] But her optimism could also fall prey to her many health issues, chronicled in passages devoted to her headaches, hemorrhoids, and heart palpitations.[53] On bad days, her writing seems to come from beyond the grave, though she was but a little past 40 years old when their correspondence began.[54] Unexpected amusements helped her shake off her illness,[55] but at other times, Eleonora's preference during excruciating pain was "to stay in bed and scream."[56] Unfortunately, it was the season of visiting, and a noble-woman had her obligations to fulfill. Her perceived proximity to death left her indifferent to the potential impending celestial doom that panicked friends and relatives during an eclipse in the summer of 1684. She was sick then too, but not too ill to get out of bed and see what all the fuss was about.[57]

But make no mistake about it, sick or well, Eleonora was a bulldozer of a woman, a force to be reckoned with, even when she acknowledged her subjugation to the men of her household. "If I were the boss of me," she hypothesized, she would spend more time with Ippolita and her son Ugo.[58] Eleonora claimed that her eldest son was now in the realm of his father but still she hesitated to relinquish control.[59] During the 1670s, rumors had circulated that it was Eleonora rather than her husband, Giovanni Battista, who was most involved in a major renovation to the Borghese palace. The Borghese prince was evidently "angry for being led around by the nose by his Consorte and the architect ..." the gossip sheets of Rome intimated.[60] Subsequently, the offending architect was fired, which attests to who had the final say in the Borghese house-hold (Eleonora's husband, as she asserted in her letters to Ippolita). As the mother of a daughter of marriageable age, Eleonora complained that she was compelled to make the rounds of comedies, dances, and conversations, despite the limitations of her health.[61] Yet, she clearly liked a good season of carnival festivities and encouraged Ippolita to enjoy them as well.[62] Her portrait by the French artist Ferdinand Voet captured her youthful beauty and the worldly and party-oriented side of Eleonora (Figure 3.2).

Eleonora's portrait mirrored the frankness of her letters, where her words were as straightforward as her gaze. "You were not pretty, in fact you were ugly as a child," she once remarked to Ippolita, "... but now you pass for beautiful."[63] She underscored that the point of such blunt-ness was to undermine Ippolita's doubts about the future beauty of her

Figure 3.2 Jacob Ferdinand Voet, *Portrait of Eleonora Boncompagni Borghese,* seventeenth century, oil on canvas, © Ville de Nantes- Musée des Beaux-Arts. Photographie: A. Guillard.

newborn girl, who was evidently not the most attractive infant, but about whom Eleonora remained defensive and optimistic.[64] Eleonora recognized that in expressing such things she took liberties, but cast her bluntness as either "true sentiment" or a sincerity that "love and duty required of her."[65] In some letters her frankness went too far, for they wounded rather than soothed the already anxious mother.[66] Eleonora then either asked pardon of Ippolita, or requested that she be judged in context of the affection and tenderness that she bore for Ippolita.[67] She was mortified in one instance that her comments might appear to Ippolita a betrayal.[68] Eleonora explained that she spoke with "confidence" because she "love[d] Ippolita like a mother [would]."[69] It was affection that inspired her revelatory bombshells, which were often on matters of health. Apologies were forthcoming, but perfunctory, since

Eleonora's blunt advice kept coming.[70] Her "interest and worry" over the ailing Ugo inspired her to share her own experience that she believed might shed light on his condition.[71] Ippolita was besieged by contradictory medical advice and hesitated at times to take Eleonora's counsel, a demurral that prompted further rumination on Eleonora's part.[72]

Ippolita Ludovisi often welcomed Eleonora's opinions anyway as she entered a new phase in her relationship to the Boncompagni. By producing offspring, Ippolita established for herself a more secure link to her marital kin: the Boncompagni, Eleonora reminded her, were "a *casa* that is your [*casa*] as long as you have children."[73] Not surprisingly, then, a significant portion of the early correspondence with Eleonora is devoted to the health problems of Ugo, who was born healthy as well as beautiful, but who then suffered a series of illnesses and physical problems.[74] Within about three years following Ugo's birth, Ippolita would bear two more children. The frequent correspondence between the two women paralleled the intensity of maternal involvement on the part of Ippolita, as she faced the dual burden of caring for an ailing child and continuing to bear other offspring. To guide Ippolita in these difficulties, Eleonora focused her attention on the issues of health and illness in the growing Boncompagni family.

The Domestic Affairs of the Aristocratic Nursery

The role of aristocratic women in the routine activities of caring for children has been downplayed because their offspring were reared in conjunction with wet nurses and servants.[75] Reliance upon wet nurses certainly raised the fertility of aristocratic women, who did not experience lactational amenorrhea, and could thus become pregnant not long after giving birth. Sexual intercourse, pregnancy, or menstruation were thought to ruin the milk for the baby's consumption, hence the reliance by elite parents upon a lactating woman to succor their offspring, so that they could return to the task of procreation.[76] Mothering and frequent birthing required the collaboration of at least two women in order to be successful.[77] Aristocratic women generated considerable epistolary evidence that indicates a deep involvement with the growth and development of their children, even if other women nursed them.

Successful childrearing began with the selection of the wet nurse, which, for Eleonora, meant attention to the quality of the milk she produced.[78] Milk was the "principal foundation" of infant care, and without it, the child was in jeopardy.[79] The quality of the milk was revealed in the infant's physiological well-being, although she acknowledged the emotional security that breastfeeding provided the child.[80] Eleonora emphasized how well Ugo was doing physically, that is, "whether he was getting strong and big was the sign that the milk suited him."[81] The mother's key task was to develop keen skills of observation of the child's body, so that she could assess how well the wet nursing was progressing.[82] Ancient and subsequent medical texts had underscored the necessity of the good character of the nurse, even if a slave or a social inferior, since such traits were believed to have an impact upon the character of the child. Eleonora ignored the long-held notion that the character of the wet nurse mattered.[83] Children took after their parents in their disposition and physical development.[84] The personal matters of the wet nurse's character were irrelevant.[85] Eleonora anticipated the most controversial and innovative ideas about wet nursing by about 50 years: physicians in London would later express similar doubts, but not until the 1730s.[86]

Close attention also had to be given to the body of the wet nurse, whose health and diet could have a significant impact on the milk she provided the child.[87] Eleonora's copious commentary on the wet nurse's milk production (or lack therof) contrasted sharply with the paucity of insight on such matters in the detailed compendium of medical knowledge in the Boncompagni household.[88] The scarcity of such references in the information-packed volume underscores the lack of medical interest in early infancy. Her loquacity on the subject of infant feeding testified instead to the significance of such matters to aristocratic mothers.[89] Eleonora dismissed the physicians' solutions to increase milk production as ineffective anyway.

Although suitable milk consumption was essential to healthy children, motherhood also involved rigorous attention to the diverse elements of their care. Swaddling, for instance, was considered a critical tool in the successful physiological development of a child, and so clearly belonged in the mother's purview.[90] Eleonora expressed her disappointment about one of Ippolita's midwives, who didn't swaddle tightly enough, in her opinion.[91] She was nostalgic for the old days, when wet nurses made some good-looking babies, and they knew how to swaddle.[92] It was the mother who had to attend to the failure or success in swaddling by her (likely) deficient wet nurses.

Even Eleonora's bitter comment that the "wet nurses were the bosses of the mother" was combined with the counsel that mothers, nonetheless, should never be far from their children, especially when they were in the wet nurses' care.[93] The frequent departures of the wet nurses meant that it was the mother, rather than the wet nurse, who remained the constant figure in the child's life and who was to guide the young child through the milestones of development.[94] Her attention was essential in the child's gradual transition from breast milk to solid foods, although breast milk was to be continued as long as possible since it would have mitigated the dangers associated with the introduction of food.[95] Eleonora had specific advice about recipes for the first foods that children could easily digest, and she had a number of empirically tested recipes.[96] She stressed the importance not only of what the young child might eat and at what age, but how such food should be presented, at what time of the day, and in what sequence.[97] Since the risks of dehydration were high and potentially deadly, the mother had to be especially attentive during weaning and knowledgeable about the proper drinks for very young children.[98] A small amount of wine mixed in with a substantial amount of water was an appropriate drink for a one-year-old, and a praiseworthy libation for a two-year-old.[99] Eleonora's mind ranged over the possibilities of healthful drinks for babies – contemplating their purgative, respiratory, and alimentary impacts.[100]

As her infants grew, Ippolita was to devote herself not only to how their body matured, but also to how they progressed through developmental stages, including the child's psychological maturity. She cautioned Ippolita to accept her children as they were, including the spirited and argumentative nature of her daughters, which was a good sign, even if such qualities could drive a mother crazy and would necessitate more careful monitoring, once the child became ambulatory and inclined to share her opinions with the relatives.[101] Eleonora acknowledged that the developmental achievements of walking and talking were the domain of the mother, but cautioned her that children's growth could be beyond her control and could vary considerably from child to child. Boys talked later than girls and this difference was not a cause for concern.[102] She urged Ippolita not to carry Ugo too much, which she thought slowed brain development and weakened eyesight and legs. Instead, the mother instead should have the child in a carriage or monitor closely his attempts at walking, or let him crawl on all fours. Outside was the ideal location for such activities: "Fresh air was the best medicine" and could also help the child get over coughs and congestion.[103] A little sweating was also recommended and to be expected as children took their first steps in the summer heat.[104]

Even what Ippolita assessed as Ugo's delay in walking (and subsequent weakness in legs) as well as his belated use of speech were not matters of concern. Her own sons had talked intelligibly only at around three years old.[105] The difficulty was that a late-walking, late-talking child lacked these amusements and might turn to eating the way infants turned to suckling – as partially a way to pass time.[106] Ugo was still, at 16 months, within the parameters of development for learning to walk. Eleonora knew of a child who had not walked independently until he was three years old, and only after the application of an unguent to his knees, which Eleonora volunteered to send Ippolita if the latter were unavailable locally.[107] Since Ugo had a history of seizures, Eleonora thought it likely that his walking would be delayed, since she believed he would have suffered minor nerve damage as a result.[108] In light of his seizures, it was not surprising that he appeared to be developing more slowly.[109] "If he gets through [all of this], he will learn to do everything," she observed and urged Ippolita to listen to an older mother's experience, rather than panic in the face of Ugo's difficulties.[110] Time and patience were the key.[111] When, in the spring of 1686, Ugo did indeed walk, Eleonora smiled to see her prophesy fulfilled.[112]

With her child, the aristocratic mother should physically demonstrate her feelings and form a strong and continuous relationship that would counterbalance what could, at times, become a rapid turnover of wet nurses. In such a scenario, the love of the mother was critical.[113] Girls and boys were all a gain to the *casa* and Eleonora would show the same affection to a child whether boy or girl.[114] Eleonora assured Ippolita that she herself would caress Ugo, if she were there, and urged Ippolita to do the same, in Eleonora's place, until she could see him again.[115] Ippolita and Gregorio evidently needed little encouragement in demonstrating their affection for Ugo, as parents and child engaged in co-sleeping in the chilly nights of September. Eleonora acknowledged the attraction of this practice (pronouncing it a "delight" of childrearing) and underscored its utility since their bed was obviously warmer than Ugo's cradle.[116] Whereas breastfeeding would in the modern era be the activity most associated with bonding between mother and child, Eleonora's comments emphasized the value of and attested to the practice of other forms of maternal bonding that could occur through holding, caressing, attending to the infant's needs, and following his or her development. Raising children from the perils of infancy to the boundaries of adulthood required the mother's scrutiny of the wet nurses, acute skills of assessment in reading children's bodies, and the ability to meet the challenge of the frequent illnesses of childhood.

Souls Held by Teeth: Childhood Illness and Medicine in Early Modern Rome

Eleonora insisted that the health of infants and toddlers rested upon the attentiveness of the mother, yet the mother could not prevent the occurrence of all childhood illnesses. Scrupulous attention and the proper equilibrium of affection and clear-sighted analysis were necessary in such scenarios. Mothering required a woman to adapt to the episodic near-death experiences of her offspring, to the moments when a child appeared to "hold his soul by the teeth,"[117] or to have been "pulled from the grave" by a last-minute intervention.[118] The mother should be on the alert for the appearance of minor and major illnesses in her children, but not become consumed with worry about them. Maternal emotions had to remain under control in order to plot a course through such storms. Mothers should be the masters of medical advice from doctors (who contradicted each other), midwives and wet nurses (who in her view could lack intelligence), and nervous family members (who could make things worse rather than better). Intertwined with the early modern bricolage of medical choices was religious faith, the notion of a deity who "either wanted or permitted" the illness of a child, in the face of which the mother should calmly resign herself to his will, while searching assiduously for a solution until the life of the child was lost.[119] Resignation was combined with steady activity and the determination to rescue the child. In the midst of difficulty with one of her offspring, the mother was also to continue to pay close attention to what might best maintain the well-being of her other children. Maternal activity required tolerance for the repetitive and mundane as well as a capacity for crisis, when visceral emotion had to be tempered by close observation and experienced diagnosis.

The foundation for such success was immersion in medical discourse and firsthand experience of illness. Epistolary activity was one vehicle for such knowledge. Eleonora valued her correspondents' information, especially that of Cardinal Albergati Ludovisi, who along with his news, sent "remedies and recipes."[120] Her interactions with Ippolita included the exchange of similar secrets, as the younger mother occasionally had something to offer the older mother in that regard.[121] Illness narratives could also impart medical insight. When Eleonora ran out of firsthand stories, she offered testimony on the dilemmas of others – a girl of youthful vigor struck down with only enough warning to commend her soul to God, or her brother Francesco's lifetime struggle with incapacitating digestive ailments and circulatory problems.[122] She could draw upon the vagaries of her own children's maladies and near-death experiences that she remembered vividly – her son Paolo, skinny as a skeleton, yellow as a lemon, phlegm-filled, weak in the stomach.[123] Urine in all its deficits, excesses, and idiosyncracies was a key factor in ascertaining health. Graphic observations were interspersed with recipes for a malady's antidotes, the appropriate blend of home purges and pomades; praise for the virtues of bloodletting; recommendations for the city with the best doctors (Naples); the proper use of swaddling and corsets; the superiority of Florentine powders that formed the basis of many of her cures.[124] Her medical know-how was interspersed with pithy proverbs to make it memorable, such as "the mouth carries the legs," which she employed to describe a specific period of childhood when diet was essential to form a child who could successfully learn to walk."[125]

From the hindsight of the twenty-first century, Eleonora's eclectic dabbling appears to be part of an early modern set of healing practices, a "medical pluralism" in which seventeenth-century people practiced a "therapeutic calculus" when faced with an illness and with the variety of healers from among whom they might seek guidance.[126] Such calculations might lead them to rely simultaneously on healers and remedies that were ecclesiastical, medical, or popular with considerable overlap between these approaches to disease.[127] Eleonora embraced the widely shared medical belief that causes of illness could be both natural and divine and that remedies should be sought accordingly in both spheres, although she tended toward the material more than the spiritual. She believed that illness could be read as a punishment from God, but she did not put much credence in the role of the diabolical, either in the cause of diseases or in exorcism as a potential cure for them.[128] The medical narratives in her epistolary outpourings typically lack the miraculous element, even if divine influence was generally acknowledged by her in sickness and in health.[129] By her own estimation, Eleonora was not particularly devout, although she occasionally mentioned the efficacy of certain devotions, including the feast of the Assumption of Mary in August, a ritual moment in the city of Rome when all of its neighborhoods and governing authorities came together in pious procession.[130] The Madonna of August was especially significant for Eleonora because she protected pregnant women and children.[131] Eleonora also put great stock in a spiritual figure in Rome who was never canonized a saint, but who had emerged as a "living saint" in the Borghese *casa*, Camilla Orsini Borghese. Camilla was the grandmother of Eleonora's husband and, once widowed, would eventually found her own convent (Santissima Annunziata) and take religious vows and the name Suor Maria Vittoria.[132] Eleonora had known well this grandmother-in-law, who had delayed her entry into religious life to mentor her young granddaughter-in-law Eleonora during her early years of childrearing.[133] She admired her virtues, but pronounced herself incapable of reaching her relative's level of sanctity, and was more drawn to her practicality than to her piety.[134] Eleonora invoked her more frequently after 1685, the year in which Camilla/Suor Maria Vittoria died and in which Ugo experienced his first seizures.[135] In the time of Ugo's greatest difficulties, Eleonora confessed that she implored her deceased grandmother-in-law to intercede for God's mercy upon the boy.[136]

Spirituality and corporeality were connected in Eleonora's mind. Maladies of the soul could result in illness in the body or worsen an existing malady.[137] The relationship was an especially close one for mothers. Eleonora noted that Ippolita's sickness was related to her son's difficulties.[138] Perfect health would likely return when the medical issues of her son Ugo were resolved.[139] Ippolita's subsequent illness after the death of Ugo was not a surprise to Eleonora, who advised the young mother to put her soul in order if she wished to be physically well.[140] "The illness of the soul," she noted, "was worse than the illness of the body."[141] The rule applied to Eleonora as well. She attributed one of her particular sicknesses as due to her worries about her daughter.[142] She noted of herself in general: "The illness of my body is that of my soul."[143] Spiritual issues could also morph into emotional ones, as she clearly subscribed to the notion that emotions contributed to the onset of ill health, as did many of her contemporaries, including medically trained ones.[144] Melancholic thoughts had to be banished in favor of happy ones for a woman to have a successful birth.[145] Such attitudes were widespread and formed a fundamental part of the medical approach to treating illness, although Eleonora emphasized its heightened implications for mothers.[146]

The calm conducive to pregnancy was critical also to successful mothering: From childrearing ("with some children all it takes is patience") to the vagaries of dealing with mysterious illnesses ("one can never lose heart") and the perplexing behaviors on the part of men ("better to recommend them to God"), a courageous forbearance was essential.[147] Patience might heal a child faster than a physician's prescriptions.[148] Childrearing, Eleonora reminded Ippolita, necessitated perseverance in the face of recurring dilemmas: "After good things, you must be prepared for bad ones," she opined to the young mother.[149] She recalled the saying of her own mentor, her grandmother-in-law turned nun, Suor Maria Vittoria, who had observed blithely, "Young children get by and they live to do it all, but [the mother] needs a great strength of spirit and an unflappable calm."[150] Many daily situations were not, in Eleonora's view, particularly serious: cradle scalp, stomach ailments, teething, and colds were among the repetitive troubles that children might outgrow or that a change in practice on the part of the mother might alleviate.[151] Philosophically (and far from Ippolita's domestic scene), Eleonora observed that even jags of infant crying were not all cause for dismay (especially in girls) since infants sometimes needed to blow off steam, though she invoked God to bring such outbursts to an end for she knew that they were difficult to bear.[152]

The mother had to consider the variety of factors that might contribute to infant discomfort. The hot weather of summer or the extreme cold of winter could worsen an ordinary illness and exacerbate the symptoms of teething.[153] Some children just fared better with the end of the perilous summer weather, but the winter chill could also slow child development.[154] Such knowledge might mitigate a mother's worry, but it could never eliminate childhood illnesses. The mother had to learn that they were part of the expected stuff of young childhood from which many children recovered but not without struggle: "Few are the children," she noted, "who grow up happily."[155] Yet, children bounced back from their setbacks, if the mother could bring patience and common sense to the situation, and if she could learn to read the details that might impinge upon the child's illness.

Maternal tenderness, while essential, could obscure the mother's view. "Affection and a lack of experience and at times ignorance can trick [the mother] into believing things that are not true," Eleonora observed. This could cause the mother to think that the child was more ill than she or he was in reality.[156] The insights of others were not necessarily helpful in this regard, and a new mother might take them too much to heart. Eleonora's own sons, many had predicted, would not live to adulthood but were now "healthy and robust men."[157] Many cases that Eleonora described had seemed disastrous, but turned out well.[158] Ippolita also worried over every possible error that she might have made. Eleonora sympathized with the novice mother's worry, confessing that she too had made mistakes in treating her own children's maladies. This common maternal shortcoming was exacerbated for Ippolita because, for a time, she had only one child, and therefore, little with which to compare his dilemmas.[159] Eleonora cautioned Ippolita against making predictions, since she lacked sufficient experience as a mother to do so accurately.[160]

In the face of a truly grave difficulty, such as the advent of Ugo's childhood seizures, the mother's expectations had to be moderated. The same emotions that caused the mother to overestimate the gravity of the illness could undermine her ability to deal with a serious matter. In such situations, Eleonora believed that the best way to help the child was for the mother to remain collected, rather than to transmit her anxiety to her offspring.[161] The same advice went for the father.[162]

Such sangfroid could be achieved by adjustments to one's outlook: "Just keeping a sick child going was an accomplishment," Eleonora remarked.[163] "After bad, you have to expect good, and after good, you have to expect bad," she commiserated. But a happy day for the child was a good sign, she observed, encouraging Ippolita to appreciate the joys of the present instead of sinking into boundless worry about the child's future.[164]

After the advent of Ugo's seizures, Eleonora continued to reiterate the necessity of the balance between the care of the child and the mental state of the mother.[165] As the years rolled by, and Eleonora thought Ippolita was ignoring her advice, Eleonora escalated her rhetoric, insisting that the health of Ippolita was more important than the health of Ugo, and if Ippolita "loved the Boncompagni *casa*, her husband and her children, then she had to tend to herself before everything else."[166] When Ippolita became pregnant for the second time, Eleonora urged the strategy even more strongly: Ippolita's panic and worry could not help Ugo, and it made Ippolita ill.[167] It would certainly damage Ippolita's second and unborn child, to whom Eleonora continued to remind Ippolita to devote her calm.[168] Though she acknowledged Ippolita's "very intense passion [*passione*]" for Ugo,[169] she cautioned against Ippolita's excessive involvement as the birth of her second child approached. "Leave him in the hands of God, his father, and his grandmother," she urged, so that Ippolita would have time for her own health since the due date for delivery of her second child had already passed.[170]

For many of us, there is no more stress-inducing advice than the admonition to keep calm or the chilling reminder of the risks created by our own anxiety. Ippolita pushed back on this counsel, prompting Eleonora to assure her that while she was within her rights to worry, it was not the best course.[171] Eleonora professed herself more concerned for Ippolita and Gregorio than she was for Ugo, since she was convinced that they would wear themselves out with apprehension.[172] She reminded Ippolita that while her suffering for her son was normal, to push herself to an overwrought state was a requirement neither of "conscience, nor of the affection owed to your *casa* and to your husband."[173] It would impede Ippolita's additional duty of bearing other children for the *casa*.[174] To preserve the life of the child she once carried, Eleonora admitted to having limited her contact with her children when they were ill, since they posed some jeopardy to herself and to the unborn child.[175] At that juncture, Eleonora consigned her ailing offspring to the care of their father and grandmother, the same counsel she urged for Ippolita.[176]

To achieve the elusive calm necessary to good parenting, Eleonora suggested reframing this phase of family life. Eleonora imagined a grown-up Ugo, already a young man,[177] an "*ometto*," alongside Ippolita's second child (still in utero).[178] She recast time for Ippolita by noting that, as mother, Ippolita was rightly bogged down in the rounds of teething and colds, but these were nothing and would pass; in fact, she predicted, the maladies of Ippolita's offspring would make them stronger in the long run.[179] It was best not to make more out of them than they were. In streams of writing that captured colloquial speech, Eleonora described the flow of maternal time which could seem circular rather than linear, a direction and a rhythm to which the mother had to adapt: "[Ugo] does well and then does badly, but you keep him going [*lo tirarete avanti*], and then he will change and then he is twice as old and the season changes."[180] Eleonora also hoped to pull Ippolita out of the terror of her particular sleepless night into the broader pattern of mothering success stories. Ippolita should regard neither her difficulties as mother nor the health problems of her son as unique.[181] Many children who hovered near death later reached healthy adulthood.[182] Eleonora's son Marcantonio had pulled through several maternal heart-stopping incidents.[183] Her sister-in-law, the Principessa Chigi, had endured even more terrible illnesses on the part of her children, yet those children had also recovered and grown up.[184] A modest hope had to underwrite all the mother's efforts in the face of such difficulties. "Through the good and through the bad times, children did grow up," she philosophized.[185] Writing specifically of Ugo, whose health deteriorated in the fall of 1685, Eleonora noted that "as long as he holds on, there's hope."[186] She mentioned only obliquely and quickly the children who did not survive, or she gently cautioned that Ippolita could not yet believe that a miracle had saved Ugo, since until he reached his seventh year, he was not out of danger, considering how ill he had been.[187]

The real worry, she advised, came with the advent of childhood seizures, as she had learned from her own grandmother-in-law turned nun.[188] Yet later, when such seizures struck Ugo, Eleonora acknowledged that they were "the most dangerous and terrible illnesses," but a child could survive and outgrow seizures as well, especially if the child's mental faculties were not damaged as a result of them, as was the case with Ugo, who remained "lively" and not "slow-witted."[189] Eleonora also attempted to mitigate Ippolita's evident terror that Ugo might be epileptic, noting that many children who had childhood seizures did not suffer long-term effects from them, nor did they continue to suffer them in adulthood.[190] Eleonora focused on the fact that Ugo's seizures occurred during fits of coughing, when he was likely short of breath. Her son Paolo, she noted, had had similar coughing spells until he was 14 months old, and though, at the time, Eleonora "believed him dead," he was fine afterward.[191] Even in the event of seizures, a change of wet nurse might well be the cure.[192] Ippolita could be confident, too, in employing the powders Eleonora had sent, which would "do no harm" and which were employed in the treatment of adult epileptics.[193]

Eleonora acknowledged that mothers faced these difficulties in conjunction with physicians and other family members, including the father. Gregorio was a devoted paterfamilias, who communicated directly to Eleonora the news of his growing family, especially its medical news.[194] He informed his sister of the news of the return of Ippolita's menstrual cycle, one clue in assessing her fertility.[195] In the tense days following what appeared to be the first seizure experienced by Ugo, Eleonora wrote to comfort her brother, who was evidently overcome with worry about the health of his son.[196] She grew impatient with him at other times, letting him know that his concern was unwarranted.[197] While Eleonora bore great affection for her brother, she had a rather dismal view of men's abilities in general to manage their own health, much less to tend to the health of their offspring.[198]

Eleonora's own medical opinions defy simple characterization, since relative to the physician advising Ippolita, some of Eleonora's views were innovative but others were ancient. She must have been influenced by the physicians who served noble households, to whom she had regular access.[199] Physicians were considered among the highest ranks of noble employees.[200] Eleonora held some physicians and some surgeons in high regard, recognizing four of them generously in her last will and testament.[201] Did medical professionals welcome her interventions? For physicians she may have only demonstrated the physician Scipione Mercurio's witticism that "every old woman wants to play the doctor."[202] She was unlikely to have been deterred by such criticism or by the injunction against women practicing medicine.[203] Midwives were the only women independently licensed to practice the healing arts, and so allowed because their activities were considered beneath the dignity of professionalizing male practitioners, since they involved menstrual blood.[204] But Eleonora's thoughts ranged more widely, as varied as the issues faced by Ippolita, Eleonora herself, and her far-flung network of family and extended relations. Like the physicians, Eleonora was squarely in the tradition of Galenic medicine – especially the idea that the humors of the body had to be balanced for optimal health – that is, that blood, phlegm, yellow and black bile should be in equilibrium.[205] Each person had her or his own "complexion," a combination of humors that had to be taken into account for good health and healing, in Eleonora's view.[206] Such characteristics could be shared among relatives.[207]

Eleonora was also not alone in her criticisms of physicians, who inspired both admiration and consternation among their seventeenth-century patients. She resisted new trends in the seventeenth century that allocated an expanded role for the physician in the treatment of very young children and that challenged the place of breast milk in child nutrition. In the event of the illness of the child, Eleonora envisioned greater duties for the aristocratic mother while simultaneously assigning more significance to the breast milk provided by the wet nurse. This bifurcated strategy was a core tenet of Eleonora's maternal practices, and sometimes it inspired an outright rejection of the opinion of the physicians who advised Ippolita. She did acknowledge the potential value of some physicians' input and so sent Ippolita the advice of physicians whose counsel she had sought on behalf of the worried younger mother.[208] She thought such advice required careful scrutiny, since not even the physicians agreed upon how to treat the ailing Ugo.[209] Their particular failures in his case illustrated their general shortcomings in treating infants. Physicians' advice could pose dangers and their prescription errors could be deadly. She counseled recourse to them only in specific circumstances.[210] In medicine, as in eating, she recommended a measured approach, "*una buona regola*," rather than excessive dosages or abrupt alternations in treatment, the latter being especially hard on infants and young children.[211] Such advice had to be weighed in conjunction with her opposition to any practice's overuse, lest Ippolita "tire out [the baby]" with repetitive remedies.[212] Alternating solutions could occasionally bring a better outcome for the child's woes.[213] A change in practice might also offer the most effective solutions. Ugo's minor digestive problems, for instance, might be alleviated by allowing him to nurse more often, so that he took in smaller quantities of milk.[214] Physicians, on the other hand, were too quick to resort to medications, when a change in daily practice might be a better solution.

As Ugo's maladies continued, she doubted that further medications or additional consultations from yet more physicians could be the answer.[215] She questioned her son's suggestion that a student of the brilliant physician of Naples, Tommaso Cornelio, could possibly offer insights, though she acknowledged that Cornelio had saved her husband's life during a troubling illness that had stumped the greatest medical minds of Rome and Bologna.[216] Ugo's maladies were likewise mysterious. Desperation and despairing relatives eventually swayed her to the idea that recourse to the best physicians in Naples could be useful.[217] She then again solicited medical opinions in Rome, as the situation with Ugo deteriorated, and Roman physicians held out some cause to be hopeful.[218] She continued to prefer their opinions (especially their emphasis on the use of quinine, one of Eleonora's favorite remedies) to those of Ippolita's local physician, with whom she had disagreed on numerous occasions.[219]

The physician's treatment of Ugo's serious maladies could not assuage Eleonora's doubts about the applicability to children of many medical procedures prescribed by physicians, including those to be carried out by surgeons, especially bloodletting. She was a great proponent of the practice, but she nonetheless shared Ippolita's dilemma at having Ugo bled, since it might cause disgust or fright in him, and thus result, at best, in a compromised benefit.[220] Surgeons were well aware of the problems with bleeding children and sought to distract them during the process.[221] Bloodletting was a complex procedure: from discerning the correct place from among 22 possible sites for bleeding to identifying the right method (leeches, knives, or cupping glasses), it required considerable skill.[222] It is perhaps not surprising that Eleonora was dubious about its application to children. Eleonora concurred that Ugo's difficulties might derive from blockages, a problem for which bloodletting could be the cure, but there were other remedies.[223] She advised the virtues of sweating over the risks of bloodletting in order to balance the body's humors, at least where children were concerned. Provided he did not catch a chill on a windy day, sweating was a good remedy for Ugo's ill health.[224] If bloodletting was absolutely necessary for a child, Eleonora believed that leeches worked better for them than other methods, but they should not be used for long.[225]

Similarly, though cauterization was frequently employed to treat wounds and infections, Eleonora cautioned against its use in Ippolita's still young son Ugo, then about one year old, who had a head wound that did not heal. Rather than apply heat to the child's head (to be avoided whenever possible), Ippolita should return to Eleonora's recommended powders, a light purge, and to a steady supply of fresh milk and broths to encourage healing.[226] After cauterization was used (against Eleonora's advice) she urged the application of butter, almond oil or other unguents to ease the child's pain from it.[227]

Eleonora maintained that in the care and treatment of children there were numerous issues that neither physicians nor men in general could understand.[228] A woman with offspring of her own was more observant and knowledgeable than the doctors about the treatment of those children, she argued.[229] "Even certain things that appear to be trifles mean a lot," she noted, despite the fact that doctors and husbands had trouble reading them.[230] A 1682 decree from Bologna, Italy's most medically sophisticated city, reiterated her view: "[women] are often wont to surpass the industry of men, especially in those things that require diligence and application."[231] Eleonora described her technique as the close scrutiny of the details necessary to understand child health and illnesses. Her reading of minute signs was a skill passed from mothers to daughters, ephemeral in its transmission through words and gestures. Eleonora's letters captured these habits of observation, assessment, and treatment of illness – the work, as she put it, of "a true mother."[232] Physicians were too little acquainted with childcare to have developed such skills.[233] The physician's failure was partly caused by defects in his powers of observation, an inability to grasp significant particulars exacerbated by a lack of sufficient experience with the very young. Any physician's remedy had to be evaluated against the mother's careful observations of the child. Prescribing a purge, for instance, might throw out the good with the bad from the child's body, and could lead to his further weakening and to an imbalance of humors that would make him even more susceptible to seizures.[234] Her skepticism regarding the utility of purges increased as Ugo's health worsened in 1686: a child's body worn out and wasted away had no need of a purge. It would be an additional jeopardy to him.[235]

Physicians violated her general principle that one needed above all to practice moderation in all aspects of living: "[Their] going overboard did harm," she admonished.[236] "Have more faith in good living than in medicines, which, the more you use them, the worse off you are," was another adage of the older mother.[237] Eleonora associated the physician's medications with outcomes that were bizarre and sometimes deadly. Had the son of the Principessa Chigi been left to the care of physicians, he would not have survived.[238] Physicians were especially ignorant about dosing infants and toddlers and tended to overmedicate them, causing them to suffer at times.[239] One physician's medical prescriptions had once turned her child yellow, then red. Only through her care and after much time did he return to his former healthy self.[240] Since physicians' medicines were particularly hard on children's digestion, she urged the use of the smallest possible quantities of medications. Too often the physician's treatment of children failed to fulfill her basic standard for medicine that it should do no harm if it did no good, a measure of good care that she applied to adults as well.[241] If a remedy did no good, it should be eliminated since no medication should be taken without a clear purpose.[242] Children required even more scrupulous ministrations, and for them Eleonora offered instead her tried, true, and less risky remedies.[243] These included simple ointments, herbs, powders from Florence, fortified wine, medicinal waters, and syrups, some of which she sent to Ippolita herself. "This remedy is a proven one," she asserted, when advising Ippolita about a particular recommended ointment or favorite powder.[244] She legitimated these remedies with reference to her numerous observations of children, including her younger siblings, her own children, and the children of the aristocratic women with whom she had close contact, especially her sister-in-law, the Principessa Chigi, a veteran mother of 12 children.

Although Eleonora praised the knowledge gained through interaction with her female peers, she disparaged the knowledge of wet nurses, or the sayings of the *donne*, or as she put it, "the women who don't know where their brains are ... They make foolish mistakes," she complained, "for which it is not easy to find a remedy ... and on account of such women, I once nearly lost a child."[245] Eleonora used the term *donne* to refer to the women who waited upon her.[246] She may have also been referring to wet nurses and midwives, or perhaps only to the subgroup among them she considered "brainless," since it is clear that she held at least one midwife, for instance, in high regard and enjoyed her company, pronouncing her "lovable" and contriving to keep her with her in Rome as long as possible.[247] Ippolita's midwife was literate and esteemed enough to pass from Ippolita's service to that of Eleonora's daughter.[248] But Eleonora urged Ippolita to remember her superior status as noble mother, especially in comparison to the wet nurses who were, after all, just peasants. Wet nurses, however, occupied a unique niche in the noble household, in comparison with other servants. In addition to their wages (which were higher than those of most servants), wet nurses were provided with decent clothing, bedding, and shoes.[249] Both the wet nurse and her offspring might continue to receive gifts from the family long after the term of her service. Their intimacy with their charges, as well as their likely proximity to other young children of the family, provided them with insights that they shared with their employers. Eleonora's diatribe against the peasant wet nurses inadvertently reveals the reality in the nursery and the extent to which it failed to measure up to her ideals. Wet nurses were not in the habit of silently nursing and swaddling, but offered opinions of their own, to which some aristocratic women, especially first-time mothers, probably gave credence, when faced with unfamiliar illnesses.[250] Any members of the lower classes holding opinions contrary to those of their superiors were typically disparaged by the latter. Nobles had particularly harsh words for peasants under their jurisdiction who challenged their authority, and in the late seventeenth and eighteenth centuries, peasants questioned noble prerogatives with increasing frequency in papal law courts.[251] Eleonora's censure of peasant wet nurses is related to this increasing class tension in Rome. The so-called "cantankerous" wet nurse may have been no more than a peasant woman with ideas of her own, including about health and illness.

Although Eleonora positioned her knowledge as superior to that of lower-class women, the source of her knowledge would have been similar to theirs – it was acquired through observation and tested practices shared among women who cared for children. Eleonora may have had access to the many printed texts on good health, but she does not refer to them directly in her correspondence.[252] Her information on health was doubtless formed through interactions with many wet nurses. According to Eleonora, the mother had to remain the authority figure in this dynamic, since the wet nurse couldn't be left alone with the child, and the mother had to follow her movements, keep track of her diet, and monitor her consumption of foods that could spoil the milk.[253] In the case of the cranky or difficult wet nurse, the mother had to manage as best she could, privileging the quality of her milk over the quality of her interactions with the mother.

Some ailments of the infant could be treated through the careful control of the wet nurse's diet, rather than by resorting to drugs.[254] Eleonora thought it best that if medicines were absolutely necessary, to have the wet nurse ingest them and thus she would pass the medicine through her milk to the child, which we know does occur in the case of some substances, sometimes to the benefit and sometimes to the detriment of the child.[255] It was the course of action recommended by medical authors since antiquity.[256] Her insistence on the continuation of this ancient practice underscores her skepticism of contemporary medical innovations that de-emphasized breast milk. She recommended purging the wet nurse in order to assist the child.[257] One has to wonder whether Eleonora was more unpopular with the wet nurses or with the physicians. The sighs of both must have been heavy whenever either she or her missives arrived.

In times of Ugo's dire difficulties, which involved inexplicable seizures, Eleonora tended to blame the wet nurse, acknowledging (as Ippolita had evidently written to her) that wet nurses *could* be the ruin of children.[258] One particularly inadequate wet nurse (whom Eleonora didn't favor) could have been to blame for the child's decline.[259] She admitted that the wet nurses in her employ had made errors nearly fatal to her children, especially in the care of her son Marcantonio.[260] Yet, in the same letter, Eleonora upheld her general principal that "if the wet nurse breastfeeds well, there is no need to think of medicines and nothing is as helpful [to him] ... as the milk that suits him."[261] So while she might critique a particular wet nurse, her faith in breast milk itself was not shaken.[262] Even in Ugo's worse crises, Eleonora continued to believe that milk was the answer and predicted that milk that suited him would be what saved him. According to Eleonora, milk was not only food but also safe medicine, in contrast to the prescriptions of the physicians. Eleonora urged Ippolita to "get out of her head" the idea that medicines or anything else could do Ugo more good than breast milk that agreed with him.[263] Good breast milk had once pulled her sister-in-law's son "from the grave." The continued use of breast milk until he was four years old (a late age for weaning even in the seventeenth century) had kept him alive.[264]

Eleonora judged as a profound error the physicians' advice to withdraw milk temporarily from the diet of the child in favor of a regimen of medications and broths, yet it appeared she lost this argument to the physician advising Ippolita.[265] She assigned the blame to Ippolita, however: "You have increased the harm to him by withdrawing [breast] milk."[266] Her critique underscored that it was the mother who would be judged for the decision, not the physician who recommended it. She called the practice of withdrawing the milk (which she also observed in Rome) a "hazard" to the survival of the child, noting that it was the child's main sustenance (along with pap) and that its withdrawal would have to be followed closely, to avoid damage to the child.[267] The withdrawal of milk had exacerbated the illness in one of her children.[268] It left a hole in the nutrition of the young that, at best, could be filled with eggs and soups, but these were not ideal in her view, though she had a careful outline of the regimen to follow when relying upon them.[269] Children could get by on little food, but some nourishment was necessary.[270]

By the spring of 1686, Eleonora acknowledged that she had relayed all the help and advice that she had to give.[271] To withdraw the milk and to rely on medicines was decidedly the wrong course, as was the physician's recommendation that Ippolita should get Ugo to lose weight since, Eleonora noted, all children typically lost weight in weaning.[272] Ugo's appetite was a good sign, far better than a poor one, and should not be discouraged.[273] If he appeared to be gaining rather than losing weight, this seemed to Eleonora to be a positive trend,[274] especially since he tended to run a fever, and such children needed more food. Eleonora further noted that "suffering consumed Ugo," further spurring on his appetite.[275] As long as he was eating, Ippolita should not despair: "his mouth would carry him away from all difficulty."[276]

Local physicians, however, may have only thought they were following some of the latest medical thinking, including the widely published and translated work of the Flemish physician Johann Van Helmont (1579–1644), who promoted the use of broth-based gruels and pronounced his skepticism about the hygiene and safety of breast milk, believing it to be spoiled by the inevitably bad passions of the nurses.[277] Eleonora dismissed the wet nurses' "passions" as a significant factor in the quality of the milk. She too, had her praise for broths, but she believed that they were no substitute for milk, thus rejecting the contemporary trend of relying on broth or gruels made without milk of any kind, which would have drastically reduced the child's intake of protein and vitamin D.[278] She favored heartier soups instead of watery broths, in the case where a child had reached the age to digest them.[279] Faced with Ippolita's concerns about a lack of strength and development in Ugo's legs, Eleonora assured her that it would happen, as it had in her own children who eventually developed "legs of steel."[280] Eleonora underscored the critical role breast milk played in the physical future of the child, including his ability to walk. A good supply of breast milk was the best barrier against rickets, as was later recognized when the promotion of broths instead of breast milk was connected to the increased incidence of rickets during the seventeenth century.[281]

Increasingly confronted with physicians' interventions, Eleonora considered their prescriptions less valuable than a wet nurse's fresh milk. Regardless of the nature of the physician's recommendations, the mother was to protect the child's ingestion of milk, regarded by Eleonora as the best guarantee of the good health of the child. As food and medicine, milk was critical. In this regard, Eleonora supported some of the longest practiced aspects of breastfeeding against seventeenth-century novelties introduced by medical authorities. She simultaneously elevated the circle of female care that had sustained children, centered upon the production and evaluation of milk, even as she disparaged the insights of wet nurses into the treatment of childhood illnesses. Class trumped the long-held view that a wet nurse's character mattered. Their role was limited to the supply of a product with an enormous impact on the body of the child, but not upon his character or personality.

Ippolita's involvement in the care of children, the supervision of wet nurses, and the review of doctors' advice was predicated upon careful observation and a wide-ranging medical knowledge of which the mother was supposed to be the master. The mother had to carefully evaluate her infant, reading the signs of his or her flesh to judge how well the breastfeeding was going and whether the milk might contain some defect. In the case of the child's illness, the mother's first role was observation, a careful assessment of symptoms and habits. After the use of remedies or a change in practices, the mother should study with care the outcome and assess the efficacy of the intervention. The mother should survey medical opinions, including and especially those of her aristocratic female peers, but also those of physicians – both those medical experts in the household as well as those consulted at a distance through the report of the child's symptoms. She should seek such input but be skeptical of it, since doctors could disagree, and their knowledge of infants was flawed. She should draw instead upon the repository of female medical knowledge represented by women such as Eleonora and her contemporaries. From these varied insights, the mother was to extract what would be the best course in the specific medical scenario she was facing with the child. Ippolita was to remain in charge of the situation, rejecting the advised medical course or change in practice suggested by her husband or by the physicians, if Ippolita thought such a plan against the best interests of her own health or that of the child.[282] Gregorio was evidently an intensely involved father, especially where Ugo was concerned. Eleonora advised Ippolita to go against his wishes as well, if her assessment of the situation told her to do so.[283] Eleonora acknowledged that this might be badly viewed but it was a modest resistance on the domestic front that was sometimes necessary. Such opposition was contrary to Eleonora's proclaimed submissiveness to the superiority of male relatives, whose authority she accepted as the will of God. By contrast, God had evidently willed that aristocratic women be the "absolute Padrone of no one except the hapless women [of their household]."[284] Men were in charge, even if they were philandering and health-squandering husbands, it was best to "commend them to God" and to require women, "to give joy" to them nonetheless.[285] This tolerant obedience extended only up to the point that male authority might interfere with the appropriate treatment of one's children. At that juncture, men could be ignored altogether, and the mother was on her own. As the health of Ugo declined, Ippolita was left more frequently in this terrifying position identified for her by Eleonora, left to weigh the options that ultimately failed to save the child, a situation in which

Eleonora urged her "not to trust anyone."[286] Eleonora did not approve of all of Ippolita's decisions and told her so. However, Eleonora continued to express her affection for Ippolita and to defend her to others who criticized her for her choices regarding Ugo's care.[287] Whether defending or criticizing the younger mother, Eleonora underscored the responsibility that Ippolita carried for deciding upon her ailing son's medical routine.

Ippolita's dilemma illuminates the shortcomings in the interpretation that a plethora of medical choices offered positive opportunities for early modern patients. In an era of increasing influence by medical professionals, this theory fails to capture Ippolita's experience of illness. If we consider the problems faced by Ippolita with her ill son, what we refer to now as "medical pluralism" should be viewed as offering not only possibilities but also elevated anxiety. Medical practitioners recommended bleeding, even for children, but Eleonora did not. Should Ippolita allow it in the case of the ailing Ugo, prone to seizures? If milk was medicine, should Ippolita change a problematic wet nurse, even though Eleonora emphasized that the bonds between nurse and child had their importance as well, and that the child might well reject the new wet nurse? Eleonora's careful directions as to how to separate a child from a wet nurse to whom he had formed an attachment testified to her recognition that the child's feelings affected the outcome. How did a mother weigh withholding milk and giving medicine versus drugging the wet nurse and leaving off the medicine for the child? Eleonora's attempt to exclude the physicians' influence from the realm of infants and toddlers was, in effect, an attempt to limit the choices Ippolita might consider. But shrinking the realm of the possible, in the face of intractable problems, is difficult – Eleonora's continued discussion of the options she hoped to exclude suggests that Ippolita considered and chose them nonetheless, further confusing her and complicating the situation.

Studies of modern patients suggest that more medical options do not necessarily generate greater happiness. If presented with a hypothetical situation of grave illness, human beings in our contemporary context typically wish for more medical choices. Once diagnosed with an actual serious illness, however, most patients state that they would prefer not to make the decision regarding their treatment.[288] The "medical pluralism" of the seventeenth century may have not been so desirable either, especially in a crisis situation, a not infrequent scenario for early modern parents. Eleonora recognized the intense suffering of Ippolita and Gregorio, as they tried to plot a medical course for Ugo through the myriad of possible treatments. Their difficulties had concomitant implications for the health of the parents, and, for the mother, they could compromise the possibility for future offspring, or, in the case of pregnancy, the health of the unborn child. The volume and the detail of Eleonora's epistolary mentoring suggest the complexity of the lessons required to learn how to balance such medical equations. During the early years of Ippolita's mothering, both clarity and success in this medical calculus eluded her.

From Eleonora's perspective, Ippolita lacked mastery of the sequencing required to utilize a multifaceted approach to illness and its worst outcome, death. As Ugo's health declined and remedies failed, Eleonora's advice shifted in the direction of trusting divine rather than human solutions. Her approach to child health (up to that point) had been primarily material – good mothering was about reading children's bodies – but at the point of irresolvable malady and eventual loss, the mother's next role was to surrender to the will of God. She urged Ippolita and Gregorio not to seek out any more medical consultations, but rather to do, in the care of their son, "what God inspired" them to do for him.[289] She no longer sanctioned even the advice of the physician highly recommended by her own son.[290] She continued to emphasize the importance of breast milk and of Ippolita's continued attention to Ugo's health. Eleonora, however, recognized that the young mother had likely reached a point where there was no more that she could do.

The Risks of Affection

In the aftermath of Ugo's death, Eleonora completely abandoned medical matters for spiritual ones. She pondered God's mystery, conceding that only He could know the reason for such sad events. She countered Ippolita's loss of her son in this life with the benefit of an angel in heaven, who would never forget the kindnesses of his mother, and who would intervene on her behalf with the Almighty, to send a new, healthier son to Ippolita.[291] God could "make another Ugo" even better than the first.[292] With a speed that Ippolita considered unfeeling, Eleonora urged Ippolita to reconcile herself to the death of her child.[293] His passing had been the will of God, and God would make Ugo a far greater prince in heaven than he could have been on earth.[294] Ugo had left the suffering of this world for the happiness of heaven.[295] Back on earth, procreation and the work of consoling the rest of the *casa* were the tasks at hand for the young childbearing mother.[296]

Eleonora was not so insensitive that she missed the pain her remarks caused Ippolita. She attempted to soften their impact with the expression of her own grief at the loss of Ugo, and with the acknowledgment of the tears in her own eyes when she read of the continued suffering of Ippolita and Gregorio.[297] Yet such suffering had to come to a close. She "begged [Ippolita] not to cry anymore."[298] For the couple's outpouring of emotion, Eleonora held both Gregorio and Ippolita at fault, critiquing them for their "bad life" and their attachment to the "disgusting mirage" of a past that was theirs no more.[299] In their sadness, they wished for the return of their ill son, rather than for subsequent healthy children.[300] The consequences of Ippolita's melancholy were far more serious than those of her husband's. The older mother cautioned that Ippolita's emotional turmoil jeopardized the whole family, including the third child she was carrying, who might indeed be that Ugo, "resurrected" (it was in fact, a girl).[301] Ippolita had to focus her attention on her own health, so that she might enjoy the possibility of other children, healthier than this first one had been.[302] Even Ippolita's husband's health difficulties could be ignored if necessary in this quest.[303]

Criticism of Ippolita's overly emotional involvement had appeared earlier in their exchanges, when Ugo's difficulties shook Ippolita to the core. The older mother had then reminded her of the necessity of quiet acceptance of the will of God.[304] Eleonora accused the younger mother of having little faith, reminding her that "God touches with His hands what you wish He would not."[305] The task of the devout was complete surrender of the will to such divine interventions, and for the mother, that included the Almighty's plans for her children, who were no more than "scraps in the hands of God."[306] Her insights echoed her attachment to the teachings of the Spanish priest Miguel de Molinos, who had been wildly popular in Rome beginning in the 1660s through the 1670s. Molinos called for the abnegation of the will, of desire, and of thought.[307] Although the cleric's views were declared heretical in 1685, Eleonora clung to them after his demise, as did other women of her generation. Following his condemnation, she had handed over writings by Molinos to a trusted cardinal, but she did not put aside his message as easily.[308] Two years later, she still recalled their verbal and epistolary exchanges, noting that, to her, his writings appeared to be those of a saint.[309] In this theological framework, humans had to accept that "God does not do things haphazardly," as she put it.[310] Though by her own admission Eleonora lacked sufficient religiosity to tend to her soul, when she did mention God in her writing, it was most frequently in reference to the necessity of submitting to His will, the core tenet of

Molinos' theology.[311] In the last years of Eleonora's life, such surrender would prove difficult for Eleonora in the face of the loss of her own son. But in her earlier correspondence with Ippolita, she stressed the necessity of such spiritual orientation for success in mothering and medical matters.[312]

Ippolita's mourning subsequently became a topic the two women rarely discussed, or a subject mentioned only obliquely.[313] An early devastating comment by Eleonora may have inspired Ippolita's silence on the subject. A few months after Ugo's passing, Eleonora observed that the link between the medical and the maternal, though necessary to good mothering, could be problematic and potentially deadly. Eleonora herself had recommended the intimate process of closely monitoring the health of Ugo. She reminded Ippolita, for instance, of the value of of her attentive presence at difficult moments, such as bloodletting: "It is necessary to be afraid and to be vigilant, for the child will be disoriented."[314] Such watchfulness was a key maternal role in isolating the "trifles" necessary to childcare, the diagnosis of childhood maladies, and their successful treatment. But affection, proximity, and attentiveness had their dangers. They had further entangled Ippolita emotionally with Ugo in ways that made his death even more difficult for Ippolita to accept.[315] The older mother had warned about the emotional risk involved in caring for a child as ill as Ugo, a situation that would tend to make the mother fearful of all she observed in him. Eleonora had noted the "passion" of Ippolita for her little son, but she had sometimes criticized Ippolita for it.[316] It led her to spend too much time with Ugo in the evenings, thus increasing his "eccentricities," when what he needed was a more regular schedule.[317] Affection that led to bad maternal practice was emotion gone too far.

After his death Eleonora turned these relatively rare observations into the origins of Ippolita's loss of her son. In a devastating comment, Eleonora observed that excessive emotional attachment to the child was a sin, a sin that God might punish with the death of the child. She hypothesized that this might be the reason for Ugo's passing – Ippolita's excessive love for him.[318] Eleonora's was a punishing God, as she had noted periodically in her letters to Ippolita. He had denied Eleonora the chance to see Ippolita "tranquil and content" because of Eleonora's sins.[319] Such a God would doubtless intervene in Ippolita's maternal wrongdoings. In love, as in medicine, mothers needed moderation.[320] Mothers of ailing children were not the only ones who might fall into such error – excessive love for a child was a sin any parent (mother or father) might commit. Eleonora, as aunt, was guilty of it herself: She pronounced her own enthusiastic affection for Ippolita's daughter Nora as bordering on inappropriate. When she sent the child gifts, she begged forgivenss for her audacity.[321] God Himself (Eleonora believed) kept Eleonora from seeing the child more often, lest her affection for the child became too great.[322] On the Roman scene, this human weakness received treatment in the writings of the priest (and later cardinal) Silvio Antoniano (1540–1603) who in his reflections on the education of children noted, "This excessively worldly tenderness (for one's child) is not appropriate in the heart of a Christian."[323] In Eleonora's estimation, however, the mother of an ailing child was particularly vulnerable to this shortcoming. That Ippolita's ministrations to the ailing Ugo had evidently rendered her particularly susceptible was a risk embedded in caring for him, yet she was required to care for him intently, in order to be a good mother, according to the maternal model of Eleonora. Thus, the medical and the spiritual were not reconcilable, at least as Ippolita had been able to practice them. Ippolita's maternal failure led her to a form of grief that revealed the emotional disconnect between the two mothers.

To Eleonora, Ippolita was misled by her passion for her son, an emotion that made her mistakenly believe that "[she] could not give [herself] peace and get over this."[324] Her grief breached acceptable boundaries, producing a "tempest" in the soul of Gregorio and Ippolita – a regrettable outcome, in the estimation of the older mother, meriting condemnation, not praise.[325] Ippolita's expression of child loss would find greater approval in the eighteenth century, when emotions were believed to enlighten rather than dupe the sufferer. Ippolita's despair presaged the storytelling of Marcello Leopardi, a painter active in late eighteenth-century Rome who narrated the moment that Hecuba, obliged to kill her son Paris since he would cause the downfall of Troy, surrendered him instead to a servant, who raised him. Unwilling to accept his passing, the mother points the child away from his destiny, in the direction of safety (Figure 3.3).

Ippolita's grief foreshadowed these eighteenth-century developments, which, with the proliferation of their visual and literary manifestations would become acceptable in the generations subsequent to Ippolita's. In the waning years of the seventeenth century, Ippolita had already arrived at this copious outpouring of unrestrained maternal feeling. It remained in vexed dialogue with its seventeenth-century alternatives – neo-Stoicism, Jansenism, and their Roman inflections, including the quietism of Molinos. In spite of their differences, Eleonora's personal devotion to Ippolita did not waiver, but she couldn't help noting the

Figure 3.3 Marcello Leopardi (*c*.1750–95) *Hecuba Giving the Infant Paris to one of Her Servants*, *c*.1791 in Palazzo Altieri, Rome. Courtesy of L'Associazione Bancaria Italiana. Photo by author.

peril in Ippolita's approach to mothering in her exegesis on the jeopardous encounter between the maternal and the medical. At the place where medicine, maternal love, and mortality intersected, there was no coherent position for Ippolita, only a God with a punishing parental love meter, ready to dole out death for emotional excess. In her later years, Ippolita mechanically employed the expression about the sin of loving a child too much, but she rejected the view of God that sustained it. Ippolita would recast the maternal by rethinking the intersection of parenting and theology, questioning how God's will manifested itself in family life. This reformulation required her to throw away some of Eleonora's cherished insights, but she would build a new future for the next generation of Boncompagni daughters from Eleonora's observation that sometimes a good mother had to rebel against authority. The independence of the Roman aristocratic mother in the face of childhood maladies was marshaled later for her children who survived childhood to adulthood. Eleonora's mock subjugation to male authority – extolled and then ignored in the nursery – was not isolated to that domain. For

Ippolita, it would spill over to other aspects of life, contained no better than her grief for Ugo. The domestic realm, with its attendant medical dilemmas and emotional entanglements, was its own battle ground and training ground for later struggles beyond the nursery in which mothers would challenge their male relations' view of family life. In comparison with the sometimes hopeless struggle against child mortality, the challenge of the patrilinear family may have seemed to Ippolita less daunting and its future an outcome upon which she might have greater control.

4
Ippolita's Wager
Letting Daughters Decide in the Early Eighteenth Century

In the first days of January 1698, Ippolita Ludovisi (1663–1733) penned a gloomy but appreciative letter to her brother-in-law, Cardinal Giacomo Boncompagni (1652–1731). The cardinal had sent her a gift to add to her glass cabinet of treasures, a keepsake in honor of the birth of her seventh child, Lavinia, born at the end of December 1697. A humiliated Ippolita expressed her gratitude for the gift but confessed the unworthiness she felt as a recipient:

> If it were not for fact that it has pleased you to remember me, I would certainly not have had the heart to place these lines before you, since I have just reached a number [of girls sufficient] for a convent of nuns, [and] especially considering that it is only on my account that the *casa* has received this great harm ...[1]

A few years earlier, Ippolita might have made this confession to Cardinal Giacomo's older sister, Eleonora Boncompagni Borghese, who had provided critical support to Ippolita. Eleonora, however, was dead.[2] Ippolita was without her older mentor's guidance. She struggled to accept her "convent" of girls and faced the failure of having produced only one son, who died at the age of two. Ippolita was prostrate with sorrow and waited for the final blow:

> I feel that grief that Your Excellency could easily estimate, knowing the obligations that I have to everyone and especially the Duke [my husband], but God on account of my sins gave to all [the Boncompagni] this humiliation. It is not worthwhile to hope in this life that I will have anything besides daughters; therefore I pray that God strike me down, so that the *casa* might find consolation in a male succession.[3]

Ippolita added that she hoped that her brother-in-law would "have the goodness to forgive the revulsion that [she] experienced every year," evidently referring to the reaction she had shared with him at the birth of her last three daughters in 1695, 1696, and 1697.[4] Her apology suggests that she knew that the cardinal would find such repugnance unacceptable, just as his older sister Eleonora had done before him. Ippolita had been exposed in her youth to the medicalized mothering of her sister-in-law Eleonora Boncompagni Borghese, with its rigorous attention to child health and its commensurate emotional entanglements. Eleonora had warned her too, about what she perceived to be Ippolita's less than positive reaction to the birth of her first daughter, Maria Eleonora (whom she called Nora). She underscored that there was far too much emphasis put on boys.[5] Both boys and girls, she noted, added to the greatness of the aristocratic lineage.[6] Eleonora would not, she had claimed, treat boys and girls any differently, and for each she would praise God and to each she would show signs of her maternal affection.[7] Eleonora swiftly and enthusiastically took to defending Nora,[8] issuing a blunt reproach to the younger mother: "I would like to believe that the poor little Nora, although badly viewed by you, was treated well during the birth and after."[9] Nora should not be blamed for being a girl, the older mother observed, because had she been allowed to choose, Nora would have wanted to be a boy.[10] That she caused her mother disgust was strictly involuntary on Nora's part.[11] Eleonora chastised Ippolita for such a reaction and reminded Ippolita that nothing was more distasteful than being "less esteemed and less loved for no other defect than being female."[12]

Ippolita's dislike dismayed Eleonora in part because she saw it as following a pattern in the Boncompagni family, in which mothers did not receive girls well. Eleonora was not sure whether her own mother (who lived with Ippolita) would ever love Nora or not.[13] Eleonora differentiated her brother Gregorio from the family pattern (he had "adored her") and from her father ("the poor man who did what he could").[14] She noted that had it not been for her brother and her grandmother, she would have chosen to enter a convent if she had not been married at 16.[15] As a teenage girl, she could no longer endure her poor treatment (presumably at the hands of her mother, conspicuously absent from the list of the people who loved her).[16]

Eleonora urged Ippolita to break the Boncompagni cycle and to "devote yourself to loving [Nora]."[17] For children to become affectionate, they had to be shown affection before they were capable of it. In a well-loved child, the Madonna of August would place affection toward the parents in return.[18] The necessity of affection extended to Nora's father, Gregorio (Figure 4.1), whom she hoped would love Nora as much as Gregorio had loved Eleonora.[19] Eleonora sniffed some hypocrisy in Gregorio's glowing words: "Sometimes I fear that you write me so much [about Nora] in order to demonstrate more affection than you feel."[20] If Ippolita (Figure 4.2) could not show the requisite affection to Nora, and hide the disgust for her that she had evidently expressed in her letters (which was so displeasing to God), then she would be better off placing Nora in a convent as soon as possible.[21] Otherwise such rejected children developed an "antipathy" (*avversione*) for the *casa*.[22]

Figure 4.1   Gregorio Boncompagni

Figure 4.2 Ippolita Ludovisi Boncompagni Both portaits by unknown artists. Original portraits in Villa Aurora, Rome. Reproductions in Giuseppe Felici, *Biography of Gregorio Boncompagni Ludovisi*, unpublished manuscript, Rome, 1927. Courtesy of Princess Rita Boncompagni Ludovisi and Prince Niccolò Boncompagni Ludovisi.

Eleonora's enthusiasm for girls may have mitigated but it could not remove Ippolita's sense of failure by the late 1690s. She had reached the end of hoping that the next child might be a boy and she despaired of bearing more children if it would simply add to the already large Boncompagni "convent" she was raising at home. Three years of such "disappointments" left her downcast. The long-ago warning of her mentor, Eleonora, that she should be careful about how she viewed her daughters, was forgotten under the strain of rapid childbearing that failed to produce its goal. If she were, as she put it, "struck down," then her much older husband might still have sufficient time to remarry and a new wife might secure for him the male heir that she had failed to provide.

Gregorio, too, eventually came to see the impossibility of producing a male heir.[23] He had, in his youth, at least once sought an extramarital solution to this problem, but this too, had yielded a daughter.[24] So in 1702, with a papal dispensation, Gregorio married off his eldest daughter, Maria Eleonora (1686–1745) to his younger brother, Antonio (1658–1731). Although such dynasty-saving scenarios were rare, they were not unheard of on the Roman scene.[25] Within four years of matrimony, and before the death of Gregorio in 1707, his daughter Maria Eleonora would bear four children (two of them boys). Although not all of these children would survive, one boy, Gaetano (b.1706), would live to adulthood and a fifth child (a boy, Pier Gregorio), born in 1709, would also survive the precarious early years of childhood and live to marry. The Boncompagni were thus eventually provided with two potential male heirs.

Ippolita lived to see her daughter succeed where she and her husband could not. There were positive changes, too, in Ippolita's financial fortune, after that desperate winter of 1697–98. With the death of her remaining siblings at the turn of the century, she eventually inherited what was left of the Ludovisi patrimony. This inheritance allowed her to provide the dowry necessary to marry off her second daughter, Costanza, to Vincenzo Giustiniani in 1706. Still, there was the matter of the remaining girls in the Boncompagni "convent" and, by the marital politics of the Italian aristocracy, the logical place for them would be an actual convent, perhaps the Roman convent of the Tor de' Specchi where Ippolita's sister had been a nun, or in one of the convents in Rome or Naples, where her husband's six unmarried sisters would finish their days on earth. It was a pattern common among noble families across the peninsula. Declining noble income and high expenditures meant that families economized on the costs of marrying daughters by placing them in convents whose required financial donations from families were far lower than the cost of a marital dowry. Although comprehensive numbers are difficult to come by, the evidence from the Venetian example is astonishing. By the mid-seventeenth century, some 80 percent of the girls of the Venetian ruling class were nuns.[26] Although the Venetian case was somewhat extreme, religious life became a common destiny for aristocratic Italian girls between the mid-sixteenth and the mid-seventeenth century.

Despite Ippolita's expressed shame at bringing the Boncompagni family nearly to a succession crisis, she did not later take the future of her four girls lightly, nor assume that the convent was their destiny. When it mattered most, the defective mother eventually declined to be an indifferent mother, at least as far as her four remaining daughters were concerned. Beginning in 1707, the first year of her widowhood, and intensifying in the subsequent years, Ippolita battled her in-laws – or, more specifically, her brother-in-law turned son-in-law Antonio and his brother Cardinal Giacomo – for the financial resources to marry all the remaining four daughters if they wished to marry or to enter the convent if they so chose.[27] To allow the Boncompagni girls such latitude, she would insist that while she could provide them with partial dowries through the wealth of the Ludovisi family, it would take some resources from the Boncompagni family as well, if they were to enter an acceptable marriage to someone worthy of their rank. According to Ippolita's design, each of her yet unmarried female offspring – Teresa (b.1692), Giulia (b.1695), Anna Maria (b.1696), and Lavinia (b.1697) – would receive a dowry of 80,000 scudi, a sum that she considered necessary to allow each girl to have a true choice between marriage and the convent.

Antonio Boncompagni regarded Ippolita's demand as the financial ruin of the family. She sparked a controversy among the Boncompagni that took multiple decades to resolve.[28] Yet, throughout the conflict, Ippolita stuck to her defense of the girls, tenaciously and determinedly. The mother once devastated by the birth of so many daughters became as brilliant a *mater litigans* in their defense as could probably be found in early eighteenth-century Rome. She eventually succeeded in this struggle: all four girls would marry within their rank, although it would take her a long time to put marriages together for the two youngest daughters.

Why did Ippolita come to insist upon this solution and with what ideas did she sustain it? How did the mother who expressed such bitterness over giving birth to a succession of girls turn out eventually to be a tenacious advocate for allowing them at least the autonomy of choosing between the convent and married life? Luigi Alonzi, the family's most systematic and sympathetic modern historian, pronounced Ippolita's behavior "eccentric," her choices "irrational," and the decision to marry all of the girls as "surprising."[29] Like other women of her class, Ippolita achieved a certain "social preeminence" enhanced, in her case, by the inheritance of the Ludovisi family patrimony.[30] Did she favor her natal over her marital dynasty, as her critics asserted?[31] Ippolita was beset, according to Alonzi, by "psychological indecisions" and "anxieties."[32]

In this model, the crises in Roman aristocratic families led to the greater social importance of women, but such preeminence produced female behaviors that might appear bizarre to their adversaries and their later interpreters.

Ippolita's behavior, considered from the perspective of dynastic ideology, could indeed be considered strange. It certainly ran counter to Boncompagni family practices. Since the late sixteenth century, one son had inherited the bulk of the patrimony and none of the other male siblings had married. Such strategies shored up diminishing noble patrimonies, which came to pass predominantly to a single male heir in Rome. Such an heir in Rome was not always the oldest son, who sometimes renounced marriage in favor of pursuing a career in the church. While hypothetically the remaining siblings could also have married, the small allocations for girls' dowries left the convent the option for all but one or two – who were allocated sums sufficient for a marriage in their rank. Sons largely excluded from much inheritance might remain single, take religious vows, or wait in the wings in case they were needed to procreate the lineage.

The widowed mother's behavior becomes more comprehensible if we consider the family from other points of view. Her "surprising" decision to insist upon her daughters' free will to choose their life's vocation was scarcely a novelty in the early eighteenth century. The Council of Trent had insisted upon it about a century and a half before Ippolita's battle with her in-laws. Yet, the proclamation that free will was integral to the sacramental validity of either marriage or religious life had instead been followed by the confinement of increasing numbers of "extra" noble daughters to convents, largely due to the financial dilemmas of nobles (although there were doubtless some sincere religious vocations among them). In Ippolita's case, the theology of free will – or "vocation" as she called it – became a sticking point, a justifying argument in favor of making marriages for the girls if that were their wish. But this had proved an insufficient argument, as the history of aristocratic families after the Council of Trent so clearly showed. To underscore the validity of church teaching on free will, Ippolita rethought the aristocratic family itself, realigning the fate of each girl with the general fate of the *casa*, recasting her four fatherless unmarried daughters as orphans, deserving of the protection and resources that the family might bestow. Her own obligations, she eventually came to believe, were limited only by the will of God to end her earthly life as her daughters' guardian. Intertwined with this intense obligation was an emotive tie that bound each family member to another, but most especially to the children, both female and male, of the aristocratic lineage. To understand how this formidable *mater litigans* reframed the Roman aristocratic family necessitates too, that we map the emotional territory to which she hoped to coax the Boncompagni, and upon which she would insist that she and Cardinal Giacomo were already standing. It is Ippolita's domestic theology, her charting of the confluence of the spiritual and the maternal, that makes sense of her "eccentric" behavior and uncovers the ambiguity of allegiance to the preceding dynastic family model – an increasingly ambivalent loyalty among women and men – to which Ippolita gave voice in the early eighteenth century.

A Successful Collaboration: Cardinal Giacomo and Ippolita in Service to the Boncompagni Dynasty

The conflict between Ippolita and her male in-laws evolved over several years, with spikes of animosity, tense ceasefires, and exasperation on all sides. Aggravation was especially acute on the part of Cardinal Giacomo (Figure 4.3), who regretted the disputes that unsettled his family. Ippolita was left to raise the issues episodically on her own, with the support of her allies, including, occasionally, Cardinal Giacomo. He lamented the presence of conflict in the Boncompagni family but ultimately recognized the rightfulness of Ippolita's vision. He eventually conceded that the conflict had to be resolved sooner rather than later, as she wished. She successfully courted his vacillating support in search of this outcome.

It was with and through Giacomo that Ippolita faced her maternal ambivalence about daughters and developed the steadfast loyalty she felt for her four younger offspring. Ippolita's correspondence with Cardinal Giacomo reveals the reasoning that helped her defeat her own prejudices as well as those of her adversaries, who summoned historical precedent as well as theological frameworks to condemn her advocacy for her daughters. Ippolita reconciled her own activities as *mater litigans* with the exigencies of Christianity, by confronting her in-laws' insistence that she must conform to the will of God as defined by Antonio Boncompagni and his allies. Ippolita's exchange with Cardinal Giacomo offers the possibility of understanding not only how she met the arguments of her detractors, but how she overcame her own disgust toward her daughters and became the mother-advocate for the "convent" she had brought into the world.

Cardinal Giacomo and Ippolita seem to have had a mutually supportive and productive relationship. Such success was not a foregone

IACOBVS S.R.E.EPISCOPVS CARDINALIS
BONCOMPAGNVS BONONIENSIS
CREATVS DIE XII DECEMBRIS M.DC.XCV.
Obijt die 24 Martij 1731.
A.Lesma Pinx. *N.Dorigny Sc.*
Dom! de Rubeis Heres Io Iacobi de Rubeis formis Romæ ad Templ S! M! de Pace cum Priuil. S. P. et Sup. perm.

Figure 4.3 Antonio Lesma and Nicolas Dorigny, *Portrait of Cardinal Giacomo Boncompagni, 1695–1731.* Courtesy of Museo di Roma, Gabinetto Comunale delle Stampe.

achievement in light of the conflict. But Ippolita's difficult widowhood was preceded by a longstanding, familial, frank, and affectionate dynamic between them. Her exchange with the cardinal offers the rare possibility of understanding Ippolita's behavior from a less formal source than the lawyers' proposals and magistrates' decrees that eventually resolved the dilemma. Cardinal Giacomo was a younger brother of Ippolita's spouse, Gregorio. A decade closer in age to Ippolita than Gregorio (who was 20 years her senior), Cardinal Giacomo had been one of the younger "extra" children of the bountiful Boncompagni family of 13. His older sibling, Francesco (1643–90), had taken clerical vows and was to advance through the hierarchy of the church. Francesco's slightly older brother, Gregorio, was to marry and perpetuate the dynasty. The Boncompagni thus followed the well-worn bifurcated pattern of Roman dynastic politics. Francesco, however, was prone to ill health and so Giacomo waited in the wings, in case Gregorio failed to produce an heir or Francesco lost a battle with one of his frequent maladies.[33]

Giacomo bided his time by studying at La Sapienza, where he earned a degree in both canon and civil law in the mid-1670s. He took up posts commensurate with his training and available to a layperson in the papal government, situating himself as governor of Orvieto in 1676 and later as the vice-governor of Fermo. While evidently not opposed to taking clerical orders, Giacomo did not enter religious life until the spring of 1690, shortly after his brother, Francesco, died.[34] He was immediately made the archbishop of Bologna and five years later promoted to cardinal.[35] His sister-in-law, Ippolita, was quick and effusive in her congratulations. She set herself to work on the embroidery of his clerical vestments, fussing about whether she had indeed secured exactly the type of garment he would need for his ordination and investiture as archbishop of Bologna.[36] As she reminded him, he need not lose sight of his family, and she encouraged him to return to the family villa at Rocca Secca for the delicate antipasti and familial conversation he had held so dear before taking up his post in the church.[37] As cardinal in the church, Giacomo was called back to Rome for papal conclaves, another opportunity to renew familial ties. During the conclave of 1700, for instance, he celebrated the sacrament of confirmation with the first five daughters of Gregorio and Ippolita. The following year, he traveled to the Duchy of Sora, to visit his mother.[38]

With Giacomo's assumption of the clerical life and his elevation to the College of Cardinals, he also rose in importance in the Boncompagni family. He would have assumed a role at least as significant as that of his older brother Gregorio, and, in the eyes of some historians, ostensibly a more crucial role than Gregorio's in guiding the family through the politics of Rome.[39] With his promotion, he certainly became the social and familial superior of Ippolita, as she acknowledged many times in her letters. Yet his late arrival to religious life, combined with various clues in Ippolita's correspondence, suggests that remnants of their earlier and less formal interactions endured. She continued to refer to these throughout their exchange and to draw upon a dynamic initiated in the old days before his ordination, when he participated more freely and more often at family gatherings. The few extant letters that survive from Cardinal Giacomo, as well as the tone of her correspondence to him, suggest that their affection was mutual.[40] Ippolita likely valued her rapport with her brother-in-law Giacomo, since her own life had been marked by a series of losses and ruptures – the early death of her parents, of her sister, and of her older brother and his infant son. The ubiquity of premature death on the Ludovisi family tree left Ippolita's life more centered on her in-laws than would have typically been the case.[41]

Among the new dynamics between Cardinal Giacomo and his sister-in-law Ippolita was his expanded role as her patron. Although this bolstered his position as her superior, it also deepened the bond between them in a number of ways. As a high-ranking cleric, Cardinal Giacomo could assist Ippolita through his new position in the church hierarchy. Throughout the controversies over the Boncompagni daughters' marital future, Ippolita would continue to seek out such assistance. She acknowledged him as "father" and "protector" of her daughters and of herself;[42] praised the "honor" of his protection;[43] and underscored her "blind obedience and subordination" to his wishes.[44] Newly widowed, she declared her willingness, "to depend upon His Excellency in everything with the same subjugation of a daughter for her father."[45] Although the language of her subjugation amplified – especially in the years immediately following her husband's death – she had professed herself beholden to him for particular favors both before and beyond this period of crisis.[46]

One frequent request on her part was for the use of his connections to help her situate her clients and acquaintances. Such individuals were typically, but not exclusively, priests, since Ippolita was well acquainted with many priests as well as high-ranking cardinals. She evidently adored one Father Filippo Sergente, whom she identified as "very fond of the *casa* [Boncompagni]" and a friend of the deceased Eleonora Boncompagni Borghese.[47] She attributed the health of her girls to his prayers, and referred to him as her "right hand."[48] She was extremely grateful for Cardinal Giacomo's recommendations of him to other cardinals.[49] She also sought the help and hospitality of Cardinal Giacomo for one of her clerical clients whose aspirations were modest (in her opinion), but who merited assistance.[50] She warned the cardinal of one supplicant's impending arrival in Bologna, where he intended to kiss the hem of Giacomo's garments.[51] Ippolita's beneficence could cast a wide net, to include a lowly would-be groom who aspired to the cardinal's household;[52] honest but poor boys looking to get into the seminary;[53] and a loyal servant whose stepfather was withholding her dowry and thwarting her marriage plans.[54]

Though she expressed regret in having to bother her cardinal brother-in-law at all ("When I can," she noted, "I do for myself"),[55] she was sometimes approached by people she could not afford to ignore. The wife of the Viceroy of Naples, for instance, sought a benefice for one of her clients and Ippolita saw to it that her request reached Cardinal Giacomo.[56] Other aristocratic women of her rank in Rome also sought her assistance in securing appointments for their clients who were priests. Occasionally, Ippolita and Cardinal Giacomo shared some amusement over the convoluted nature of the requests, including that of one aristocratic woman who sought chaplaincies for priests she refused to name, in one case because she thought if her husband found out the identity of her candidate, that he would oppose him.[57]

The bestowal of favors made possible by Cardinal Giacomo's elevated status in the church hierarchy not only solidified his superior status relative to Ippolita, but it also become an additional occasion for exchanging observations on people and events in Rome. Such tangentially related gossip underscored their common opinions. Ippolita divulged her worry over the outcome of events in a convent where one of the nuns had exited the community and then been allowed to return to religious life, causing some upheaval in the convent upon her return.[58] Giacomo enlisted her input for a troubling situation in a small town near Bologna, where the priests were accused of offenses grave enough to inspire civil magistrates to proceed against them, rather than leave the matter to ecclesiastical tribunals.[59] Ippolita expressed horror at what she perceived as this overstepping of ecclesiastical immunity.[60] She pledged to assist the cardinal by passing the documents related to this case to their ally, Monsignor Bonaventura, who would then convey the evidence to the pope himself.[61] She kept herself as informed as possible regarding the controversy and eschewed any thanks from him regarding her contributions to the matter.[62]

In this delicate situation – and in many more ordinary ones – Ippolita was especially mindful of her role as sister-in-law to the highest-ranking cleric in the family,[63] a cleric who happened to be often away from Rome, tending to his archbishopric in Bologna, an obligation he apparently took very seriously. His new life buried him under an avalanche of petitions for his help from in and beyond Bologna, along with good wishes from monarchs across Europe.[64] Ippolita encouraged him in his devotion to his "wife" and his "sheeplings" in Bologna.[65] She, by contrast, was usually present in Rome, wife and then widow in the Boncompagni enterprise. Since Antonio and her daughter, Maria Eleonora, were ensconced in Sora about 70 miles from Rome, Ippolita remained a critical conduit of information and informal maneuvers among the powerful of Rome, gathering insights great and small to pass on to Cardinal Giacomo.[66] She was especially fond of some allies, many of whom evidently frequented her home and helped provide her with information for the cardinal. These included fellow clerics such as Cardinal Tommaso Ruffo (1663–1753), the Acquaviva d'Aragona family, including Cardinal Francesco Acquaviva d'Aragona (1665–1725), and Monsignor Sebastiano Pompilio Bonaventura (1651–1734).[67] Her contacts with the greatest European noble families were significant. In 1715, she accompanied Elisabetta Gonzaga to Madrid for her marriage with Philip V.[68] With Ippolita's web of clerical acquaintances and well-born aristocratic friends, her love of walking in Roman gardens and in religious processions – whatever the weather and no matter how many slippers she left stuck behind in the mud – she became a skilled observer of the Roman scene.[69] She could provide rapid news ranging from the tragic (Cardinal Coloredo lost his life due to the same damp procession that had proved so perilous to her footwear)[70] to the political (providing news of the Roman court and the possible appointments of various cardinals to legations in the Papal States)[71] to the extraordinary (observing that perhaps only hermits would survive the upheavals in central and southern Italy caused by the War of Spanish Succession).[72] About the latter invasion, Ippolita voiced her despair when the subjects of the Kingdom of Naples surrendered to Austrian troops.[73] She rejoiced when a settlement with Austria in early 1709 appeared to promise some peace, at least to the subjects of the Papal States.[74] Ippolita had her own trail of informants on such international matters, men who sent her accounts of battles, troop movements, grain shipments, and diplomatic maneuvers.[75] She was indeed a well-informed correspondent.

Other activities were more mundane but tangible signs of her support and affection for Cardinal Giacomo and his new life in the church. These included making his vestments and sending tapestries to his titular church and offering to host him on his return trips to Rome.[76] She regularly pronounced herself willing and desirous to do more for the cardinal despite the limited skills that she had, amplified as she hoped they would be by her affection for him.[77] Another key role for her as cardinal sister-in-law was as informal ambassadress to the other aristocratic families, especially the women of those families.[78] This explained her special devotion to the requests of women for their clerical clients, however odd she might have found their wishes. Early in his cardinalate, she wrote specifically to ask him which ally among the aristocrats in Rome he considered especially important, so that she might serve with particular attention the wife of that lord, as she evidently had done for his brother Francesco, when he was alive.[79]

Although other mothers in this study had their difficulties with the clerics who also happened to be their relatives and in-laws, the collaboration of Cardinal Giacomo and Ippolita reminds us that the dynamic could be collaborative and affectionate.[80] Ippolita certainly stressed her role as ardent supporter of the Boncompagni *casa,* her service on behalf of the next generation of the family, and her consolation in knowing that she had not been remiss in her duty or attention to the Boncompagni interests.[81] The *"bella unione"* of the Boncompagni was a prized attribute that she worked to preserve.[82] Cardinal Giacomo and Ippolita also seem to have had a genuine affection for each other that reached beyond their socially assigned roles and transcended the conflicts and the distance that separated them after he became a cardinal. Their correspondence was rich in concerns about mutual good health along with specific advice and detailed reports on the maladies that afflicted each of them. She worried about him in the (relative to Rome) frigid temperatures of Bologna; in the tramontane winds; in the cold of late-night holiday processions; in the drafty churches; and traveling to the mountainous parishes at the remote part of his diocese.[83] She encouraged his frequent visits to the country for walks and for dabbling in his agricultural pursuits.[84] She urged him in illness to leave off the Lenten fasting, since the right kind of fish wasn't sold in Bologna anyway.[85] He, evidently, responded with similar advice to her, especially when she was bedridden and wracked by a variety of maladies, including the dark moods that emerged in early widowhood, when she, in her sorrow, "should have been ashes one thousand times over," or experienced the spasms of grief "blacker than crow."[86] He also received news of her more quotidian struggles against her "rotundity" and her secret love of the sedentary life "so comfortable but so prejudicial to her health."[87] She was too immersed in the culture of peripatetic diversion to sit still, walking in her house when it was too cold outside and encouraging him in return to never abandon the activity.[88] He sent medicines for her and the children that she couldn't find in Rome. She concurred on the prognosis that a trip to the baths was the remedy for sour blood.[89] While he encouraged her to get out and about, she hinted that he might be overdoing it in the endless round of comedies and spectacles available to him in Bologna, a swirl of entertainments he evidently preferred to the Roman scene. She begged to differ with his negative assessments of Roman theater.[90]

Cardinal Giacomo's departure from Rome seems to have expanded exponentially their epistolary exchange, a textual extension of their face-to-face discussions. She confessed, in the spring 1691, that she could not wait to see him.[91] Though she appreciated his letters, they could not match the "grace of his person."[92] Nor could the "gallantry" of his gift giving – miniature ivory carvings, cups, feathers for writing letters, the congratulatory gifts at the birth of her babies – match the pleasure of his presence in Rome.[93] The hours, she complained, were long until she saw him, to say nothing of her days.[94] His departures were painful for her; their separations, insufferable.[95]

Given the desperate struggle of Ippolita against her in-laws, Ippolita's affection for Cardinal Giacomo might be read for its strategic value – he was an ally she could not afford to be without. Yet this affectionate language colored all of their correspondence, even before her husband's death. It intensified in her widowhood, but it was not new compared to what had come before. She recalled, for instance, that only the year before her husband's death, they had been together in Bologna. She reminded him of the walks they used to take together along the garden paths in Rome.[96] Seized by melancholy and anger by turns after Gregorio's death, Ippolita observed in her early widowhood that she "recognized her husband's soul in [Giacomo]," and that he was "all that was left to [her]." [97] Without his letters to her, we can only map his continued affection in her acknowledgment of his concern, his advice for her, and the chronicle of his continued gift giving – a reliquary of Pius V, a book on Venetian customs, books dedicated to him, candles, collectibles for her glass cabinet, an image of Saint Catherine that she placed over her bed.[98] Presents and letters were fine, she noted again in 1710, but he was taking too long to get back to Rome.[99] His departures apparently stirred great emotion in her, which he teased her about, sometimes to deleterious effects. A cruel joke that he would never see her again uttered at the moment of his departure one October took months to resolve by epistolary means, and could only be settled (he insisted) if she came to Bologna with her daughters.[100]

Mapping the parameters of this affectionate exchange is not a simple undertaking. She did not, as she claimed, merely transfer her dedication from her husband to him after Gregorio's death. An intimate bond already linked them and continued to bind them, despite their differences over the marriage of her daughters. In the remnants of surviving correspondence from the late teens, she still admired his devotion to his "sheeplings" but lamented that with her own difficulties in traveling, they could see each other "neither here nor there."[101] He had been the confessor of her maternal failures but also the sounding board for her ruminations on matters that were as much theological as they were familial in nature. The controversy over her daughters would test their affection and challenge the categories in which they considered matters as earthly as the family and as ethereal as divine will. They would disagree, but never entirely part company, despite their differences.

The Errant Mother: Ippolita against
the Patrilinear Lineage

Despite Ippolita's expressed determination to die on the disappointing occasion of the birth of her sixth daughter, it was Gregorio who passed away first on February 1, 1707.[102] At Gregorio's death, Ippolita's four unmarried daughters ranged in age from nine to fifteen years old. The ensuing struggle over their destiny would test Ippolita's relationship with Cardinal Giacomo and weaken her rapport with her brother/son-in-law Antonio. Early in her widowhood, Ippolita had insisted that each girl who did not wish to become a nun be provided with a dowry sufficient to marry, or about 80,000 scudi, in her calculations. Antonio's side countered with historical arguments and the longstanding and continuing financial difficulties of the Boncompagni, who could not – in their view – afford such a never-before-attempted strategy of marrying a large number of girls. Her detractors claimed the plan would sink the financial prospects of the new primogenitor, Antonio, and his heirs. Ippolita's first dilemma in confronting such differences was to combat the negative image of her created of her by her in-laws, specifically, that she had been a corrupting influence on a weak spouse, a failed mother in her marriage for bearing only girls, and a worse parent in widowhood, precisely because of the aspirations she had for her daughters. Ippolita had to rewrite this script with care in order to maintain Cardinal Giacomo's allegiance. She found it difficult to do so without resorting to the same Manichean terms as her critics, although ultimately she would have to do much more than this in order to persuade Cardinal Giacomo.

As Antonio would continue to emphasize, the year following Gregorio's death ushered in another period of crisis for the family, but one not entirely made by the Boncompagni. Gregorio, after all, had left this world with some longstanding struggles successfully resolved. It appeared that the intense financial difficulties of the Boncompagni–Ludovisi might instead be drawing to a close.[103] Piombino, Sora, Vignola, the Villa Ludovisi in Rome, and the Villa Sora in Frascati were gradually integrated to form the core of the joint patrimony of Gregorio and Ippolita. Eyewitness accounts of Gregorio's last days stress his failing health, which must have alerted him that he was running out of time to make a will. Romans typically did as Ippolita's father had done on his deathbed – they specified the exact amount each unmarried daughter should have for her dowry, so that there would be clarity after his passing.[104] Even Ippolita's sister, losing consciousness in the aftermath of a difficult childbirth, managed to dictate a will, so that she could die "without leaving lawsuits."[105] But Gregorio was ambivalent about doing so, despite the urging of one trusted advisor, who worried about the potential claims that Ippolita might make on the Boncompagni patrimony. Her dowry and other Ludovisi incomes had been employed in service to the Boncompagni family.[106] Financial affairs were a tangle. While the issue of the dynastic succession was resolved, the matter of the inheritance of Gregorio's four unmarried daughters was left undecided. A father's will could clarify their individual inheritance. Gregorio lamented that he had not the resources to provide sufficient dowries for his four remaining daughters.[107] He expressed confidence, however, that Ippolita would use her Ludovisi inheritance to situate the remaining four girls in the best manner possible.[108]

Gregorio's failure to leave a will allowed the subsequent conflict to unfold. There were legal guidelines to help guide families in such scenarios: legislation in Rome and Naples attempted to sort out how the inheritance of girls might be handled in such cases. In Rome, the division of the patrimony was supposed to be in *favor agnationis* – to preserve the inheritance for the male lineage. The daughter in the Roman family had the right to sufficient maintenance and to a dowry suitable to her rank and commensurate with her share of the inheritance, while one of her brothers would receive the bulk of the patrimony. In the case of no sons, a daughter might inherit more.[109] Ippolita Ludovisi herself eventually was heir to her family's patrimony. Legal precedent and courts in the Kingdom of Naples favored Antonio Boncompagni's claims on the Boncompagni patrimony in entail: he was recognized as the legitimate primogenitor and heir.[110] Yet Ippolita's insistence on higher dowries for her daughters found sympathy in Rome even if it was counter to the legal practice of the Kingdom of Naples.

Ippolita eventually succeeded in marrying off all four daughters by employing a number of strategies. She never abandoned the threat of legal recourse, even if she did not ultimately pursue the dispute formally in a law court. She did seek direct intervention by the *auditore* of Pope Clement XI (Albani, 1700–21).[111] Cardinal Corradini, who considered the case in May of 1711, found in favor of Ippolita's claims on behalf of her daughters, decreeing that the Boncompagni wealth delineated as part of the *fedecommesso*, as well as the Boncompagni wealth outside the *fedecommesso*, could indeed be tapped to provide sufficient dowries for the girls.[112] Antonio and his lawyers protested this decision by the papal *auditore*, taking their grievance to the viceroy of Naples, Carlo Borromeo. Borromeo would only agree that the proper jurisdiction of the case was not in Rome, but in Naples, where (he observed), it should be heard without prejudice to the girls. He declined to say that the Boncompagni men were necessarily in the right: a Neapolitan court of law would have to decide.[113]

The stalled familial dispute finally moved forward in February 1713, when the parties agreed to choose judges in Rome to resolve the dispute. The judges' decision brokered a modified plan for the girls' dowries: each of the girls' dowries should be constituted with no more than 40,000 scudi of the Boncompagni wealth, 20,000 scudi to come from the non-allodial inheritance of Gregorio, and 20,000 scudi to come from Antonio Boncompagni's patrimony in the Regno.[114] It was considerably less than Ippolita had originally insisted upon, but considerably more than Duke Antonio hoped to provide. Ippolita then married Teresa Boncompagni to Prince Urbano Barberini in 1714 with an 80,000 scudi dowry by promising 40,000 additional scudi from her own extra-dotal funds.[115] Duke Antonio protested even the lowered demands on his patrimony, turning again to Vienna and to Neapolitan tribunals to try to stop Ippolita from using the decision to make more marriages for her daughters. Options were running out for Antonio.[116] Ippolita married Giulia to Marco Ottoboni later in 1714.[117] Duke Antonio, meanwhile, continued to reiterate that the price of the girls' dowry was too high, claiming that even the greatest families of Naples did not marry their daughters with such dowries.[118] In 1715, he received the support of Vienna with another proclamation from Naples that refuted the legitimacy of Roman jurisdiction over feudal incomes in the Kingdom of Naples.[119] In 1716, Antonio returned to the strategy of negotiation, successfully settling with his niece Giulia and her husband Marco Ottoboni to lower his contribution to her dowry to only 10,000 scudi.[120]

Ippolita continued to tend to the future of her remaining two daughters, who evidently did not wish to become nuns. Her daughter Anna Maria married Gian Vincenzo Salviati in 1719, but the couple formally agreed first to receive only 10,000 scudi from Duke Antonio.[121] Ippolita and Duke Antonio clearly found it difficult in the 1710s and early 1720s to navigate all the payments on the dowries. Teresa's in-laws, the Barberini family, were particularly vexing.[122] Such disputes were at last settled in 1723, the same year that Ippolita was finally able to marry her youngest daughter, Lavinia (at nearly 26 years old) to Marino Caracciolo.[123] Ippolita's granddaughter by her daughter, Maria Eleonora, was married at about the same time, a generational displacement that was inevitable given the longstanding difficulties of the dowry controversy. It thus took Ippolita 16 years after her husband's death to marry all four of the girls, none of whom evidently had the vocation to become a nun. By the late 1720s, Ippolita, her brother/son-in-law Duke Antonio, and her daughter Maria Eleonora, settled the outstanding differences among them and renounced suing each other any further.[124]

Ippolita probably did not foresee her future success in the tense months following the death of Gregorio. Nor is it likely that she could have anticipated the long duration of her endeavor to provide her daughters with dowries. Initially, she was likely struggling to find her equilibrium in a difficult transition in the Boncompagni family. Even in a city that was accustomed to the upheaval of transitions between pontiffs, there was something particularly bitter about this passing of the patriarchal role from brother to brother. Ippolita recoiled at what she regarded as the outpouring of animosity against her deceased husband. Familial congregations (*congregazioni*), or the formal meetings of family members – sometimes in the presence of lawyers or advisors – were hostile. Ippolita was dismayed by their tone in the spring and summer of 1707. Her first act as widow was to answer the charges against the man who was for her "a saintly soul" but whose life was being made "into a satire."[125] Clearly, she felt herself also under attack. She had to remind the new Duke of Sora (Antonio) that he could not speak to her during family meetings in a tone appropriate only for the subjects of the family estate of Sora.[126] She further insisted that only inventories and accounting records could determine whether Gregorio had increased or decreased the *fedecommesso*; whether in fact, he had failed to do as the primogenitor was charged to do – to increase the value of the *fedecommesso*.[127]

In the interim, Ippolita was left to address the rest of Gregorio's so-called errors, since such shortcomings reflected upon her as well. Did Gregorio undermine the Boncompagni financially by living in Rome?[128] Was it Ippolita who had tempted him to lead the Boncompagni into ruin?[129] As a border dynasty, the Boncompagni had an ambiguous identity between Rome and Naples, but critics charged that Gregorio pulled the family too close to Rome, wrecking family finances to keep up with the expensive demands of the papal city.[130] Ippolita's adversaries conveniently ignored the triangular strategy of the Boncompagni brothers – Gregorio had tended to family affairs in Rome; his brother, Antonio, to the family holdings in the Kingdom of Naples, especially the main territory of Sora; Cardinal Giacomo, to the matters of Bologna, and the family's holding at nearby Vignola.[131] Gregorio had neatly summarized their peninsular sprawl, which required "a foot in Spain, a foot in Naples, a foot in Rome, and a foot in Bologna."[132] No Boncompagni brother alone had enough limbs to manage it. It even necessitated the input of an organized and formidable nun (a sibling of the Boncompagni brothers), Suor Maria Gerolama, who, though in a Neapolitan convent, kept her brothers informed on affairs at the court of Naples through a trusted agent.[133] If the family's collective management practices were conveniently forgotten after Gregorio died, an even more glaring failure of Ippolita and Gregorio could not be: Were the two of them at fault for having had only daughters (and six of them at that)?[134] Or was Ippolita the "reason" for "so many girls," although, as she noted, "God in his righteous judgment had permitted it."[135] In answering such charges, Ippolita would argue that she had acted the role of the good wife and mother. She would continue to do so, defending her departed husband's reputation and protecting her girls as a *mater litigans* would, despite her continued suffering from "the greatest blow of her life," the loss of her beloved Gregorio.[136]

Some of the difficulties between Ippolita and her in-laws were the common dilemmas that emerged in women's early widowhood, when complex issues related to the potential return of a woman's dowry had to be settled. In Ippolita's case, her in-laws noted that the full amount of her dowry had never been paid and thus they calculated that the payments that needed to be made to her should be based upon the amount paid by the Ludovisi, rather than the sums promised at the time of her marriage.[137] Ippolita would eventually concede that point and settle for much less for herself, although she noted that by legal right she should have been allocated more.[138] Matters were further complicated by the situation of Maria Eleonora. She also initiated claims on her father's estate, noting that she had been married without a dowry and thus deserved some of the property from which her mother hoped to carve dowries for the unmarried daughters.[139] She also claimed to have married with the understanding that her children would inherit the fiefs in the Kingdom of Naples. Her mother's claims on that patrimony potentially compromised Maria Eleonora's inheritance as well as the inheritance of Maria Eleonora's children.[140]

Antonio and his advocates underscored the negative side of Ippolita's staunch advocacy. After being designated to the guardianship of her girls in 1707 in the court of the Vicario, Ippolita moved quickly to try to establish dowry amounts for the girls.[141] According to Antonio and his advocates, Ippolita went against both family history and good financial accounting by insisting that the remaining four girls be allowed dowries sufficient to marry. Initially, the Boncompagni hoped to delay consideration of the issue, by stressing that the girls were too young to be married, and that some would eventually become nuns anyway. It was pointless at the death of Gregorio to consider a formal allocation of dowries sufficient for their marriage.[142] While issues related to Ippolita's own dowry were eventually resolved, the future of the unmarried girls remained uncertain. The family lawyer, Filippo Viscardi, drew up a document outlining the differences between family members. He attempted to act as mediator in the dispute, but succeeded only in cataloguing their differences, not in brokering a solution.[143]

Ippolita's wealth from the Ludovisi family was also cited as a reason for the Boncompagni to delay decisions about the girls' dowries. By their accounting, Ippolita had enough money from her status as heir to the Ludovisi patrimony, especially the Duchy of Piombino. But Piombino was encumbered by debts from her deceased brother, whose ruinous renting of the territory Ippolita had been unable to stop.[144] She faced legal difficulties in securing the right to bequeath Piombino to her offspring, and her hold on the territory remained tenuous.[145] Another Ludovisi property in southern Italy, Venosa, had been similarly encumbered by debts generated by her brother. Ippolita and her sisters had thrown themselves into the rescue of that property as well.[146] By Ippolita's reckoning, there was no way to make a sufficient dowry for each girl out of the debt-encrusted Ludovisi fiefs alone. For her part, she discounted the Boncompagni's own financial difficulties, but the Boncompagni also had economic dilemmas.[147] In the years following Gregorio's death, their ownership of properties in southern Italy was potentially compromised. The succession crisis of the Spanish monarchy led to the occupation of the Kingdom of Naples by Austrian troops in 1708. Would the Boncompagni successfully maintain their fiefs under the Austrians, a new ruling dynasty? Too much seemed in jeopardy for Antonio to promise sufficient future income to allow the marriages of all four of his nieces. It was unreasonable, in his view, for Ippolita to expect him to come to an agreement at such an uncertain moment.

Even if the international scenario had been calmer or with less import for the Boncompagni, Antonio and his critics could call upon the history of the Boncompagni family to bolster their claims. They cited the longstanding practice of primogeniture and the exclusion of girls from any significant inheritance from it. These trumped any claims that Ippolita might make upon the Boncompagni holdings in the name of her daughters. In a variety of extensive reports on the problems of Ippolita's demands, the same key turning points in the family history were repeatedly referenced. In the late sixteenth century, Gregorio's great-grandfather, Giacomo (1548–1612), had already operated within the confines of "the masculine primogeniture, excluding all the girls, and their descendants."[148] To those family holdings, the patriarch Giacomo added the *stato* of Vignola in Modena, imposing the rules of primogeniture upon it.[149] Gregorio's father, Ugo (1614–76), had taken special care to reconfirm that all the holdings in the Kingdom of Naples, especially the Stato di Sora, were designated for the male line of the Boncompagni family.[150] At the death of Ugo, Gregorio's position as primogenitor was confirmed in the Corte della Vicaria in the Kingdom of Naples.[151] At the death of Gregorio Boncompagni in 1707, Antonio, his brother, successfully had himself declared primogenitor through the same court in Naples, and thus assumed peaceful possession of the Stato of Sora, along with the other fiefs belonging in the Boncompagni primogeniture.[152] From the perspective of Antonio Boncompagni, male lines of succession had been clear, transitions between generations were smooth, and the girls, plainly excluded for generations.

In addition to the overwhelming evidence of the notarial documents establishing male primogeniture, Antonio and his allies could point to a longstanding pattern of allowing only one or at most two daughters in each generation of the Boncompagni family to marry. In the sixteenth century, girls had not been particularly numerous among the Boncompagni. By the generation of Gregorio's father, three girls out of four had taken religious vows. Among the seven sisters of Gregorio, six of them would become nuns. Antonio's advocates described such practices as crucial to the best families of the Kingdom of Naples, indeed, for all families, anywhere, who practiced primogeniture in the seventeenth century:

> One cannot destroy the right of primogeniture instituted *favore familiae*. Additionally, no *casa* which practiced primogeniture or which had the status of nobility of the first rank has ever had the practice or now has the practice of marrying all the girls.[153]

Ippolita's insistence on the necessity of providing a marriage-worthy dowry for each of her girls violated history and potentially undermined the status of the family. She was – in the words of her adversaries – "the mistaken mother who intended to marry her four remaining daughters with the intention of ruining if not destroying the little family of Sora."[154] The defender of daughters was thus also the injuring party of the "*famigliola*" of her own eldest daughter, brother/son-in-law, and their children, who were in line for the rightful succession to the Boncompagni primogeniture.[155]

From the point of view of the Boncompagni, there were a variety of ways in which the behavior of Ippolita could easily be framed as untoward, as conduct unbefitting the behavior of a female member of the Boncompagni *casa*, especially the matriarch and collaborative partner of the cardinal while he was away from Rome. As her frequent reiterations of her subservience to Cardinal Giacomo make clear, her subordination to him – and by extension to the male Boncompagni – was an expected part of her behavior. While such statements were clearly part of the standards of good epistolary rhetoric, their effusive repetition suggest that she hoped to counteract a negative narrative that questioned whether she did indeed love the Boncompagni *casa* and whether she did what she did for her daughters, or in fact for her own gain, or as some monument to her status as "Principessa di Piombino."[156] The good fortune of such an inheritance was a decided improvement from the Ludovisi's longstanding financial difficulties. Her elder brother, Giovanni Battista, had been a spendthrift, subtracting significantly from the family riches and failing to add a male heir to the family tree.[157] Debts had mounted against the territory, but Ippolita fought to stabilize her ownership of it against creditors.[158] With her inheritance from the Ludovisi, Ippolita had been able to help provide a dowry to her second daughter, Costanza. As heir to the Ludovisi fortune, Ippolita's standing in the city of Rome rose. Yet, such success also cast her in some suspicion for the Boncompagni.[159] Did she truly love her younger daughters, or was she throwing them out of the house without dowries sufficient to allow them to live within their rank?[160] Perhaps she wasn't even a good mother, despite her panegyric to the virtues of maternal affection.

Ippolita attempted to counter their criticisms by underscoring the perils that the Boncompagni brothers were running by failing to resolve the situation. She acknowledged that the "domestic controversies" of the family were scarcely remaining domestic. In an especially impassioned text, she tossed out a warning to the Boncompagni brothers, noting that, "the city laughs and talks about us."[161] She claimed the better part of discretion, noting that the "theater of Rome" was no place for this conflict, and arguing that it should be settled more quickly and more quietly.[162] The reputation of the family held considerable import for its future in Rome, for the advancement of both the clerical and the lay branches of the family. Ippolita's ultimate aim was to avoid a lawsuit and settle the matter within the family meetings that her advisors and legal advocates might also attend. She cast her aims in the blunt saying of her ancestors: "Better a bad agreement than a good lawsuit."[163]

Ippolita had to remain within the realm of general observations about their situation. It was too risky for her to respond in kind to the Boncompagni criticisms of her. In the months following the death of Gregorio, Antonio was evidently engaged in a number of political struggles for the fiefs in the shifting political future in the Kingdom of Naples.[164] An earlier rebellion of the nobility in Naples in 1701 had shown Antonio and the other Boncompagni brothers to be clearly supportive of the cause of the Spanish monarchy rather than the disobedient nobles of their own caste.[165] With the occupation of southern Italy by the Austrians, in 1707, Antonio faced the uncomfortable task of reconfiguring his strategy for his dynasty, shifting his allegiance from Madrid to Vienna. The Kingdom of Naples would be ruled by Vienna until 1735, when a Spanish Bourbon would be placed on the throne.[166] As the controversy unfolded in the 1710s, Ippolita pursued a more varied strategy in light of these new political configurations, turning to Rome (her home city) and to her contacts in Madrid in order to help her situate her daughters.[167]

Any critique of Antonio in this precarious international context was bound to be badly viewed by Cardinal Giacomo. Ippolita had to reiterate her loyalty to Antonio as well as to Cardinal Giacomo. Although the image was somewhat forced, she cast herself in the role of the sister/mother-in-law anxiously awaiting Antonio's return in the summer of 1707. He was to provide direction "for we two women and for all of the *casa*."[168] She expressed her admiration for Antonio, observing that he "had a good heart."[169] The trouble in the *casa* was stirred up by others, especially his lawyers. She rewrote the scene in the *casa* in eschatological terms, declaring the duke to be an "angel" but the unnamed "ministers of the devil" [*ministri del Diavolo*] used "diabolical arts" [*arte diabolica*] to profit from the Boncompagni disorders [*pescar nel torbido*].[170] She had especially dire words for Antonio's advisor, Riccardelli, noting that he used his influence to stir up further controversy and to make more business for himself in Rome. She, by contrast, relied upon the tried and true counsel of Viscardi, who had been the lawyer of her husband.[171] Not surprisingly, Viscardi was later similarly condemned by Duke Antonio's side: he was referred to as "the viper" who stirred up trouble between mothers and sons in Rome.[172] Duke Antonio noted that Viscardi was a cleric but "more deserving of a jail cell."[173]

For his part, Cardinal Giacomo was clearly concerned that the strains between his sister-in-law and his brother could tear the family apart. Given the physical separation between Antonio, in the Duchy of Sora, and Ippolita, holding together the family's position in Rome, distance likely played a role in increasing the potential acrimony between the two.[174] Cardinal Giacomo reminded her of his misgivings about familial discord, since she reiterated frequently that she also loved and valued the peace and unity of the *casa*.[175] Ippolita was asked to wait until more propitious times to push the issue of the girls' dowries, and yet she found the waiting game a difficult one to endure. She expressed hurt at some of Cardinal Giacomo's criticisms, and offered apologies and promises of future good behavior. "I silence myself," she pledged in May of 1707. She offered to retract whatever she had said that was so offensive.[176] But broken silences could be forgiven (she apparently thought) if they were motivated by her "maternal affection," and her affiliation with the cardinal might also allow her the occasional "filial outburst."[177]

If emotional entanglements might help fudge the boundaries between what she promised and what a good *mater litigans* would feel compelled to do, her apologetic retractions also served a lawyerly purpose. She expressed herself quite frankly, and although she would then take it back, she likely knew that her counter-claims would linger – and they survived in the preservation of her letters by him.[178] Ippolita's obstinacy was never too far below the surface of her epistolary apologies. She had pledged "blind obedience" to his will in the months following her husband's death, but she had never said anything about remaining mute.[179] To disentangle her arguments requires understanding the frameworks she employed, as well as the theological interpretations that she rejected in order to wage the dowry battle for her last four girls. Ippolita moved the disagreement from the clarity of dynastic practice to the complexities of religious interpretation. The potential barriers posed by divine will were the last sticking points between Ippolita and her brother-in-law. If dynastic politics failed her, Ippolita came to believe that God would not.

A Matter of Great Conscience: The Ethics of Mothering in an Era of Religious Controversy

The Boncompagni brothers' vision of the family had a coherent set of practices and clear historical and legal precedents to support it. By comparison, Ippolita's efforts to reimagine other possibilities for the dynasty appeared new and their foundations vague. Her improvisations cannot be simply explained as further evidence of her "eccentric" behavior. They also had their connections to the dilemmas she shared with many of her generation who struggled to lead a moral life amidst contemporary controversies over Christian ethics and confusion over the boundary between God's will and human will. Ippolita, like many of her contemporaries – including her male in-laws – was influenced by the Jesuits, especially their teaching on probabilism, a mode of ethical reasoning that circulated widely if controversially in the late seventeenth century.[180] Probabilism encouraged the faithful to consider carefully the recognized moral authorities and to be absolutely certain of the morality of the action they chose. Yet, probabilism recognized that in some situations there could only be "speculative certainty," or probability, regarding the decision about which moral opinion applied to a specific context.[181] Ippolita's recourse to probabilism is captured most clearly in her explanation that her decision to support her daughters rather than Boncompagni familial practice was "a matter of great conscience."[182] This phrase, coming at the end of a series of letters in which she reviewed various arguments with the cardinal, was not an accidental choice on her part. Such a phrase had clear links to the contemporary practice of examining one's conscience as a preparation for confession. The Jesuits used cases of conscience in their teaching of the probabilist method at the Collegio Romano of Rome and in the many other schools the Jesuits established throughout Europe.[183] The appearance of the phrase within the larger argumentative framework she employed suggests that the noblewoman resolved her dilemma and found comfort in a time of great difficulty by leaning into the insights of Jesuit probabilism. Ippolita announced her moral certainty in a context in which she acted against established authorities within her marital family, including an authority who was a cardinal in the Roman Catholic Church.

Ippolita did not need advanced theological training in order to encounter probabilism in seventeenth-century Rome, since it was already widespread in Roman Catholic culture. The proliferation of probabilism owed a great deal to the Society of Jesus, although it had its origins among the Spanish Dominicans.[184] Its subsequent development suggests some of the reasons for its enduring influence upon Roman Catholicism. In the sixteenth century, the Jesuits insisted on the importance of frequent confession. They subsequently gravitated toward probabilism as an outcome of their close and frequent contact with the faithful. The teachings of probabilism spread rapidly through the Jesuits' role as confessors, especially to the great and powerful across the Catholic Europe, including and especially Rome.[185] Probabilism also had connections to the Jesuits' increasing devotion in the late sixteenth century to classical learning, especially to the moral skepticism of their most beloved classical author, Cicero.[186] Jesuit probabilism emphasized the dynamic obligation of the penitent to consider the opinions of recognized moral authorities and to come to a nuanced understanding of what did and did not constitute sin in a particular context.[187] Probabilism acknowledged and analyzed moral complexity and simultaneously attempted to provide penitents with consolation and spiritual sustenance.[188]

By the late seventeenth century, when Ippolita was then in her twenties, the tenets of probabilism and its competition with Jansenism were under scrutiny in Rome. But the Jesuit mode of reasoning was only modified in this period, not defeated. Its influence likely expanded under attacks from the Jansenists.[189] Ippolita might easily have encountered Jesuit probabilism in sermons, in conversations with her many acquaintances who were priests, or through her confessors. Probabilism helps makes sense of Ippolita's "eccentric" decision to challenge the authority of the brother-in-law to whom she had pledged steadfast loyalty. It emboldened her to present to him the moral alternative to forcing all of the remaining unmarried daughters to become nuns, whether they wished to do so or not. Ippolita used Jesuit theology to support her domestic theology, that is, to help her legitimate a new version of family life that was more in accord with Christian principles. She connected such principles to the emotional bonds between family members, integrating familial affection and Christian spirituality as her generation came to understand it.

Ippolita's line of reasoning to Cardinal Giacomo might appear in its myriad formulations as though she were desperately throwing anything possible at the dilemma. But her approach had its connections to the Jesuit confessional mode of weighing moral opinions before settling on the ethical course of action in a particular context. Alternative theologies – such as Jansenism – as well as earlier views of religious ethics had stressed the need for the faithful to *"deponere conscientiam,"* that is, to put aside their own moral doubts and follow the consensus of opinions of higher authorities.[190] Jesuit teaching countered that following the dictates of even the greatest or the plurality of higher authorities did not necessarily mean that a moral choice had been made, nor did it quell a person's reservations about whether following such authorities represented a moral course of action.[191] Jesuits' insistence on human freedom rested on their focus on individual choice of the path that one was convinced is moral, even in the face of contrary opinion from a higher authority, one's confessor or one's ruler.[192] Probabilism thus had potentially radical implications, a mode of ethics that could, in certain circumstances, legitimate rebellion.[193] In the case of Ippolita's rejection of the male authorities of the Boncompagni family, one of whom also happened to be a cleric, Ippolita decided that she could not accept their version of the appropriate course of action for her daughters, despite the solidity of their legal reasoning, the evidence of dynastic practice, and the theologically superior training of her cardinal-brother-in-law, Giacomo.[194] En route to making this moral rupture, Ippolita offered a variety of perspectives to undermine the Boncompagni dynastic practices of concentrating the inheritance in one son, and leaving the rest of the children only small sums upon which to build their adult lives, leading to the de facto placement of the girls in convents.

Ippolita attempted to shift the moral terrain of the dispute to the issue of how the girls should be viewed in the family. Like the good widow who settled her husband's accounts with the help of Cardinal Giacomo, Ippolita defended her actions in the name of her emotionally entangled mothering and the demands of their guardianship that had been entrusted to her. She was inspired by her "tenderness as mother" not because she wished to "eat off of her daughters" as her critics charged.[195] "Her last loaf of bread" would be used "to get her girls decently settled and for all the *casa*."[196] In order to legitimate the spirited defense of her daughters she gravitated toward the centuries-old language of Italian charity, whereby social and economic superiors defended the lives (as she put it) "of such impoverished innocent orphans."[197] To care for such foundlings was among the highest forms of Christian charity – Ippolita charged herself with nothing less than the "salvation" of the girls.[198] She reminded Cardinal Giacomo that such obligations implicated him in their future as well, noting that her four innocent orphans would pray for the intentions of their benefactor, much as recipients of charity were charged to do in institutional contexts.[199]

If Christian charity was insufficient to motivate the Boncompagni brothers to take seriously the "orphans" of their dynasty, Ippolita reframed the aristocratic family in order to move the seemingly peripheral interests of the extra daughters closer to its core. Specifically, the phrase "to get her girls decently settled and for all the *casa*" conflated the two enterprises and underscored the connections between daughters and *casa*.[200] She also reminded Cardinal Giacomo that the four younger daughters were also the offspring of the primogenitor of the dynasty, or "of your first born brother," as she reiterated to the Cardinal.[201] She emphasized to Cardinal Giacomo that they too shared the "blood" of "your first born brother," as she referred to her husband.[202] She stressed the connections between all family members, especially in light of the collaborative enterprise that the Boncompagni and Ludovisi became after she had inherited the Stato di Piombino, which she co-ruled with her husband Gregorio until his death.[203] The two dynasties were, in her view, "our two common families,"[204] a definition further reinforced by the marriage of Antonio Boncompagni and Maria Eleonora.[205] She professed herself shocked at the divisions that emerged after the death of Gregorio, noting that she had believed that she would finish her days on earth without ever hearing, "this is yours and that is mine."[206] Ippolita assumed that men as well as the women of the family would share such attitudes and that they were not particular to either gender. She insisted on dynastic practices that would attend to the well-being of each child (even if the child were a girl) as a measure of how well the dynasty was doing as a whole.

Ippolita connected what she called the "common good" of the *casa* to the future of the individual girls, whose choices (either for the marriage or the convent) had to be respected.[207] Such practices were scarcely invented by Ippolita, since Italian nobles had not always practiced the rigid marriage restrictions that so deeply troubled her in the early eighteenth century. Familial patterns of the late Middle Ages in Rome had their parallels to the family later envisioned by Ippolita, with several members of a generation sharing in the inheritance of the family property, rather than it mostly being allocated to a single son.[208] In those earlier times, more siblings had been allowed to marry. More of the inheritance was split more equitably among the children in comparison to the later rigid practices of primogeniture. Such precedents were likely beyond Ippolita's historical knowledge, or at least she made no reference to them. She was probably inspired by growing up and growing older amidst the Ludovisi, where she had experienced firsthand the potential catastrophe of tightly restricted marriage, including the loss of all her siblings and all her siblings' children in her generation of the Ludovisi family. As an avid watcher of the Roman scene, Ippolita was doubtless also aware that a plethora of lawsuits in late seventeenth-century Rome challenged the practice of reducing entail (*fedecommesso*) to strict primogeniture, the devolution of most familial holdings to a single son.[209] She had ample examples of hostility or ambivalence toward the practices of primogeniture in Rome. The failure of her husband to make a will was likely related to this shift in attitudes toward primogeniture's rigid application. Although Gregorio could not bring himself to advocate for his daughters, he also could not bring himself to limit their inheritance to a sum that would only have allowed them entry into a convent.

Ippolita nuanced this call for change by reminding Cardinal Giacomo that she was not radical in her thinking about the options for girls within the family. She had no opposition to her girls' residence in convents, a means typically employed to help socialize girls to convent life and to encourage them to take vows as nuns when they came of age. Her daughter, Anna Maria, was already in the Tor de' Specchi convent in 1707, where she was "very favored by the ladies there" and where "she hoped [the convent's founder and patron saint] Santa Francesca [Romana] would want Anna Maria for a [spiritual] daughter."[210] Later in 1707, her daughter Giulia also entered a convent to tend one of her Boncompagni aunts.[211] Where Ippolita diverged from familial practice was in her insistence that each girl should be allowed to decide whether or not she had the vocation to be a nun. If, as in the case of Teresa, a daughter decided that taking religious vows was not her choice, then the family should see to it that she should be able to marry, rather than place her in a convent against her will. Ippolita thus echoed the theological significance that the Roman Catholic Church placed upon free will, insisting by extension that a similarly oriented domestic theology was necessary to support free will in daily practice. Cardinal Giacomo knew firsthand the dilemmas raised by coercing girls to become nuns. While archbishop of Bologna, cases of nuns who protested being forced to be nuns against their will passed Giacomo's review. With his approval, such cases were forwarded to the Holy Congregation of the Council in Rome for adjudication.[212]

Integral to Ippolita's conception of the family was the preeminence of the emotional bonds between its members. Ippolita reminded Cardinal Giacomo that he, too, occupied the same emotional terrain that she did with her daughters. Just a few years after she had written him the discouraged note on the birth of her sixth daughter, Ippolita rejoiced in the good health of her two youngest daughters, focusing specifically on the sixth girl, who, as she noted, was good in every way and about whom she commented, "I don't believe that Your Excellency would have wished her to be a boy, even if God granted the grace to make it so."[213] Cardinal Giacomo took a keen interest in his nieces and nephews. Any news of the family's offspring he expected to receive immediately and from Ippolita – he was vexed, for instance, that she had failed to write him right away following the birth of her grandson by her daughter Costanza, though she pleaded that her role in the birth had detained her from this obligation.[214] She continued to underscore the familial tie between her unmarried four girls and Cardinal Giacomo, when she sent him warmest greetings from her two daughters who remained at home as well as the two girls then residing in the convent.[215] She challenged the cardinal to see the four girls "at his feet" from a variety of perspectives – as innocent orphans deserving of his Christian charity; as sharing in the blood of the Boncompagni lineage; and as children the two of them loved and accepted as they were, even with the "defect" of their gender.[216]

Brother and sister-in-law also exchanged the warm sentiments they shared for Niccolò, the eldest son of Maria Eleonora and Antonio Ludovisi Boncompagni. Ippolita wrote emotionally about her eldest grandson and suggested in the sad aftermath of his death that he had died in punishment for the sin of her excessive love for the child. Or, as she explained to Cardinal Giacomo:

> I found myself especially sensitive to this blow and still it doesn't seem to me that a misfortune of this kind has ever happened to a son who was as robust and who flourished as Niccolò did. But my sins merited this scourge because I loved him too tenderly and I longed for the moment that I had him with me ... but I did not merit this comfort and now must conform myself to the will of God ... [217]

That a mother's love (if too great) was a sin was a refrain that Anna Colonna had also employed in the 1630s. It was the same charge that Ippolita's sister-in-law had made against Ippolita when her only son died in 1686.[218] The expression was a figure of speech,[219] but one linked to priorities dictated by Christian teaching. Ippolita noted that the cardinal himself bordered on the same error, yet simultaneously it was a failing that earned him a compliment from her: "I understand from your most sympathetic letter that your humanity of feeling made you especially sensitive to the death of our dear little angel Niccolò, even if your virtue led you to reaffirm the most holy Passion of our Lord."[220] A deity who doled out child mortality for excessive parental love was a powerful image, especially in a culture that increasingly valorized maternal emotion and yet still feared its potentially deadly consequences. Mothers in particular were intimately close to this impossible contradiction in demands. As in the case of Anna Colonna, Ippolita seemed to regret the sin and go right on sinning, hinting in her correspondence that such an error was shared by Giacomo himself, who also walked the emotional tightrope between loving his nephew and "conform[ing] ... to the will of God."[221]

But this was not the only jeopardy in the kind of love celebrated by Ippolita. Critics charged that if emotional attachments played a role in decision-making, they could create fractured loyalties within the same family or within the same person. Ippolita's adversaries, for instance, insisted that her advocacy for her daughters compromised her love for her grandson, the future primogenitor of the Boncompagni family. Her precarious emotional balancing act was reminiscent of that of widowed mothers who – if they remarried – stood to lose custody of their children since their life with a new husband and new children supposedly undermined their loyalties for their children from their first marriage.[222] In the view of her critics, Ippolita's interests as mother collided with her interests as grandmother. Ippolita stood in a web of complex and potentially compromised affections, in this case between her daughters by Gregorio and her grandchildren by her daughter and brother/son-in-law. So, though she might love Niccolò too much in the eyes of God, she also loved him too little in the eyes of her in-laws.

Ippolita's multifaceted domestic theology, though indebted to probabilism, could not resolve the contradictory implications of maternal love. Such paradoxes had continued unabated since the humanists captured them in their fifteenth-century texts on the family. An increasing emphasis on the value of maternal love created new dilemmas, difficulties in which mothers like Ippolita expected the men in their family to share. Such predicaments confounded the cardinal's ability to side unequivocally with his brother Antonio. Drawn into this web of arguments that were theological, dynastic, familial, and emotional, Cardinal Giacomo vacillated – he encouraged Ippolita to have patience and keep the peace and simultaneously urged his brother to reach an accord more quickly. Cardinal Giacomo's strategy worked for a time but it could not be sustained beyond a few years. By 1709, the failed marriage negotiations for Teresa Boncompagni stretched the fragile accord to the breaking point, and forced Ippolita to declare herself fully on the side of the girls as "a matter of great conscience."[223] She appealed in the end to the highest authority, God himself, and challenged the theological conclusions of her in-laws, who determined that the failure to marry off Teresa (and by extension the rest of the girls) was more than a matter of dynastic politics and finances, but rather it was the will of God himself. God's will was a familiar adversary for the "failed" mother who had not produced an adult son, but it was not one against which Ippolita was willing to admit defeat. She faced her own worse doubts in this critique and declared that reading divine adjudication was a difficult matter in which there might be divergent interpretations.

God's Will and the Boundaries of Maternal Advocacy

In the face of her in-laws' opposition, Ippolita emphasized that she had to "save" her daughters in order to be a good mother.[224] Religious language intertwined with parental devotion was not a spiritual approach unique to Ippolita, though it only began to gain ground in the late seventeenth century.[225] For Ippolita, the conflict of 1709 over the potential marriage of her eldest unmarried daughter, Teresa, was a critical turning point in her maternal commitment. That was the year that Ippolita faced the spiritual and familial differences between herself and the Boncompagni men, and laid to rest her last doubts about whether she should patiently wait for her brothers-in-law to decide the fate of the girls or push the fight forward on their behalf. Ippolita's maternal resolution emerged as she settled her internal qualms about matters of faith that disturbed many Roman Catholics. In 1709, Ippolita took both a theological and familial stand, and staked her earthly life and future salvation on the kind of *mater litigans* she could become for her daughters.

In the same decades that Rome bristled with the debate over probabilism, residents of the city became fascinated by the spiritual practices of quietism, especially as articulated by Michele de Molinos, a Spanish priest who resided in Rome.[226] The popularity of quietism crested between the mid-1660s and mid-1670s, when Ippolita was no more than a child, but at which time the adult Ludovisi and Boncompagni princesses were among Molinos's best known supporters.[227] His following continued among women close to Ippolita, including her older sister, Olimpia, who became Suor Anna and to whom the second Italian edition of Molinos's spiritual guide was dedicated.[228] Ippolita's beloved older sister-in-law, Eleonora Boncompagni Borghese (1642–95), was also among the Roman women who followed him avidly and abandoned his teachings reluctantly when he was later condemned by the church.[229] In addition to widespread favor in Roman convents, quietism gained followers among the clergy as well, including high-ranking prelates, such as Pier Matteo Petrucci (1636–1701), who would eventually become a cardinal in the church.[230] The future pope Innocent XI (Benedetto Odescalchi, r.1676–89) also fell under the spell of Molinos, though as pope he would later condemn aspects of his teaching.[231]

Quietism's popularity is not surprising considering its solution to human anxiety about the place of God in an individual's life. It provided a means by which human beings might reconcile themselves to his will. In a century torn apart by warfare, plague, and economic crises, Catholicism offered an inconsistent answer to whether believers should see God in such events as merciful or angry, forgiving or punishing. In quietism, such tensions melted away as its spiritual practice, the *"via interna,"* encouraged the faithful to dissolve their personal aspirations and concerns: "man must annihilate his powers ... the desire to do anything actively is offensive to God and hence one must abandon oneself entirely to God and thereafter remain as a lifeless body."[232] Quietism privileged this interior surrender and de-emphasized both good works and the sacraments in the spiritual life of the faithful.

By the time Ippolita had grown to adulthood, married Gregorio Boncompagni, and begun her life as a mother, quietism was already under criticism by the church. Though papal bulls officially chipped away at its legitimacy, its practices doubtless endured and some of its more famous adherents in Rome, including Cristina of Sweden, never distanced themselves from Molinos.[233] Quietism elicited a vivid rejoinder from the Jesuits, since it challenged the contemplative practices they had extolled and taught since Ignatius Loyola founded their order a century before.[234] The Jesuit preacher Paolo Segneri was among the more measured critics of quietism.[235] The peripatetic orator came to Rome in 1692, invited by Pope Innocent XII (Antonio Pignatelli, r.1691–1700) to preach the Lenten sermons to the College of Cardinals.[236] Yet his fame long preceded him, as his far-flung preaching and publications in the vernacular sought to provide spiritual consolation for those who, like Ippolita, struggled to live an ethical life amidst the social complexities of their times.[237] Although Ippolita never specifically referenced Segneri in her letters to Cardinal Giacomo, she was clearly an avid reader in general, as the books in the gift exchange between Cardinal Giacomo and her suggests. There is much in her spiritual manner and the orientation to her earthly life that echoes Segneri's reflections in his popular calendar of spirituality, *Manna of the Soul*, and his collection of printed sermons, *Il Quaresimale*. The calendar provided the faithful with readings, meditations, and guidance for each day of the year.[238] Widely popular – despite its length (it was originally published in four volumes) – *Manna of the Soul* was printed in nine different editions in the city of Venice alone between the late seventeenth and early eighteenth centuries.[239] It was translated into French, German, Spanish, and Latin in those same decades. Catholicism's most famous preacher since Bernardino of Siena thus reached a wide audience beyond those who were able to hear him preach in person.

Ippolita was doubtless in need of guidance and consolation as she navigated a crisis that was at once familial and theological, maternal and historical. Her unmarried daughters were not getting any younger and yet her brothers-in-law encouraged her to wait. By the end of December 1708, Ippolita broke her temporary silence and began to venture again with the cardinal into the territory of the controversy. Her scarcely veiled threat of a lawsuit was followed by an immediate apology that excused her outburst on the basis of her "breaking heart" and the "goodness [of Cardinal Giacomo] that gave me liberty to speak my mind."[240] Biding her time was difficult because of the pernicious effects on the future of her daughter Teresa. In 1709, Teresa would turn 17 years old. That same year there emerged in Rome some interest in her as potential bride on the part of at least two aristocratic families. The conflict between Ippolita and Antonio, which had been subdued somewhat by Cardinal Giacomo's call for patience, once again crossed over into acrimony. The disagreement over Teresa's marriage became the struggle that inspired Ippolita to break her barely sustained silence and write a comprehensive manifesto on her vision of the divine as mother of the Boncompagni "convent."

From the beginning of her widowhood, Ippolita was clearly torn between advocating for her daughters and demonstrating obedience to the Boncompagni brothers. As late as the summer of 1709, Ippolita expressed calm regarding the possibility of making a match for Teresa with the Barberini family, who expressed an interest in the girl. In her equanimity, Ippolita emphasized her willingness to work as a team player in the future marriage negotiations for her eldest unmarried daughter.[241] Later that year, however, a different family, the Rospigliosi, also inquired after Teresa. Gauging the Rospigliosi to be a better choice, Ippolita was ready to move toward finalizing a match, but she faced objections from Cardinal Giacomo and Antonio. Ippolita's bluntness ultimately got the better of her patience. She began by confessing that she found any point of view opposing her own incomprehensible, including the one evidently offered by Cardinal Giacomo that the Rospigliosi match could wait:

> In every matter and on every occasion my own feeling will never be without its connection to the sentiments of Your Excellency and I do glory in my eternal submission to the very wise opinion of You. But to tell you the truth my lord and most reverent brother-in-law, in the matter of the matrimony of my daughter Teresa it would be very difficult to have a feeling different from my own. Even after the reply of Your Excellency I still have no basis for believing that there could be any other reasonable way of seeing the situation.[242]

The limbo of these "blessed domestic controversies" as she referred to them, would only make them worse over time and their long lack of resolution would damage the reputation of the Boncompagni.[243] Ippolita's predictions were frequently dire – and increasingly so in the case of Teresa's marital negotiations. In her opinion Antonio's side was only stirring up further obstacles rather than seeking solutions. Her adversaries raised what she regarded as extraneous issues, such as the fate of her husband's illegitimate daughter, rather than staying focused on the matter at hand.[244] She, by contrast, was motivated by her obligations as the guardian of the girls to set things right, not in order to pursue her own gain but rather "for the peace and advantage of the *casa*."[245]

By summer's end, Cardinal Giacomo had evidently come around to her way of thinking about the Rospigliosi offer, and even Antonio later gave his approval of the match for Teresa.[246] Yet problems remained, since along with his consent Antonio presented other obstacles: specifically, that he lacked the means to offer his niece a dowry sufficient to her rank. Ippolita was forced again to make her case to Cardinal Giacomo:

> But if you could permit me my Lord and venerable brother-in-law that I might unburden myself to you ... . I do so that I might know what reply to give to these Signori [Rospigliosi] for after I received the approval of Your Excellency and the Lord Duke [Antonio], who must initiate the agreement about the Dowry, there has yet been nothing negotiated and we are even further behind [in the discussion among ourselves] than when we started. I must admit that after I received the most kind letter from the Lord Duke [Antonio] that he approved of the negotiation but that he was sorry that he could not allow the daughter to exit [the House] without that which Justice would have circumscribed.[247]

Ippolita recoiled at the stalemate, and unleashed a torrent of frustration upon Cardinal Giacomo. She declared her unwillingness to acquiesce to the waiting game any longer. She withdrew her trust from Antonio and from the whole process that had led to this debacle:

> ... it can no longer be claimed nor should anyone now claim that there will be a *Congregazione* [to settle these matters]. And I had formerly believed that the Lord Duke had already given the order to hasten the conclusion of the matter, as he promised in the letter in which he said he desired the conclusion of the matter for the tranquility [of the *casa*].

But if anyone was expecting to hear a decisive strategy, it's all to the contrary now and against what was gained in the previous *congregazione*. As I told Your Excellency, I hoped that the matters could take a good turn but now all is lost and we are back to the beginning when the *congregazione* was so difficult and the negotiations were broken off.[248]

In spite of their supposed approval of the Rospigliosi match, the Boncompagni continued to express their disappointment with Ippolita's tenacious insistence upon a dowry for Teresa. As they had in 1707 at the beginning of her widowhood, they questioned in 1709 whether her motives were as selfless as she claimed. Ippolita again brushed off the criticism:

I am not the Princess of Piombino who proposes her own interest against the peace and good service of the *casa*, and even if my good heart neither persuades nor pleases anyone, my heart accepts none of these accusations if I am defending my daughters to whom I am already obligated by the demands of their guardianship.[249]

She had since early widowhood expressed her indifference to adversaries' criticism, because she knew that "God who sees all hearts knew if she were speaking with sincerity" in her wish to help her daughters.[250]

Ippolita's recourse to her good heart as sufficient to justify her resistance echoes a number of cultural and religious metaphors diffuse in seventeenth-century society. The human heart was increasingly viewed as the sincere expression of the self and Ippolita inserted it into the debate in this fashion.[251] She professed herself ready to be viewed as in the wrong in the conflict and she certainly was in the wrong, from the point of view of the established dynastic practices of the Boncompagni. But God, rather than the in-laws, would judge the purity of her heart and that was consolation enough for her in the face of adversity. God, the preacher Segneri reminded his listeners, "principally looks at our hearts."[252] Similarly in her disputes with Antonio, she had also declared his heart good, and the deeds of his evil councilors as the cause of familial disputes.[253]

Ippolita's recourse to the heart and to her sincerity helped her distinguish herself from Boncompagni history and legal precedent. She asserted a separate standard of assessment of her behavior – an evaluation that could be made by God alone. Recourse to the human heart helped Ippolita elaborate an image of herself as an altruistic mother, a maternal identity that helped her separate herself from what she viewed as the misguided family practices of her in-laws. Fulfilling the mandates of this earthly role was sufficient for Ippolita's path to holiness.[254] Yet it also bound her ever more tightly to the familial, albeit a relatively new definition of the familial that she hoped to convince Cardinal Giacomo to accept. She defined herself and her morality by what she did for her daughters, even if she simultaneously liberated herself from the dynastic family practices insisted upon by her adversaries.

Ippolita took comfort that a direct recourse to a merciful God would legitimate her rebellion. But how far would the noblewoman go in these aims? As summer gave way to fall in 1709, Ippolita and her in-laws began reading intently the signs of the faltering marriage negotiations with the Rospigliosi. Antonio's allies implied that the failure of the marriage negotiations for Teresa was, more than merely the will of God, the "vendetta of God,"[255] a divine judgment which must contain clues about how mortals were to orient themselves to outcomes. In this case, the Boncompagni should accept the failed negotiations as divinely ordained and recognize that they would probably never be able to marry off all the daughters.

Ippolita would ultimately reject this particular conclusion (declaring it an impiety). Yet, initially the Boncompagni brothers' verdict struck a spiritually vulnerable part of Ippolita. She had previously expressed to Cardinal Giacomo her anxiety about how to interpret God's will in family crises. Dilemmas about divine will are sprinkled throughout the correspondence but are especially prevalent in the years following her husband's death. Although at that time she declared herself willing to "conform to the will of God," how could she know the intentions of the Almighty? Ippolita herself had wondered whether it was God's will that the Boncompagni were faced with so many disasters.[256]

Death offered Ippolita clearer insights about the wishes of the Almighty. She noted that the death of the pope's brother was a "tribute" that everyone must pay.[257] Death appeared more complex to her as an instrument of God's will when she tried to guess at God's motivation for dealing out death or extending life. God, she claimed in one desperate missive, had taken her husband out of punishment for her sins.[258] In a similar vein, Ippolita went so far as to suggest that her grandson died in punishment for the sin of her excessive love for the child, an argument her sister-in-law had also stressed over 20 years earlier at the death of Ippolita's only son, Ugo.[259] The most popular contemporary figures in Roman Catholic culture undermined such simple equations as appropriate analysis of events, or in the words of Segneri, "because adversity is a sign of the love which God bears the chastiseth."[260] Such a perspective complicated how the noblewoman should respond to the crisis and assess the role of divine will within it. The rupture between Ippolita and her in-laws underscores the contradictory image of God among Roman Catholics. In some versions of Catholicism, an angry God wreaked havoc on human affairs in punishment for sin. This God inflicted illness to bend human beings away from their depravity toward salvation. This was "Heaven's invisible intestinal war," according to one seventeenth-century physician.[261] A punishing God took Ippolita's son and grandson because of her sin of loving him too much. Although quietism may have offered some comfort to an earlier generation of Roman women, Ippolita clearly found no peace in its spiritual surrender and the effacement of her own will and feelings in the face of such losses.

Alternative readings of God underscored his loving mercy and clemency toward the faithful. These were also popular in the seventeenth century, especially among Jesuit writers.[262] The works of Segneri in particular underscored this alternative theological vision even if he never completely abandoned the references to the vengeful God who hated the sinner as well as the sin.[263] We have already seen how Ippolita's mode of arguing with Cardinal Giacomo was indebted to Jesuit probabilism. It is not surprising that the larger theological vision to which she would ultimately align herself was similarly shaped by the Jesuit version of Catholicism. Such a view underscored the value of patience in the face of hardship and acknowledged complexity in the interpretation of disaster. God's will operated in all things, but interpreting his will was profoundly difficult. As she reminded the cardinal early in her widowhood, in the face of adversity Catholics were supposed to put as much faith in God's mercy as in God's divine will: "I recognize your anxiety over the condition of our *casa* about which I don't know what to say except that we must recognize everything as the judgment of God in whose clemency we must hope for relief."[264]

Empowered by this more merciful interpretation of the Almighty and with the realization that interpreting his will was difficult, Ippolita disputed her in-laws' interpretation that the failed marriage negotiations were a sign of God's will to which she must resign herself. She insisted instead that such a failure indicated the shortcomings of human beings. She interpreted the Boncompagni brothers' declaration that it was impossible to provide Teresa a dowry sufficient to marry within her rank, as a sign to turn to lawsuits to solve the dispute. She underscored

her insight with some drama and a Latin interjection to bolster the
validity of her realization:

> I take this as a sign that I cannot hope to obtain an agreement even
> though it was what the Duke said he desires and what I yearn for
> and yet here we are *sicut erat in principio,* which we are supposed
> to consider a great and obscure justice of God, and I fear that it
> will not finish well. I regret it but I can't find another remedy and
> the [girls'] matrimonies will not be settled for the little fortune that
> the girls have.[265]

She reiterated her earlier visions of the familial, rejecting the notion
that the failure to resolve the situation in any way reflected "what is fair
or appropriate according to the potential of the *casa,*" which she clearly
aligned with the interests of the girls, "since they no longer know what
to hope for or what to wait for and when they might receive it."[266] The
girls were, as she reminded him, an integral part of the Boncompagni
casa. She vehemently refused the suggestion that the failed marriage
negotiations could be said to be the will of God – or, as she clarified it
for it the cardinal, "It seems to me an impiety to call this the vendetta
of God."[267] The breakdown in negotiations brought her greater clarity as
to how she had to orient herself toward Cardinal Giacomo and Antonio.

Ippolita elaborated her message further just in case the cardinal had
failed to follow her, as unlikely as that could have been. She threatened,
as she had not done anywhere else in the correspondence, to withhold
the subservience to him that she had expressed so many times before.
She interspersed this threat with requests for forgiveness for her mater-
nally motivated rebellion:

> I am resolved to finish it in whatever form necessary; and if this
> matrimony is not pulled off with the Rospigliosi (even if with them
> we lack little to conclude the possibility), I want to have a [marriage]
> agreement written with the offer in mind, because others could come
> for this daughter who has already declared that she does not have the
> vocation to become a nun.
>
> Excuse me, Your Excellency, for this outburst but it is caused by the
> maternal affection that foresees that from the prejudice towards this
> daughter the damage [that will fall] to the others if instead of finish-
> ing with an amicable accord we have to go forward with litigation
> in the courts. It seems that you can use your authority to approve
> these appropriate [marriage] agreements so the matter can be settled

since there is no time to suffer further delay. [If you will do so] then I will submit and place myself again under your powerful protection. I place at your feet the four daughters of your first-born brother who ask nothing more than true justice [in their regard] ...[268]

Evidently Cardinal Giacomo saw enough justice in her request or danger in her threat to try to move the matter along. Letters subsequent to this diatribe suggest that, by October, Cardinal Giacomo was again in her camp, insisting that the affair of the dowries be settled soon and giving the specific command that Antonio go to Frascati to finalize the matter.[269] It was, however, already too late to rescue the negotiations with the Rospigliosi. By the year's end, Ippolita had to recognize defeat. Teresa had lost out on a good potential match, and Ippolita feared that worse would follow for the other girls, who, she predicted, would grasp the desperation of their situation. Rather than resign herself to failure, however, she reiterated the broadest possible motivation for continuing the fight for her daughters, declaring that it was "a great matter of conscience" that drove her forward.[270]

Ippolita rebelled in a family in which (she had to know) there would likely be little support for resistance against established male authorities, as the staunch loyalty of the Boncompagni to the king of Naples in 1701 had so clearly shown. Ippolita attempted, nonetheless, to draw the Boncompagni out of the labyrinth of historical documents and practices that they regarded as hitherto successfully sustaining the dynasty. Ippolita had to face their accusation that she would not conform to the will of God as her in-laws defined it and accept the failure of the negotiations for Teresa's matrimony and, by extension, the likely possibility that such problems would be repeated for all the other girls. Ippolita countered with what she regarded as the surer boundary of God's will – death itself. Though she herself had once wished for death in the wake of her husband's passing, she speculated that it was a "God's judgment" that she was still in this world.[271] In her struggle to retain the Ludovisi properties, Ippolita had once observed to Cardinal Giacomo that it was God "who gave me the health and the strength to resist."[272] Those same resources were now to be employed in the defense of her daughters.

Throughout her life Ippolita had expressed fear of God's deadly judgment in punishment for her sins. Yet many of her spiritual qualms seem to have been settled by the conflict of 1709: the defense of her daughters was the most ethical course of action even if God alone could recognize that. She would not be turned back, even by the failure of Teresa's dowry negotiations. As Segneri reminded his readers in the words of

Ecclesiastes, "Even unto death fight for justice."[273] The presence of difficulty was no indication that a cause was misguided. This was the kind of surety she eventually brought to her role as *mater litigans*: she declared herself willing to fight until God no longer granted her the means or the physical force with which to wage her battle. Ippolita arrived at a material boundary for the maternal role, defining its limits in the physical duration of her own body. Death was scarcely an idle threat in the early eighteenth century; it was a frequent event and one with which Ippolita was particularly well acquainted. While it might be taken as a direct enjoinder to the Almighty, it might also be read as an injunction to the in-laws, to whom she had declared the tactics that they would have to employ if they wished to stop her.

Ippolita's mothering evidently evolved over multiple decades and in complex ways, not all of which are captured in her correspondence with the cardinal, nor by her struggles in the second half of her life to allow all four of her daughters to marry if they wished. That between resigned acceptance to the will of God as defined by the Boncompagni men and the commitment to do more she would choose the latter is not entirely surprising. Her domestic theology emerged amidst endless activity – from childbearing, the struggle to keep ailing children alive, and failure in the case where it mattered most to the male Boncompagni: in the death of her only son and the inability to bear any more male children. It was not a life in which the practices of quietism and a spirituality of passive resignation could find a place. Motherhood and Christianity necessitated motion. While acting as Cardinal Giacomo's eyes and ears in Rome, she had also worked tirelessly to recover the territories of her own Ludovisi family, and battled internationally for that inheritance so that she could pass it on to her daughters. She later turned those same skills on the Boncompagni, when they postponed her demands to secure her girls' future.

The failure of 1709 delayed her but ultimately did not stop her. Tense negotiations resumed with Ippolita's lawyer, Viscardi, and the lawyers of Duke Antonio, but they were without success.[274] Relying on her contacts with the Spanish court, in 1709 Ippolita secured written permission from the Spanish king Philip V to withdraw 100,000 scudi from the incomes of the principality of Piombino. The promissary note would provide dowries for her daughters, though the money was not to be withdrawn until her life was over.[275] The document only came to light after her death, but she likely used it in her negotiations with potential in-laws since her negotiations for their dowries included promises of payments after her death.

Despite what might appear to be the irrational mortgaging of the resources that were supposed to belong to the male lineage, Ippolita also thought in terms of the long-term goals of primogeniture. She did eventually recognize a male heir and acknowledge the "demands of eternity" in the system of primogeniture[276] by designating her grandson by Maria Eleonora, Gaetano, as the later heir of the Ludovisi patrimony, including Piombino.[277] But in the meantime, eternity could wait. In 1709, when she secretly approached the Spanish sovereign in a legal maneuver to secure her daughters' dowries, Gaetano was then about two years old. Gaetano's older brother, Niccolò, had died that same year, at the age of five. What future awaited the Boncompagni Ludovisi? Would it have any boys in it? Did one sacrifice the girls' in the present to such an indefinite tomorrow? Such reasoning explains Ippolita's decision to place a promissory note on the Ludovisi inheritance in the hopes that it would gain her enough financial leverage to marry off her daughters in the short term and leave sufficient time for the inheritance to be put back together for her grandson in the long term.

This was a highly modified form of primogeniture, and it was a gamble, but not one undertaken due to a lack of commitment to her grandchildren, as her critics charged. She remained involved with her grandson Gaetano throughout her life, professing to love him "more than a son," helping him make connections in and beyond Rome, and taking interest in his education.[278] She followed his deliberations about what future he might wish for himself – for marriage or the religious life – a choice that Gaetano evidently had difficulty making.[279] It was nerve-wracking for Maria Eleonora, who observed to her mother, "My children leave me in a continual state of agitation."[280] Ippolita reminded her (in reference to Gaetano), "To never abandon nor undermine her son, but to allow for his liberty to speak [his mind]."[281] So for sons as well as daughters, their opinion on their own future had to be considered. Ippolita also insisted on mortgaging what he would receive, to provide for her remaining unmarried daughters.[282] Her grandson did eventually inherit the Ludovisi family patrimony of Piombino, and his siblings also each inherited enough to marry. Maria Eleonora, like her mother before her, insisted that all her offspring be allowed to marry if they wished, even against the wishes of her eldest son, Gaetano, who resisted this relative novelty, but could not prohibit it. The marriage pattern of the Boncompagni family was broken as a result of Ippolita's efforts, and continued by her eldest daughter.[283] What appeared eccentric in one generation became the norm in another.

Ippolita's rethinking of the family and her role as mother likely owes much to the early influence of Eleonora Boncompagni Borghese, who sternly admonished her to think seriously about her girls. Was her advocacy also driven by the memory of her unhappy older sister, confined to the convent, but openly dissatisfied with her life there? Was it forged in dialogue with her beloved Gregorio, with whom she cultivated a parental tenderness for the girls that later helped her defy her in-laws' insistence that they be forced to take religious vows? Gregorio's failure to make a will suggested at least ambivalence on his part, an unwillingness to choose between the reigning practices of his *casa* and the affection he bore his daughters. Leaving the matter in Ippolita's trustworthy hands left her also with the fight of her life, and it was her own life she declared that she would stake upon it.

Even Gregorio's younger brother, Antonio, who fought to defend the Boncompagni patrimony from the claims of his sister/mother-in-law Ippolita, was evidently open to negotiation regarding his nieces' future. In the early 1720s, Antonio solicited legal advice and commissioned two reports that pointed in different directions. One strategy urged Antonio to solidify the Boncompagni *fedecommesso* and to make it inviolate against the maneuvers of challengers such as Ippolita. Antonio himself is criticized in the report for his ambivalence toward resolving the fight with his nieces.[284] Yet an alternative text pointed instead toward a flexible strategy of negotiating with the nieces in the name of "familial decorum."[285] Its anonymous author recognized the potential impact of lawsuits, noting that their formidable costs made it more advantageous to settle "rather than make oneself the slave of Doctor Lawsuit,"[286] a lament that recognized the peril to familial finances and familial honor that lawsuits posed in the early eighteenth century.[287] Antonio challenged Ippolita but he also waivered in his attempts to fight her and his nieces, as his own solicited reports acknowledged. He wished to preserve the Boncompagni patrimony as Neapolitan law courts upheld his right to do. But a patchwork of accords and settlements with his nieces suggested that he, too, like his deceased brother, Gregorio, was ambiguous about whether he should disinherit his nieces to the extent that previous generations of the Boncompagni had done with their daughters.[288]

Sharing in this fraternal ambivalence to an even greater degree was Cardinal Giacomo, with whom Ippolita had been closely involved, as was the Roman familial pattern for clerics and their sisters-in-law. More than simply his collaborator in advancing the interests of the Boncompagni dynasty, Ippolita was also the recipient of his comfort and his advice in the last unsuccessful years of childbearing, and as she endured the travails of raising her "convent" after the death of her husband. Cardinal Giacomo evidently shared his brothers' doubts about forcing monacalization on the next generation of Boncompagni girls. He pushed his younger brother Antonio to negotiate even as he recognized the especially precarious financial position in which the Boncompagni found themselves. Yet to deny the girls' free will to choose their vocation was a heinous spiritual offense, as the Cardinal doubtless knew. Ippolita also implicated him in the same praiseworthy but problematic emotional connections to the children of the dynasty that she herself expressed. She played upon the Cardinal's growing unease with the reality that to deny his unmarried nieces their dowries would be an offense to this emerging domestic theology, to which he and the other men of his generation found themselves increasingly, if cautiously, drawn.

5
Extravagant Pretensions
The Triumph of Maternal Love in the World of Rome

Ippolita Ludovisi (1663–1733) lived to see all her daughters marry, but married lives, as she well knew, were not without their painful difficulties. A few short years after the marriage of her youngest daughter in 1723, Ippolita found herself with one older daughter already a widow: Teresa (1692–1744), married in 1714 to Urbano Barberini, was widowed at 30, and subsequently entrenched in a battle with her brother-in-law for the custody of her only daughter, Cornelia (1716–97). Ippolita, by then in her sixties, appeared to Teresa's adversaries still a formidable force, an aging *mater litigans*, politically clever but reduced to tears when the controversy seemed to go against her daughter.[1] Ippolita's interlocutors critiqued both her arguments and her emotion. Some opinions of her daughter Teresa were scarcely better. A dispatch by the Holy Roman Emperor Charles VI referred to the behavior of Teresa as "resistance" to his royal will.[2] Because Teresa wished to continue to reside with her only daughter, the nine-year-old Cornelia, she had refused the emperor's order to place her in a convent in 1725. Since Cornelia was heir to fiefs in southern Italy, then ruled from Vienna, Cornelia was a kind of collateral subject of the emperor, although as a daughter of Roman nobles she was also a subject of the pope.[3] In contrast to the emperor, Teresa eschewed the terminology of resistance, insisting instead that maternal affection justified her unwillingness to surrender Cornelia. Resistance in Vienna was good mothering in Rome, at least as far as Teresa was concerned.

The interpretive dissonance between the Holy Roman Emperor and Teresa was scarcely new. Since the seventeenth century, Italian mothers had attempted in controversial matters to persuade law courts, princely courts, and popular opinion that their love for their children should be factored into decisions about their future. Such mothers articulated a view of parenting as a maternal affair. They centered the family on the emotional attachment of the mother for the child, rather than focusing exclusively on larger dynastic ambitions, or on political or financial aims.[4] While the Holy Roman Emperor claimed not to be persuaded by such views in the 1720s, by the mid-eighteenth century this maternal perspective would reach a popular apogee, usually attributed to the author Rousseau and the cult of sentimentalized motherhood. The painter Angelika Kauffman would offer a powerful visual argument for such notions in her historical painting, *Cornelia, Mother of the Gracchi*, later exhibited to great acclaim in Rome in 1785 (Figure 5.1).[5] The exemplary mother of Roman antiquity presented her children as her greatest achievement, her finest adornment, the center of a praiseworthy domestic life. Looking back from the perspective of late eighteenth-century Europe, emotive mothering would appear as far from resistance as one could imagine.

But Teresa Boncompagni and her predecessors promoted the preeminence of emotional ties between mothers and children before its sanitized

Figure 5.1 Angelika Kauffman (Swiss, 1741–1807, active in England and Italy), *Cornelia, Mother of the Gracchi, Pointing to her Children as her Treasures*, c.1785. Courtesy of Virginia Museum of Fine Arts, Richmond. Adolph and Wilkins C. Williams Fund.

representation made it palatable to a broader audience. She faced adversaries for whom motherly affection was still characterized as resistance – as dangerous, inappropriate, unreasonable, or simply irrelevant to the family's future. Yet, other maternal activity had long been integral to dynastic aims, since mothers worked as informal ambassadors in their families' interests,[6] as intermediaries between dynasties,[7] as marriage brokers,[8] and as legal advocates and skilled consumers of the judicial possibilities of the Papal States. That they employed such skills in service of their children was not surprising. It was expected.

Teresa's resistance to the loss of her daughter captures these two halves of seventeenth-century mothering, since she insisted on the integrity of an intimate domestic space that would include her only daughter, yet she also lived a public life in Rome, courting allies, litigating, frequenting the theater, moving expertly in networks that could help her advance her cause. Her primary adversary in Rome claimed to find both aspects of Teresa's mothering outrageous. But by the early eighteenth century, the activities of a *mater litigans* and the validity of her emotional claims for mothering were so interwoven in Roman life that they were an integral (if for some still controversial) aspect of the papal capital. Rousseau in print and Kauffman on canvas were subsequent successful sanitizers of maternal tenderness, but their interpretations were also epilogues to and truncations of what was once an older view of mothering in which love and advocacy were linked, potent, potentially dangerous but an expected part of Roman life.

Teresa's struggle helps to excavate this earlier history of maternal affect. During the course of the controversy (1725–27), Teresa's opinions were remarkably consistent, even under threats from the Holy Roman Emperor and with only shaky support from Roman law courts. As mother to her daughter Cornelia, and as the flesh-and-blood predecessor to the pictorial Cornelia who later moved Roman audiences, Teresa navigated a world in which an emotional commitment to her daughter was not yet sufficient to allow her to mother as she wished. Yet, she made no apologies for it, nor did she couch it in terms of her service to the aristocratic *casa*, as her predecessors had done. In Teresa, emotion and advocacy were expressed openly and unapologetically. The potential discourses of danger surrounding them were abandoned altogether in her writing. Maternal affection had made considerable gains, especially in Rome. The determination of Teresa and her cohort in facing down residual suspicions and criticisms would allow subsequent generations to see the ancient Cornelia and the contemporary Cornelia in a very different light.

The Will of God and Monarch, or Why Women Should Obey Men

At issue for Teresa and the relatives of her deceased husband was the residence of her daughter Cornelia in 1725. Widowed only three years before, Teresa continued to reside in the Palazzo Barberini alle Quattro Fontane, and she placed a premium on allowing her daughter to grow up with her and gradually, perhaps in her mid to late teens, to come to a decision about her own marriage (Figure 5.2). The rival for Teresa was an aging fixture on the Roman scene, Cardinal Francesco Barberini Junior (1662–1738), then in his sixties, who sought to have control of Cornelia's future since she was the sole legitimate heir of his now deceased brother, the spendthrift Urbano Barberini (1664–1722), who had taken Teresa as his third wife in 1714 (see Figures 2.3 and 2.4).

Figure 5.2 Anonymous artist, *Maria Teresa Boncompagni*. Courtesy of Galleria Nazionale D'Arte Antica in Palazzo Barberini, Galleria dei Ritratti.

Cardinal Francesco had considerable legal, historical, and dynastic precedent for the removal of his niece from her mother and for her placement in a convent. From there, he believed, she would be married to a man of Cardinal Francesco's choosing, so important was her marital future to the future of the Barberini. Teresa resisted both the removal of Cornelia from their shared residence and the settlement of her marital future at a time when Cornelia was still of a "tender age" (nine years old), far too young to give her consent to any marriage proposal.

Into this dispute would step many of the most famous political players on the European scene: the Holy Roman Emperor Charles VI, Pope Benedict XIII, the magistrates of Rome's highest court, the Rota, and Count Carlo Borromeo of Milan, considered one of the learned luminaries and esteemed statesmen of the Italian peninsula. Each of these would support Cardinal Francesco to some degree, sometimes reluctantly, sometimes with more enthusiasm. Allies occasionally backed the cardinal while trying to persuade him of the appropriateness of his adversary's concerns. Cardinal Francesco won in the end, placed Cornelia in a convent in 1727, and married her off the following year to a man of his choosing, Giulio Cesare Colonna di Sciarra. She was 12 years old. Giulio Cesare was 20. He added Barberini to his name and agreed that one of his sons would provide the Barberini with a direct male heir to continue the lineage. Paradoxically, it was Cardinal Francesco who helped to promote the legitimacy of Teresa's views, by underscoring the extent to which it was her opinions, not his, that won the day in what he called the "world" of Rome. The Roman public, the cardinal believed, sided with Teresa's insistence on the centrality of maternal love and maternal care to the upbringing of Cornelia. Key allies found more reasonable Teresa's wish that, in the choice of marital partner, both Cornelia and her mother should have some say.

Cardinal Francesco characterized his victories as a series of defeats. While he succeeded in having his way, he did so against what he perceived to be the larger and deleterious trends in Roman society that accepted the intertwined practices of affection and advocacy associated with the figure of the *mater litigans*. Cardinal Francesco began by railing against the dangers of allowing emotion to overturn legal precedent and dynastic practices. By the end of the controversy, he had embraced the language of his opponent and acknowledged that public sympathy was with her, not with him.

Cardinal Francesco had been in charge of the management of some Barberini properties since the first years of the eighteenth century, a time when his brother Urbano proved himself incapable of doing anything but wrecking family finances and running through wives.[9] Cardinal Francesco was a man accustomed to struggle, but not to defeat. At the time of his brother Urbano's death in 1722, he was already empowered to settle issues of succession to the Barberini primogeniture.[10] When Urbano Barberini died, he left behind Teresa and their daughter Cornelia, not yet six years old. Cornelia was Urbano's only legitimate offspring after three marriages. Although Urbano had failed to appoint a guardian for Cornelia before he died, this initially seemed to pose only minor problems between Teresa and her brother-in-law, Cardinal Francesco. An informal agreement between the two was sufficient to organize Cornelia's life immediately following the death of her father. A negotiator appointed by the Holy Roman Emperor worked out a solution that allowed mother and daughter to remain together in Teresa's apartments in the Palazzo Barberini alle Quattro Fontane, with the proviso that Cardinal Francesco would continue to manage what was left of the Barberini patrimony.[11] At the mediation, Cardinal Francesco pledged to "maintain his sister-in-law and his niece as she required, provided that, by the Holy Year (1725), Cornelia Costanza would be placed in the Convent of the Incarnation (a convent long associated with the Barberini family, in which some Barberini daughters had resided)."[12] Teresa came to later accords with Cardinal Francesco on her use of carriages, her allotments for food, and the annual payments she was to receive from the Barberini income. She worried about the drafty chapel where her daughter went to Mass and insisted that she be given access to another chapel where Cornelia would be less likely to catch a bad cold, as she already had done.[13] This was the stuff of typical relations between widowed mothers and brothers-in-law. It was (at first) relatively amicable, by comparison with similar negotiations in neighboring Tuscany.[14]

More problematic for Cardinal Francesco was the matter of Cornelia's future residence. Cardinal Francesco claimed that he and Teresa had agreed that Cornelia would be moved by 1725 to a convent for the remainder of her childhood. Many of Cornelia's aunts and great-aunts had passed at least a period of their childhood in convents. Teresa declined to sign any statement to such effect, and she resisted attempts by the cardinal to control the terms of Cornelia's education and upbringing.[15] Cardinal Francesco's own allies urged caution. One of the cardinal's mediators questioned the purpose of such pressure in 1722. What did the cardinal gain? This pragmatic counselor reasoned in his report to Cardinal Francesco that if in 1725 the cardinal were unhappy with the girl's upbringing, he would be able to insist that she be moved to a convent.[16] Thus, between 1722 and 1725, the supposedly mutually agreed-upon future for Cornelia took the form of an "oral agreement" to which Teresa would continue to assert that she had never agreed.[17]

Despite Teresa's protests, it was probably very easy for Cardinal Francesco to believe that, as the head of the Barberini family, he was in the right when he asserted his authority over the mother and child. A typical clerical brother in a Roman aristocratic family would have wielded considerable power, and Cardinal Francesco's authority was further enhanced by the failure of his brother, Urbano, to behave as an heir-producing brother should. Cardinal Francesco's intense desire to control his niece's future was also driven by the pitiful state of the Barberini family in the early eighteenth century. He had spent most of the preceding three decades attempting to rescue the family patrimony from sale. Urbano had scarcely cooperated with Cardinal Francesco's efforts, endangering with ever more debt what his diligent brother rescued by ingenuous financing and his own cash. Assisted by his mother, Olimpia Giustiniani, the cardinal had successfully wrested control of key territories from the spendthrift Urbano.[18] Cardinal Francesco probably believed himself further justified in determining Cornelia's fate because he had, after all, saved the patrimony upon which her financial future depended.

Legal evidence and political authorities bolstered his claims. A papal dispensation by his ancestor, Urban VIII (Maffeo Barberini, r.1623–44), had established patrilinear control of all Barberini children.[19] The Holy Roman Emperor, Charles VI, concurred that Cardinal Francesco was right to insist on the convent for Cornelia. The papal sovereign, Benedict XIII (Pietro Francesco Orsini, r.1724–30), who had to endure Cardinal Francesco's relentless badgering, eventually agreed that, in 1725, Cornelia should be moved from her mother's residence to a convent until her marriage. However, Pope Benedict added that he hoped such a transfer could be accomplished "without violence" and "without uproar [*strepito*]."[20]

About midway through 1725, however, the transfer of Cornelia Costanza to the convent had yet to occur. From Cardinal Fabrizio Paolucci, the cardinal Vicar, Cardinal Francesco secured papal permission to place his niece in the convent. As cardinal Vicar, Paolucci tended to issues related to morality and familial disputes in and around Rome.[21] He authorized taking the girl to the convent and insisted upon the pope's point, that this had to be accomplished "without uproar and without violence."[22] Cardinal Paolucci was known in Rome for his compassion for the poor and for his expertise and moderation in the affairs of Rome's secular government.[23] His view of how the transfer of Cornelia to the convent should be handled was, therefore, probably in keeping with mainstream views on the family within its urban aristocratic context.

By Cardinal Francesco's own account, however, this was going to be difficult. So he attempted to bribe one of his niece's servants, one Anna Maria (sometimes also called Angela). Angela was to provide peaceful or non-violent entry for him to the niece's apartments in the Palazzo Barberini alle Quattro Fontane. A small monthly stipend for life was to be the servant's reward.[24] Alas for Cardinal Francesco, the plan was spoiled by Angela, who confided the bargain she'd made to her lover, a priest. The priest then spilled the plan to Teresa. By whatever means she learned of the plans, Teresa alerted the servants and double-locked the doors of her apartments in the Palazzo Barberini to prevent the cardinal from seizing her daughter.[25]

Barely slowed by these setbacks, Cardinal Francesco returned to international channels to achieve his aims. He looked to his sister Camilla (1660–1740), who lived in Lombardy with her husband Carlo Borromeo (1657–1740), to provide support for his effort to secure aid from the Austrians, who then ruled Lombardy directly. Cardinal Francesco's correspondence with his long-distance relations began to focus on making a match for the still very young Cornelia. Camilla and Carlo Borromeo had a son, Federico, in his late twenties, who had not yet married, while Carlo also had an older son by his first wife who would carry on the Borromeo family. So began a dialogue among Cardinal Francesco, his sister Camilla, and brother-in-law Carlo Borromeo regarding the possibility of a marriage between Federico and his cousin, Cornelia. The Borromeo family tightened their ties to Rome, purchasing a lovely fief, Monte Rotondo, that belonged to the Barberini until the last years of the seventeenth century. Cardinal Francesco Barberini dreamed of joining Monte Rotondo to one of the Barberini's most extensive territories in the same area of the countryside, the *stato* of Monte Libretti.[26] Cardinal Francesco could thus regain a lost Barberini fief and regenerate the Barberini family with a spouse for his niece. Her husband would add the Barberini name to his own and provide one of his sons for the continuation of the Barberini line.[27]

Although a number of complexities stood in his way, the cardinal was persuaded that the marriage of his niece by his brother to his nephew by his sister was the most advantageous union. He drafted a detailed contract, which included the demand that the Borromeo family pay the papal dispensation for the cousin-marriage.[28] The prospective husband,

Federico Borromeo, was then sent to Rome in the spring of 1726 to acquaint himself with his potential in-laws and with "the governing of the Barberini *casa*."[29] Extended contact between nephew and uncle seemed to exacerbate differences between the generations, leading Cardinal Francesco to offer detailed and unsolicited advice on how to remedy what he saw as his nephew's faults. According to the cardinal, Federico had talents, but because he was an "enemy of fatigue," he would rather leave matters too much in the hands of his employees and officials, thus becoming their slave rather than their master.[30] He wasted his time rearranging his wig and straightening his stockings, spent too much money, slept by day and partied through the night, and confessed (despite his nocturnal habits) that he was tempted to retire to a hermitage and take holy orders.[31] Cardinal Francesco thought greater industry the cure for Federico's shortcomings and confusions. Camilla defended her son, but other observers in Milan found him as baffling as Cardinal Francesco did.[32] He wondered to his sister whether Federico was another Urbano Barberini in the making, an irresponsible spendthrift.[33]

While Federico had been allowed to pursue a protracted adolescence, Cornelia was expected to marry at a very young age, the man of Cardinal Francesco's choice – and if Federico did not measure up, the cardinal had a number of alternative negotiations under way.[34] In his eyes, the best setting for such a micro-managed childhood was the convent. Cardinal Francesco preferred the Convent of the Incarnation, where both his sisters had spent their childhood.[35] He also considered putting Cornelia in the convent of San Domenico e Sisto, where his niece Anna Costanza Caetani resided. From Cardinal Francesco's perspective, the Barberini family had a long and wise tradition of placing daughters in convents until they were old enough to marry or take religious vows. Even his aunt, Lucrezia Barberini (1632–99), had lived in a convent when the family was in exile in Paris during the 1640s.[36] To bolster his case against Teresa, he summoned this family history, but it was only a partial history – his grandmother, Anna Colonna, had protested the placement of her daughter Lucrezia Barberini in a convent, preferring that the child remain with her.[37] By ignorance or by intent, Cardinal Francesco muted the protests of the most famous Barberini mother, who was opposed to the practice of placing girls in convents. The recurrence of the practice was sufficient evidence of its legitimacy for the cardinal.

The nature of Cornelia's upbringing and marriage seemed to belong rightfully under the control of her long-suffering uncle, who had pulled the Barberini back from the financial abyss into which her father,

Urbano, had been determined to throw them. Legal precedent, local and distant monarchs, and aristocratic family practice supported the cardinal. He corresponded personally with one of the judges of Rome's most powerful court, the Sacra Rota, the court from which he would eventually demand a formal decision regarding Cornelia's custody.[38] He continued to seek the support of his sympathetic brother-in-law, Carlo Borromeo, the well-connected correspondent of some of Italy's greatest minds. Borromeo forwarded Cardinal Francesco the equally supportive correspondence from Marchese Rials, a personal friend who served as minister of the Holy Roman Emperor.[39] In that correspondence, Marchese Rials offered advice to Carlo Borromeo and Cardinal Francesco on how to deal with the difficult Teresa. After Teresa wrote to Carlo Borromeo in 1726, lamenting how much she had suffered since the death of her husband, the Milanese noble advised her that the solution to her problems was in her own hands – she should agree to place her daughter in the convent as Cardinal Francesco insisted. It was, he noted, both God's will and the emperor's will that it be done. Yet, there was no higher authority than the emperor's that could "bring the Señora to reason," observed an ally of the emperor in Rome.[40] By comparison, a mother's wish to remain with her daughter seemed a flimsy argument, "an extravagant pretension," as Cardinal Francesco put it.[41] What kind of mother would withstand pressure from so many distinguished authorities, and for what reason would she do so?

Playing for Time: Making a Childhood for Cornelia

Despite the prestige of his allies and the solidity of his legal advice, Cardinal Francesco was extremely concerned about Teresa, whom he considered the center of a cabal of Barberini enemies, controlled by evil counselors, and wildly unreasonable in her desire "to keep her daughter with her, always."[42] He went so far as to claim that Teresa would rather kill Cornelia with her own hands than see her go to the convent, contorting a mother's affection into vengeful murder.[43] By contrast, her polished, if all-too-rare letters reveal a confident and articulate mother with straightforward and reasonable concerns about her daughter. Teresa's primary claim was that the emotional bond between mother and daughter required their co-residence. Her second related and more elaborated concern was that Cornelia had to have a childhood without the pressure of decisions that she was far too young to make in 1726, at the age of nine, the time at which Cardinal Francesco began actively seeking a husband for her. Teresa was always bargaining for more time for Cornelia, in the hope that her daughter would make a better choice, of her own free will, when she was a bit older. In Teresa's writing and conversations with the Holy Roman Emperor's minister in Rome, Cardinal Cienfuegos, she made the argument for the significance of emotional ties and free will with a detached but determined calm. Such appeals found their audience. Even Cardinal Francesco later admitted that popular opinion in Rome sided with the sentiment that mothers and children belonged together.[44]

We can speculate about the origins of Teresa's ideas and her determination to fight for her daughter. In her case, resistance followed the maternal line. One *mater litigans* evidently begat another. Her mother, Ippolita Ludovisi, was by then well known for her successful struggle to provide a dowry for each of her daughters, after the death of her husband Gregorio Boncompagni in 1707. Insisting upon the preeminence of free will in her daughters' choice of marriage or the convent, she eventually convinced her in-laws that, despite the dynastic tradition, the girls should not be forced into the convent against their will. Ippolita pursued the arduous but ultimately successful strategy of pledging pieces of the family patrimony in southern Italy and of offering payments after her death in order to give her daughters sufficient dowries to marry if they wished.[45]

Cardinal Francesco and his allies hoped to frighten Teresa into surrendering Cornelia with the threat that they would deprive Cornelia of Barberini fiefs in southern Italy. His allies in Vienna advised him to return to this strategy periodically in order to "terrorize the mother."[46] This threat was considerable, since Teresa's own mother had relied on such territories to construct her daughters' dowries. It was probably not clear to Teresa whether Cornelia would inherit all (or part) of the Barberini patrimony held in primogeniture. In response, Teresa laid claim to the fiefs in southern Italy in 1725, a claim the cardinal successfully contested.[47] Cardinal Francesco also hinted that he would disinherit Cornelia altogether unless she married the man of his choosing.[48] Both threats undermined what Teresa doubtless saw as a vital role for herself as a mother – to see that her daughter married well. Without the fiefs in southern Italy or any of the Barberini property held in primogeniture, this would be impossible to do. Despite her concern about the fiefs in the south, Teresa did not pursue the custody of Cornelia for her own financial gain. Although her adversaries suggested to Cardinal Francesco that bribes might be enough to move her, she accepted no money in exchange for surrendering her daughter, and monetary issues did not dominate their disagreement. Cornelia's residence and young age remained the key issues. Despite threats and bribes, Teresa never willingly relinquished her daughter.

In the fall of 1725, Cardinal Francesco took his demand for the formal custody of his niece to the Rota, the highest law court of the papal capital. Teresa aired her own arguments for custody in an alternative civic tribunal in Rome, which granted her custody.[49] The higher status of the Rota meant that the lesser court's judgment would not prevail, but it indicated to the cardinal that the mother remained unwilling to surrender the girl. In a statement protesting Cardinal Francesco's attempt to move Cornelia to a convent, Teresa pronounced Cardinal Francesco "legally suspect," claiming that much of the property he administered rightfully belonged to Cornelia, an assertion which, if true, would have rendered the cardinal an inappropriate guardian since he could, theoretically, profit from her death, to put the matter more bluntly than Teresa actually did.[50] Magistrates elsewhere in Italy had found similar conflicts of interest on the part of male relatives to be sufficient reason to give custody of children to their mothers.[51] Teresa also frequently referred in her petition to the "tender age" of Cornelia (too young to be separated from her mother) and to the emotional costs of their separation for Teresa herself:

> At her age [Cornelia] is still so raw and immature ... that it is an affront to her very nature to be torn from the arms of her mother, whose tender affections have surrounded her growing up. It is also repulsive to the mother to lose her dearly beloved daughter, the only reminder of the great loss of her husband, the now deceased Prince [Urbano Barberini].[52]

Teresa acknowledged that Cardinal Francesco produced the names of girls who spent their childhood in convents, but noted that they were sent there because their parents wished it.[53] As Cornelia's parent, she would not sanction her placement in a convent. Also, none of Cardinal Francesco's examples was an only child, as Cornelia was. Teresa asserted the naturalness of maternal feeling as a factor in Cornelia's residence and claimed her prerogative as parent to be more important than Cardinal Francesco's larger dynastic machinations (which, Teresa noted, were both poorly managed and irrelevant to the bond between mother and child). To remove a child without the mother's consent was such an affront to a woman's mothering that "it wasn't even permitted in the case of an indifferent mother."[54] Certainly, a woman of Teresa's rank never expected to be subjected to such a fate. If Cardinal Francesco wished to tear Cornelia from her mother, it must be, she surmised, because he wished to be "the arbiter of the girl's will and to avoid having to render an account of the debts that he had with her."[55]

Teresa's critique of the financial implications of the cardinal's guardianship rarely resurfaced in the subsequent years of her dispute. Although a legal loophole to which some widows made successful recourse, such a critique did not capture the issues central to her mothering. Instead, her insistence on the importance of nurturing the affection between mother and daughter through their continued co-residence and her emphasis on the autonomy of Cornelia's will never wavered during the conflict. These arguments were, for the cardinal and his allies, suspicious and vague. They necessitated some explanation. Why was Teresa always stalling for more time for Cornelia?[56] What alternative vision of childhood and free will drove her to continue to do so despite the threats, harassment, and bribes offered by the cardinal and his allies? Teresa claimed that her mothering was based on a deep affection for Cornelia, yet she also acknowledged Cornelia's separateness from her. Each premise rested on the notion that Cornelia was in a particular phase of life, a "*tenera età*" [tender age], separated from her later life as a betrothed and then married woman. By contrast, Cardinal Francesco usually presented this period of Cornelia's life as a danger zone of perilous attachments, best avoided in the controlled environment of the convent, followed shortly by marriage to the spouse he designated for her.

Cardinal Francesco's perspectives have clear roots in the history of the Barberini family, which he knew well. Her ideas, by contrast, struck him as strange, and she never named their origins with precision. Perhaps an early inspiration for the stubborn mother was the childhood trajectory of the Boncompagni sisters. Though her elder sister, Maria Eleonora, was only 16 at the time of her marriage, the remaining sisters all married later, one at the age of 25. Financial difficulties may have been the origin of those late marriages, but the extension of girlhood for most of the Boncompagni sisters into the late teens or early twenties must have shaped how Teresa saw the boundaries between childhood and adulthood. Cardinal Francesco's machinations, aimed as they were at concluding marriage negotiations for his niece before she had even reached her eleventh birthday, evidently horrified Teresa. She insisted that the girl needed at least three or four more years before she was ready to make such a decision.[57] At a minimum, she wanted Cornelia to have as much time before marriage as her sister Maria Eleonora had been allowed.

Teresa insisted that Cornelia had to decide about her marital future by her own free will, just as Teresa's mother had insisted that her daughters should take religious vows only if they chose to do so. Teresa gave an extensive presentation of her position on these issues in a lengthy letter to Carlo Borromeo. In the Roman mother's view, it looked terrible that Cardinal Francesco contemporaneously pursued a variety of potential spouses for Cornelia, even offering her to the Borghese family, who recoiled from the match simply due to Cornelia's young age. Teresa argued that Cardinal Francesco could not recognize Cornelia's free will because he was driven by his desire to "possess the Innocent creature only to sacrifice her to his interests."[58] Reminding Borromeo that she had neither opposed the marriage with his son, Federico, nor failed to treat the young man with anything but respect and hospitality during his visit to Rome, Teresa nevertheless reiterated that she could not promise her daughter to Federico, since Cornelia was "too immature" to know what she wanted. Therefore, she concluded that even as the mother, she "could not usurp for herself something that God himself could not take from Cornelia, ... her free will, to choose her husband according to her own liking."[59]

As a cardinal in the Roman Catholic Church, Francesco Barberini must have understood the concept of free will. Indeed, he would later resort to Teresa's own concern, charging the mother with wanting to be the "arbiter of the will of that poor Innocent."[60] But his approach to free will in girls was a negative one, in which the primary concern was the curtailing of unsavory influences, including and especially the people with whom the girl socialized. As early as 1722 – that is, immediately following the death of Urbano – Cardinal Francesco had begun to question the extent to which Teresa would provide the girl the proper upbringing and education [*buona educazione*].[61] Teresa was clearly seeing to Cornelia's education, since Teresa was a highly literate woman herself. Cornelia (perhaps under her mother's direct tutelage) became a fluent writer, with clear handwriting, an excellent grasp of grammar and spelling, and a certain talent for sarcasm.[62] It is clear from a number of Cardinal Francesco's complaints that Teresa believed part of Cornelia's upbringing also had to be focused on what we could call her social literacy, daily lessons in living that struck the Cardinal as scandalous.

Those lessons, however, can easily be understood as ordinary and necessary in a Roman context. Accepting that her daughter would have to marry (rather than take religious vows), Teresa saw to it that Cornelia moved in the best aristocratic circles and that she participated with her peers in public events. Teresa accompanied her daughter to the theater, where Cardinal Francesco claimed her mother was fomenting a relationship between the ten-year-old and a suitor of her mother's choosing.[63]

When her mother could not accompany her, Cornelia was chaperoned by paid female companions, upon whom her mother kept a watchful eye.[64] Such had been the habits of aristocratic mothers and daughters for half a century. Through her observations and conversations, Cornelia was very slowly being prepared to assume a public role on the part of her marital and natal families. To do so, Cornelia could not be cloistered in the noble palace or in a convent, but rather had to move among other aristocrats. Along the way, Cornelia also appeared to have had a bit of fun with her peers and to have formed a number of strong attachments, including with her attendants and with some members of the Borghese family, a family whose company Teresa especially enjoyed, and to which Teresa was allied through marriage.[65] She and Cornelia visited the Borghese on sojourns to their villa in Frascati. Such visits to country retreats were also a routine part of Roman life.[66]

Cardinal Francesco, however, had a pronounced suspicion of the Borghese. Many of his criticisms of Cornelia's upbringing revolved around the time she spent with that family. The Borghese, despite their status as the greatest landowners in Rome, were relatively removed from some typical aristocratic behaviors. For instance, for several generations, none of the Borghese daughters had professed religious vows – all married instead. In that regard, Teresa and her sisters had fates more similar to the Borghese family than to the Boncompagni and Ludovisi from whom they had descended, families that had placed some daughters of each generation permanently in convents. When they did marry, the Borghese daughters of Teresa's acquaintance had also married relatively late, in their twenties, as Teresa and her sisters did. Perhaps because of these somewhat unusual practices, Cardinal Francesco derided one of Cornelia's visits with the Borghese *in villeggiatura* as bringing the innocent to a *"macello"* [slaughterhouse, or a whore house], though the accusation's closest connection to reality seems to have been related to the Cardinal's annoyance at Cornelia's genuine delight in spending time with the Borghese family. During his intense period of negotiating with his Borromeo in-laws, the Borghese appeared to Cardinal Francesco to be rivals. He worried that Teresa would marry Cornelia off to one of the Borghese, a match that would not have been a bad one considering the status of the family, although he likely feared the loss of the Barberini name and the absorption of Barberini properties into Borghese holdings.[67]

Cardinal Francesco regarded Cornelia's social interactions in Roman society as allowing the child "the greatest liberty possible," since they potentially allowed her to form attachments that would be contrary to his plans. Teresa, by contrast, regarded Cornelia's activities and childhood affections as essential parts of her growing up, although she did not assign them much long-term significance. She did not, in fact, oppose Cardinal Francesco's ideas for Cornelia's future, nor did she make any specific marriage plans for the child. To Teresa, Cornelia's likes and dislikes at the age of nine or ten years old constituted only a phase of the girl's life, not a prediction about her future. Teresa operated under the assumption that Cornelia should have some relatively carefree years that would come to a close as the child approached her mid-teens, at which time the topic of her marital future could be more appropriately raised. What Cornelia thought as a child, in other words, didn't have much bearing in Teresa's mind on her later choices, which were many years in the future. Teresa valued Cornelia's childhood years in a radically different way from Cardinal Francesco. Cardinal Cienfuegos, who served as negotiator between Cardinal Francesco and Teresa, summarized Teresa's position at the end of 1725, when tensions between the two rivals fighting for Cornelia were escalating. Although the cardinal believed that he had found the perfect match for the girl, a match Teresa admitted to liking, Teresa, nevertheless, still considered her daughter to be "of tender age, and thus unable to give her consent [to a marriage]," adding "that as mother she was not able to promise now what the will of the daughter would be once the daughter were in the position to know for herself what suited her." Time, Teresa asserted, was the critical variable, with three or perhaps four more years needed for the marriage to be concluded "with a true foundation."[68] Although Cardinal Cienfuegos cautioned Teresa that he didn't consider her answer an answer, she was "unmoved by any reason" that he could offer.[69]

Resistance Old and New in the Struggle for Cornelia

Both Teresa and Cardinal Francesco were sustained by networks of allies. Roman aristocratic women, as well as men, had webs of allies, male and female, whose strengths they carefully analyzed before plunging into a conflict, especially a judicial controversy.[70] Teresa, in other words, did not face Cardinal Francesco alone. To the consternation of the cardinal, she won the sympathies of Cardinal Coscia (the favorite of Benedict XIII) and Cardinal Corsini. Although Cardinal Coscia was a controversial figure in Rome, such a contact was useful in presenting Teresa's demands.[71] Teresa, however, considered herself the organizing and directing force behind such a network. As she reminded Carlo Borromeo, the rumors, spread by Cardinal Francesco and Cardinal

Cienfuegos, that she was merely following the dictates of evil counselors, ought not be believed:

> Please don't think that I am so weak that I would allow myself to be led by counselors of evil inclination, because God in his mercy has given me sufficient knowledge to distinguish evil from good, and it is only circumstances that have obliged me to do what I have done thus far, in order to escape those who viciously oppressed me and who oppress me still, and thus it was most certainly not done in order to acquiesce to [the wishes of] counselors.[72]

By her own initiative, through writing petitions, consulting with lawyers, and seeking the advice of powerful patrons, Teresa engaged in the broadest possible campaign to keep her daughter with her. She was sustained by a network, but not, in her estimation, controlled by it. Teresa's blatant assertion suggests that a woman could know very well how to drive the networks and secure the legal knowledge that she might lack.

Despite his prestigious international allies, Cardinal Francesco expressed frustration with the inconsistent support Roman authorities gave to his side. He admired instead the "heroic piety of the Austrians," though probably as much for their support of him as for their religiosity.[73] Perhaps the remoteness of the controversy to authorities in Vienna helped them distinguish what the cardinal saw as the resistance of the mother to the conformity of legal precedent and dynastic practice. In Rome, by contrast, ambiguity rather than clarity was in abundance. The results of Cardinal Francesco's sending the case to the law court, the Rota, illustrates this ambivalence clearly. Cardinal Francesco probably hoped that his connections would produce a decision from the Rota in his favor. Yet the clerics of the Rota employed a variety of tactics to avoid making a definitive decision about the case. The court began by stalling, granting him control of Barberini property and the right to name its successor, but then delaying the naming of Cornelia's guardian (November 1725); it next awarded him custody, but allowed the mother to appeal (April 1726); it subsequently responded to Teresa's appeal by finding in favor of Cardinal Francesco, yet it allowed the mother another chance to contest the decision (February 1727). Thus, she could tie up the case for an even longer time period. These decisions were consequently limited victories at best for Cardinal Francesco. Just as the clerics on the court dodged rather than rendered a final judgment, so too the beleaguered Pope Benedict XIII grew weary (and perhaps confused) about what to do, first granting Cardinal Francesco permission to kidnap the girl, then withdrawing such permission and then granting his permission again. The pontiff sometimes hid behind the excuse that he had to allow the Rota to decide.

Teresa also found it difficult to remain in limbo and to engage repeatedly in lawsuits. She must have understood by the fall of 1726 that local institutions might yield no definitive results, yet she offered Cardinal Francesco only a partial surrender. By the end of 1726, she was ready to offer a compromise – that Cardinal Francesco would have legal custody of Cornelia, control of her inheritance, and oversight of her education, but that Cornelia would remain with her mother and not be forced to make decisions about her future until she was of "sufficient age." Cardinal Cienfuegos, one of Cardinal Francesco's most loyal allies, exploded with frustration. Teresa was still under the influence of "perfidious counselors." There was "no way to bring the señora to reason."[74]

Since Teresa doubtless realized that recourse to law courts could sustain the conflict, but not necessarily resolve it, she decided to write directly to Carlo Borromeo, questioning whether a man of such fine qualities could actually be involved in the plot "to rip by force from my arms my only daughter." She probably hoped to weaken Borromeo's support for Cardinal Francesco, and to cultivate a rapport with the Milanese nobleman based on a shared set of emotional and ethical premises. Teresa underscored the incongruity between Borromeo's participation in the affair and what she knew to be his reputation as a person: "Anyone who knows the noble soul [of Carlo Borromeo] considers himself very fortunate, and thus I could not imagine that you are capable of feelings so very contrary to your rare qualities and character."[75] Teresa claimed that she approved of her daughter's marriage to Federico because Cornelia could find in Carlo Borromeo a comfort for the loss of her own father. She emphasized, however, that she could not decide for her daughter, who needed to reach a mature age in order to make such a choice.[76] Teresa refrained from recounting every horrifying offense committed by Cardinal Francesco, but she reminded Borromeo that the Cardinal had attempted to take Cornelia from her mother's rooms. Now she lived in constant fear for her daughter.[77] Cardinal Francesco appeared to use Cornelia as a pawn, offering to give the girl in marriage to many possible suitors at the same time.[78] She urged him to stop Cardinal Francesco from saying that he was doing these brutal deeds "in Carlo Borromeo's name."[79] She closed by appealing to feelings that she assumed he shared: "hoping in his goodness, and that he would show compassion for my miserable state, and for the doting love that I have for this daughter, which is the source for my suffering and for [my efforts] to defend her."[80]

Teresa appealed to the noble sentiments of Carlo Borromeo and underscored that her primary objections in this case concerned the violation of her own feelings and lack of proper consideration for her daughter's young age. Although she was vilified as the woman with whom one could not "reason," she appeared quite reasonable in her self-presentation to Borromeo. With legal precedent, family tradition, and dynastic politics all seemingly outside the scope of her defense, she had recourse only to maternal feelings and to a mother's body – to her arms (from which Cornelia would be torn) and to her eviscerated love [*Amor sviscerato*].[81]

The pleading of Cornelia's mother to Carlo Borromeo seems to have had an effect, although he had to state it obliquely. Borromeo emphasized, in his reply, his respect for her and his hope that she could recognize him as a man of honor.[82] With God and Cardinal Cienfuegos as his witnesses, he swore that he had never had the idea of using violence in this situation.[83] He assured her that he, too, agreed that, "when Cornelia would reach the years of reason, she would have all the liberty to make the decision that is most proper for her and for Your Excellency."[84] He recognized the significance of leaving the choice up to Cornelia and the practice of Roman aristocratic mothers playing key roles in arranging their children's marriages, especially the marriages of their daughters. Still he urged Teresa, as we have seen, to surrender to Cardinal Francesco's wish to place Cornelia in the convent.[85] In a later letter to the cardinal, Carlo Borromeo underscored his agreement with Teresa on the issues she had raised, and transmitted to the cardinal a letter along the same lines that he wrote to Cardinal Cienfuegos in Rome. Clearly Borromeo hoped to convince both cardinals that no violence was to be used against the will of Cornelia. He reminded them that contracts made in such bad faith were "without foundation and without fruit," a thinly veiled criticism of Cardinal Francesco's desire to seize Cornelia and marry her to whom he chose.[86] Borromeo gently leaned toward the mother's point of view, even if he did not acknowledge her as the source. Carlo Borromeo also transmitted the letter that Teresa wrote to him, so the Cardinal was likely to have seen the connection between the nobleman's and the noblewoman's points of view.

In the waning months of 1726, when the cardinal insisted that he cared only about "the good education of his niece," he found his plans "violated by the arts used by her mother ... to engage Signore Borghese in the affair," critiquing Teresa's prestigious connections. He conceded that he could do nothing to stop what he called "the frequent and continual conversation ... the supplicating letters written to the Pope, including letters written by his own mother."[87] Now in her mid-eighties, his mother was a veteran petitioner of the pope. She suggested that a compromise might be struck if the girl were moved to a different convent from the one long associated with the Barberini – a convent perhaps more acceptable to the child's mother. Teresa, however, declined such overtures.

The year 1727 should have been the time of Cardinal Francesco's triumph over the scheming and negotiating women. In February, the Rota ruled in his favor, declaring that the guardianship and the education of Cornelia Costanza belonged to the cardinal.[88] But there was a hitch. An official of the court counseled him to get the order to seize the girl from the pope, because what Francesco had won by law, he had lost in fact. This "enigma" was explained by the particularities of the Rota's judgment. The Rota left open the possibility that the mother could contest the judgment, and in the interim (until the court ruled on the appeal), the girl could not be removed from the mother by the court. Since Cornelia was already past 11 years old, she was likely to be past 12 years old by the time the court made the final decision, at which point she could already have been married "ad placitum della Madre," and so the question of her guardianship would be rendered moot.[89]

This enigmatic triumph spurred Cardinal Francesco to frenetic begging of his allies for assistance.[90] He eventually succeeded in getting the order to seize her and hatched several plans for doing so during the week of carnival – February 15 through February 22. He was still constrained to take her without violence (for he had not won the release from that clause).[91] He planned to meet her on the street, and if she was in the company of only her ladies-in-waiting, he would "exchange courtesies with her, offer her money, and if these allurements weren't enough he would embrace her, throw her in his carriage and take her directly to the convent."[92] Cardinal Francesco had an accurate sense of the limits of his charms, but it was rain or the presence of her mother that thwarted him every day. Finally, accompanied by Cornelia's confessor, who (he hoped) would win the girl's confidence and "exhort her to obedience," plus two other priests and six servants, he accosted Cornelia with two ladies-in-waiting while their carriage was stopped before the Palazzo Barberini alle Quattro Fontane.[93] He attempted to

caress his Niece, telling her to come with him, but she started screaming along with the two other women [accompanying her], resisting as best she could. The Cardinal attempted to take her with the greatest pleasantries possible, but seeing that he wasn't obeyed, he started to raise his voice and to grab the other two women and throw them out of the carriage. Then embracing his niece, he removed her from the carriage and placed her on the ground. He gave her a purse of money, that she took voluntarily, although showing disgust, while calling that she wanted her lady-in-waiting Marianna with her ... and asking that her father confessor not leave her.[94]

For the day, it seemed that Cardinal Francesco's connections at the papal court had trumped those of Teresa. But Teresa also had some support from "counselors, friends, and relatives" who raised their voices against the seizure of the girl. Cardinal Niccolò Coscia, whom Cardinal Francesco pronounced the pope's "Favorite," was sympathetic to Teresa's plight and managed to secure, in a few days, a papal order that would allow Teresa, accompanied by three ladies-in-waiting, to enter the convent.[95] Horrified, he appealed to the pope, using allies to accompany him all the way to the pontiff's bedchambers, where he tried without success to win him over to his side. In fact, the pope's solution was simply to propose moving Cornelia to another convent altogether (this had been her grandmother's idea, some months before).[96] Cardinal Francesco confided to his sister that he was sure that Teresa would succeed in spiriting her daughter away from the other convent.[97] Finally, the cardinal returned a second time to the pope's chambers. He carried with him a clarification from the Rota that, if the court's decision withstood appeal, it allowed Francesco to place Cornelia in a convent of his choosing. Along with this new detail from the ambiguous legal victory, the Barberini cardinal brought Cardinal Alessandro Albani, an ally who delivered a reasoned and calm presentation of the case as a great injustice, emphasizing the evidence of the Rota's new clarification.[98] The pope was still inclined to have the girl removed from the Barberini convent.[99] Hearing this, Cardinal Francesco was "overwhelmed by passion and driven to the edge by his desperation." How could the pope make such a decision, given "the seventeenth-century dispensation of Pope Urban VIII, the decree by the Barberini pope that definitively established patrilinear control of Barberini children, and despite the decision of the law court"?[100] The Barberini cardinal envisioned (as he frequently did) the "extermination of his own house," and so carelessly spoke in "terms that were hardly proper of a servant toward his Prince."[101] The pope's response was a loud command to his servants: *"Mi volete fare perdere la Deputazione."* ["Get the delegation out of here!"][102]

Cardinal Francesco became (in his words) "furious" and "out of his senses": "Holy Father, I don't ask for anything from your Holiness but justice, I don't want anything but a true vigorous justice."[103] Turning to those in the antechamber who were supposed to be seeing him to the door, he exclaimed, "I know the reason that His Holiness won't give me justice, it's because the knave Cardinal Coscia has been corrupted by my sister-in-law. He spent the entire carnival in her box at the theater, but I tell you that if I don't get justice from the pope I will get it by my own hands."[104] Cardinal Francesco's outburst cleverly drew on two critiques circulating in Rome during the 1720s. He aligned himself with popular criticism of Cardinal Coscia, the pope's protégé from Benevento, upon whom the pontiff had bestowed much responsibility with which, it was rumored, Cardinal Coscia behaved venally and irresponsibly.[105] Cardinal Francesco combined his insult of his rival cardinal with an issue he doubtless knew to be of great concern to Benedict XIII, in keeping with his religious piety – the blurring distinction between clerics and laity. Benedict was known, for instance, to become emotional to the point of insomnia over the persistence of wig-wearing among his cardinals and prelates.[106] The two-pronged outburst, doubtless delivered with intensity worthy of the Roman stage, convinced the beleaguered Benedict XIII, who, in his "innate clemency," issued the order that allowed Cornelia to remain in the Convent of the Incarnation.[107] So the Barberini cardinal had won at last, and the pope likely spent another evening in his modestly furnished apartments in the Vatican, regretting that he had ever left Benevento.[108]

Transcending Gender Roles, the Child's Will, and the Charge of Tyranny

The battle for Cornelia certainly cannot be reduced entirely to Teresa's maternal tenderness versus the cardinal's avuncular domination of the family, although Cardinal Francesco acknowledged that this was one interpretation of their conflict in Rome. He would certainly have preferred a world of avuncular domination if he could have gotten away with it. One alternative interpretation of their struggle is that, for each combatant, Cornelia was no more than a financial pawn. Reading between the lines of some of Cardinal Francesco's narrative, it does seem that he squeezed Teresa of some of her financial support in 1725, probably to encourage her to give up her daughter. In retaliation, Teresa tried to lay claim to the Barberini fiefs in the Kingdom of Naples, but she did not pursue this very far.[109] Immediately after the cardinal seized Cornelia, Teresa's allies secured a declaration from the papal auditor that her mother would continue to have the "enjoyment" of her apartment in the Palazzo Barberini alle Quattro Fontane.[110] Later, Teresa also insisted that Cornelia write Cardinal Francesco about the whereabouts of a cross of diamonds that the noble mother insisted belonged to her.[111] Attention to one's rooms and personal articles were familiar concerns for a woman of Teresa's station: they were markers of status to which her mother-in-law Olimpia and other noblewomen also paid close attention (as did Venetian women of the artisan class, for that matter).[112] Cardinal Francesco may have saved the child's letter to illustrate her mother's selfishness, but there is remarkably little of this kind of attack made on Teresa by Cardinal Francesco. He was certainly not above using such tactics, as was clear from his conflict with his mother in the 1710s.[113] Teresa gave him little evidence for the charge of gold-digging, and this doesn't seem to have been the source of their disagreement.

Teresa's and Cardinal Francesco's disagreement was certainly a battle between competing aristocratic networks. They were, however, also overlapping networks, since brother-in-law and sister-in-law were in contact with clerics in the same alliances. Cardinal Lercari, for instance, attempted to be of assistance to Cardinal Francesco in his role as Secretary of State, but Lercari was closely allied with Cardinal Coscia, who was identified by Cardinal Francesco as a supporter of Teresa.[114] Teresa was clearly in the company of well-connected and well-born women and men, clerical and otherwise. She could not go to the pope's private chambers (a privilege reserved for high-ranking clerics like Cardinal Francesco) but she knew clerics who could. We can't say whether she shared with men like Cardinal Coscia more than a taste for theater, but some conviviality with him at the theater was not outside the norms of women of her station.[115] In a letter to his sister in Milan, Cardinal Francesco claimed that, after he spirited Cornelia away, her mother went to the house of a friend, Duchessa di Fiano (born Anna Camilla Borghese) and "from there was off to the banquets."[116] The detail was probably intended to underscore that Teresa was a social gadfly, but in fact, it was probably at those same banquets that she was rallying her allies to her side, since it took her about 48 hours to over-turn the cardinal's total control of Cornelia at the convent. Numerous details in Cardinal Francesco's account reinforce the impression that Teresa was a typical Roman aristocratic woman – she knew her servants and her servant's lovers; she accompanied her daughter to carnival festivities; she wrote petitions and persuasive letters; she socialized in Rome and furthered her interests at the same time. Aristocratic women in Rome had been engaged in such practices for a long time.

Considering how well connected and active Teresa was in aristocratic society, Cardinal Francesco's charge that she would marry off her daughter to any old *"cavaliere"* was absurd. As a Roman aristocratic woman, she would have felt obliged to fulfill one of her most important functions – to arrange her daughter's marriage – and she wouldn't have betrothed her to just anyone.

More than any other issue, the contest for Cornelia was a battle for the arrangement of her marriage, as can be seen in the few details of Cornelia's life after Cardinal Francesco's successful negotiations in the pope's bedchambers. That night, he actually won only a compromise, because Cornelia's mother was still allowed to visit her every day in that convent, and whenever the nuns attempted to interfere with that, they were ordered to allow the mother to see the daughter as much as she liked, and in private. A letter from the Prioress of the convent claimed that their talk centered on whom Cornelia should marry, long the critical topic for Cardinal Francesco, one that not even enclosing his niece in the convent of his choosing had been able to prevent.[117]

In the struggle between Cardinal Francesco and Teresa, it is Francesco, according to conventional Roman practice, who would be seen as usurping the role assigned to Teresa by reasons of her caste and her gender. Many aristocrats, apparently, were married, "ad placitum della Madre," as the court put it. Such had long been one of their roles in Roman society. This pattern is evident in the Barberini family – Cardinal Francesco's mother had clearly arranged the marriage of her daughters, including the marriage of Camilla to Carlo Borromeo. This match inspired considerable complaining on Cardinal Francesco's part about the size of his sister's dowry, since Olimpia evidently threw in the promise of extra cash after her death during the negotiations.[118] Yet it was worth the price, apparently, since this tie proved to be valuable to Cardinal Francesco during the custody battle and offered at least the potential of remaking the Barberini by the marriage of two cousins.

The cardinal's excessively controlling behavior and insistence that he could simultaneously fulfill the roles of cardinal and Roman aristocratic woman finds some explanation in the peculiarities of Cornelia's circumstances. He refers to her frequently as "the total subsistence"[119] of his aristocratic *casa* because, in Roman dynastic terms, his Cornelia is a girl and a boy. Reading backwards from what Cardinal Francesco insisted upon in her eventual marriage, he was looking for a man who would take the Barberini name, or, at least, combine it with his, and who would give at least one of his sons to the Barberini dynasty, by giving that son the Barberini name as well as the inheritance that belonged originally to the Barberini dynasty. Cardinal Francesco needed an aristocratic man who would act like an aristocratic woman, at least in some aspects of his life. Such a scenario was not outside Roman practice, but it was not an everyday event. If Cardinal Francesco could successfully act the part of a woman, and find a man willing to engage briefly in the same "transgression," then the curtain need not fall on the Barberini family drama, to put it in theatrical terms.

The question of Cornelia's residence, her co-residents, and her visitors had consequence for the cardinal because if the cardinal could find such a hybrid, Cornelia had to agree to the match. According to canon law, Cornelia could not be forced into a marriage against her will, or such a marriage could potentially be declared invalid. Cardinal Francesco apparently believed that he was contesting his sister-in-law for the will of the girl. In a letter to the Counselor and Secretary of State at the court of Vienna, he stated most clearly that the extravagant pretensions of the mother were "to never separate the daughter from her, indicating that she wants to remain the arbiter of the will of that poor Innocent."[120] Given the aristocratic woman's role in arranging marriages, a mother would have been (under ordinary circumstances) close to the intersection of dynastic interests and individual will. By placing her in the convent, Cardinal Francesco hoped to end this potential influence, as well as a second potential foil to his plans. Cornelia, outside the convent, lived part of her day on the street. She apparently went sometimes accompanied only by her ladies-in-waiting. Cornelia's potential displeasure with a particular match would be more likely to become public knowledge than if she were confined to a convent, especially one controlled by the Barberini.

As a cardinal in the church, Cardinal Francesco was obviously familiar with canon law, hence his scrupulous attention to the clause that he must take his niece "without violence." Aside from issues of decorum, given her age (11) and her inevitable approaching marriage, taking her by violence could have been seen as a prelude to forcing her into a marital choice. "Reverential fear" of one's parents was acceptable but "grave fear" was not.[121] Cardinal Francesco risked crossing this line if he took Cornelia away by violence. He emphasized his own unwillingness to do so in hopes of winning favor with the pope (even as he simultaneously pursued a strategy to get the clause lifted). In a letter to the pope in September 1726, Cardinal Francesco noted that, while he had been granted papal permission to remove his niece, he hesitated to do so in order not to create "the opportunity for even minimal criticism." He hoped instead for praise for his "moderation" in respecting the opinion so counter to his own.[122] When he did seize Cornelia in February 1727, he wanted witnesses to attest that "there was no violence" (although by his own account he threw two women out of a carriage, this did not count since he didn't use violence against the niece). Cornelia's willingness to go with the cardinal (demonstrating what might be termed only "reverential disgust" for him) was crucial, since whatever legal and familial precedents Cardinal Francesco had in his favor, it was apparently not socially acceptable to take a child against her will from her mother.[123]

The cardinal bristled at such constraints. From his letters, petitions, and lengthy narratives, it is clear that he idealized a world in which his total control of the matter would not be an issue. He recognized the potential critiques of such behavior, but noted that it was inspired by the potential demise of his family. By Cardinal Francesco's own account, his fervent belief that he was (again) witnessing the "extermination of his *casa*" drove him out of his mind.[124] A letter to his sister in Milan explained how he had personally passed from the purgatorial torments caused by the "bestialities" of Urbano's illegitimate son (whom Cardinal Francesco disinherited) to the hell created by his diabolical sister-in-law, whose allies were capable of "fooling and seducing" the pope on her behalf. Terror, combined with delusions of grandeur, drove his assessments of his allies in a letter to his sister in Milan: "I am now the master of 291; I am also sure of 269 69 60 32 30 ..." The epistolary code continued incomprehensibly.[125]

His admiration for what he called the "heroic piety of the Austrians" probably derived from what he perceived as their willingness to privilege dynastic interests as defined by men above all other interests, a clear set of priorities that in Rome encountered opposition.[126] Cardinal Francesco occasionally revealed the "absolute *padrone*" side of his character. He wrote in code to his sister about the men of whom he was "master;" he declared himself the "absolute *padrone*" of the Convent of the Incarnation (something that might have come as a shock to its prioress); he preferred secret late-night meetings in his private garden near Saint John Lateran, and he thought he would get more from a late-night rendezvous in the pope's chambers, where he would benefit from the pope's unwillingness to be an absolute *padrone*, indeed, from the pope's unwillingness to engage in the secular aspects of governing at all.[127]

Mostly, however, Cardinal Francesco had to avoid the appearance of absolutist inclinations. In the same letter in which he claimed to his sister that he was the "absolute *padrone*" of the convent, he admitted that he would never be able to prohibit Teresa from seeing her daughter, now resident in that Cardinal Francesco-controlled convent. If he did, "people would be moved by compassion for her, and say 'what Tyranny, that the mother can't see her,' and with this persuade the will of the magistrates."[128] By the late seventeenth century, the charge of tyranny was probably the worst insult one could throw at a family member, an enemy, or a person who happened to be both. It had become what insults to honor were for males in the early seventeenth century. Even Cardinal Francesco tried to use the insult, complaining that the Cardinals Corsini and Coscia used "injustice, barbarity, and tyranny" against him and his *casa*, meaning that they prevented him from enjoying the rights that the papal tribunal declared belonged to him. This had become the conventional political charge against a tyrant (he usurped rights and property).[129] His mother, however, had also used the term in the 1690s to describe her son Urbano's unacceptable way of governing the household as an absolute *padrone*, which (for her) was a mistaken way to view his authority in the family.[130] Cardinal Francesco was anxious to avoid this charge, hence his emphasis in his narrative on working in concert with his sister-in-law. He also collected letters from his mother to illustrate that she supported his seizure of the girl.[131]

While the charge of tyranny is clear, what he violated, vis-à-vis his sister-in-law, was harder for her allies to define. The day after Cornelia was seized, Cardinal Corsini intervened with the pope to convince the pontiff that "a grave offense was done to such a great Lady, to take from her her only daughter, and with such impropriety."[132] All that Cardinal Francesco could be accused of was a violation of good manners. While the cardinal clearly found frustrating the idea that "justice" could be thwarted in service to such outrageous concepts, he fully acknowledged their power in his society. If he kept Teresa from Cornelia, then he would be accused of tyranny, and this perception by the public would persuade the court against him. It is an interesting chain of causality, on Cardinal Francesco's part, that public compassion for Teresa – not legal precedent – moved the magistrates of the Rota. Cardinal Francesco had learned well the lessons of his enigmatic victory at that court. The court had acknowledged the considerable legal evidence for Cardinal Francesco's custody, including the seventeenth-century papal chirograph by the Barberini pope Urban VIII that denied women the right to custody of Barberini children unless there was no male relative capable of doing so or their deceased husbands had designated them in this role.[133] Yet the eighteenth-century court still affirmed that the mother was likely to protest the decision, and that the magistrates were inclined to leave this option open. They hadn't definitively ruled until she had spoken and, not surprisingly, she did.[134] Cardinal Francesco dared not push them too far as long as the matter was pending and dependent (in part) on public opinion about Cardinal Francesco's behavior toward the mother's "right" to be with her daughter. The power of public opinion was clear, even if the terms in which it is inclined in favor of the mother are not. Cardinal Francesco's recourse to kidnapping his niece acknowledged his loss in this arena.

Despite Cardinal Francesco's success at seizing his niece and placing her in a convent, the cardinal was still by turns enraged and desperate. His dismay alerts us to how much Roman aristocratic mothers had shaped public opinion, which, while without the clarity of legal terms, constrained the cardinal's behavior. In his conflict with his mother a decade before, he had identified a similarly troubling context – he referred derisively to the scrutiny of his actions by the "world." His mother's transgression was bringing what he thought of as the private business of the family into public view, since she had written petitions to papal officials and received support from them.[135] Cardinal Francesco's idealization of the Austrians indicated how alien he felt in the Roman scene, especially its comparatively out-of-control "world" of law courts, theaters, and banquet conversations. Unlike the Habermasian "public sphere," Cardinal Francesco's "world" did not neatly delineate reason and emotion – both had their place.[136] By the "world" the cardinal meant the generalized "talk" of the piazza and city streets: ubiquitous, pro-maternal, and against him, he thought in his more despondent moments.

Cardinal Francesco despised the Roman "world" as insufficiently Catholic. Emphasizing the moral laxity of Teresa and her supporters suggests that Cardinal Francesco aligned himself with the more austere faith and the call for the reform of the clergy associated in Rome with Jansenism. He framed the struggle in terms that suggested that papal support of Teresa sanctioned an intimate interaction between the laity and the clergy, something that Roman Jansenists believed to be in need of reform. While the split between the cardinal's allies and Teresa's allies doesn't quite support this interpretation (Teresa received support from Cardinal Corsini, and the Corsini family was closely identified with Jansenism), Cardinal Francesco's presentation of what was at stake echoed Jansenist critiques of Rome and the apparently sincere desire on the part of Benedict XIII to reform the clergy.[137]

Cardinal Francesco risked public scrutiny in the law courts because he hoped for a definitive legal resolution from them. In Italy, such institutions were the critical vehicles for cultivating allegiance between rulers and subjects, the site for politics and political change, to the extent that they allowed marginal members of society to bargain for their rights.[138] Eighteenth-century Italy produced a large number of lawyers who sustained a legal culture with profound impact on the peninsula's political and cultural evolution.[139] It is estimated that there was one lawyer for every 140 persons in eighteenth-century Rome, a city with a population of approximately 160,000,[140] hence the continued and increasing importance of the *mater litigans*, savvy about using courts as well as petition writing to push legal possibilities. Cardinal Francesco lamented the legal milieu that created the "cultural capital" of early modern Rome. Such capital multiplied in the myriad of legal avenues that grew up in Rome. Benedict XIII did not challenge this profusion of sites of power; he acknowledged and relied on it occasionally as an excuse to get the Barberini cardinal to leave him alone.

In Teresa's case, the Rota guarded her interests, positioning itself as a mediator between conflicting parties, rather than as simply the defender of legal precedents. That's why the magistrates left open the possibility of her appeal. Since litigants could also seek alternative decisions by other courts, this further reinforced the impression that courts served as sites for airing grievances, but did not begin by offering definitive answers on them. Cardinal Francesco wandered foolishly into the realm that he claimed he despised – where details of the cases were widely discussed, sometimes printed, and under the scrutiny of many more individuals than the members of the aristocratic dynasty.

Furthermore, when women and other marginalized members of society, such as peasants, took up their grievances in the Roman judiciary or by petition writing, they were frequently unwilling to give up the fight. Cardinal Francesco's nephew-in-law, Giulio Cesare Colonna di Sciarra, would later loathe the villagers of Monte Flavio for just this reason – they were "insolent ... the most rebellious ... crassly ignorant people" (diatribes equal in intensity to Cardinal Francesco's for his sister-in-law).[141] Aristocratic rage was the typical response to persistence by inferiors. Such adversaries also created dilemmas for magistrates, who would sometimes have to ignore legal precedents if they wanted to side with those inferiors. According to Giulia Calvi, seventeenth-century Tuscan magistrates faced a similar conceptual problem in trying to sort out what to do with fatherless children – maternal love, Calvi argues, was invented in the interactions between women and magistrates as an ideal to counterbalance the legal rights the father's family held to the custody of the child.[142] In Cardinal Francesco's conflict with his mother a decade before, an exasperated Pope Clement XI accused Cardinal Francesco of being "overly legalistic" and too obsessed with legal and financial particulars rather than behaving in the caring way a son should toward his mother.[143] In the 1720s, Cardinal Francesco argued that compassion moved the public, who moved the court. Sentiments overturned historical precedents, imbalances in account books, and laws that violated human feelings.[144]

Although the legal answers Teresa's side provided were insufficient to sway the Rota, the emotional argument for the significance of the tie with her daughter eventually shaped the rhetoric, if not the mentality of Cardinal Francesco himself. Frustrated by his inability to place Cornelia in the convent, by the fall of 1726 he was ready to petition the pope in terms of familial sentiment. Since the controversy with Teresa began, he claimed that neither he nor or his aging mother, Olimpia Giustiniani, had seen Cornelia. Removing Cornelia from Teresa's apartments and placing her in a convent was the only hope that the 90-year-old grandmother and the 64-year-old uncle had of seeing their only granddaughter and niece. Their sole consolation would be to see her at the grate of the convent parlor.[145] Both petitioners, of course, exaggerated, but their embellishments were inspired by the arguments of Teresa. Cornelia was not the only niece of Cardinal Francesco, nor was she the only grandchild of Olimpia. In a later letter to the pope, Olimpia essentially acknowledged that maternal arms and wombs defined a core of human meaning when she wrote of seeking "the consolation of being able to hold in her maternal arms the only offspring of her womb."[146] Emotional and bodily ties had to be factored in among other concerns, as Teresa had all along insisted.

Cardinal Francesco had begun the struggle to control his niece's destiny by exerting his paternal authority, by claiming his right to place her in a convent when he wished, and by exhibiting his disgust at the thwarting of his plans to re-establish his dynasty with the marriage of his niece and nephew. Four years later, he resorted to the affective tie to his niece as the most important issue at stake in the affair. He echoed the language of emotional loss that Teresa had expressed since the beginning of the controversy.

At this difficult juncture of simultaneous failure and success in early 1727, by which time his own mother's womb had been brought into the controversy, Cardinal Francesco found his victory to be ambiguous at best. Cornelia was in the convent, but her mother was then given the right to visit her daily. He would never be able to prevent this, he noted, because the public hue and cry would be, "What Tyranny, that the mother can't see her!"[147] Thus, whether as a framework for his petitions or as a strategy for navigating Rome, Cardinal Francesco was obliged to admit that maternal affection, so little present in the law, was a force to be reckoned with in the aristocratic circles that constituted the Roman world.

In her deliberative responses to the Cardinal's claims and in her interviews with his intermediaries, Teresa repeatedly underscored the value of allowing Cornelia a childhood sustained by her mother's love. Such a childhood would evolve toward closure with discussions about her marital future, not end in rupture with her placement in a convent. Teresa mitigated the effects of that rupture by continuing to visit her daughter after she had been placed in the convent. From our perspective, this might appear a modest victory for maternal love. Teresa likely imagined that the wishes of girls like her daughter should be considered in conjunction with larger dynastic interests. Teresa did not question the notion that Cornelia would marry, nor that Cornelia's choices would have to be constrained by the options her family offered her or by the advice of her elders, including her mother. Teresa located her emotional life, including maternal love, along a continuum of concerns, rather than in opposition to the "reason" promoted by her adversaries. To paraphrase the philosopher Martha Nussbaum, Teresa claimed that her affection offered her insight, and that it deserved consideration.[148] In the mother's view, the girl's wishes had to be included as a variable among other issues, but only once Cornelia had reached an age to know her mind – somewhere in the mid-teens, according to the mother's chronology. Cardinal Francesco, by contrast, dreaded the unpredictability such ideas introduced, the way in which they might contravene the interests of the Barberini or potentially erode his authority in the family. Yet, mother love had weakened his best ally in Milan, captured the imagination of the Roman public, and even permeated the cardinal's own rhetoric.

This type of resistance on the part of a *mater litigans* was subtler than the institutionalized form of the courts and more dangerous to the things Cardinal Francesco held dear. It rested on a shared emotional register as a basis for human decisions. Combined with a sense of the separateness of each person (a concept Teresa elaborated for her daughter using the idea of free will), it has been posited as the foundation for human rights in the West, a liberating and destabilizing force in European history.[149] The cardinal's dread of future slippage may not have been merely the product of his pessimistic tendencies. The ancient Cornelia's maternal tenderness gave way to the rebellions of the Gracchi, as any informed viewer of the painting would have known.

In her adult life, Cornelia Barberini would throw off the terms of the marital contract that Cardinal Francesco had made for her and attempt to make a new future for the Barberini in her own terms, bringing the family into decades of upheaval.[150] Perhaps the Cardinal's success in placing her in the convent did come too late, after all, as resistance along matrilines became at least as much her inheritance as was the patrimony of the Barberini family.

Conclusion

As the varied experiences of these Roman mothers illustrate, a successful *mater litigans* had to reach beyond the limitations of law and culture, history and daily life, if she wished to challenge the decisions of her male peers. She eroded the distance between her experience as the physical reproducer of the dynasty and her more public role in the theater of Rome. Her arguments breached the boundaries of dynastic practice and imported the terminology of other spheres to probe the weaknesses of its claims. Anna Colonna struggled to describe a new familial form that we would define as nuclear, but which floundered in the lexical void and under the pressures of the Barberini's fall from political grace. Olimpia Giustiniani rejected the use of absolutism as a model for governing the family and resisted the intrusion of the master ledger as the arbiter of familial relations. Her model of the familial imagined it as a consortium of interests in which women played a recognizable role but also maintained some separation between themselves and the dynastic. Eleonora Boncompagni affirmed maternal independence against the intrusion of the medical professionals and the meddling of well-meaning male family members. In the nursery, the *mater litigans* faced her greatest adversaries, death and illness, and in her choices rested the future of the patrilinear family. Surrounded by her children, she was alone in a medical crisis with only an irreconcilable theology to console her. Ippolita Ludovisi built new possibilities for the family by employing the theological underpinnings of Jesuit probabilism. In so doing, she uncovered the link between the future of the patrilinear family and the well-being of its girls, whose free will had to be recognized and in whose defense rebellion might be not only justified but required. By the early eighteenth century, Teresa expressed simply and firmly the centrality of maternal affection to the family, for which she made no apology and which guaranteed, in her view, the appropriate transition for children from a "tender age" to the life-defining decisions of adulthood, including marriage.

This examination of mothers in seventeenth-century Rome reveals the means, modes, and methods by which women advocated for change to the aristocratic family along the lines of matrilinear critique. They sought to improve but not to replace the patrilinear family. Enshrined in legal documents, crafted by venerable ancestors, and sustained (if reluctantly at times) by law courts, the patrilinear family was woven into the fabric of the city in its prestigious palaces and in the ubiquity of family crests that celebrated the deeds of great men who shaped the city as clerical rulers but who never severed their familial ties. Their family trees, traced through men, reaffirmed continuity and solidity. Sometimes, they included the names of women who had born their much-desired male heirs. Such women could be the supporters of the patrilinear family as well as its critics, since Roman aristocratic women had lineages to which they proudly belonged. Olimpia Giustiniani's status as the great-niece of a pope likely sustained her in many a battle with her aggravating Barberini sons. Eleonora Boncompagni's pride in her *casa* was a source of personal belonging and affection for her much younger sister-in-law, who did the propagating of the dynasty she admired so much. Anna Colonna lent moral and financial support to her female and male kin throughout even the most difficult years of her life with the Barberini.[1]

Yet, as this study of resistance along matrilines has emphasized, in Rome it was the rapport with marital families that was more frequently problematic – the other side, as it were, of the patrilinear coin. The marital family was the domain in which women spent most of their lives – serving and physically reproducing their marital dynasties, with whom, as we have seen, they could form very strong connections. The Boncompagni, Eleonora reminded her sister-in-law, were "your [*casa*] as long as you have children."[2] Affection for children helped contemporaries to understand how a seventeenth-century woman could position herself between two dynasties and serve one which, in theory, was only temporarily her own. As children reached adulthood and became situated in their careers and marriages, the mother's rapport with her marital dynasty could weaken and dissolve, as happened in the case of Anna Colonna. The difficulties of Olimpia Giustiniani further underscore this perilous moment of the mother's life course. What place had she in the future of her husband's dynasty, especially while at war with her two sons? But Olimpia continued to affirm her commitment to her marital family, with which she had been involved since the age of 12. Although early modern women have been called "passing guests" to their husbands' families,[3] by the time Olimpia entered the fight for her granddaughter's custody in 1725, she had been visiting the Barberini for more than 70 years, decades which were fraught with financial difficulty, genealogical disaster, and warring offspring — home sweet home, in sum, if you were a *mater litigans* in the contentious world of Rome.

The struggles of Roman aristocratic women were part of a larger pattern of maternal advocacy on the Italian peninsula and of the celebration of the maternal in the seventeenth century. In neighboring Tuscany, mothers litigated for custody of their children after the death of their husbands. More than 70 percent of such cases were settled in favor of the mother, although legally such children belonged to the patrilinear family. A shared set of assumptions about motherhood emerged between mothers and magistrates.[4] Mothers argued that their love was superior to that of their husband's male kin because mothers, unlike patrilinear kin, could never inherit from their children. Their love was thus "pure" and "free." It was "above suspicion," unlike the attitudes of her husband's relatives, who stood to inherit in the event of the death of the children.[5] Patrilinear relatives had more to lose than to gain by the survival of their dead relative's offspring. Since the mother was cut out of the patrilinear inheritance of her husband, she was motivated by love alone in her devoted and highly qualified care of her children.[6] Not even remarriage could compromise the depth of attachment a mother felt for her child, since, as one widow explained in the 1630s, she "loved her son more than herself."[7] From her marginality to the patrilinear arose her greater capacity to love and parent.

The dilemma of how love varied according to gender was not confined to the law courts of Rome or Florence. It was also a popular topic in the contemporaneous debate about the role of women in society, the *querelle des femmes*, a literary movement discussed in the Introduction. We return to this famous and 300-year-long literary conversation in order to illuminate its connections to and departure from the situation of Roman aristocratic women. The *querelle des femmes* attempted to reverse many arguments against women that were typical of the misogyny embedded in European society. Its deliberate contestation of gender roles connects the literary *querelle des femmes* to the strategies deployed by Roman mothers. To counter the hegemony of male superiority, some passages of the literary debate reversed the sign of gender inferiority in favor of women. Both men and male culture sometimes take a considerable beating in this literary inversion of gender villains in the early modern world. Such accounts contrast the unshakable love of women with the limitations of men's capacity for such emotion.

Living and dying as a mother in service to a dynastic family in Rome required a more nuanced packaging of the maternal role. Such mothers had to refrain from the soaring praise for the superior humanity that was womanhood in the *querelle des femmes*. A damning indictment of all male behaviors similarly had to be avoided. A comparison of the approaches of the Venetian author, Arcangela Tarabotti, with the strategies of Ippolita Ludovisi is instructive. It underscores the particular dilemmas of Roman women who tried to reinvision the family while living alongside the men to whom they addressed their complaints. The two women's rhetoric and their construction of gender differences diverge widely, despite the considerable overlap in their areas of interest. Yet, both the *querelle* and the arguments of Roman aristocratic women illustrate the precocity of women's ideas about the family in society, pushing both in directions that would emerge in European and male culture only many decades later.

Both Tarabotti and Ippolita were concerned with the circumstances of girls' entry into convents. Neither appears to have been opposed to the voluntary choice of religious life, but resisted instead the coercion of such a choice by the girls' families. Each woman recognized that the theological paradigm of free will was not enough to defeat forced monarchalization of daughters. Roman Catholic theology had to be embedded in a reconfiguration of the family in order to be relevant, especially to aristocratic and well-to-do families. Tarabotti launched a two-pronged attack on the failure of Venetian patriarchal authority, demonstrating how it both negated the principle of free will and failed to exhibit the proper emotive parental response. In contrast to Tarabotti's account, in which the Venetian mothers was completely absent, in Ippolita's analysis the Roman mother was ever-present. She was a central figure in the drama of one generation situating the next into adult life. Tarabotti thoroughly vilified Venetian men, and she could thus draw a stark contrast between right and wrong behavior according to gender. In the day-to-day dilemmas of Roman aristocratic life, Ippolita could scarcely make such a drastic comparison and hope to be heard. Even for her more muted critiques, she was severely taken to task and yet she went on making them, finessing them as well as she could in the hopes that her opinions would become acceptable.

According to Tarabotti, men's diminished emotional capacity wreaked havoc on the family. Enclosed in a convent against her will, Tarabotti confronted the flaws in the financial and theological underpinnings of the patrilinear family. She launched a protest that, in writing (if not in practice), systematically destroyed justifications for the forced confinement of "extra" girls to religious institutions. According to Tarabotti, Venetian fathers perverted the very core of Roman Catholicism, denying its focus on the role of free will in human salvation.[8] Her outrage knew no bounds, as she imagined the postmortem reunions of such families, all cast into hell for their respective roles in this perversion of Christianity.[9] Despite her excoriation of Venetian fathers (who drank, whored, or gambled away the money they saved by placing their daughters in convents), Tarabotti called for a new kind of fatherhood as the foundation for a better Venetian family – for a father who could be moved to tears by the tenderness of love rather than remain the slave of his unbridled lust; a father more like the loyal and beloved apostle John (an honorary woman in Tarabotti's view) than a severe and heartless patriarch.[10] Tarabotti anticipated by decades the arguments made by Jean-Jacques Rousseau, who swept European readers away with his intuitive links between the emotional, the political, and the familial in his critique of society. Tarabotti had already unraveled the connections among the Venetian political order, patrilinear authority, and the appropriate emotional parameters for human beings, long before Rousseau's novels and Carlo Goldoni's comedies asked readers or audiences to do the same.[11]

Tarabotti's impact was stifled by the Roman Catholic Church when her works were placed on the index of prohibited books in 1660. She is nonetheless a northern iteration of what Roman women also addressed in law courts and in letters, in words and in daily practice. Roman women could not readily employ the stark rhetoric of Tarabotti except in cases of extreme misbehavior, such as the kind Olimpia Giustiniani faced with her violent wayward son, Urbano. Although Roman aristocratic women's adversaries were formidable, they did not typically threaten them with bodily harm. Since the men with whom they argued might be seen often, some on a daily basis, the debate had to occur in a different register.

By contrast, the author Tarabotti spoke in the non-negotiable terms of innocent outrage, and although she called for a new emotive basis for family life, it was far from clear how the perverted male monsters who currently ruled the family in her treatise could transform themselves into the "virtuous honorary women" who might remake it. Ippolita was, by her own admission, immersed in her varied and sometimes ambivalent emotional ties. Her own feelings about her daughters in the early stages of her mothering were at times negative. She herself was implicated in the attitudes she hoped to reform. Like Tarabotti, her audience was predominantly male – specifically, one clerical male who, she thought, might aid her in her dilemma. Although she directed her arguments to a cardinal in the Roman Catholic Church, she knew as well as Tarabotti that an exclusive focus on free will and the girls' vocations would be insufficiently persuasive. Unlike Tarabotti, however, she addressed her brother-in-law not as the enemy, but as a co-participant in the problem, likely to be on her side because they lived (she argued) in the same emotional and familial territory. And then there was the further complication of their evidently mutual affection for each other. Arguing with such a male relative left Ippolita in a more complex rhetorical bind, without the simple effectiveness of assigning right and wrong according to gender. But the implications of their relationship also helped Ippolita substantiate the validity of a family that resolved domestic controversies in part based upon emotional connections, such as the ones that bound Ippolita and Giacomo to each other and bound him to her daughters. While the critique thus had to be more nuanced, the path to the kind of family imagined by Tarabotti was clearer and forged in a lengthy epistolary exchange that forecast its future existence. Ippolita, too, anticipated the insights of Rousseau and Goldoni by about a half a century.

To grasp such shifts in the Roman aristocratic *casa*, the powerful cardinal brother-in-law has also to be taken into account. Something of a curiosity of the Roman scene, he was a figure not exactly like any other in the Italian or broader European context. Although aristocratic Catholic families typically had clerical brothers and uncles, they seem to have lacked the power and the autonomy of such figures in the Roman context, where they might eclipse the standing of the brother who was designated to carry on the lineage.[12] The performance of the patrilinear in Rome thus involved two kinds of men, the carefully controlled cleric and his sometimes brash and less predictable brother.[13] Between them was the latter's wife. Aristocratic mothers spent much of their adult lives entangled with clerical relatives and, in the case of Ippolita, intimately and enduringly. Such relationships doubtless had a significant bearing on the direction of the Roman family. Cardinal Giacomo seems to have shared his deceased brother Gregorio's doubts about the wisdom of forcing the next generation of Boncompagni girls into convents – hence his tendency to agree with Ippolita, more explicitly than Gregorio had done, even as he recognized the especially perilous financial position in which the Boncompagni found themselves. Ippolita declared Cardinal Giacomo guilty of the same emotional connections to the children of the dynasty that she felt. He acted as if her assessment were true.

It was in dialogue with her cardinal brother-in-law that Ippolita Ludovisi elaborated her argument that affection transcended gender, an assertion that echoed the one Anna Colonna had tried to make earlier in the seventeenth century. Both mothers implied that women and men should be equally participatory in familial affection, which outweighed the perils that such emotional entanglements might bring. They downplayed the differences between genders in describing the ideal practices and attitudes toward family members. Behaving appropriately in the family meant acting in accordance with maternal love: the highest measure of familial affection and one that men could also achieve. Tarabotti's honorary woman John would have fit perfectly into this familial landscape. A man who combined the apostolic with the tenacity of love resonated best with the figure of the cardinal brother-in-law but had implications for his lay brother as well.

The most avidly patriarchal figure in this study was a cardinal who, in the face of fraternal failure, seems to have tried to play all the roles of the family at once. Yet, even the irrepressibly patrilinear Cardinal Francesco Barberini Junior conceded that his opponent Teresa Boncompagni's assertion of maternal love and insistence on time for a childhood for her daughter found widespread support in Rome, though its legal justifications were weak. The dangers of such views seemed to him widely forgotten although they remained all too real to the cardinal. But Cardinal Francesco also resorted in the end to the emotional bond with his niece as the variable of the greatest import in the battle for her custody with her mother. The weakening of patrilinear allegiance expressed itself elsewhere in a failure to act. Flavio Orsini and Gregorio Boncompagni both died intestate by choice. Each man thus left his spouse in the fight of her life, should she choose to oppose the wishes of the men of her husband's family, as each ultimately did. Fence-sitting while on one's deathbed had its connections to the increasing number of lawsuits that challenged the tighter limitations on inheritance that were established in the late sixteenth and seventeenth centuries in Rome.[14] Such limitations were undermined in a number of ways – passively on the part of some (in the refusal to make a will) and actively by others through the law courts. Attack and retreat were related manifestations of the weakening of loyalty to the strict enforcement of the patrilinear in Rome. As the agonizing of the Boncompagni men during their dispute with Ippolita Ludovisi makes clear, ambivalence permeated even their attempts to reassert the centrality of male primogeniture as the foundation of aristocratic family life. The aristocratic *casa* required a strong performance of the patrilinear and a reiteration of its significance for each generation of the dynasty if it were to endure.[15] Some men, however, no longer easily enacted these gender roles, and as the seventeenth century drew to a close, men like Cardinal Francesco Barberini found that it was they, rather than their female family members, who met with criticism in the theater of Rome. Men at such transition points in their roles as heads of aristocratic families were caught between the obligations to their ancestors in the past and the implications of their ties to the women and the children in their present.[16]

The male audience for the *querelle des femmes* must have emerged in part among those for whom the patrilinear and its concomitant performances of male gender did not fit easily into the practice of family life. Such observations were still risky and, therefore, it was likely less disconcerting to early modern readers that the critique of men in the *querelle* was performed by a female speaker, even if the readers of the *querelle* who may have agreed with her were not exclusively women. The sheer popularity of the *querelle* implies large numbers of male readers, many of whom were used to hearing women speak in its mode, a strong voice amidst the collapsing confidence in the beliefs that the choices of one's ancestors were the correct ones; that the wishes of a child had to be ignored for the future of the dynasty as a whole; that service and duty were superior to the shaky claims of love. In rebellions literary and quotidian – either women or men masquerading as women – occupied the space of protest and were permitted transgressions in the name of higher ideals, either empty bellies at home or anger over injustices.[17] Such doubts then reverberated across the eighteenth century, and to the female voices of the seventeenth century was added the eighteenth-century talk of men. In Italy's most famous treatise of the Enlightenment, *On Crimes and Punishments* (1764), Cesare Beccaria derided the subjugation required to the father by the family configuration of his times. The laws of such families "inspire submissiveness and fear," when what was needed in society was "courage and free spiritedness."[18] In a more lighthearted and comic fashion, the wildly popular playwright Carlo Goldoni lampooned the bumbling patriarch who resisted following the inclinations of children or the advice of his wife. By the comedy's end, such a character had typically yielded on some points (usually regarding a child's matrimony) and, though he remained in charge, he did so with more equanimity for the wishes of others.[19] The primary shift in the eighteenth century was to add real and fictional men's voices to those of women in recognizing the defects of the patrilinear and the advantages of affection to the well-being of the family.

Yet, fulfilling what a living seventeenth-century woman saw as her responsibilities as a mother could still leave her vulnerable to the charges of irrationality and ill-advised resistance to authority, "extravagant pretensions" that dangerously sought to overthrew legal precedent and familial order.[20] Ippolita argued for her daughters' future in the context of this uncertainty, when the rules of primogeniture were challenged, but the arguments for doing so were still in formation, and the vision of the kind of family that might emerge in its place remained vague. Still, Rome remained more tolerant than elsewhere, and Teresa Boncompagni faced criticism from beyond Rome that was harsher than its local expressions. Within Rome, Teresa Boncompagni operated openly in a world where her affection for her daughter and her pleasure in mothering required little explanation. The discourses of love's perils had retreated, too, no longer remaining in her writing even as the residue of a mode of speech. Even her mother, Ippolita, though she had still employed the phrase of "loving too much," refused to orient her behavior to such strictures and fought for her daughters with the theological certainty of a matter of conscience that she believed her role as mother required.

Both detractors and supporters of new alignments in the family were influenced by the nature of the judicial regime in Rome. Such a system encouraged the settlement of family conflicts prior to launching a lawsuit – by means of family meetings or *congregazioni*; in consultation with agreed-upon mediators; and by epistolary negotiations with the contesting party. When a dispute did at last emerge in a legal arena of Rome, magistrates privileged the mediatory aspects of the law court, often refusing to render definitive judgments on the first hearing of the case. Male adversaries of a *mater litigans* looked to tribunals beyond Rome for definitive mandates, but Roman tribunals might overturn, ignore, or modify these judgments that came from beyond the papal realm. Popes themselves might intervene in such dilemmas, offering the conciliatory possibilities of recognizing that it was love, especially parental and filial love, that held the dynastic enterprise together. In contrast, Cardinal Francesco Junior's outraged cry to Pope Benedict XIII, "Holy Father, I don't ask for anything from your Holiness but justice, I don't want anything but a true vigorous justice," played upon the image of the popes that they assiduously cultivated in building the Papal States.[21] For since the late sixteenth century, it was the administration of justice that symbolized papal sovereignty.[22] The papal right to rule was predicated upon the monarch as the "dispeller of discord."[23] When it came to familial disputes, however, the papal regime preferred mediation between conflicting parties, defining justice as what might emerge from a settlement of differences. To Cardinal Francesco's dismay courts might modify or ignore clear legal precedents, encouraging, in the case of the aristocratic family, the emergence of practices closer to the emotional parameters outlined by litigating mothers than to the intentions of venerable ancestors enshrined in law. The papal regime weighed the interests of its subjects and behaved according to the consortium of interests model that Olimpia Giustiniani described as the way the family ought to operate.[24] With their still tight marital ties, the College of Cardinals was a large family as well as a ruling body.[25] Its judicial regime acted like both.

The experiences of the five mothers of this study also reveal the distance between the celebratory maternal ideals of the seventeenth century and the messy realities of everyday practice. Close attention to these points of dissonance illuminated the impossibility of motherhood to circumvent the paradoxes at the core of the domestic and the political in seventeenth-century Rome. If, in contrast to the negative view of maternal love in the fifteenth century, seventeenth-century mothers successfully constructed a positive image of maternal affection that challenged the vaunted superiority of paternal love, they could not do so without encountering new dilemmas that this study has also acknowledged and analyzed. The evolution of the maternal emerged at precisely such points of impossibility and in women's negotiation of them. What mothers and daughters might do with their lives in the domestic realm and in the world of Rome was an ongoing project subject to negotiation and conflict across the generations. In a single mother, such as Ippolita Ludovisi, such roles might never cohere, and so the life of the Roman aristocratic mother must also be recognized for its disconnects between ideals and daily practice – the inexplicable outcomes of child loss, children who did not turn out as expected, husbands who failed the family, uncles who dabbled in kidnapping. No encomiums to motherhood could obviate such dilemmas, but, in the face of such things, the mother was to remain nonetheless affectionate and steady in her actions, the backbone of the family, as Eleonora Boncompagni had admiringly called her, and the embodiment of the successful papal subject, petition-writing, navigating the law courts, and engaging in the conversations in the public events of the papal city, where things also got done.

In the face of familial problems, Roman mothers did not think in terms of the binaries with which later historians sought to demarcate society – as shaped either by the triumph of the family or by the emergence of the individual emancipated from the family.[26] Roman mothers argued instead for the recognition of the individuals within the family (demarcating them by objects possessed, by their free will, or by their right to a childhood). They also recognized the significance for the individual of the family, where individuals were reproduced and nurtured, sustained by affection and a sense of belonging in a larger historical and dynastic enterprise, which included daughters as well as sons. Such nuances necessitated maternal love as the emotional standard for familial affection. It could and should be emulated by men, not limited to the world of women. Situating such emotions as a source of information along the continuum of accepted practices and legal ideals made for a better quality of family life, in their view.[27]

In their embrace of such ideas, Roman mothers did not limit the maternal role either to what they called their domestic affairs or to the theater or the world of Rome. Affect and advocacy intertwined, and effective mothering required attention to both. It made murky the boundaries between them. Motherhood in seventeenth-century Rome spoke the language of power and affection; it connected the latest religious controversies to the dilemmas of the domestic; it redefined the maternal in the face of medical novelties; and it recognized the significance of parental attachment to the future of the dynasty. For their critics, this matrilinear resistance was dangerous, in part, because it produced more flexible familial practice that had yet to achieve universal acceptance or solidify in historical repetition. An additional weakness was the fact that that although matrilinear politics functioned well in practice it was not supported by changes in law. Yet, it was law (associated by its critics with the "end of love") that underwrote the familial and political order of Europe's states.[28] Popes and their magistrates recognized law's limitations and employed law courts as sites of negotiation rather than as strict enforcers of patrilinear hegemony. They recognized the emotional parameters of family life as integral to rule, but they did not enshrine them in legal change or significantly challenge the patrilinear emphasis in society, except by the practices of judicial delay and papal admonishment. The only substantive reform of the law undertaken anywhere in the eighteenth century was in criminal law.[29] It was difficult, therefore, to extend the impact of the matrilinear beyond the specific political configuration that had helped produce it. The subsequent revolutions and unrest that undermined the foundation of the early modern political order swept aside some of its achievements along with its shortcomings.

A Europe reeling from the late eighteenth-century revolutions and then episodically convulsed by political upheaval turned toward a more restrictively apportioned gender regime, typified by the Napoleonic code, in which women would lose more ground than they gained. The domestic and the political, so tightly intertwined in seventeenth- and eighteenth-century Rome, were subsequently delineated along segregated gender boundaries in most European states. Increasingly, the domestic was supposed to deliver what the political could not and vice versa. Although the epistolary would remain the female genre, organizing the connections of nineteenth-century bourgeois society, its behind-the-scenes work was little recognized in the political sphere as it came to be constituted in the nineteenth century.[30] Though the detractors to the idea of a separate public and domestic sphere appeared as quickly as it was formed, there was little space in the liberal political order of the nineteenth century for the voices of women. The battle to return to women a portion of the public presence they had known in the premodern world and a legitimate share in modern regimes would extend into the twentieth century. The political implications of the domestic and the familial remain unresolved. The mothers in this study would have likely recognized that in moments of upheaval, a reassertion of patriarchy was a predictable if regrettable scenario. What happened before often happens again. Family life emerged amidst this zigzagging pattern of historical change, which had to be confronted between the swaddling and the needlework, between protesting in letters and letting girls decide, at the interstices between reproducing the children and unmaking the inevitable future, one struggle at a time.

Appendices: Family Trees

Appendix 1: The Barberini Family

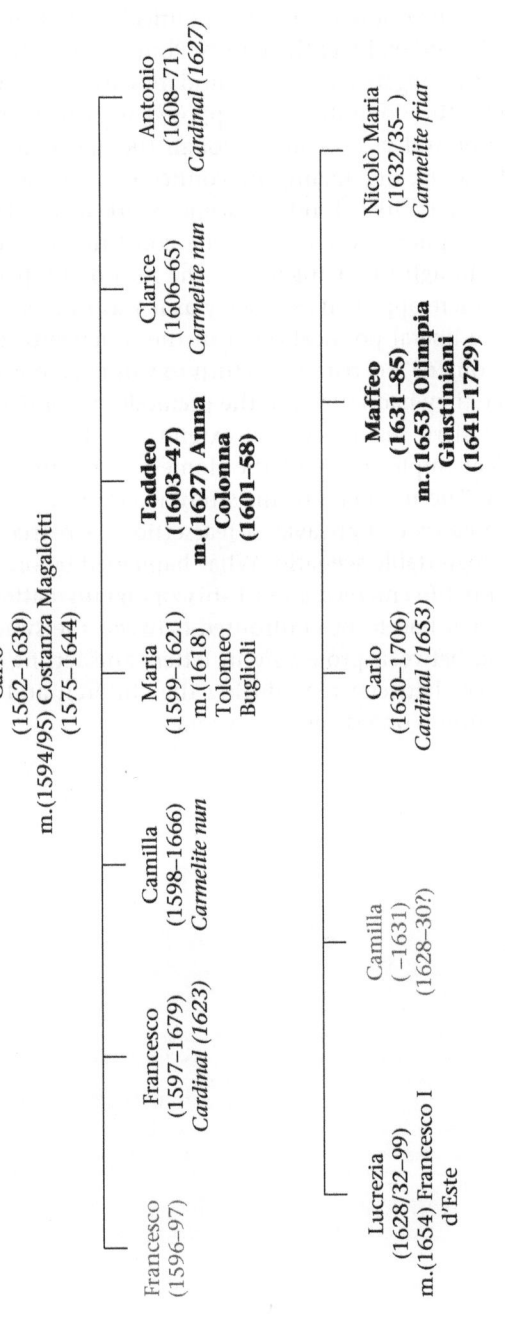

Carlo
(1562–1630)
m.(1594/95) Costanza Magalotti
(1575–1644)

Francesco
(1596–97)

Francesco
(1597–1679)
Cardinal (1623)

Camilla
(1598–1666)
Carmelite nun

Maria
(1599–1621)
m.(1618)
Tolomeo
Buglioli

**Taddeo
(1603–47)
m.(1627) Anna
Colonna
(1601–58)**

Clarice
(1606–65)
Carmelite nun

Antonio
(1608–71)
Cardinal (1627)

Lucrezia
(1628/32–99)
m.(1654) Francesco I
d'Este

Camilla
(–1631)
(1628–30?)

Carlo
(1630–1706)
Cardinal (1653)

**Maffeo
(1631–85)
m.(1653) Olimpia
Giustiniani
(1641–1729)**

Nicolò Maria
(1632/35–)
Carmelite friar

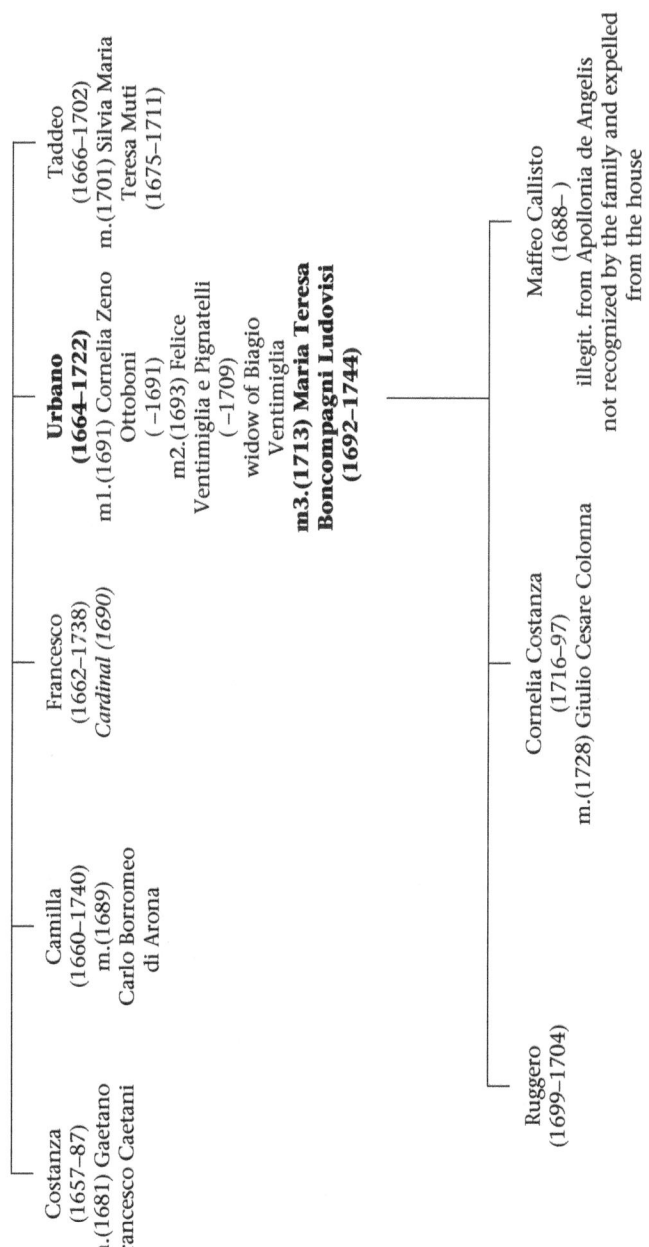

Costanza
(1657–87)
m.(1681) Gaetano
Grancesco Caetani

Camilla
(1660–1740)
m.(1689)
Carlo Borromeo
di Arona

Francesco
(1662–1738)
Cardinal (1690)

**Urbano
(1664–1722)**
m1.(1691) Cornelia Zeno
Ottoboni
(–1691)
m2.(1693) Felice
Ventimiglia e Pignatelli
(–1709)
widow of Biagio
Ventimiglia
**m3.(1713) Maria Teresa
Boncompagni Ludovisi
(1692–1744)**

Taddeo
(1666–1702)
m.(1701) Silvia Maria
Teresa Muti
(1675–1711)

Ruggero
(1699–1704)

Cornelia Costanza
(1716–97)
m.(1728) Giulio Cesare Colonna

Maffeo Callisto
(1688–)
illegit. from Apollonia de Angelis
not recognized by the family and expelled
from the house

220

Appendix 2: The Boncompagni & Boncompagni Ludovisi Families

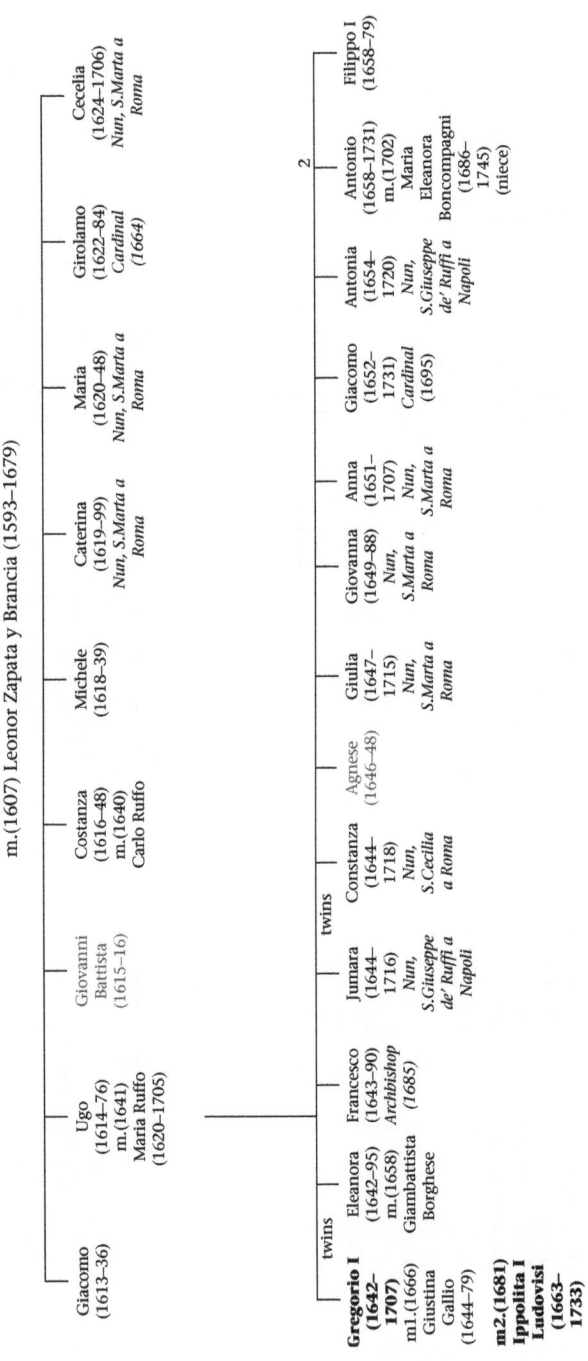

Gregorio
(1590–1628)
m.(1607) Leonor Zapata y Brancia (1593–1679)

Giacomo
(1613–36)

Ugo
(1614–76)
m.(1641)
Maria Ruffo
(1620–1705)

Giovanni
Battista
(1615–16)

Costanza
(1616–48)
m.(1640)
Carlo Ruffo

Michele
(1618–39)

Caterina
(1619–99)
Nun, S.Marta a
Roma

Maria
(1620–48)
Nun, S.Marta a
Roma

Girolamo
(1622–84)
Cardinal
(1664)

Cecelia
(1624–1706)
Nun, S.Marta a
Roma

twins

Gregorio I
1642–
1707)
m1.(1666) Giustina
Gallio
(1644–79)

m2.(1681)
Ippolita I
Ludovisi
(1663–
1733)

Eleanora
(1642–95)
m.(1658)
Giambattista
Borghese

twins

Francesco
(1643–90)
Archbishop
(1685)

Jumara
(1644–
1716)
Nun,
S.Giuseppe
de' Ruffi a
Napoli

Constanza
(1644–
1718)
Nun,
S.Cecilia
a Roma

Agnese
(1646–48)

Giulia
(1647–
1715)
Nun,
S.Marta a
Roma

Giovanna
(1649–88)
Nun,
S.Marta a
Roma

Anna
(1651–
1707)
Nun,
S.Marta a
Roma

Giacomo
(1652–
1731)
Cardinal
(1695)

Antonia
(1654–
1720)
Nun,
S.Giuseppe
de' Ruffi a
Napoli

Antonio
(1658–1731)
m.(1702)
Maria
Eleanora
Boncompagni
(1686–
1745)
(niece)

2

Filippo I
(1658–79)

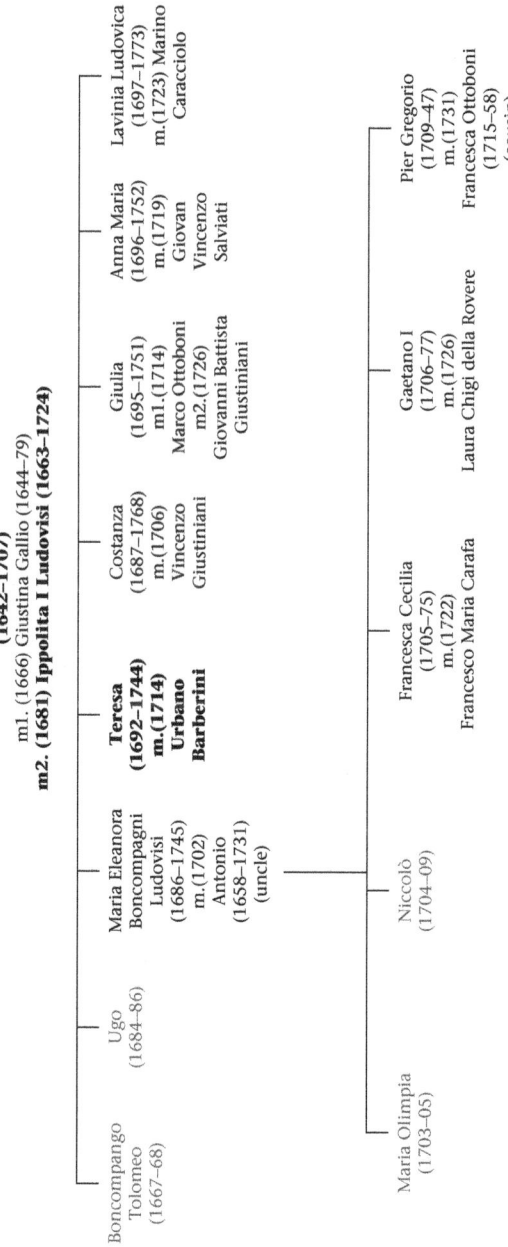

**Gregorio I
(1642–1707)**
m1. (1666) Giustina Gallio (1644–79)
m2. (1681) Ippolita I Ludovisi (1663–1724)

Boncompango
Tolomeo
(1667–68)

Ugo
(1684–86)

Maria Eleanora
Boncompagni
Ludovisi
(1686–1745)
m.(1702)
Antonio
(1658–1731)
(uncle)

**Teresa
(1692–1744)
m.(1714)
Urbano
Barberini**

Costanza
(1687–1768)
m.(1706)
Vincenzo
Giustiniani

Giulia
(1695–1751)
m1.(1714)
Marco Ottoboni
m2.(1726)
Giovanni Battista
Giustiniani

Anna Maria
(1696–1752)
m.(1719)
Giovan
Vincenzo
Salviati

Lavinia Ludovica
(1697–1773)
m.(1723) Marino
Caracciolo

Maria Olimpia
(1703–05)

Niccolò
(1704–09)

Francesca Cecilia
(1705–75)
m.(1722)
Francesco Maria Carafa

Gaetano I
(1706–77)
m.(1726)
Laura Chigi della Rovere

Pier Gregorio
(1709–47)
m.(1731)
Francesca Ottoboni
(1715–58)
(cousin)

222

Appendix 3: The Colonna Family

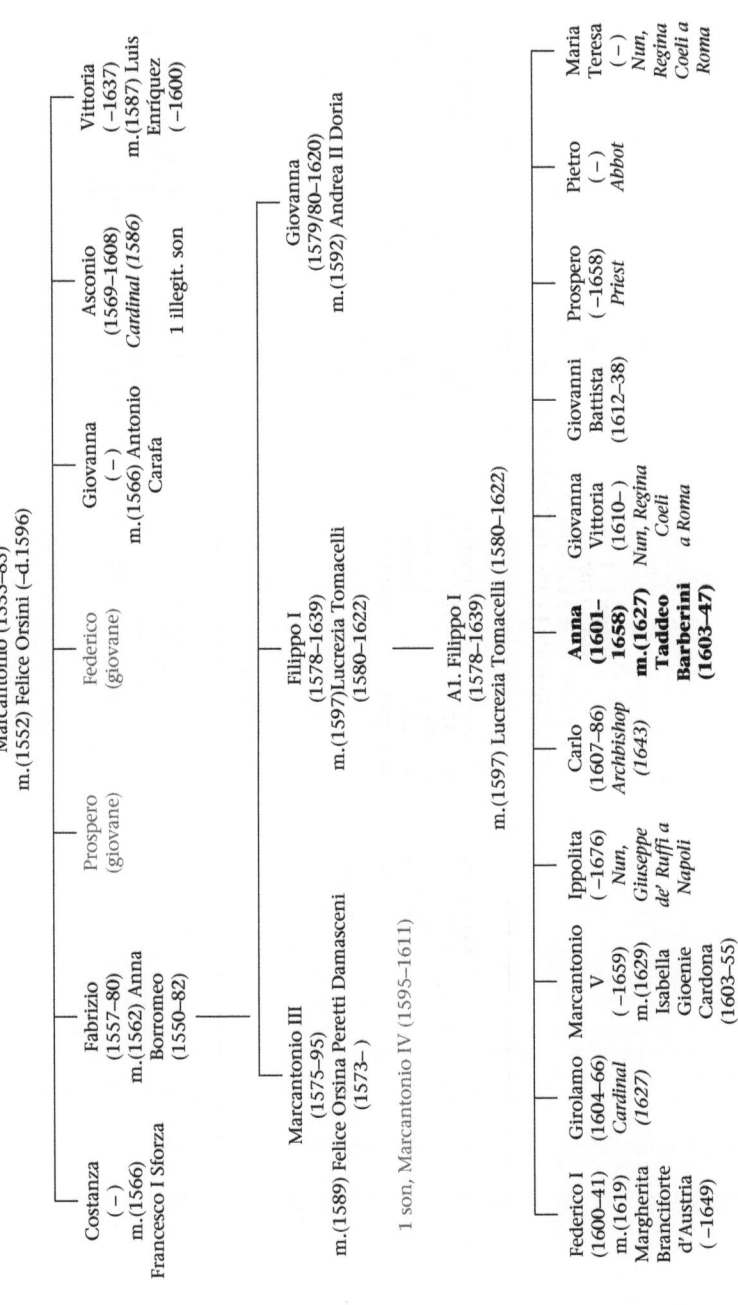

Marcantonio (1535–85)
m.(1552) Felice Orsini (–d.1596)

Costanza
(–)
m.(1566)
Francesco I Sforza

Fabrizio
(1557–80)
m.(1562) Anna
Borromeo
(1550–82)

Prospero
(giovane)

Federico
(giovane)

Giovanna
(–)
m.(1566) Antonio
Carafa

Asconio
(1569–1608)
Cardinal (1586)

1 illegit. son

Vittoria
(–1637)
m.(1587) Luis
Enríquez
(–1600)

Marcantonio III
(1575–95)
m.(1589) Felice Orsina Peretti Damasceni
(1573–)

1 son, Marcantonio IV (1595–1611)

Filippo I
(1578–1639)
m.(1597)Lucrezia Tomacelli
(1580–1622)

Giovanna
(1579/80–1620)
m.(1592) Andrea II Doria

A1. Filippo I
(1578–1639)
m.(1597) Lucrezia Tomacelli (1580–1622)

Federico I
(1600–41)
m.(1619)
Margherita
Branciforte
d'Austria
(–1649)

Girolamo
(1604–66)
Cardinal
(1627)

Marcantonio
V
(–1659)
m.(1629)
Isabella
Gioenie
Cardona
(1603–55)

Ippolita
(–1676)
Nun,
Giuseppe
de' Ruffi a
Napoli

Carlo
(1607–86)
Archbishop
(1643)

**Anna
(1601–
1658)
m.(1627)
Taddeo
Barberini
(1603–47)**

Giovanna
Vittoria
(1610–)
Nun, Regina
Coeli
a Roma

Giovanni
Battista
(1612–38)

Prospero
(–1658)
Priest

Pietro
(–)
Abbot

Maria
Teresa
(–)
Nun,
Regina
Coeli a
Roma

Appendix 4: The Ludovisi Family

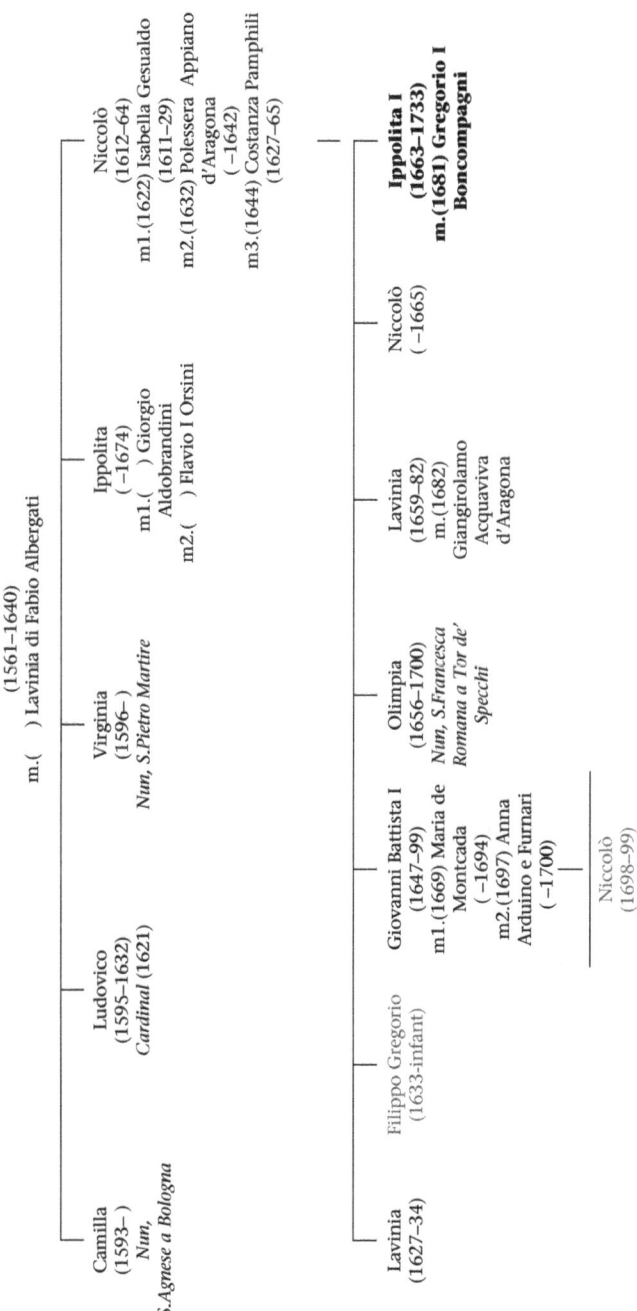

Orazio
(1561–1640)
m.( ) Lavinia di Fabio Albergati

Camilla
(1593–)
Num,
S.Agnese a Bologna

Ludovico
(1595–1632)
Cardinal (1621)

Virginia
(1596–)
Num, S.Pietro Martire

Ippolita
(–1674)
m1.( ) Giorgio
Aldobrandini
m2.( ) Flavio I Orsini

Niccolò
(1612–64)
m1.(1622) Isabella Gesualdo
(1611–29)
m2.(1632) Polessera Appiano
d'Aragona
(–1642)
m3.(1644) Costanza Pamphili
(1627–65)

Lavinia
(1627–34)

Filippo Gregorio
(1633–infant)

Giovanni Battista I
(1647–99)
m1.(1669) Maria de
Montcada
(–1694)
m2.(1697) Anna
Arduino e Furnari
(–1700)

Olimpia
(1656–1700)
Num, S.Francesca
Romana a Tor de'
Specchi

Lavinia
(1659–82)
m.(1682)
Giangirolamo
Acquaviva
d'Aragona

Niccolò
(–1665)

Ippolita I
(1663–1733)
m.(1681) Gregorio I
Boncompagni

Niccolò
(1698–99)

Notes

Acknowledgments

1. Quoted in Lloyd deMause, ed., *The History of Childhood* (London, 1974), p. 2.
2. Moderata Fonte, *The Worth of Women*, trans. Virginia Cox (Chicago, 1997), p. 67.
3. Erma Bombeck, *Motherhood: The Second Oldest Profession* (New York, 1983), p. 2.

Introduction

1. For these details, see Giacinto Gigli, *Diario Romano (1608–1670)*, ed. Giuseppe Ricciotti (Rome, 1958), pp. 274–5. The Barberini family had built a magnificent palace on the Quirinal hill, but Anna, Taddeo, and the children subsequently relocated to an older palace on the via dei Giubbonari, near Campo de' Fiori. See Patricia Waddy, *Seventeenth-Century Roman Palaces* (Cambridge, 1990), pp. 154, 242–4; John Beldon Scott, *Images of Nepotism: The Painting Ceilings of the Palazzo Barberini* (Princeton, 1991), pp. 198–9.
2. Biblioteca Apostolica Vaticana [hereafter BAV], Barb. Lat. 10043, 69r [11 January 1642).
3. For the place of women in the Roman aristocratic family, see the bibliography in note 20 below. Critics of powerful seventeenth-century women charged that Roman women in general exercised too much power. See Marina D'Amelia, "La nuova Agrippina. Olimpia Maidalchini Pamphilj e la tirannia femminile nell'immaginario politico del Seicento," in *I linguaggi del potere nell'età barocca*, vol. 2, *Donne e sfera pubblica*, ed. Francesca Cantù (Rome, 2009), pp. 45–95, esp. pp. 56–7. I am grateful to Françoise Hamlin for conversations on the difficulties of tracing women's political activities in the past and to Paula Findlen for her insights on writing early modern women's lives. Audiences at the following institutions and conferences sharpened my thinking on early modern women, politics, and society: University of California at Los Angeles; Sixteenth-Century Studies; and Renaissance Society of America.
4. Giulia Calvi, "'Cruel' and 'Nurturing' Mothers: The Construction of Motherhood in Tuscany (1500–1800)," *L'Homme* 17.1 (2006): 75–92. Early modern motherhood is now receiving greater scrutiny as a historical topic. See Marina D'Amelia, "La presenza delle madri nell'Italia medievale e moderna," in D'Amelia, *Storia della maternità* (Rome, 1997), pp. 3–52. For a wide-ranging set of essays on motherhood in literature and art history, see Naomi J. Miller and Naomi Yavneh, eds., *Maternal Measures: Figuring Caregiving in Early Modern Period* (Burlington, 2000), especially the introductory essay by Naomi J. Miller: "Mothering Others: Caregiving as Spectrum and Spectacle in the Early Modern Period," ibid., pp. 1–25; Caroline Castiglione, "Mothers and Children," in *The Renaissance World*, ed. John Martin (New York: Routledge, 2007), pp. 381–97.

5. On matriarchy, see Helen Nader, ed., *Power and Gender in Renaissance Spain* (Urbana, 2004), pp. 3–4. On the beginning of women's political lives in motherhood, see Calvi, "'Cruel' and 'Nurturing' Mothers," esp. pp. 79–80; 90–1.

6. On the ideal behavior for women in the family, see Ian Maclean, *The Renaissance Notion of Woman* (Cambridge, 1980), pp. 57–64. For a more recent summary, see Merry E. Wiesner, *Women and Gender in Early Modern Europe*, 3rd ed. (Cambridge, 2008), especially chapter 1: "Ideas and Laws Regarding Women." For a comparison of humanist discourse and familial practice, see Stanley Chojnacki, "'The Most Serious Duty': Motherhood, Gender, and Patrician Culture," in *Women and Men in Renaissance Venice: Twelve Essays on Patrician Society* (Baltimore, 2000), pp. 169–82.

7. The edition of Baldassare Castiglione's *The Book of the Courtier* by Daniel Javitch (New York, 2002) offers valuable insight on its gender politics, interpreted alternatively as pro- and anti-women, depending on the scholar. See pp. 281–400. For an insightful synthesis of gender attitudes in Renaissance culture, see Elissa B. Weaver, "Gender," in *A Companion to The Worlds of the Renaissance*, ed. Guido Ruggiero (Malden, MA and Oxford, 2002), pp. 188–207.

8. Jeffrey Merrick, "Fathers and Kings: Patriarchalism and Absolutism in Eighteenth-Century French Politics," *Studies on Voltaire and the Eighteenth Century* 308 (1993): 281–303.

9. Paolo Prodi, *The Papal Prince: One Body and Two Souls: The Papal Monarchy in Early Modern Europe*, trans. Susan Haskins (Cambridge, 1987); Mario Caravale and Alberto Caracciolo, *Lo Stato pontificio da Martino V a Pio IX* (Turin, 1978).

10. The larger European pattern of maternal advocacy is emerging in a growing European historiography. Its roots are in the Middle Ages, when women, especially widows, demonstrated a pattern of seeking redress in the courts. On the continent, beyond Italy, the best known case is France. See Harry A. Miskimin, "Widows Not So Merry: Women and the Courts in Late Medieval France," in *Upon My Husband's Death: Widows in the Literature and Histories of Medieval Europe*, ed. Louise Mirrer (Ann Arbor, MI, 1992), pp. 207–19. For the early modern dynamic in France between women and courts, see Sarah Hanley, "Social Sites of Political Practice in France: Lawsuits, Civil Rights, and the Separation of Powers in Domestic and State Government, 1500–1800," *American Historical Review* 102: (1997): 7–52.

11. For an analytical synthesis of women's writing in Italy, including their contribution to the *querelle*, see Virginia Cox, *Women's Writing in Italy, 1400–1650* (Baltimore, 2008).

12. A careful reading of this work and the work of Virginia Cox, cited in note 11, will reveal that both of our narratives posit a period of retrenchment beginning in the seventeenth century, followed by a reclamation of the possibility of women's writing or familial participation in the latter part of the century. In the case of women's writing, Cox locates the resurgence of misogyny and the marginalization of women's writing in the mid-seventeenth century. In roughly the same time period, Roman families embraced – in greater numbers and to a greater degree – the practice of primogeniture, with the latter part of the century the period in which women and cadet sons challenged the paradigm in and out of the law courts. For further discussion, see the section in this chapter, "Roman Aristocrats in a Resurgent Monarchy," and the works in notes 26 and 27, below.

13. Moderata Fonte, *The Worth of Women: wherein is clearly revealed their nobility and their superiority to men*, ed. and trans. Virginia Cox (Chicago: University of Chicago Press, 1997). In her introduction to Fonte's text, Virginia Cox underscores its deviation from its more formulaic predecessors, but reminds the reader that it is difficult to assess the radicalness of its call for change. See pp. 1, 15–17.

14. Fonte, *The Worth of Women*, pp. 67–8.

15. On the weakness of maternal versus paternal love in the Renaissance, see the discussion of Montaigne and Alberti in Calvi, *Il contratto morale: Madre e figli nella Toscana moderna* (Rome, 1994), pp. 30–1.

16. Giulia Calvi has proposed the seventeenth-century judicial origins of the matrifocal family. Magistrates and mothers collaborated in casting mothers as the superior parents. See *Il Contratto morale*, esp. pp. 28–32; 130–4. On the alliance between ecclesiastical authorities, state institutions, and women, see Joanne M. Ferraro, *Marriage Wars in Late Renaissance Venice* (New York, 2001).

17. Microhistory as elaborated by Carlo Ginzburg has inspired the method employed here. Microhistory is a groundbreaking subcategory of the larger genre of the case study and has greatly influenced cultural history. I have employed it for its attention to dissonance, difference, and confusion about meanings among historical actors in order to explore the history of mothering in Rome. An early exemplar is Carlo Ginzburg, *The Cheese and the Worms*, trans. John and Anne Tedeschi (Baltimore, 1980).

18. Charles L. Stinger, *The Renaissance in Rome* (Bloomington, 1985), esp. pp. 2–3.

19. Barbara McClung Hallman, *Italian Cardinals, Reform, and the Church as Property* (Berkeley, 1985), pp. 158–62, 167.

20. The combination of male and female efforts to the family was first elaborated by Renata Ago, "Giochi di squadra: Uomini e donne nelle famiglie nobili del xvii secolo," in *Signori, patrizi, cavalieri in Italia centro-meriodionale nell'età moderna*, ed. Maria Antonietta Visceglia (Rome, 1992), pp. 256–64 (esp. pp. 260–3). For an overview of this argument in English see her "Ecclesiastical Careers and the Destiny of Cadets," *Continuity and Change* 7 (1992): 271–82. Ago elaborated the argument further in *Carriere e clientele nella Roma barocca* (Rome: Laterza, 1990); see pp. 67–71 for a specific treatment of the clerical brother in this familial configuration. The model is further confirmed in Marina d'Amelia, "Becoming a Mother in the Seventeenth Century: The Experience of a Roman Noblewoman," in *Time, Space, and Women's Lives in Early Modern Europe*, ed. Anne Jacobson Schutte, Thomas Kuehn, and Silvana Seidel Menchi (Kirksville, MO, 2001), pp. 223–44. D'Amelia underscored that both the cardinal brother and the women were important in marriage negotiations (pp. 225–6). Benedetta Borello tracked the interplay of women's and men's efforts and networks through their correspondences in *Trame sovrapposte: La socialità aristocratica e le reti di relazioni femminili a Roma (XVII–XVIII secolo)* (Naples, 2003). Several politically active mothers figure in the collection of essays, *I linguaggi del potere nell'età barocca*, Vol. 2, *Donne e sfera pubblica*, ed. Francesca Cantù (Rome, 2009). Specific case studies from that volume are cited in subsequent chapters.

21. Ago, "Giochi di squadra," p. 256.

22. On the bilinearity of families in Rome, see note 20. For the Venetian case, see Stanley Chojnacki, *Women and Men in Renaissance Venice: Twelve Essays on Patrician Society* (Baltimore, 2000), pp. 14, 96, 129, 140, 149.

23. On male honor in Rome, see Ago, "Giochi di Squadra," pp. 260–1. Ago hypothesized that the origins of female activity are in Roman law, because women could have heirs, but not successors, so therefore their honor risk was not the same as men, who were bound to perpetuate the family. See "Giochi di Squadra," p. 263.

24. Guendalina Ajello Mahler, "The Orsini Family Papers at the University of California, Los Angeles: Property Administration, Political Strategy, and Architectural Legacy," *Viator* 39.2 (2008): 297–321.

25. Waddy, *Seventeenth-Century Roman Palaces*, pp. 193–4.

26. Maura Piccialuti, *L'Immortalità dei beni: Fedecommessi e primogeniture a Roma nei secoli xvii e xviii* (Roma, 1999), pp. 12, 81, 99.

27. Richard Ferraro persuasively argued that the terms of *fedecommesso* meant that the holder "could freely alienate only earnings, and was supposed to preserve in good condition the capital inherent in all property under entail ..." He notes that in theory male members of a family could split entailed holdings and each marry under the terms of *fedecommesso*. Primogeniture was a "specialized form of entail" which designated family holdings for a single heir. For primogeniture's increasing popularity in the seventeenth century and its synonimity with the term *fedecommesso*, see Richard Ferraro, "The Nobility of Rome, 1560–1700: A Study of Its Composition, Wealth, and Investments" (PhD diss., University of Wisconsin-Madison, 1994), pp. 139–42.

28. Ibid., p. 211, note 78.

29. Thomas Kuehn posits that the *fedecommesso* was the family. Although I dispute this interpretation, see his valuable study of the Orsini's *fedecommessi*, "Fideicommissum and Family: The Orsini di Bracciano," *Viator* 39.2 (2008): 323–41. I thank Tom Kuehn for his conversations on the institution of *fedecommesso*, and his insights on the legal literacy of women and men in Italy.

30. Renata Ago, "Maria Spada Veralli, la buona moglie," in *Barocco al Femminile*, ed. Giulia Calvi (Rome, 1992), pp. 51–70. On pregnancy and the diplomatic work of women, see Borello, *Trame sovrapposte*, pp. 31–2.

31. For women's general rise in literacy and the changes in its character, see R. A. Houston, *Literacy in Early Modern Europe: Culture and Education 1500–1800* (New York, 2002), pp. 144–6. On women as letter writers, see Gabriella Zarri, ed., *Per Lettera: La scrittura epistolare femminile tra archivio e tipografia secoli XV–XVII* (Rome, 1999) and Jane Couchman and Ann Crabb, eds., *Women's Letters Across Europe, 1400–1700: Form and Persuasion* (Burlington, 2005). See the recent bibliography on women and letter writing in Giovanna Benadusi, "The Gender Politics of Vittoria della Rovere," in *Medici Women: The Making of a Dynasty in Gran Ducal Tuscany*, ed. Giovanna Benadusi and Judith Brown (Toronto: Centre for Reformation and Renaissance Studies, forthcoming). For the evolution of women as letter writers, see Adriana Chemello, "Il codice epistolare femminile. Lettere, 'Libri di lettere,' e letterate nel Cinquecento," in Zarri, *Per Lettera*, pp. 43–78. On female letter writing in Rome, see Marina D'Amelia, "Lo scambio epistolare tra Cinque e Seicento: scene di vita quotidiana e aspirazioni segrete," in Zarri, *Per Lettera*, pp. 79–110; and Barbara Scanzani, "Camilla e Costanza Barberini: lettere a Urbano VIII," in *Scritture di donne: La memoria restituita*, ed. Marina Caffiero and Manola Ida Venzo (Rome, 2004), pp. 167–83.

32. Gabriella Zarri, "Introduzione," in *Per Lettera*, p. xiv.

33. Zarri insists upon the paramount influence on women's writing of mystics in general and of Saint Teresa in particular. See "Introduzione," in *Per Lettera*, pp. xiv–xv, xxiv. See Elisabetta Marchetti, "Le Lettere di Teresa di Gesù: Prime traduzioni ed edizioni italiane," in ibid., pp. 263–84. For the earlier influence of Catherine of Siena, see Adriano Prosperi, "Spiritual Letters," in *Women and Faith: Catholic Religious Life in Italy from Late Antiquity to the Present*, ed. Lucetta Scaraffia and Gabriella Zarri (Cambridge, MA, 1999), pp. 113–28.

34. Marilyn Dunn, "Piety and Patronage in Seicento Rome: Two Noblewomen and Their Convents," *Art Bulletin* 74.4 (1994): 644–64 (p. 652).

35. BAV, Barberini Carteggi 41, 751r (1 December 1662): Letter from Costanza Pamphilj Ludovisi in Sassari, Sardinia, to Olimpia Giustiniani Barberini in Rome.

36. On the lack of the training among Roman aristocratic women, see Borello, *Trame sovrapposte*, p. 69.

37. For Anna's writing difficulties, see Chapter 1 of this volume.

38. Piccialuti identified but did not analyze 237 cases in the 1670s and 1680s in the archive of the Congregation of the Barons. See *L'Immortalità dei beni*, p. 258.

39. For noteworthy illustrations of specific litigating mothers, see Piccialuti, *L'Immortalità dei beni*, pp.182, 184–6, 246, 249–51.

40. Raymond Grew, "Finding Social Capital: The French Revolution in Italy," *Journal of Interdisciplinary History* XXIX (1999): 407–33, esp. pp. 413–14.

41. Hanns Gross, *Rome in the Age of Enlightenment* (Cambridge, 1990), p. 48. His precise numbers are 1,200 lawyers in a city of 166,000.

42. For more on Roman notaries, see Laurie Nussdorfer, *Brokers of Public Trust: Notaries in Early Modern Rome* (Baltimore, 2009).

43. On the legal literacy of late medieval and Renaissance cities, see Thomas Kuehn, *Law, Family, and Women: Toward a Legal Anthropology of Renaissance Italy* (Chicago, 1991), especially chapters 8–10, on the legal activities involving women. On the legal constraints imposed by gender (and their circumvention), see Kuehn, "Person and Gender in the Laws," in *Gender and Society in Renaissance Italy*, ed. Judith C. Brown and Robert C. Davis (New York, 1998), pp. 87–106; "Daughters, Mothers, Wives, and Widows: Women as Legal Persons," in *Time, Space, and Women's Lives in Early Modern Europe*, ed. Anne J. Schutte, Thomas Kuehn, and Silvana Seidel Menchi, (Kirksville, MO, 2001), pp. 97–115. On the legal activities of widows seeking custody of their children, see Calvi, *Il contratto morale*. On the legal status of Roman women, see Simona Feci, *Pesci fuor d'acqua: Donne e Roma in età moderna (diritti e patrimoni)* (Rome, 2004).

44. BAV, Archivio Barberini, Indice IV, 1572, 354r–354v. See Chapter 5 of this volume for more on this assertion.

45. I thank Ron Martinez for his advice on the formulation of this term for my study.

46. Archivio Segreto Vaticano [hereafter ASV], Archivio Boncompagni Ludovisi, busta 899 (24 March 1685 [letter to Eleonora's brother Gregorio Boncompagni, letter miscatalogued in packet of letters "1687–1689"]).

47. Donna Spivey Ellington, *From Sacred Body to Angelic Soul* (Washington, DC, 2001), pp. 143–8.

48. For a judicial overview, see Irene Fosi, *Papal Justice: Subjects and Courts in the Papal State, 1500–1750*, trans. Thomas V. Cohen (Washington, 2011).

49. On the Cardinal Vicar in the eighteenth-century, see Gross, *Rome in the Age of Enlightenment*, p. 54.
50. See Laurie Nussdorfer, *Civic Politics in the Rome of Urban VIII* (Princeton, 1992), pp. 46–9; Maria Grazia Pastura Ruggiero, *Le Reverenda Camera Apostolica e i suoi archvi (secoli XV–XVIII)* (Rome, 1984), pp. 211–17.
51. For more on the Congregation of the Barons, see Chapter 2; Jean Delumeau, *Vie économique et sociale de Rome dans la seconde moitié du XVIe siècle* (Paris, 1957–1959), 2 vols (vol. 1: pp. 457, 471, 475; vol. 2: 817).
52. Gross, *Rome in the Age of Enlightenment*, p. 345.
53. On Marianna as letter writer and diplomat, see Marianne Cermakian, "La Princesse des Ursins: Sa vie et ses lettres" (PhD diss., University of Paris, 1969). For a fuller account of her Roman years and activities, see Caroline Castiglione, "When a Woman 'Takes' Charge: Marie-Anne de la Trémoille (1642?–1722) and the End of the Patrimony of the Dukes of Bracciano," *Viator* 39.2 (2008): 363–79.
54. On Flavio's retreat to Bracciano, see Cermakian, "La Princesse," p. 95. On the late life surrender of both Flavio and Lelio to the direction of Marianna, see Orsini Family Papers (Collection 902), Department of Special Collections, Charles E. Young Research Library, University of California, Los Angeles [hereafter, OFP], Box 254, ff. 118–19 (30 March 1696).
55. Archivio Capitolino [hereafter AC], Archivio Orsini, I Serie, 304, Letter number 153 from Marianna (in Paris) to Flavio Orsini (27 December 1694).
56. On the terms of her dowry, see OFP, Box 236, folder 3, "doti 12." Further information on the dowry can be found in ibid., Box 257, 18r (17 February 1675). On the use of her dowry to hide Orsini assets, see ibid., Box 20 and Cermakian, "La Princesse," p. 139, note 4. On Marianna's securing of payments from the French King to Flavio Orsini, see AC, Archivio Orsini, I Serie, 304, Letter number 146 from Marianna (at Versailles) to Flavio Orsini (2 February 1692).
57. OFP, Box 301; a long-running dispute with the Collegio Germanico named the two of them as co-litigants: ibid., Boxes 69–76, 292. On lawsuits she continued, see ibid., Boxes 29–30, 62. On her activity with lawyers, see AC, Archivio Orsini, I Serie, 303, Letter number 122, from Marianna (in Bagnaia) to Flavio Orsini (22 August 1685). On her attentiveness to pending cases during her Paris sojourns, see AC, Archivio Orsini, I Serie, 304, Letter number 154, from Marianna (in Paris) to Flavio Orsini (30 May 1694).
58. OFP, Box 302; Box 46, folder 1 (draft of will June 1696).
59. On the difficulties faced by Marianna's siblings and their advancement in Rome by her, see Cermakian, "La Princesse," pp. 105–6, 131–2, 135–7.
60. The Palazzo di Pasquino was approximately where the current Palazzo Braschi is located today. See Carlo Pietrangeli, *Palazzo Braschi* (Rome, 1958), pp. 7–21. For the recovery of the Orsini of Bracciano archive by the Orsini of Gravina, see OFP, Box 46 (papal chirograph of 5 September 1729).
61. On the rapport between the La Trémoille and the Orsini, see Cermakian, "La Princesse," p. 187 and AC, Archivio Orsini, I Serie, 304, Letter 156 Marianna (in Paris) to Flavio Orsini (22 January 1695). On Marianna's diplomatic work, see Cermakian, "La Princesse," pp. 193–474. On Marianna's defeat of her rival heirs and her successful maneuvers against Livio Odescalchi, see ibid., p. 197 and OFP, Box 257.

62. ASV, Archivio Boncompagni Ludovisi, 899 (13 December 1687).
63. I base my calculations on the recourse of women to the tribunal by analyzing two extant inventories of the Congregation of the Barons in the Archivio di Stato in Rome. I used MS 303, an early index containing some information omitted in the later and more extensive modern inventory Number 122, "Congregazione dei Monti e Baroni." I counted all women who were involved as litigants, defendants, or petitioners of any kind to the tribunal. I did not count women whose inheritance was in dispute by their heirs after the woman's death, since I was trying to track women's activity in the Congregazione. Women were involved in 258 cases of the 1,084 catalogued for the tribunal, or about 24 percent of all the cases. There were 176 women whose issues were deliberated by the Congregazione in those 258 cases. The discrepancy between total number of cases and the number of women is explained by those women (19 in all) who were involved in three or more cases and an additional 25 women who were involved in two cases brought before the tribunal. The remaining 132 women were involved with the tribunal's proceedings only once in their lifetime. One weakness of this analysis of the litigants is that the data includes cases into the early nineteenth century and the modern inventory does not make the dating of the cases easy to verify, except for the first 11 volumes of materials, where the incidence of women in the cases is slightly higher, about 27 percent. The broad pattern for the early modern period is clear, however, even if more precise change over time cannot be tracked through these preliminary findings.
64. On the Tuscan widows, see Calvi, *Il contratto morale*. On servants, see Giovanna Benadusi, "Investing the Riches of the Poor: Servant Women and Their Last Wills," *American Historical Review* 109.3 (June 2004): 805–26. On exits from bad marriages, see Ferraro, *Marriage Wars in Late Renaissance Venice*.
65. Caroline Castiglione, *Patrons and Adversaries: Nobles and Villagers in Italian Politics, 1640–1760* (New York, 2005), p. 13.
66. Wayne Te Brake, *Shaping History: Ordinary People in European Politics, 1500–1700* (Berkeley, 1998), p. 6.
67. Edward Muir, "The Sources of Civil Society in Italy," *Journal of Interdisciplinary History* 29.3 (Winter, 1999): 379–406.
68. Grew, "Finding Social Capital," pp. 413–14.
69. The notion of "hidden" and "public" transcripts was introduced by the anthropologist James C. Scott. See note 73, below.
70. Elizabeth S. Cohen, "The Trials of Artemisia Gentileschi: A Rape as History," *Sixteenth-Century Journal* 31.1 (2000): 47–75.
71. For the expression "*il mondo romano*," see See BAV, Fondo Boncompagni Ludovisi, E 119, 24r.
72. Carlo Ginzburg, "The Inquisitor as Anthropologist," in *Clues, Myths, and the Historical Method*, trans. John and Anne Tedeschi (Baltimore, 1989), pp. 156–64, esp. pp. 159–63. For an overview of issues related to microhistory, see Edoardo Grendi, Carlo Ginzburg, and Jacques Revel, "Sulla microstoria," in a special section of *Quaderni storici* 86.2 (1994): 511–75.
73. James C. Scott, *Domination and the Arts of Resistance: Hidden Transcripts* (New Haven, 1990), esp. pp. 135, 156–7, 164–6. On the relation of the hidden transcript to resistance and moments of rebellion, see pp. 191, 223.

74. On the public circulation of letters, see Tiziana Plebani, "La corrispondenza nell'antico regime: lettere di donne negli archivi di famiglia," in Zarri, *Per Lettera*, pp. 43–78, esp. p. 49.

75. See Armando Petrucci, *Scrivere lettere: una storia plurimillenaria* (Rome, 2008), pp. 109, 119–20. I thank Professor Irene Fosi for her insights and bibliography on this important issue.

76. For other European examples of male ambivalence, see Jonathan Dewald, *Aristocratic Experience and the Origins of Modern Culture: France, 1570–1715* (Berkeley, 1993), pp. 69, 73–4, 77. For more on this theme, see Chapter 4 and the Conclusion of this volume. Anne Jacobson Schutte emphasizes that the study of epistolary sources in familial archives may be the key sources for understanding change in the patrilinear family. See Anne Jacobson Schutte, *By Force and Fear: Taking and Breaking Monastic Vows in Early Modern Europe* (Ithaca, 2011), esp. pp. 254–5.

77. Judith Butler, *Gender Trouble* (New York, 1999), pp. 198–9.

78. Thomas Kuehn, "Reading Microhistory: The Example of Giovanni and Lusanna," *Journal of Modern History* 61.3 (1989): 512–34, esp. p. 522.

79. On this theme, see Chapter 3 of this volume.

80. Family history today encompasses a variety of methodologies and approaches. This study engages with specific works on motherhood and the family that have emerged in recent decades within the vast research enterprise on the family, women, and gender. The history of the family in Europe still contends with some of the earliest conclusions of its first professional researchers. Among such works was the path-breaking volume by Philippe Ariès, *L'enfant et la vie familiale sous l'Ancien Régime* (originally published in Paris in 1960; English translation, 1962). Ariès almost singlehandedly invented family history and the history of childhood, at a time when a generation of historians trained in the emerging methodology of quantitative history explored household size and kinship, and historians of various methodological inclinations began to examine marriage and sexuality, childhood and adolescence. Lawrence Stone's *The Family, Sex and Marriage in England, 1500–1800* (New York, 1977) was one of the more controversial interventions that is still widely cited even if its conclusions have been largely refuted. Stone drew a sharp contrast between the family of the Middle Ages and the modern family, positing without much evidence that prior to modernity parents were relatively indifferent to their children. This interpretive leap along with a confused chronology of change (but an insistence upon positive change in the family unit over time) gave way to many subsequent studies aimed at debunking its conclusions. The research of Linda Pollock offered insightful correctives. See especially her essay "Parent–Child Relations," in *Family Life in Early Modern Times, 1500–1789*, ed. David I. Kertzer and Marzio Barbagli, vol. 1 *The History of the European Family* (New Haven, 2001), pp. 191–220. Recent family history has focused on more limited chronological periods; incorporated more fully gender and class analysis; and explored the links between the history of the state and the development of the family. The outcome of such investigations has produced greater interest in understanding the forces of change in familial relations, problems that Ariès located in the clergy and the school, and which Stone neglected to discuss at all. A useful critique of the long enduring and much criticized theoretical model of European family development is Arland

Thornton, *Reading History Sideways: The Fallacy and Enduring Impact of the Developmental Paradigm on Family Life* (Chicago, 2005).

81. Martha C. Nussbaum, *Upheavals of Thought: The Intelligence of Emotions* (Cambridge: Cambridge University Press, 2001), pp. 3–4.
82. Nussbaum, *Upheavals of Thought*, p. 12.
83. Ibid., p. 370.
84. Lynn Hunt, "The Paradoxical Origins of Human Rights," in *Human Rights and Revolutions*, ed. Jeffrey N. Wasserstrom, Lynn Hunt, and Marilyn B. Young (Lanham, MD, 2000), pp. 3–17. Linda Pollock stresses the importance of examining emotions in historical context in "Anger and the Negotiation of Relationships in Early Modern England," *The Historical Journal* 47.3 (2004): 567–90. See the lucidly written and extensively researched dissertation by Tiziana Plebani, "Un Secolo di sentimenti: Amori e conflitti generazionali nella Venezia del Settecento" (PhD diss., Università Ca' Foscari Venezia, 2008). Some historians remain skeptical about the extent to which emotions such as love can ever be incorporated into the study of history. See Renata Ago, "Young People in the Age of Absolutism: Paternal Authority and Freedom of Choice in Seventeenth-Century Italy," in *A History of Young People in the West*, Vol. 1, *Ancient and Medieval Rites of Passage*, ed. Giovanni Levi and Jean-Claude Schmitt and trans. Camille Naish (Cambridge, MA, 1997), pp. 283–322, esp. p. 322. Or historians issue extreme calls for caution in such study: Élisabeth Crouzet-Pavan, "Les faux-semblants d'une histoire des relations affectives: L'exemple italien," in *The Household in Late Medieval Cities: Italy and Northwestern Europe Compared*, ed. Myriam Carlier and Tim Soens (Leuven, 2000), pp. 147–63.
85. Joan Landes, *Women and the Public Sphere in the Age of the French Revolution* (Ithaca, 1988); Lieselotte Steinbrügge, *The Moral Sex: Woman's Nature in the Enlightenment* trans. Pamela E. Selwyn (New York, 1995).
86. On the significant rise in interest in the emotions in the seventeenth century, see Plebani, "Un secolo di sentimenti," pp. 7, 9, 41–2. Roman aristocratic women, though outside the printed discourse on this subject, attempted to move their families in parallel to this change.
87. Natalie Zemon Davis has most effectively articulated this view for judicial testimony, noting that it provides insights into the boundaries of what contemporaries considered acceptable behavior. See *Fiction in the Archives* (Stanford, CA, 1987), pp. 3–6.
88. I was inspired here by similar insights on the impact of early arguments for capitalism by Albert O. Hirschman in *The Passion and the Interests* (Princeton, 1977), esp. pp. 129–30.

1 Practicing Motherhood When the Definition of "Family" Is Ambiguous: Anna Colonna and the Barberini Dynasty, 1627–47

1. For insights on the archives and problems related to the Barberini family, I thank Dr. Luigi Cacciaglia of the Vatican Library and Professor Angela Groppi for their generous expertise. Anna Colonna's life has inspired scholars in a number of fields. See Giuseppe Lodispoto Sacchi, "Anna Colonna Barberini ed il suo monumento nel monastero di Regina Coeli," *Strenna dei romanisti* 43 (1982): 460–78.

For an account of Anna's religious vocation and her patronage of the Roman convent, see Marilyn Dunn, "Piety and Patronage in Seicento Rome: Two Noblewomen and Their Convents," *The Art Bulletin* 74.4 (1994): 644–64; "Spiritual Philanthropists: Women as Convent Patrons in Seicento Rome," in *Women and Art in Early Modern Europe: Patrons, Collectors, and Connoisseurs*, ed. Cynthia Lawrence (State College, PA, 1997), pp. 154–88. Anna's relationship to her distant cousin, Cesare, and her dispute with the Barberini for her dowry after the death of her husband is outlined in Simona Feci, *Pesci fuor d'acqua: Donne a Roma in età moderna: diritti e patrimoni* (Rome, 2004), pp. 197–226. Simultaneously in 2009 appeared two articles on Anna: Caroline Castiglione, "To Trust is Good but Not to Trust is Better: An Aristocratic Woman in Search of Social Capital in Seventeenth-Century Rome," in *Sociability and its Discontents: Civil Society, Social Capital, and Their Alternatives in Late-Medieval and Early-Modern Europe*, ed. Nicholas A. Eckstein and Nicholas Terpstra (Turnhout, 2009), pp. 149–70; and the synthetic biography, Simona Feci and Maria Antonietta Visceglia, "Tra due famiglie: Anna Colonna Barberini "prefettessa" di Roma," in *I linguaggi del potere nell'età barocca*, Vol. 2, *Donne e sfera pubblica*, ed. Francesca Cantù (Rome, 2009), pp. 257–327. On the emotional dynamics of the Barberini family after the return from Paris, with a focus Anna's daughter Lucrezia, see Angela Groppi, "La Sindrome Malinconica di Lucrezia Barberini D'Este," *Quaderni Storici*: 129.3 (2008): 725–749; "La Malinconia di Lucrezia Barberini D'Este," in *I linguaggi del potere nell'età barocca*, Vol. 2, *Donne e sfera pubblica*, ed. Francesca Cantù (Rome, 2009), pp. 197–227.

2. On women's roles, see Renata Ago, "Giochi di squadra: Uomini e donne nelle famiglie nobili del xvii secolo," in *Signori, patrizi, cavalieri in Italia centro-meriodionale nell'età moderna*, ed. Maria Antonietta Visceglia (Rome, 1992), pp. 256–64, esp. pp. 260–3; Patricia Waddy, *Seventeenth-Century Roman Palaces: Use and the Art of the Plan* (Cambridge, MA, 1990), pp. 25–30.

3. Christiane Klapisch-Zuber, *Women, Family, and Ritual in Renaissance Italy* (Chicago, 1995), p. 117; Merry E. Wiesner, *Women and Gender in Early Modern Europe*, 2nd ed. (Cambridge, 2000), pp. 74–5.

4. Waddy, *Seventeenth-Century Roman Palaces*, pp. 31–46.

5. Renata Ago, "Giochi di squadra," idem, *Carriere e clientele nella Roma barocca* (Rome, 1990), pp. 67–71; "Ecclesiastical Careers and the Destiny of Cadets," *Continuity and Change* 7 (1992): 271–82; Marina d'Amelia, "Becoming a Mother in the Seventeenth Century: The Experience of a Roman Noblewoman," in *Time, Space, and Women's Lives in Early Modern Europe*, ed. Anne Jacobson Schutte, Thomas Kuehn, and Silvana Seidel Menchi (Kirksville, MO, 2001), pp. 223–44.

6. A formulation of the family as *madre-figli* is discussed in Giulia Calvi, *Il Contratto Morale: Madre e figli nella Toscana moderna* (Rome, 1994).

7. Anna was most certainly a cultural bricoleur, in the positive sense described by Wendy Doniger, *The Implied Spider* (New York, 1999), pp. 106–7, 144–51.

8. On Anna's early years and religiosity, see Lodispoto, "Anna Colonna Barberini ed il suo monumento," pp. 460–1.

9. Waddy, *Seventeenth-Century Roman Palaces*, pp. 129, 375, note 6.

10. Waddy, *Seventeenth-Century Roman Palaces*, p. 130. On the Barberini's other potential choices of bride for Taddeo, see Feci and Visceglia, "Tra due famiglie," pp. 257–60.

11. On the perks awarded to the nephews, see von Pastor, *History of the Popes from the Close of the Middle Ages*, vol. 28 (London, 1938), pp. 40–3. On the significance of the Colonna match, see Waddy, *Seventeenth-Century Roman Palaces*, pp. 129–30, 277; Feci and Visceglia, "Tra due famiglie," pp. 260–1.

12. On the unique nature of the design, see Waddy, *Seventeenth-Century Roman Palaces*, p. 172.

13. Ibid., p. 180; According to Waddy, Taddeo moved into the new Palazzo Barberini alle Quattro Fontane in May 1632, while the apartments of his brother Cardinal Francesco were not yet complete (p. 197). See also John Beldon Scott, *Images of Nepotism: The Painting Ceilings of the Palazzo Barberini* (Princeton, 1991), p. 34.

14. Waddy, *Seventeenth-Century Roman Palaces*, pp. 179, 201–2.

15. Waddy, *Seventeenth-Century Roman Palaces*, p. 193. Visitors to Anna could enter her apartments separately from those of Taddeo (ibid., p. 213).

16. Waddy, *Seventeenth-Century Roman Palaces*, pp. 26–8; Scott, *Images of Nepotism*, p. 62.

17. Waddy, *Seventeenth-Century Roman Palaces*, pp. 27, 29, 195.

18. Scott, *Images of Nepotism*, pp. 5–6.

19. Scott, *Images of Nepotism*, pp. 55–6.

20. Scott, *Images of Nepotism*, pp. 61–2.

21. Waddy, *Seventeenth-Century Roman Palaces*, p. 4.

22. Waddy, *Seventeenth-Century Roman Palaces*, pp. 27–8.

23. Scott, *Images of Nepotism*, p. 62.

24. Scott, *Images of Nepotism*, pp. 56–7.

25. The phrase "lovers of wisdom" is Scott's (p. 58).

26. Scott, *Images of Nepotism*, pp. 62–3.

27. Scott, *Images of Nepotism*, p. 63.

28. Scott, *Images of Nepotism*, pp. 65–7.

29. Waddy, *Seventeenth-Century Roman Palaces*, p. 30.

30. Scott, *Images of Nepotism*, p. 66.

31. Scott, *Images of Nepotism*, p. 67; Waddy, *Seventeenth-Century Roman Palaces*, p. 28.

32. Biblioteca Apostolica Vaticana [herafter BAV], Barb. Lat. 10043, 96r (24 May 1642).

33. Dunn, "Piety and Patronage," pp. 644, 653.

34. Dunn, "Piety and Patronage," p. 645. Contemporary assessments of Taddeo's character are in ibid., p. 644, note 8. John Beldon Scott explores the deleterious changes in Taddeo's character caused by Pope Urban VIII's bestowal of the title of Prefect upon his nephew. See *Images of Nepotism*, pp. 55–6, 60–2.

35. Two heartfelt letters written by Anna to her son Carlo are transcribed at length by Pio Pecchiai, *I Barberini* (Rome, 1959), pp. 182–7. In his diary, Giacinto Gigli recounted an anecdote that suggests that the destination of the men was indeed kept from her until the moment of the Barberini departure. See Giacinto Gigli, *Diario Romano (1608–1670)*, ed. Giuseppe Ricciotti (Rome, 1958), pp. 274–5. The incident is recounted in this volume in the Introduction.

36. Pecchiai, *I Barberini*, p. 184.

37. The lawsuit is briefly mentioned in Pecchiai, *I Barberini*, p. 188, and Dunn, "Piety and Patronage," p. 647. It is treated in more detail in Feci, *Pesci fuor d'acqua*, pp. 197–226; Feci and Visceglia, "Tra due famiglie," pp. 310–14.

38. On Taddeo as a careful steward of Barberini properties, see Waddy, *Seventeenth-Century Palaces*, pp. 281–90. On her specific assessments of his character, see ibid., pp. 129, 131, 193, 288–90.

39. Waddy, *Seventeenth-Century Palaces*, p. 193; Scott, *Images of Nepotism*, pp. 55–6, 60–2.

40. Dunn credits her return to her desire to continue her religious patronage, Dunn, "Piety and Patronage," pp. 647–8. See her other reason to be "of some service to the *casa* and to ... my children," in BAV, Barb. Lat. 10491, 377r (5 April 1647). On the dates of her trip, see Gigli, *Diario romano*, pp. 278, 309. The dates of her return are easier to verify than those of her departure since she carefully kept an account of her expenditures for her return trip (April 1647 through June 1647). See BAV, Archivio Barberini IV, 47.

41. A nearly contemporary example that illustrates well the conflict between mothers and children over the dowry is Giulia Calvi, "Maddalena Nerli and Cosimo Tornabuoni: A Couple's Narrative of Family History in Early Modern Florence," *Renaissance Quarterly* 45.2 (Summer, 1992): 312–39.

42. According to Waddy, the birth order and ages of the children were as follows: Camilla (1628–30?); Carlo (1630–1706); Maffeo (1631–85); Lucrezia (1632–98); Nicolò (1635–?). See Waddy, *Seventeenth-Century Roman Palaces*, Table 50.

43. For a discussion of women's writing practices, see "The Making of the *Mater Litigans* in Rome," in the Introduction to this volume.

44. She couldn't write on 26 March 1633 because she had a pain in her hand. See BAV, Barb. Lat. 10043 [16r]. Her excuses chronicle recurring health issues in the 1640s. See BAV, Barb. Lat. 10491, 84r (6 November 1641); 133r (9 March 1642); 151r (23 April 1642); 169r (9 June 1642). On additional notes in her own hand on one of the secretary's letters, see BAV, Barb. Lat. 10043, 38r–39v (29 April 1633).

45. On Taddeo's apartments and possessions and on the new boy among his pages, BAV, Barb. Lat. 10043, 3v (11 March 1633). She was especially concerned about investigating a theft that occurred in the palace, see ibid., 30r (20 April 1633). On the changing of *parati* in her room and the children's room and on the furnishing of the casino at Castel Gandolfo with furnishings from her apartments, see ibid., 35r–35v (24 April 1633). On damage at Monte Rotondo and the harvest in Palestrina, see ibid., 43r (13 November 1641).

46. BAV, Barb. Lat. 10043, 31v (20 April 1633). The pages remain a problem in the 1640s. See ibid., 55r (14 December 1641). The trouble with the servants seemed to intensify due to Taddeo's lengthy absence. Ibid., 205r–206r (12 December 1643).

47. BAV, Barb. Lat. 10043, 9r (19 March 1633). She recounts how she doesn't write as much as she should because she was tired from her care of the children and felt alone without his "oblationi [*sic*] sollevamento et aiuto." She refers to her loneliness in a later letter, noting that her father and Taddeo are the only people she has in the world. Ibid., 21r (12 April 1633). Similar complaints continued in the 1640s, when his absence went on for much longer, and her father had passed away: "io sento grandem.te lassenza [*sic*] di VE." Ibid., 40r (2 November 1641). She also repeats the loss she feels without their combined advice: "io sto qui senza aiuto ni Consiglio. Per che [*sic*] quando

V.E. era lontano che c'era vivo mio Padre di felice memoria mi pareva di havere pur qualche uno in questo mondo per me" (82r [March 29, 1642]).

48. On her purges, see BAV, Barb. Lat. 10043, 26r (16 April 1633); 32r (20 April 1633); 36v (24 April 1633); 47r (13 December 1641). He sent her an extract of cinchona bark as medicine for her ailments. Ibid., 94r–94v (17 May 1642).

49. BAV, Barb. Lat. 10043, 83v (29 March 1642); 115r–115v (12 November 1642); 125v (22 November 1642); 137v (13 December 1642); 157r (6 May 1643).

50. See the psychoanalyst Donald Winnicott, *Holding and Interpretation: Fragment of an Analysis* (New York, 1986), p. 96.

51. Schematic notes are added to the back of Anna's letters, but these are typically brief reminders of the content of her letters. It is clear from her correspondence that she was receiving regular responses from Taddeo. I thank Dr. Luigi Cacciaglia, archivist of the Vatican Library, for his insights on the current state of family letters in the Barberini archives.

52. BAV, Barb. Lat 10043, 198v (31 October 1643).

53. The reference to Camilla in the biography of Taddeo is in BAV, Archivio Barberini Indice IV, 1254, ff.15v–16v. Waddy has transcribed a significant portion of the biography in *Seventeenth-Century Roman Palaces*, appendix 3; she discusses Camilla on p. 130.

54. Valerie Fildes, *Breasts, Bottles, and Babies: A History of Infant Feeding* (Edinburgh, 1986), pp. 30–2. The qualities of a good wet nurse were most explicitly spelled out by Soranus of Epheseus in the first century CE and endured in European culture until the nineteenth century. Ibid., pp. 168–73. For more on wet nursing and childcare among Roman aristocratic women, see Chapter 3.

55. BAV, Barb. Lat. 10043, on the wet nurses, 6r (16 March 1639); 8v (19 March 1639); 11r (29 March 1639); 16r (26 March 1633); 19v (9 April 1633); 22r (12 April 1633); 26r (16 April 1633); 28v (20 April 1633); 33r (23 April 1633); 36r (24 April 1633). On the search for the wet nurses and their shortcomings, 9r (19 March 1633) and 11r (29 March 1639).

56. On Anna's moving to the children's quarters, see BAV, Barb. Lat. 10043, 9v. On their illnesses, ibid., 1r (8 March 1633); 3r (11 March 1633).

57. Ibid., 12r (29 March 1633).

58. Ibid., 9v (19 March 1633); 143r–143v (14 January 1643).

59. Ibid., 143v (14 January 1643).

60. Ibid., 82r (29 March 1642).

61. Ibid., 63v (29 December 1641). On their health and her delight with their good health, ibid., 64r. On remaining health problems with Maffeo, ibid., 81r (29 March 1642). On her disagreements about expenditures, ibid., 22r–23r (12 April 1633).

62. Ibid., 36r (24 April 1633); 83r–83v (29 March 1642). On his "absolute dominion" over her, see ibid., 198r (31 October 1643).

63. BAV, Barb. Lat. 100491, 235r (14 February 1643).

64. BAV, Barb. Lat. 10043, 23r (12 April 1633).

65. Through her hands passed all the letters for his ministers. She read them and imprinted them with Taddeo's seal. Ibid., 52r (14 December 1641).

66. She offered Taddeo an account of her own expenditures, doubtless to illustrate numerically her accountability for Taddeo's affairs. See BAV, Barb. Lat. 10491, 135r–138v (8 March 1642). The letters eventually became a medium

for the transmission of financial information. Ibid., 120r–121v (8 February 1642); 222r (25 January 1643). On her investigation of the financial transactions involved in the seemingly never-ending purchase of Monte Lanico, for which she had to nudge a number of Barberini employees, including the accountant, see BAV, Barb. Lat. 10043, 73r–74v (15 February 1642); 163r (7 June 1642); 226r (25 January 1643); 229r (31 January 1643). Feci and Visceglia also treat the problem of debtors and Anna's attempts to deal with them. See "Tra due famiglie," pp. 268–9.

67. BAV, Barb. Lat. 10043, 128r (29 February 1643).
68. On her critique of servants, see ibid., 71r (11 January 1642). On her advocacy for servants, see BAV, Barb. Lat. 10491, 266r (21 August 1643); 268r (21 August 1643); 290r (10 December 1643); 292r (13 December 1643).
69. BAV, Barb. Lat. 10043, 74r (15 February 1642).
70. Ibid., on absolute padrone and missing Taddeo, 83r–83v (29 March 1642). On Maffeo, ibid., 115r–115v (12 November 1642); 125v (22 November 1642).
71. Waddy stresses the demure nature of their mother, Costanza Barberini, who would not even attend the comedies in the Palazzo Barberini alle Quattro Fontane in the performances exclusively devoted to female audiences. Waddy, *Seventeenth-Century Palaces*, pp. 26–7.
72. BAV, Barb. Lat. 10043, 22r–23r (12 April 1633).
73. Ibid., 23r (12 April 1633).
74. Ibid., 13r–13v (29 March 1633); 20r (9 April 1635).
75. Ibid., 82r (29 March 1642).
76. On the trial of the astrologers, the laws against them, and the rituals against their potential evil on the part of Campanella, see Scott, *Images of Nepotism*, pp. 73–5. For more on the furor over astrological predictions of Urban's death, see Brendan Dooley, *Morandi's Last Prophecy and the End of Renaissance Politics* (Princeton, 2002).
77. Scholars differ on the source of the conflict between the Farnese and the Barberini, that is, the degree to which it was a personal versus a political dispute. On the larger political problems posed by the Farnese, see Pastor, *The History of the Popes*, vol. 29, pp. 383–85. On the personal animosity between the two families, see Scott, *Images of Nepotism*, pp. 6, 11, 18.
78. For summaries of the perils of the conflict for the Barberini, see Laurie Nussdorfer, *Civic Politics in the Rome of Urban VIII* (Princeton, 1992), pp. 208–9, 217–27; Pastor, *History of the Popes*, vol. 29, pp. 386–8, 390, 392, 398.
79. Ibid.
80. Pastor, *History of the Popes*, vol. 30, pp. 18–19, 51; Waddy, *Seventeenth-Century Roman Palaces*, p. 170; Scott, *Images of Nepotism*, pp. 198–9.
81. BAV, Barb. Lat. 10043, 82r (29 March 1642).
82. In 1634, Taddeo returned with his wife and children to the original family palace on the via dei Giubbonari. Waddy surmises, based on contemporary sources, that Taddeo moved because Anna found the new palace damp, whereas the old palace had been healthier for the children and more conducive to the birth of boys. See Waddy, *Seventeenth-Century Roman Palaces*, pp. 154, 242–4). For additional reasons cited by contemporaries, see Scott, *Images of Nepotism*, p. 118. Despite the separation of their living arrangements, Cardinal Francesco and Anna continued to exchange pleasantries, especially at the birth of children. See BAV, Barb. Lat. 10491, 9r–9v (20 October 1631).

83. BAV, Barb. Lat. 10043, 107r–108v (5 July 1642).
84. Among the most detailed requests from Anna to Cardinal Francesco are those in BAV, Barb Lat. 10491, 20r (20 April 1635); 22r (7 October 1635); 28r–28v (28 February 1636); 30r (20 July 1636); 32r (28 July 1636); 35r (23 August 1636); 37r (15 September 1636); 43r–43v (18 April 1637); 49r–50v (15 July 1637); 56r (7 March 1638); 60r–61v (21 April 1638); 76r–76v (11 March 1640). Feci and Visceglia concur that Anna's criticisms likely undermined her relationship with Cardinal Francesco. See "Tra due famiglie," p. 271. For their account of the distance between them when they were away, see ibid., p. 274.
85. BAV, Barb. Lat. 10043, 28v (20 April 1633). By contrast, she wrote to Francesco to inform him about the illness of Taddeo and to seek the Cardinal's advice about physicians and treatments for her ailing husband. BAV, Barb. Lat. 10491, 70r–70v (3 October 1638).
86. BAV, Barb. Lat. 10043, 82r (29 March 1642).
87. BAV, Barb. Lat. 10491, 147r (16 April 1642) and repeated in a second letter of the same day 149r. On rumors, see ibid., 218r (21 January 1643). She used them to follow his movements, if not his return, ibid., 260r (5 August 1643).
88. BAV, Barb. Lat. 10043, 202r (5 December 1643). The tone of the Christmas letter of 1643 echoes the loneliness apparent in her Christmas letter of 1642. Ibid., 188r (24 December 1642).
89. Ibid., 70v (11 January 1642).
90. Ibid., 83r–83v (29 March 1642); 202r (5 December 1643).
91. Ibid., 69r (18 January 1642).
92. On Campanella's vision as origin of the iconography of the painting, see Scott, *Images of Nepotism*, pp. 88–94. On the connection among Filippo Colonna, Tommaso Campanella, and Urban VIII, see ibid., p. 90.
93. For additional insights on Anna's rapport with the Colonna family, based upon documents in the Colonna Archive, see Feci and Visceglia, "Tra due famiglie," pp. 287–91.
94. BAV, Barb. Lat. 10043, 52r (14 December 1641).
95. Ibid., 96r (24 May 1642).
96. Ibid., 45v (13 November 1641); 52r (14 December 1641); 60v (28 December 1641).
97. Ibid., 87r–90v (9 April 1642).
98. Ibid., 88r (annotated reply of Taddeo written on her letter of 9 April 1642); 105r (2 July 1642).
99. Ibid., 87r (second letter of 9 April 1642).
100. Ibid., 83v–84r (29 March 1642). For more on the conflict over the *soglio* and its ceremonial significance for the Colonna, see Feci and Visceglia, "Tra due famiglie," pp. 290–2.
101. BAV, Barb. Lat., 10043, 105r (2 July 1642).
102. Ibid., 145r (14 January 1643).
103. Ibid., 200v (31 October 1643).
104. Ibid., 96r (24 May 1642).
105. See Prospero Colonna, *I Colonna* (Rome, 1927), pp. 266–267.
106. Gianna Pomata, "Practicing Between Earth and Heaven: Women Healers in Seventeenth-Century Bologna," *Dynamis: Acta Hispanica ad Medicinae Scientiarumque Historiam Illustrandam* 19 (1999): 119–43, esp. p. 135.

107. Marilyn Dunn, "Piety and Patronage," p. 645 is the source for the quote. Gigli also narrates the incident, relating that the body of the saint was eventually returned to the chapel from its hiding place in an armoire. Gigli, *Diario Romano*, p. 177.
108. Dunn, "Piety and Patronage," p. 646 and p. 647, note 33.
109. Ibid., p. 653.
110. Dunn dates the vow to the birth of Carlo in 1630, but Anna's letter to Taddeo actually says her resolution to build the convent was about seven years old (dating it to the birth of Nicolò in 1635): "al mio volere maturato da me per lo spazio di sette anni." BAV, Barb. Lat. 10043, 198r (31 October 1643). She may have made several vows, all related in some way to her wish to build a convent to the Virgin Mary.
111. The crucial letter by Anna to Taddeo regarding the convent is BAV, Barb. Lat. 10043, 198r–201r (31 October 1643). Urban VIII's approval of the project is noted in Dunn, "Piety and Patronage," p. 645. Her wish for the papal indulgence is BAV, Barb. Lat. 10043, 200r (31 October 1643).
112. On the convent, BAV, Barb. Lat. 10043, 200v (31 October 1643). On his earlier visit to the Colonna sisters, see BAV, Barb. Lat. 10491, 74r–74v (4 December 1639).
113. "suplicando [sic] VE di promessarmi di fare eseguire subito il detto legato successa la mia morte acciò io habbia la mia sodisfatione [sic] et VE il merito da Dio benedetto." BAV, Barb. Lat 10043, 200v (31 October 1643).
114. Ibid., 199v (31 October 1643).
115. I base my estimate on her statement in the letter that she hoped to pay for the convent with the nearly 20,000 scudi she had already saved or earned in interest, combined with the 18,000 scudi she claimed the Barberini owed her for her dowry. Dunn, however, notes that Anna probably spent as much as 94,000 scudi to construct and furnish the convent. See "Piety and Patronage," p. 653.
116. Pecchiai argues that Anna's claims about the worth of her dowry were mistaken. Although she cited the number 180,000 scudi, Pecchiai notes that the Colonna only paid 67,000 scudi. Pecchiai, *I Barberini*, p. 183. Hence, Anna's claims to 18,000 scudi in her letter to Taddeo are based on 10 percent of the promised dowry, not of the paid sum, which would have given her substantially less money for her religious undertaking (only about 6,700 scudi).
117. BAV, Barb. Lat. 10043, 198r (31 October 1643).
118. Ibid., 200v (31 October 1643).
119. BAV, Barb. Lat 10491, 286r (13 November 1643).
120. BAV, Barb. Lat. 10043, 202r–203v (5 December 1643). See also 210r (21 December 1643).
121. Dunn, "Piety and Patronage," pp. 647–8.
122. BAV, Barb. Lat. 10043, 203v (10 December 1643).
123. Pastor, *The History of the Popes*, vol. 30, pp. 18–19, 51; Waddy, *Seventeenth-Century Roman Palaces*, p. 170; Scott, *Images of Nepotism*, pp. 198–9.
124. The Barberini left Rome gradually. Cardinal Antonio departed first in September 1645, followed by Cardinal Francesco, Taddeo, and the four children of Anna and Taddeo in January 1646. See Pastor, *The History of the Popes*, vol. 30, pp. 52–5, 57–8; Emete Rossi, "La Fuga del Cardinale Antonio

Barberini," *Archivio della Società Romana di Storia Patria* 59 (1936): 303–27; Scott, *Images of Nepotism*, p. 198.

125. Pecchiai, *I Barberini*, p. 184.
126. Ibid., 183–4.
127. Ibid., 183.
128. Ibid., 184.
129. Ibid., 186.
130. Ibid., 185.
131. BAV, Archivio Barberini, Ind. IV, 123. The date of the defense was 20 February 1646. The reading of the defense was done by Anna Colonna's cousin, Cesare Colonna. See Feci and Visceglia, "Tra due famiglie," p. 299.
132. On the misgivings on the part of the Colonna brothers about her defense, see Feci and Visceglia, "Tra due famiglie," p. 303. On the doubts of the Roman Senate on the Barberini–Colonna bond, see ibid., p. 300.
133. On her return, see BAV, Archivio Barberini IV, 47; "of some service," Barb. Lat. 10491, 377r (5 April 1647).
134. On Anna's activities in the rural fiefs, see Castiglione, *Patrons and Adversaries: Nobles and Villagers in Italian Politics, 1640–1760* (New York, 2005), pp. 33–4.
135. On the return of the Barberini to Rome and Cardinal Francesco's direction of the family, see Pastor, *The History of the Popes*, vol. 30, p. 64; Pecchiai, *I Barberini*, pp. 214–15.
136. BAV, Barb. Lat. 10043, 96r (24 May 1642).
137. Ago, *Carriere e clientele*, esp. pp. 67–71.
138. For more on Lucrezia Barberini, see Groppi, "La Sindrome Malinconica di Lucrezia Barberini D'Este."
139. On Anna's separate residence from the Barberini, see Waddy, *Seventeenth-Century Roman Palaces*, pp. 29, 170.
140. Anna remained closest to the youngest child, Nicolò. Waddy, *Seventeenth-Century Roman Palaces*, p. 170; Lodispoto, "Anna Colonna Barberini ed il suo monumento," pp. 467–70. She named him as her heir, though he eventually passed the inheritance to his brothers, under considerable pressure from them. See Feci and Visceglia, "Tra due famiglie," pp. 316–18.
141. See Calvi, *Il contratto morale*, esp. pp. 70, 159–61.
142. Waddy, *Seventeenth-Century Roman* Palaces, p. 29. For more on Anna's life in widowhood, see Feci and Visceglia, "Tra due famiglie," pp. 310–18.

2   The Interests Common to Us All: Olimpia Giustiniani on the Governing of the Roman Aristocratic Family

1. For an analysis of the strength and the limits of the *fedecommesso*, see Maura Piccialuti, *L'immortalità dei beni: Fedecommessi e primogeniture a Roma nei secoli xvii e xviii* (Rome, 1999). A compelling case study that also offers a broad overview of such inheritances and their role in creating and sustaining families is Thomas Kuehn, "*Fideicommissum* and Family: The Orsini di Bracciano," *Viator* 39.2 (2008): 323–41.
2. As Cardinal Francesco Junior Barberini (1662–1738) lay dying in the family palace in 1738, his accountants buzzed over his financial records to balance

his revenues against his expenses. The cardinal's books were 100,000 scudi short. Biblioteca Apostolica Vaticana [hereafter BAV], Archivio Barberini, Indice IV, 961.

3. BAV, Archivio Barberini, Indice II, 2742. Her birthdate is noted as 18 May 1641. Olimpia Giustiniani has drawn less scholarly interest than her more famous mother-in-law, Anna Colonna. See Caroline Castiglione, "Accounting for Affection: Battles between Aristocratic Mothers and Sons in Eighteenth-Century Rome," *Journal of Family History* XXV (2000): 405–31. Subsequently, Renata Ago further emphasized the significance of Olimpia Giustiniani's possessions to her identity. See "Le Stanze di Olimpia. La principessa Giustiniani Barberini e il linguaggio delle cose," in *I linguaggi del potere nell'età barocca*, vol. 2, *Donne e sfera pubblica*, ed. Francesca Cantù (Rome, 2009), pp. 171–95. Ago offers valuable insights on the condition of Olimpia's apartments and their objects (pp. 182–7) and the ceding of her apartments to her son Urbano and his wife in 1690 (p. 187). Both our approaches concur on the link between objects and identity. See Ago, p. 192; Castiglione, "Accounting for Affection," and the conclusion of this chapter.

4. See Chapter 5 of this volume.

5. Archivio Doria Pamphilj [hereafter ADP], Archiviolo, Busta 349, 197r (4 August 1657).

6. Ago also makes specific reference to the "intransigence" and the "point of honor" of the father-patriarch of the family. See *Carriere e clientele nella Roma barocca* (Bari, 1990), p. 71.

7. Lawrence Stone was the pioneer in this approach in his *Crisis of the Aristocracy, 1558–1641* (London, 1965). During the seventeenth century, the great noble families rescued themselves from financial chaos. The poorer ones derogated into the ranks of commoners. Although the numbers of nobles decreased, the caste as a whole solidified its position in society for centuries to come. See Jonathan Dewald, *The European Nobility: 1400–1800* (Cambridge, 1996), esp. chapters 3 and 4.

8. For some of the dilemmas raised by conceptualizing the family as a collective organization that has an individual will, see "Family Strategy: A Dialogue," *Historical Methods* 20 (1987): 113–25, with essays by Leslie Page Moch, Nancy Folbre, Daniel Scott Smith, Laurel L. Cornell, and Louise Tilly.

9. Hans Medick and David Warren Sabean, "Interest and Emotion in Family and Kinship Studies: A Critique of Social History and Anthropology," in their anthology, *Interest and Emotion: Essays in the Study of Family and Kinship* (Cambridge, 1984), pp. 9–27. On the oscillations in family sentiments and family strategies, see Linda Pollock, "Rethinking Patriarchy and the Family in Seventeenth-Century England," *Journal of Family History* 23 (1998): 3–27.

10. Gender was of early interest to scholars of Italy, although they did not all employ the word "gender" in their analyses. See Christiane Klapisch-Zuber, *Women, Family, and Ritual in Renaissance Italy*, trans. Lydia G. Cochrane (Chicago, 1985); Renata Ago, "Giochi di squadra: Uomini e donne nelle famiglie nobili del xvii secolo," in *Signori, patrizi, cavalieri in Italia centro-meridionale nell'età moderna*, ed. Maria Antonietta Visceglia (Bari, 1992); idem, "Maria Spada Veralli, la buona moglie," in *Barocco al femminile*, ed. Giulia Calvi (Bari, 1992), pp. 51–70.; idem, *Carriere e clientele nella Roma barocca* (Bari, 1990); idem, "Ruoli familiari e statuto giuridico," *Quaderni Storici*

88 (1995): 111–33; Giulia Calvi, *Il contratto morale: Madri e figli nella Toscana moderna* (Bari, 1994); idem, "Reconstructing the Family: Widowhood and Remarriage in Tuscany in the Early Modern Period," in *Marriage in Italy, 1300–1650*, ed. Trevor Dean and K. J. P. Lowe (Cambridge, 1991), pp. 275–96; Irene Fosi and Maria Antonietta Visceglia, "Marriage and Politics at the Papal Court in the Sixteenth and Seventeenth Centuries," ibid., pp. 197–224. See also the volume of *Quaderni Storici* 86 (1994) devoted to the family: "Costruire la Parentela," ed. Renata Ago, Maura Palazzi, and Gianna Pomata.

11. On male honor in Rome, see Ago, "Giochi di squadra," esp. pp. 260–3.

12. BAV, Archivio Barberini, Indice II, 2756: Letter of Olimpia to Maffeo Barberini.

13. Scholarly literature on the threat of blood relatives to each other's honor is still rare, aside from daughters threatening the honor of the family by a sexual transgression. James Farr reminds us that even among French artisans, "honor was a collective possession, shared by all members of the family." *Hands of Honor, Artisans and their World in Dijon, 1550–1650* (Ithaca, 1988), p. 193. Elizabeth S. Cohen and Thomas Cohen note the uniqueness of the battle between two brothers over honor in their *Daily Life in Renaissance Italy* (Westport, CT, 2001), p. 98. Frederick Robertson Bryson similarly assessed the situation in the sixteenth-century manuals about honor: "there could be no insult between a father and his son; for in questions of honor the two were considered to be one." *The Point of Honor in Sixteenth-Century Italy: An Aspect of the Life of the Gentleman* (New York, 1935), p. 33. It may be the peculiarities of the Roman aristocratic families that produced the honor conflict here described, but the events chronicled in this chapter suggest that one family member could indeed jeopardize the honor of the other. For an analysis of the epistolary dynamic between Roman aristocratic brothers, see Benedetta Borello, "Parlare e tacere di potere. La conversazione epistolare tra fratelli aristocratici (secoli XVII–XVIII)," in *I linguaggi del potere nell'età barocca*, vol. 2, *Donne e sfera pubblica*, ed. Francesca Cantù (Rome, 2009), pp. 143–69. Borello analyzes a few specific examples from Roman letters to underscore the importance of honor and hierarchy among siblings. Ibid., pp. 149–53.

14. BAV, Archivio Barberini, Indice II, 2756: Letter of Olimpia to Maffeo Barberini.

15. A. Merola, "Francesco Barberini," in *Dizionario Biografico degli Italiani* (Rome, 1964), vol. 6, pp. 164–5. Merola gives Francesco Senior's death date as 10 December 1679.

16. BAV, Archivio Barberini, Indice II, 2756: Letter of 1675 from Olimpia to the nuns of the Convent of the Incarnation in Rome.

17. BAV, Archivio Barberini, Indice II, 2756: Letter of Olimpia to Maffeo Barberini.

18. Ibid.

19. BAV, Archivio Barberini, Indice I, 837, on Cardinal Francesco's funeral.

20. Jonathan Dewald, *Aristocratic Experience and the Origins of Modern Culture: France, 1570–1715* (Berkeley and Los Angeles), pp. 69–73, 99–103.

21. For an excellent survey of noble income, see Richard Ferraro, "The Nobility of Rome, 1560–1700: A Study of Its Composition, Wealth, and Investments" (University of Wisconsin-Madison, 1994). A brief overview of the impact of the easing of credit on the expenditure is in Dewald, *European Nobility*, pp. 103–4.

22. S. Andretta, "Francesco Colonna," in *Dizionario degli Italiani*, vol. 6, pp. 303–4, and Prospero Colonna, *I Colonna* (Rome, 1927), pp. 266–7. Francesco Colonna

sold his prestigious fief of Palestrina to the Barberini in 1629. See Chapter 1 of this volume.

23. Pio Pecchiai puts the cost of the two spectacles at 60,000 scudi. They would have had to have been bought on credit, considering the financial state of the family. See Pio Pecchiai, *I Barberini* (Rome, 1959), p. 224.

24. Barbara McClung Hallman, *Italian Cardinals, Reform, and the Church as Property* (Berkeley, 1985), pp. 164–8.

25. Teodoro Amayden, *A New Relation of Rome as to the Government of the City; the Noble Families Thereof... Taken out of one of the Choicest Cabinets of Rome; and English'd by Gio. Torriano, an Italian, and Professor of the Italian Tongue* (London, 1664), p. 10.

26. Richard Ferraro, "Nobility of Rome, 1560–1700: A Study of its Composition, Wealth, and Investments" (PhD diss., University of Wisconsin-Madison, 1994), pp. 139–42. Ferraro also provides a valuable overview of more than one hundred families who converted their form of entail from *fedecommesso* to primogeniture. See p. 205, note 75.

27. On the "absorption" of properties into primogeniture, see Ferraro, "Nobility of Rome," p. 211, note 78.

28. Jean Delumeau, *Vie économique et sociale de Rome dans la seconde moitié du XVIe Siècle*, 2 vols. (Paris, 1957–59), vol. 1, pp. 471, 475.

29. Delumeau, *Vie économique et sociale*, vol. 2, p. 817.

30. Delumeau, *Vie économique et sociale*, vol. 1, p. 484.

31. Delumeau, *Vie économique et sociale*, vol. 1, pp. 457, 471, 475.

32. For a more complete analysis of the women in the Congregation of the Barons archive, see the Introduction to this volume.

33. Delumeau, *Vie économique et sociale*, vol. 1, pp. 471, 475; vol. 2: 804–5.

34. Pecchiai, *I Barberini*, p. 227.

35. For more on the complexities of Rome's institutions, see "The Making of the *Mater Litigans* in Rome," in the Introduction to this volume. Good institutional overviews of the papal bureaucracy include Laurie Nussdorfer, "Curia and City," in her *Civic Politics in the Rome of Urban VIII* (Princeton, 1992), pp. 46–50; Hanns Gross, "The Government: State and City" in his *Rome in the Age of Enlightenment* (Cambridge, 1990), pp. 40–54. In Italian, see Niccolò Del Re, *La Curia Romana. Lineamenti storico-giuridici*, 3rd ed. (Rome, 1970), and Maria Grazia Pastura Ruggiero, *Le Reverenda Camera Apostolica e i suoi archvi (secoli XV–XVIII)* (Rome, 1984). For a survey of juridical institutions, see Irene Fosi, *Papal Justice: Subjects and Courts in the Papal State, 1500–1750*, trans. Thomas V. Cohen (Washington, 2011).

36. See Nussdorfer, *Civic Politics*, p. 48; Ruggiero, *Reverenda Camera Apostolica*, pp. 211–17.

37. The phrase is Laurie Nussdorfer's. See her chapter by that title in her *Civic Politics*, pp. 45–53.

38. BAV, Archivio Barberini, Indice II, 2776, 5r. Among Urbano's debts listed at that time was the dowry of his first wife, Cornelia Zeno Ottoboni, and there seemed to be little doubt in his mother's mind that he would soon exhaust the dowry of his second wife, Felice Ventimiglia Pignatelli d'Aragona, as well. On the wives of Urbano, see Pecchiai, *I Barberini*, p. 224.

39. Urbano's demands to alienate property continued periodically up to his death in 1722.

40. BAV, Archivio Barberini, Indice II, 2772, for roughly written statements of complaint; and ibid., 2773, for an accounting of what the Barberini owed her in in 1697.

40. BAV, Archivio Barberini, Indice II, 2772, for roughly written statements of complaint; and ibid., 2773, for an accounting of what the Barberini owed her in in 1697.
41. BAV, Archivio Barberini, Indice II, 2776. The archivist dates the document 1702, but I could not find any internal evidence that would suggest that it was written at that time. A comment on folio 2r implies that the first part of the document was written in the fall of 1697, and that the original copy in her own hand has been deposited with Giuseppe Isoldi, *auditore* of Monsignor Grimaldi. The Vatican Library document is a copy of that original. The second part of the document (which is a list of the properties Urbano had "consumed") contains the reference to a letter from Cardinal Francesco asking his brother not to sell Monte Rotondo (5r).
42. BAV, Archivio Barberini, Indice II, 2776. For other examples of Olimpia's handwriting, see BAV, AB, Indice II, 2756. The writing in these letters matches the annotating hand in BAV, Archivio Barberini, Indice II, 2776.
43. Ibid., 1r.
44. Ibid., 1v.
45. Ludwig von Pastor, *The History of the Popes from the Close of the Middle Ages*, trans. Ernest Graf et al. (London, 1891–1953), vol. 30, p. 64. See also Chapter 1 of this volume.
46. Pastor, *History of the Popes*, vol. 30, p. 92.
47. According to Mirka Beneš, Donna Olimpia Pamphilj, sister-in-law of Innocent X, organized the marriage of her niece to Maffeo Barberini. See her "Villa Pamphilj (1630–1670): Family, Gardens, and Land in Papal Rome" (PhD diss., Yale University, 1989), p. 236.
48. For the origins and purposes of the very negative contemporary opinion on Olimpia Maidalchini, see Marina D'Amelia, "La nuova Agrippina. Olimpia Maidalchini Pamphilj e la tirannia femminile nell'immaginario politico del Seicento," in *I Linguaggi del potere nell'età barocca*, vol. 2, *Donne e sfera pubblica*, ed. Francesca Cantù (Rome, 2009), pp. 45–95. On her patronage and political maneuvers, see idem, "Nepotismo al femminile. Il caso di Olimpia Maidalchini Pamphilj," in *La Nobiltà romana in età moderna*, ed. Maria Antonietta Visceglia (Rome, 2001), pp. 353–99.
49. Pietro Ercole Visconti, *Città e famiglie nobili e celebri dello stato Pontificio: Dizionario Storico* (Rome, 1847), vol. 4, p. 762.
50. The libretto was by Giulio Rospigliosi, the future Clement IX. See Margaret Murata, *Operas for the Papal Court, 1631–1668* (Ann Arbor, 1981), p. 4. Murata valiantly chronicles the plot (pp. 348–9).
51. On the significance of the dowry and the jewels for women, see Olwen Hufton, *The Prospect Before Her* (New York, 1996), pp. 227–8. For the Roman scene, see Renata Ago, *Il Gusto delle Cose* (Rome, 2006). For specific insight on Olimpia's conception of the jewels given to her at her wedding as belonging to her, and identified as such in inventories, see Ago, "Le Stanze di Olimpia," pp. 190–2.
52. BAV, Archivio Barberini, Indice II, 2776, 1r.
53. Ferraro, "Nobility of Rome," pp. 145–6; Ago, "Ruoli Familiari," pp. 126–30.
54. BAV, Archivio Barberini, Indice II, 2776, 2r.
55. BAV, Archivio Barberini, Indice II, 2756: Letter of 1675 from Olimpia to the nuns of the Convent of the Incarnation in Rome.

56. Ibid., 1v.
57. Ibid., 5r.
58. Ibid., 3r.
59. Ibid., 4v.
60. Ibid., 3r.
61. Ibid., 2r.
62. Ibid., 2v.
63. Ibid., 1r–1v.
64. For a summary of anti-Louis positions in Europe, see Peter Burke, *The Fabrication of Louis XIV* (New Haven, 1992), pp. 137–42.
65. Pastor, *History of the Popes*, vol. 32, pp. 246–342. On the public knowledge of the strain between the two capitals, see pp. 263–4. On the escalating tensions between the French King and Pope over ecclesiastical appointments, see Richard Place, "Bavaria and the Collapse of Louis XIV's German Policy, 1687–1688," *The Journal of Modern History* 49.3 (1977): 369–-93; see also Jean Orcibal, *Louis XIV contre Innocent XI: Les appels au future concile de 1688 et l'opinion française* (Paris, 1949). Rome had its own critique of "despotic government," launched against women who were believed to have usurped authority. For a survey of such literature against Olimpia Maidalchini, see D'Amelia, "La nuova Agrippina," pp. 47–8, 51, 56.
66. BAV, Archivio Barberini, Indice II, 2776, 3r.
67. For the cultivation of the land as a suitable aristocratic pursuit, see Beneš, "Villa Pamphilj (1630–1670)"; Tracy L. Ehrlich, "... dall'Agricoltura venne la Nobiltà ...": The Rural Landscape of the Villa Mondragone near Frascati," in *Villas and Gardens in Early Modern Italy and France*, ed. Mirka Beneš and Dianne Harris (Cambridge, 2001), pp. 114–37. The Roman fascination for flower and fruit tree cultivation was part of a larger European pattern. See Elizabeth Hyde, "Use and Reception," in *A Cultural History of Gardens in the Renaissance, 1400–1650*, ed. Elizabeth Hyde (London, 2013), pp. 99–125, esp., pp. 102–4.
68. BAV, Archivio Barberini, Indice II, 2772, 14r.
69. BAV, Archivio Barberini, Indice II, 2776, 2v. For the pawning of items dating back to her husband's time, see her statement in BAV, Archivio Barberini, Indice II, 2759.
70. BAV, Archivio Barberini, Indice II, 2776, 2v.
71. Ibid., 3r.
72. BAV, Archivio Barberini, Indice II, 2772, 17r–17v.
73. BAV, Archivio Barberini, Indice II, 2776, from a list of Olimpia's grievances, apparently annotated in her hand.
74. See Ferraro, "Nobility of Rome," p. 211, note 78. See also BAV, Archivio Barberini, Indice IV, 1212.
75. Ferraro, "Nobility of Rome," p. 499.
76. This contrasts with men's tendencies to link their honor to that of the wealth, "acquired without the possessor's own labor." Bryson, *Point of Honor*, p. 16. Venetian women held views similar to Olimpia's regarding their property and their handiwork. See Federica Ambrosini, "Toward a Social History of Women in Venice," in *Venice Reconsidered*, ed. John Martin and Dennis Romano (Baltimore, 2000), pp. 420–53 (p. 435). On women's attention to objects rather than property in their wills, see Sandra Cavallo, "Proprietà o possesso?

Composizione e controllo dei beni delle donne a Torino (1650–1710)," in *Le Ricchezze delle donne: Diritti patrimoniali e poteri familiari in Italia (XIII–XIX secc.),* ed. Giulia Calvi and Isabelle Chabot (Turin, 1998), pp. 187–207.

77. BAV, Archivio Barberini, Indice IV, 368.

78. Urbano criticized Olimpia for being the only one to "enjoy" Palestrina, but she claims that this wasn't true. If she had taken over Palestrina, the financial obligations related to it would scarcely leave her sufficient money to support herself.

79. BAV, Archivio Barberini, Indice, II, 2785, 14v.

80. BAV, Archivio Barberini, Indice II, 4408. The agreed upon sum in 1698 was 2250 scudi per year.

81. BAV, Archivio Barberini, Indice, II, 2785. The text exists in draft form. The draft differs slightly from the better copy in its closing. All folio numbers given below refer to the folio numbers that I assigned the better of the two copies.

82. On her dowry donation during Monte Rotondo crisis, see BAV, Archivio Barberini, Indice II, 2253.

83. BAV, Archivio Barberini, Indice, II, 2785. The transcription of the letter begins on 19r.

84. Ibid., 11r.

85. Ibid., 11r.

86. Ibid., 26r.

87. Ibid., 17r–17v.

88. Ibid., 8r.

89. Ibid., 17v–18r.

90. Ibid., 9v.

91. Ibid., 10r.

92. Ibid., 10r; a description of Corcolle in the Barberini archive lists its size as about 559 rubbia, or approximately 2,515 acres. See BAV, Archivio Barberini, Indice II, 1183.

93. BAV, Archivio Barberini, Indice, II, 2785, 10v–11r.

94. Ibid., 11r.

95. Ibid. A document from 1720 explains more clearly (if not more accurately) how Francesco succeeded in saving Corcolle. Francesco combined all the outstanding debts against the tenuta into new loans (*censi*) amounting to 242,455 scudi, for which he took total responsibility. He paid 40,000 scudi in interest on these and other debts and agreed to satisfy up to 70,000 scudi for the outstanding debts. In exchange, Urbano gave all of the income related to Palestrina, the Terra di Capranica, Castel S. Pietro, and the jurisdictional tenuta of Corcolle, with its "Casale, Mill, and half wooded lands." What remained for Urbano was the income from the baronial jurisdiction and chancellery, *danno dato,* and palace. Urbano had the option of recuperating all the income on the lands in question if he could ever succeed in repaying Francesco, which, given Urbano's previous financial success, was extremely unlikely. See BAV, Archivio Barberini, Indice II, 2281. This was one attempt by Francesco to stem the tide of Urbano's debt. See the juggling by the cardinal as early as 1695 in BAV, Archivio Barberini, Indice II, 4399.

96. BAV, AB, Indice II, 2785, 10v.

97. Archivio di Stato (Roma) [hereafter ASR], Congregazione dei Monti e dei Baroni, vol. 12.

98. BAV, Archivio Barberini, Indice II, 2543.
99. Ferraro, "Nobility of Rome," p. 883.
100. He combined this critique with the view that his mother had posed a danger to the *casa*: she was too independent and too rigid in her ideas (he refers to her demand for a yearly cash payment as a "fixation" *[fissatione]*). See BAV, Archivio Barberini Indice II, 2785, 16v.
101. Ibid., 3r. A separate document contains a copy of the agreement about the dowry that supports Francesco's statement – 70,000 scudi was the actual amount, rather than the stated 100,000 scudi of the marriage agreement. See BAV, Archivio Barberini, Indice II, 2743.
102. Ann Christiansen and Barbara Sebek, "The Traffic in/by Women: Placing Women in Real and Symbolic Economies," in *Attending to Early Modern Women*, ed. Susan Amussen and Adele Seefe (Newark, 1998), pp. 105–7.
103. BAV, Archivio Barberini, Indice, II, 2785, 4r.
104. On the jewels in Francesco's account, see ibid., 3v–9v, *passim*.
105. Ibid., 4v.
106. Ibid., 6v.
107. Ibid., 7r.
108. Innocent XII authorized the sale in 1699, and the estate passed to Francesco Grillo. See Mario Tosi, *La società romana dalla feudalità al patriziato (1816–1853)* (Rome, 1968), p. 153.
109. BAV, Archivio Barberini, Indice, II, 2785, 6v–7r.
110. Ibid., 6r–7v.
111. Ibid., 8r.
112. Ibid.
113. Ibid., 8v–9r.
114. Ibid.
115. Ibid.
116. Ibid., 13r–13v.
117. Ibid., 15r.
118. Ibid., 15v–16r.
119. Ibid., 17v; 26r.
120. Ibid., 16r–16v.
121. Ibid., 25r.
122. Ibid., 16v–17r.
123. Ibid., 17v–18r.
124. BAV, Archivio Barberini, Indice II, 2543.
125. For a persuasive interpretation of how noble families prioritized such choices, see the treatment of the Caracciolo family by Tommaso Astarita, *The Continuity of Feudal Power: The Caracciolo di Briena in Spanish Naples* (Cambridge, 1992).
126. Antonio Adami, *Il Novitiato del Maestro di Casa* (Rome, 1636); Bartolomeo Frigerio, *L'Economo Prudente* (Rome, 1629).
127. Adami, *Il Novitiato del Maestro di Casa*, pp. 47–8, 61.
128. Francesco Liberati, *Il Perfetto Maestro di Casa* (Rome, 1658, 1665, 1668). The Barberini library contains the ottavo edition printed by Bernabò in Rome in 1658. It has not been possible to determine when this book entered the Barberini library. It is not in the inventory compiled in 1681 (Index Bibliothecae Qua Franciscus Barberinus S.R.E. Cardinalis Vicecancellarius Magnificentissimus suae Familiae Ad Quirinalem Aedes) but it is listed in

the nineteenth-century inventory of the family's books. I am grateful to Massimo Ceresa and Christine Grapfzinger of the Vatican Library for their help in understanding the history of the family's library.

129. Patricia Waddy, *Seventeenth-Century Roman Palaces: Use and the Art of the Plan* (New York and Cambridge, MA, 1990), pp. 281–90.
130. Ferraro, "Nobility of Rome," pp. 493–535.
131. BAV, Archivio Barberini, Indice II, 2776, from a second list of Olimpia's grievances, annotated in Olimpia's hand. For more on the significance of objects to identity, especially in the wills of women and cadet sons, see Ago, *Il Gusto delle cose.*
132. BAV, Archivio Barberini, Indice II, 2785, 12r. For more on the significance of friendship to European nobles, see Dewald, "Friendship, Love, and Civility," in *Aristocratic Experience and the Origins of Modern Culture.*
133. Calvi, *Il contratto morale*, pp. 29–32.

3   At the Nexus of Impossibility: The Medical and the Maternal in Seventeenth-Century Rome

1. I thank Richard Parks and the other fellows of the Cogut Humanities Center at Brown University (2013–14) for their comments on this chapter. I am indebted to Hal Cook for his generous advice on the history of medicine and to Evie Lincoln for her insights on medical practice. David Konstan offered early and invaluable insight on the study of emotion in past cultures. Participants at the following institutions and conferences sharpened my thinking on women and medicine: History Department Seminar, University of South Florida and the Renaissance Society of America Conference.
2. For health and illness as contentious familial issues, see Sandra Cavallo and Tessa Storey, *Healthy Living in Late Renaissance Italy* (Oxford, 2013), p. 279.
3. Marina D'Amelia, "Becoming a Mother in the Seventeenth Century: The Experience of a Roman Noblewoman," in *Time, Space, and Women's Lives in Early Modern Europe*, ed. Anne Jacobson Schutte, Thomas Kuehn, and Silvana Seidel Menchi (Kirksville, MO, 2001), pp. 223–44.
4. Archivio Doria Pamphilj, Archiviolo, 349, 197r (4 August 1657).
5. On the paucity of such sources for southern Italy, see David Gentilcore, *Healers and Healing in Early Modern Italy* (Manchester, 1998), pp. x, 177–202. On epistolary sources as materials for medical history, see Cavallo and Storey, *Healthy Living*, p. 56. On the dilemmas of such sources, see Willemijn Ruberg, "The Letter as Medicine: Health and Illness in Dutch Daily Correspondence 1770–1850," *Social History of Medicine* 23.3 (2010): 492–508.

   Eleonora's letters are in the Archivio Segreto Vaticano [hereafter ASV], Archivio Boncompagni Ludovisi, busta 899 and busta 900. Busta 900 is identified as containing letters from an administrator to Ippolita Ludovisi, but it contains Eleonora's letters as well. See Gianni Venditti with Beatrice Quaglieri, *Archivio Boncompagni Ludovisi. Collectanea Archivi Vaticani* (Vatican City, 2008) vol. IV, p. 249. Busta 899 is without folio numbers, so all citations contain a date only as a reference. Busta 900 contains both folio numbers and dates for the letters.
6. ASV, Archivio Boncompagni Ludovisi, 900, 66r (an undated letter, likely from the summer of 1686).

7. David Gentilcore, "The Organisation of Medical Practice in Malpighi's Italy," in *Marcello Malpighi: Anatomist and Physician*, ed. Domenico Bertoloni Meli (Florence, 1997), esp. pp. 107–8; Gianna Pomata, "Practicing Between Earth and Heaven: Women Healers in Seventeenth-Century Bologna," *Dynamis: Acta Hispanica ad Medicinae Scientiarumque Historiam Illustrandam* 19 (1999): 119–43, esp. pp. 121–3, 125.

8. On the role of surgeons in the treatment of infants through the sixteenth century, see Valerie Fildes, *Wet Nursing: A History from Antiquity to the Present* (Oxford, 1988), p. 69. On the limited attention of English physicians to children in the Middle Ages, see Valerie Fildes, *Breasts, Bottles and Babies: A History of Infant Feeding* (Edinburgh, 1986), p. 47. For similar limitations among Italian physicians, see James Bruce Ross, "The Middle-Class Child in Urban Italy, Fourteenth to Early Sixteenth Century," in *The History of Childhood*, ed. Lloyd De Mause, (London, 1974), pp. 183–228, esp. p. 210. Care of infants is treated in most detail in midwifery texts until the eighteenth century, when pediatric texts begin to appear. See Fildes, *Breasts, Bottles and Babies*, p. 134.

9. For more on Anna Colonna, see Chapter 1.

10. Pomata, "Practicing Between Earth and Heaven," pp. 130–1; Tessa Storey, "Face Waters, Oils, Love Magic and Poison: Making and Selling Secrets in Early Modern Rome," in *Secrets and Knowledge in Medicine and Science, 1500–1800*, ed. Elaine Leong and Alisha Rankin (Burlington, VT, 2011) pp. 143–63. Storey argues that books of secrets were largely produced for and by men in Italy, in contrast to their use by women in Spain and England (p. 145). Yet, one of the more successful books of secrets in Italy seems to have been the work of a woman. Chicca Gagliardo has located eight editions of Isabella Cortese's book: *I secreti della signora Isabella Cortese ne' quali si contengono cose minerali, medicinali, arteficiose & alchimiche et molte de l'arte profumatoria* (Milan, 1995), p. 7. In the introduction to their recent volume on secrets and medical knowledge, Elaine Leong and Alisha Rankin suggest that the gender identity of Cortese remains a mystery. See "Secrets and Knowledge," in Elaine Leong and Alisha Rankin, *Secrets and Knowledge in Medicine and Science, 1500–1800* (Burlington, VT, 2011), p. 17. William Eamon concludes instead that Cortese's identity was female and noble. See his article, "How to Read a Book of Secrets," in ibid., esp. pp. 28–9.

11. Pomata, "Practicing Between Earth and Heaven;" Montserrat Cabré, "Women or Healers?: Household Practices and the Categories of Health Care in Late Medieval Iberia," *Bulletin of the History of Medicine* 82.1 (2008): 18–51.

12. On the attention to health by women in the Veralli-Spada family, see Cavallo and Storey, *Healthy Living*, p. 57. For an analysis of another Roman matron, Maria Spada, who was a "medically informed aristocratic lady," see ibid., pp. 59–61.

13. A constellation of secondary work has appeared in recent decades which helps us construct the medical practices of Rome, including at its highest intellectual levels. See Richard Palmer, "Medicine at the Papal Court in the Sixteenth Century," in *Medicine at the Courts of Europe, 1500–1837*, ed. Vivian Nutton (London, 1990), pp. 49–78; Maria Pia Donato and Jill Kraye, eds. *Conflicting Duties: Science, Medicine and Religion in Rome, 1550–1770* (London, 2003); Nancy Siraisi, "*Historiae*, Natural History, Roman Antiquity, and Some Roman Physicians," in *Historia: Empiricism and Erudition in Early*

Modern Europe, ed. Gianna Pomata and Nancy Siriaisi (Cambridge, 2005), pp. 325–54; Elisa Andretta, *Roma medica: anatomie d'un système médical au XVIe siècle* (Rome, 2011). Silvia De Renzi has uncovered the world of elite Roman physicians and their clients in several recent studies: "Medical Competence, Anatomy and the Polity in Seventeenth-Century Rome," *Renaissance Studies* 21.4 (2007): 79–95; "A Career in Manuscripts: Genres and Purposes of a Physician's Writing in Rome, 1600–1630," *Italian Studies* 66.2 (2011): 234–48; "Tales from Cardinals' Deathbeds: Medical Hierarchy, Courtly Etiquette and Authority in the Counter Reformation," in Être médecin à la cour: Italie, France et Espagne, XIII-XVIII siècles, ed. Elisa Andretta and Marylin Nicoud, (Florence, 2013). On medical knowledge among Rome's prostitutes, see Storey,"Face Waters, Oils, Love Magic and Poison."

14. Gentilcore, "The Organisation of Medical Practice," pp. 99–100.
15. Pomata, "Practicing Between Earth and Heaven," p. 123.
16. ASV, Archivio Boncompagni Ludovisi, 900, 80r (18 October 1688). Eleonora and her husband placed such value on a good physician and surgeon that they sent both to their daughter in Mirandola, rather than have her rely on the locals.
17. ASV, Archivio Boncompagni Ludovisi, 899 (7 September 1686); ASV, Archivio Boncompagni Ludovisi, 900, 76r (12 September 1688).
18. ASV, Archivio Boncompagni Ludovisi, 331, fascicolo 11, 57r, 58v.
19. On the duration of the winter snows, see ASV, Archivio Boncompagni Ludovisi, 899 (24 April 1687).
20. ASV, Archivio Boncompagni Ludovisi, 906, 18r (9 September 1681).
21. Ibid., 40r (25 October 1681).
22. ASV, Archivio Boncompagni Ludovisi, 899 (8 September 1685; 14 June 1686; 3 July 1686).
23. Ibid. (13 October 1684).
24. ASV, Archivio Boncompagni Ludovisi, 900, 130r–130v (18 March 1688). For more on the Boncompagni family's collective admiration of Ippolita, see ibid., 132r, (6 March 1688).
25. ASV, Archivio Boncompagni Ludovisi, 900, 118r (21 June 1688).
26. ASV, Archivio Boncompagni Ludovisi, 899 (6 September 1686). For a similar comment see ASV, Archivio Boncompagni Ludovisi, 900, 135v (10 February 1688).
27. ASV, Archivio Boncompagni Ludovisi, 899 (1 September 1685).
28. Agricultural products allowed Eleonora to provide gifts to her own social circle by sharing them with others: ASV, Archivio Boncompagni Ludovisi, 900, 147v (14 January 1688). For more on the bounty of fish and agricultural produce: ASV, Archivio Boncompagni Ludovisi, 899 (24 January 1685; 24 March 1685 [both miscatalogued in packet of letters "1687–1689"]; 31 October 1687; 15 December 1687; ASV, Archivio Boncompagni Ludovisi, 900, 136v (10 February 1688); 124v (24 April 1688); 81r (27 September 1688); 157r (7 December 1690).

Exchanges of other items are chronicled in ASV, Archivio Boncompagni Ludovisi, 899 (7 September 1684; 27 September 1684; 14 September 1685; 19 September 1685; 5 November 1685; 6 November 1685; 3 February 1686; 31 May 1686; 12 July 1686; 30 July 1686; 2 August 1686; 24 August 1686;

6 September 1686; 6 December 1686); ASV, Archivio Boncompagni Ludovisi, 900, 76r (12 September 1688).

29. ASV, Archivio Boncompagni Ludovisi, 899 (9 March 1685; 24 March 1685 [both miscatalogued in packet of letters "1687–1689"]; 21 November 1687). In ASV, Archivio Boncompagni Ludovisi, 900, 78v (7 October 1688).

30. ASV, Archivio Boncompagni Ludovisi, 899 (28 June 1686); ASV, Archivio Boncompagni Ludovisi, 900, 99r (4 February 1688).

31. On her embarrassment for being able only to offer thanks and remembrance, see ASV, Archivio Boncompagni Ludovisi, 899 (24 August 1686); ASV, Archivio Boncompani Ludovisi, 900, 105r (2 August 1688); 110v (13 August 1688); 101r (1 September 1688); 53v (11 February 1689). On French fashion, ASV, Archivio Boncompagni Ludovisi, 900, 143r (23 January 1688). On gifts for Ippolita's two daughters, ibid., 88v (10 December 1688). On her remedies, ibid., 95r–95v (7 September 1688); 75v–76r (12 September 1688).

32. "Another like you," ASV, Archivio Boncompagni Ludovisi, 899 (11 August 1686). On why she did not deserve a daughter like Ippolita, ibid. (6 September 1686; 29 November 1687).

33. ASV, Archivio Boncompagni Ludovisi, 900, 112r (10 July 1688); 118v (21 June 1688).

34. "only medication," ASV, Archivio Boncompagni Ludovisi, 899 (26 October 1686). For similar sentiments, see ibid. (an undated letter, likely written circa Christmas Day, 1684); 24 March 1685 [both miscatalogued in packet of letters "1687–1689"]; 1 November 1686; 17 November 1686; 1 October 1687; ASV, Archivio Boncompagni Ludovisi, 900, 52v (14 February 1689). Eleonora refers to the sight of Ippolita's family as the "antidote" for her maladies in ibid., 130r (18 March 1688); 124v (24 April 1688).

35. Her specific bovine metaphor was Pergolese cows, ASV, Archivio Boncompagni Ludovisi, 899 (26 October 1686).

36. Ibid. (6 May 1687; 10 July 1689).

37. Ibid. (6 October 1684; 20 April 1685, 11 May 1685; 18 May 1685; 1 June 1685).

38. Ibid. (15 June 1685; 11 May 1686).

39. Ibid. (22 December 1686).

40. Ibid. (13 October 1685).

41. Ibid. (19 August 1684; 7 December 1684; 3 March 1685; 11 May 1685; 1 June 1685; 15 June 1685; 19 October 1685, 3 November 1685).

42. ASV, Archivio Boncompagni Ludovisi, 899 (11 August 1684).

43. See the Boncompagni family genealogy in the Appendix for details of their family.

44. Gregorio's illegitimate daughter evidently co-resided with her father in the 1680s. Eleonora suggested placing her in a monastery, where she predicted that she would amuse "the poor nuns." ASV, Archivio Boncompagni Ludovisi, 899 (28 July 1684).

45. Ibid. (27 June 1684).

46. Ibid. (20 April 1685). This is the first reference to him having a seizure, mentioned in a letter from Eleonora, to her brother Gregorio. Eleonora refers to Ugo's death only on 22 December 1686, whereas the date of 19 October 1686 is indicated on the family genealogy included in the recent published inventory of the Archivio Boncompagni Ludovisi. See Venditti et al., *Archivio Boncompagni Ludovisi*, vol. V: *Indici e alberi genealogici*.

47. ASV, Archivio Boncompagni Ludovisi, 899 (3 August 1687). Marchese Tiberio Astalli was charged with the financial guardianship of Ippolita and her sisters. See ASV, Archivio Boncompagni Ludovisi, 297, fascicolo 47a. It was their uncle, Cardinal Niccolò Albergati Ludovisi, who situated the three Ludovisi girls in their adult lives, an arduous process in part due to the chronically bad misbehavior of their brother. See ASV, Archivio Boncompagni Ludovisi, 331, esp. 143r. Ippolita and her sister Lavinia appear to have resided at the Roman convent the Tor de' Specchi up to the time of their matrimony. See ASV, Archivio Boncompagni Ludovisi, 316, 61r, 378r; ASV, Archivio Boncompagni Ludovisi, 317, 15r, which contains expenses while in the Tor de' Specchi.
48. Ibid. (6 June 1686).
49. Ibid. (11 November 1684; 19 January 1685).
50. Ibid. (23 May 1686).
51. ASV, Archivio Bongcompagni Ludovisi, 900, 73v (6 October 1688).
52. ASV, Archivio Boncompagni Ludovisi, 899 (3 August 1684; 1 November 1686).
53. Ibid. (27 June 1684; 3 July 1684; 8 July 1684; 19 February 1685; 5 November 1685; 6 July 1686; 2 August 1686; 1 November 1686; 7 September 1686; 26 September 1686; 24 April 1687). Eleonora's symptoms worsened as the correspondence continued and came to include insomnia, ibid. (19 April 1689; 24 June 1689), and anxiety, ibid. (1 March 1687); ASV, Archivio Boncompagni Ludovisi, 900, 92r (26 August 1688). On her difficulty eating, see ASV, Archivio Boncompagni Ludovisi, 899 (24 June 1689). On the variety of her hard to diagnose digestive maladies, ASR, Archivio Boncompagni Ludovisi, 900, 92r (26 August 1688). On swelling in the legs and extreme thirst, ibid., 50v (8 February 1689). On the loss of hope for any remedy, ibid., 85v (27 November 1688). On fainting, ibid., 75r (12 September 1688).
54. ASV, Archivio Boncompagni Ludovisi, 899 (7 September 1686; 26 September 1686 [a letter to her brother, Gregorio]; 17 November 1686; 23 November 1686; 21 March 1687); ASV, Archivio Boncompagni Ludovisi, 900, 10v (1 September 1688); 87v (10 December 1688).
55. ASV, Archivio Boncompagni Ludovisi, 900, 120v (27 June 1688); 113r (10 July 1688).
56. ASV, Archivio Boncompagni Ludovisi, 899 (21 November 1687). Her hand and arm pain intensified as she aged, making writing difficult. See ibid. (6 May 1687; 7 June 1687).
57. ASV, Archivio Boncompagni Ludovisi, 899 (21 July 1684; 28 July 1684).
58. ASV, Archivio Boncompagni Ludovisi, 899 (13 October 1685). For a long reflection on this matter, see ibid. (6 February 1686).
59. ASV, Archivio Boncompagni Ludovisi, 899 (20 September 1686).
60. According to the art historian Howard Hibbard, the *avvisi* reported the familial discord. See "Palazzo Borhese Studies I: The Garden and Its Fountains," in "Palazzo Borghese I: The Garden and its Fountains," *The Burlington Magazine* 100.663 (1958): 205–15. For his transcription of the *avvisi* from the Vatican Library (*Barb. lat.* 6409) see p. 206, note 12.
61. ASV, Archivio Boncompagni Ludovisi, 899 (3 March 1685).
62. Ibid. (19 February 1685 [miscatalogued in packet of letters "1687–1689"]; 3 March 1685; 9 March 1687).

63. Ibid. (31 May 1686).
64. Ibid. (31 May 1686).
65. "true sentiment," ibid. (31 May 1686); "that love and duty," ibid. (24 August 1686). On sincerity, ibid. (23 June 1684; 18 May 1685; 1 June 1685). Her liberty of speech was to serve Ippolita's family, ibid. (7 February 1687).
66. Ibid. (21 July 1685).
67. Ibid. (1 September 1685; 18 December 1685).
68. Ibid. (18 December 1685).
69. Ibid. (1 September 1685). On her liberty of speech, see ibid. (15 March 1686). On loving Ippolita "as a mother," see ibid. (31 May 1686). Eleonora offered the excuse that because she loved Ippolita as a mother she spoke freely. See ibid. (undated letter, most likely from 1685 [miscatalogued in packet of letters "1687–1689"]).
70. Ibid. (26 October 1685). See also the perfunctory apology in ibid. (5 April 1686), when she urged Ippolita to get her next child on a better schedule and hope for better luck with the wet nurse.
71. Ibid. (19 October 1685; 13 September 1686).
72. Ibid. (27 July 1685).
73. Ibid. (19 September 1685). Diane Owen Hughes underscored the necessity of the offspring being a boy for the link to be forged between the woman and her in-laws; "Representing the Family: Portraits and Purposes in Early Modern Italy," in *Art and History: Images and their Meaning*, ed. Robert I. Rotberg and Theodore K. Rabb (Cambridge, 1986), p. 18.
74. ASV, Archivio Boncompagni Ludovisi, 899 (3 November 1685; 6 June 1686).
75. For more on Eleonora's ideas on the relations between Roman aristocratic women, wet nurses, and infants, see Caroline Castiglione, "Peasants at the Palace: Wet Nurses and Aristocratic Mothers in Early Modern Rome," in *Medieval and Renaissance Lactations – Images, Rhetorics, Practices*, ed. Jutta Sperling (Burlington, VT, 2013), pp. 79–99. Early attention to wet nursing in modern scholarship includes the work of James Bruce Ross, "The Middle-Class Child in Urban Italy." The pathbreaking interpretive and archival work of Christiane Klapisch-Zuber shaped a generation of scholarship about mothering and wet nursing, even if some of her conclusions have since been contested. See "Blood Parents and Milk Parents: Wet Nursing in Florence, 1300–1530," in *Women, Family, and Ritual in Renaissance Italy* (Chicago, 1985), pp. 132–64. The most comprehensive treatment of wet nursing is Valerie Fildes, including *Breasts, Bottles, and Babies* and *Wet Nursing: A History from Antiquity to the Present*. A shorter overview is offered by Sara Matthews Grieco, "Breastfeeding, Wet Nursing and Infant Mortality in Europe (1400–1800)," in *Historical Perspectives on Breastfeeding* (Florence, 1991), pp. 15–62. For a summary of the sixteenth-century literature in the vernacular on breastfeeding, see Rudolph M. Bell, *How to Do It: Guides to Good Living for Renaissance Italians* (Chicago, 1999), pp. 124–53.
76. These beliefs had been repeated since antiquity. See Fildes, *Breasts, Bottles, and Babies*, pp. 12, 179–81. The use of animal milk was maligned due to the erroneous belief that through it the child would imbibe the qualities of the animal into her or his character. See Fildes, *Breasts, Bottles, and Babies*, pp. 53–4, 179–82. On the substitution of human milk for animal milk, see Barbara Orland, "Enlightened Milk: Reshaping a Bodily Substance into a

Chemical Object," in *Materials and Expertise in Early Modern Europe: Between Market and Laboratory*, ed. Ursula Klein and E. C. Spary, (Chicago, 2010), pp. 163–97, esp. p. 172. Animal milk substitutes had long been used, however, in emergency situations. See Fildes, *Wet Nursing*, p. 73. Eleonora remained dubious about their use. See ASV, Archivio Boncompagni Ludovisi, 899 (12 June 1686).

77. The necessity of this corrective to our understanding was hypothesized first by Fildes, *Breasts, Bottles, and Babies*, p. 203.

78. Similar comments are throughout the correspondence, but esp. ASV, Archivio Boncompagni Ludovisi, 899 (13 October 1684; 15 April 1685; 13 December 1686).

79. Ibid. (3 November 1685; 23 August 1687).

80. Ibid. (19 February 1685 [miscatalogued in packet of letters "1687–1689"]; 27 September 1687; 13 December 1687).

81. ASV, Archivio Boncompagni Ludovisi, 899 (27 June 1684).

82. Ibid. (24 March 1685 [miscatalogued in packet of letters "1687–1689"]).

83. Fildes, *Breasts, Bottles, and Babies*, pp. 30–2. The qualities of a good wet nurse were most explicitly spelled out by Soranus of Epheseus in the first century CE and they endured in European culture until the nineteenth century. Ibid., pp. 168–73.

84. Eleonora connected Ugo's childhood behaviors to those stories she heard about her brother: ASV, Archivio Boncompagni Ludovisi, 899 (8 July 1684); see also, ibid. (8 July 1684; 19 September 1684; 7 September 1686; an undated letter, likely from the summer of 1685 [miscatalogued in packet of letters "1687–1689"]); ASV, Archivio Boncompagni Ludovisi, 900 (7 September 1688). On the spiritedness and intelligence of the girls being inherited from Ippolita, see ASV, Archivio Boncompagni Ludovisi, 900, 102v (1 September 1688). For more on this theme, see Castiglione, "Peasants at the Palace," pp. 88–9.

85. ASV, Archivio Boncompagni Ludovisi, 899 (27 June 1684).

86. Fildes, *Wet Nursing*, pp. 111–13.

87. ASV, Archivio Boncompagni Ludovisi, 899 (19 September 1684; 17 August 1685; 24 August 1685). On not allowing the wet nurse to gain too much weight, ibid. (30 March 1685). On keeping the wet nurse covered, ibid. (9 September 1684; 19 September 1684). On the problem of fresh foods and acidic foods, which could damage the milk, ibid. (9 June 1685). On the recommended diet of wet nurses in printed sources, see Ken Albala, *Eating Right in the Renaissance* (Berkeley and Los Angeles, 2002), pp. 151–3. For further elaborations in the eighteenth century of the connection between diet and breast milk, see Orland, "Enlightened Milk," pp. 173–4.

88. Biblioteca Vaticana Apostolica (hereafter BAV), Fondo Boncompagni Ludovisi, I 55: "Raccolta di diversi Segreti e Rimedj," ff. 199v, 230v.

89. On the failure of remedies to increase milk production, ASV, Archivio Boncompagni Ludovisi, 899 (13 October 1684); and ibid. (9 March 1685 [miscatalogued in packet of letters "1687–1689"]).

90. Ibid. (21 August 1686). If the swaddling was eliminated too early, Eleonora believed that the infant would not develop properly. See ibid. (3 May 1686; 9 May 1686; 8 July 1684; 2 August 1686; 12 November 1687).

91. Ibid. (9 May 1686).

92. Ibid. (27 June 1684; 9 September 1684).
93. Ibid. (8 July 1684).
94. Continuity in the wet nurse was advisable but not always possible, in her view. See ibid. (9 March 1685; 21 March 1687). For further discussion see Castiglione, "Peasants at the Palace," pp. 91–2.
95. Diarrhea typically accompanied the introduction of solid foods. Fildes, *Breasts, Bottles, and Babies*, p. 253. On continuity of breast milk even during the transition to foods, see ASV, Archivio Boncompagni Ludovisi, 899 (3 August 1687).
96. ASV, Archivio Boncompagni Ludovisi, 899 (17 August 1685; 1 September 1685; 13 October 1685; 30 March 1686; 5 April 1686).
97. Ibid. (9 March 1685; 27 March 1685; 21 July 1685; 27 July 1685; 24 December 1687). In ASV, Archivio Boncompagni Ludovisi, 900, 58v (28 June 1685); 97v–98r (7 September 1688).
98. ASV, Archivio Boncompagni Ludovisi, 900, 111r (13 August 1688).
99. ASV, Archivio Boncompagni Ludovisi, 899 (21 July 1685; 11 May 1686; 23 May 1686). Medical writings since antiquity had differed on the use of wine for infants. It was highly regarded in the early modern period, due to problems with the sanitation of water. Fildes, *Breasts, Bottles, and Babies*, pp. 34–5, 236–7.
100. ASV, Archivio Boncompagni Ludovisi, 899 (6 April 1685 [miscatalogued in packet of letters "1687–1689"]; 9 June 1685; 21 July 1685).
101. Ibid. (13 December 1687; 20 December 1687; 31 January 1688; 10 February 1688; 14 February 1688; 14 July 1688; 26 August 1688; 2 April 1689).
102. ASV, Archivio Boncompagni Ludovisi, 900, 64v–65r (22 June 1685).
103. ASV, Archivio Boncompagni Ludovisi, 899 (21 July 1685).
104. Ibid. (21 July 1685; 27 July 1685).
105. Ibid. (21 July 1685).
106. Ibid. (12 January 1686).
107. Ibid. (8 September 1685).
108. Ibid. (8 September 1685).
109. Ibid. (23 March 1686).
110. Ibid. (12 July 1685; 9 May 1686; 14 June 1686).
111. Ibid. (3 January 1686).
112. Ibid. (21 August 1686). Ugo continued to experience weakness in his legs and a lopsided gait in the year following his walking; see also ibid. (17 November 1686; 23 November 1686).
113. Ibid. (8 July 1684).
114. Ibid. (28 November 1685; 4 February 1686; 3 May 1686; 7 March 1687).
115. Ibid. (28 January 1685 [miscatalogued in packet of letters "1687–1689"]).
116. Ibid. (7 September 1684). Eleonora's sympathetic praise was accompanied by the precaution against allowing their co-sleeping to make Ugo "an enemy of the cradle." She expressed no concern about co-sleeping as a possible moment for suffocation, as did some medical authorities. See Fildes, *Breasts, Bottles, and Babies*, pp. 195–7.
117. ASV, Archivio Boncompagni Ludovisi, 899 (5 October 1686).
118. Ibid. (26 October 1685).
119. Ibid. (3 November 1685).
120. Ibid. (28 July 1684).

121. Ibid. (26 August 1684; 9 September 1684; 19 September 1684; 27 September 1684; 2 August 1686; 21 August 1686).
122. Ibid. (11 August 1684; 21 July 1684; 9 September 1684; 21 November 1687; 13 December 1687). In ASV, Archivio Boncompagni Ludovisi, 900, 146r (10 January 1688).
123. ASV, Archivio Boncompagni Ludovisi, 899 (13 October 1685).
124. On purges, see ibid. (25 November 1684; 12 July 1685; 21 July 1685; 30 March 1686; 21 August 1686]. On her pomade, ibid. (11 August 1684). On bloodletting, ibid. (23 June 1684; 21 July 1684; 28 July 1684; 11 August 1684). On swaddling and corsets, ibid. (28 July 1684; 3 November 1685). On powders, ibid. (26 August 1684; 3 March 1685). On her various testimonials (and gifts) of powders, see ibid. (21 July 1684; 9 June 1685; 24 May 1685; 15 June 1685) and ASV, Archivio Boncompagni Ludovisi, 900, 57r (2 June 1685). Eleonora also included advice on the use of plants in various letters. See ASV, Archivio Boncompagni Ludovisi, 899 (19 April 1685 [miscatalogued in packet of letters "1687–1689"]).
125. ASV, Archivio Boncompagni Ludovisi, 899 (15 April 1685).
126. Both expressions are David Gentilcore's. See his *Healers and Healing*, pp. 2–3. For a description of therapeutic calculus and medical pluralism in the kingdom of Naples, see ibid., pp. 1–28. Gianna Pomata has underscored the extent to which "legal and illicit practice formed, in the eyes of the sick, a single pool of medical resources, out of which one could pick and choose at will." *Contracting a Cure: Patients, Healers, and the Law in Early Modern Bologna* (Baltimore, 1998), esp. pp. 122–3. Gentilcore's "medical pluralism" emerged when the concept of the "medical marketplace" was widely debated among historians of medicine. The marketplace approach to the history of medicine was advanced by Roy Porter but simultaneously appeared among the work of several scholars, including Harold J. Cook, *The Decline of the Old Medical Regime in Stuart London* (Ithaca, 1986) and Katherine Park, *Doctors and Medicine in Early Renaissance Florence* (Princeton, 1985). Such an approach contributed to shifting the focus from practitioners to patients (consumers, in the marketplace model) although the patient's perspective remains the least developed in the history of medicine, scattered as it is in archives beyond those of medical institutions. See Roy Porter's early call for this approach, "The Patient's View: Doing Medical History From Below," *Theory and Society* 14.2 (1985): 175–98. For a synthesis and critique of the medical marketplace concept, see Mark S. R. Jenner and Patrick Wallis, "The Medical Marketplace," in their edited volume, *Medicine and the Market in England and its Colonies, c. 1450–1850* (Basingstoke, 2007), pp. 1–23.
127. Gentilcore identified three categories of healers: popular, medical, and ecclesiastical, but acknowledged that these groups overlap. See his diagram and analysis of the three spheres in Gentilcore, *Healers and Healing*, p. 3.
128. A rare reference to the diabolical emerges in Eleonora's letters, but it is quickly dismissed. ASV, Archivio Boncompagni Ludovisi, 899 (16 November 1687). On sin as the root cause of illness, see Gentilcore, *Healers and Healing*, p. 12. Gentilcore also emphasizes the connection between the devil and disease as outlined by Francesco Maria Guazzo, *Compendium maleficarum* (1608). See ibid., *Healers and Healing*, pp. 158, 160–3.

129. By contrast, see the miraculous narratives analyzed by Gentilcore, *Healers and Healing*, pp. 177–202.
130. Anna Esposito, "Men and Women in Roman Confraternities," in *The Politics of Ritual Kinship: Confraternities and Social Order in Early Modern Italy*, ed. Nicholas Terpstra (Cambridge, 1999), pp. 82–97, esp. p. 90.
131. ASV, Archivio Boncompagni Ludovisi, 899 (28 July 1684; 3 August 1684; 11 August 1684; 9 May 1686; 30 August 1687).
132. On Camilla Orsini Borghese, see Marilyn Dunn, "Piety and Patronage: Two Noblewomen and their Convents," *Art Bulletin* 76.4 (1994): 644–63. Eleonora discusses her grandmother-in-law in ASV, Archivio Boncompagni Ludovisi, 899 (27 March 1685; 30 May 1685; 20 April 1685; 12 July 1685). A short and intriguing biography of Camilla Orsini Borghese is in BAV, Fondo Boncompagni Ludovisi, F 34.
133. Dunn, "Piety and Patronage," p. 655.
134. ASV, Archivio Boncompagni Ludovisi, 899 (30 March 1685).
135. Ibid. (27 March 1685).
136. Ibid. (20 April 1685).
137. Ibid. (24 April 1687).
138. Ibid. (6 September 1686).
139. Ibid. (3 June 1685).
140. Ibid. (7 August 1686; 6 September 1686; 23 November 1686; 29 November 1686; 9 December 1686; 22 December 1686; 18 January 1687).
141. Ibid. (11 May 1685).
142. Ibid. (11 May 1685; 13 August 1686).
143. Ibid. (24 March 1685 [miscatalogued in packet of letters "1687–1689"]).
144. Ibid. (27 September 1685; 13 August 1686). For more on the connections between illness and emotions, see Gentilcore, *Healers and Healing*, p. 184.
145. ASV, Archivio Boncompagni Ludovisi, 899 (1 March 1686).
146. The early modern link between health of the body and the health of the soul is summarized in Cavallo and Storey, *Healthy Living*, pp. 179–208. Gentilcore emphasizes the connection that in the "longstanding Catholic tradition … care of the soul had to accompany that of the body." See *Healers and Healing*, p. 11. Medically speaking, emotions were believed to cause changes in the corporeal processes. See also Sandra Cavallo, *Artisans of the Body in Early Modern Italy* (Manchester, 2007), pp. 21–7.
147. "with some children," ASV, Archivio Boncompagni Ludovisi, 899 (3 February 1686; 4 February 1686); "one can never lose heart," ibid. (3 July 1686); "better to recommend them to God," ibid. (6 February 1686); ASV, Archivio Boncompagni Ludovisi, 900, 57r (2 June 1685); 59r (28 June 1685). On the necessity of patience with Ippolita's spendthrift brother, ASV, Archivio Boncompagni Ludovisi, 899 (25 November 1684; 23 May 1686; 6 June 1686).
148. ASV, Archivio Boncompagni Ludovisi, 899 (1 June 1685). On patience, see ibid. (24 May 1685; 12 July 1685; 5 January 1686; 28 June 1686; 2 August 1686; 7 September 1686; 26 September 1686).
149. Ibid. (11 August 1685).
150. Ibid. (12 July 1685).
151. Ibid. (23 June 1684; 27 June 1684; 8 July 1684).
152. Ibid. (20 October 1684]; later she acknowledged their problems for the child, ibid. (4 February 1686], but mostly the "stravaganze" of small children were

part of normal development or temporary discomfort. See ASV, Archivio Boncompagni Ludovisi, 900, 58r (28 June 1685). On the difference between girls and boys, see ASV, Archivio Boncompagni Ludovisi, 899 (21 November 1687; 29 November 1687).

153. ASV, Archivio Boncompagni Ludovisi, 899 (21 July 1684; 11 August 1685; 31 May 1686; 6 December 1686; 14 March 1687; 22 July 1687; 23 August 1687).
154. Ibid. (26 October 1686; 4 February 1686).
155. Ibid. (24 May 1685).
156. "Affection and a lack of experience," ibid. (1 June 1685). For a similar insight, see ibid. (6 June 1686): "the will and the passion of mothers makes things appear greater [than they are]."
157. Ibid. (24 May 1685).
158. Ibid. (9 June 1685).
159. Ibid. (3 June 1685).
160. Ibid. (3 June 1685).
161. Ibid. (27 June 1684; 8 May 1685; 17 August 1686).
162. Ibid. (21 April 1685).
163. Ibid. (3 July 1686).
164. "After the bad," ibid. (23 February 1686; 31 May 1686). On a happy day for the child, see ibid. (23 November 1686).
165. Ibid. (24 May 1685).
166. Ibid. (11 August 1686).
167. Ibid. (23 November 1686).
168. Ibid. (27 September 1685; 19 October 1685; 26 October 1685; 31 November 1685 [*sic*]; 30 March 1686; 13 August 1686).
169. Ibid. (18 December 1685).
170. Ibid. (5 April 1686).
171. Ibid. (19 October 1685).
172. Ibid. (12 July 1686; 5 October 1686).
173. Ibid. (5 October 1686).
174. Ibid. (10 October 1686).
175. Ibid. (5 October 1686).
176. Ibid. (5 October 1686).
177. Ibid. (11 August 1684).
178. "all'età sarà un uometto [*sic*]." Ibid. (24 August 1685).
179. On the ordinary nature of Ugo's maladies, see ibid. (23 June 1684; 19 September 1684; 30 March 1685). Similar advice by Eleonora continued regarding Ippolita's subsequent children: ibid. (2 June 1687; 4 April 1687; 8 October 1687); ASV, Archivio Boncompagni Ludovisi, 900, 104v (1 September 1688); 82r (27 September 1688).
180. ASV, Archivio Boncompagni Ludovisi, 899 (6 February 1686).
181. Ibid. (5 October 1686).
182. Ibid. (11 May 1685; 24 May 1685; 13 October 1685).
183. Ibid. (21 August 1686). For other anecdotes from Eleonora's experiences, see ibid. (24 May 1685; 3 June 1685; 13 June 1685).
184. Ibid. (15 April 1685; 20 April 1685; 11 May 1685; 14 September 1685).
185. Ibid. (17 August 1685).
186. Ibid. (28 November 1685).

187. The child in question died from a malady different from that of Ugo. See ibid. (28 November 1685). On the significance of Ugo's seventh year, see ibid. (9 May 1686).
188. Ibid. (27 June 1684; 20 April 1685). In ASV, Archivio Boncompagni Ludovisi, 900, 99v (4 February 1688).
189. ASV, Archivio Boncompagni Ludovisi, 899 (21 April 1685); "lively," ibid. (9 June 1685).
190. Ibid. (9 June 1685).
191. Ibid. (13 June 1685; 23 March 1686).
192. Ibid. (20 April 1685; 21 April 1685; 22 April 1685; 26 April 1685; 11 May 1685; 9 June 1685).
193. Ibid. (9 June 1685; 27 September 1685).
194. Either Eleonora corresponded much less frequently with Gregorio, or their correspondence has been lost. A few letters from Eleonora to Gregorio surface within the collection of those of Eleonora to Ippolita. See ASV, Archivio Boncompagni Ludovisi, 899 (20 April 1685; 11 August 1685). For the engaged parenting of British and French fathers, see Lisa Smith, "The Relative Duties of a Man: Domestic Medicine in England and France, circa, 1685–1740," *Journal of Family History* 31.3 (2006): 237–56. In the Italian context, the role of men's participation in the medical care of their families can be documented since the Renaissance. See Sandra Cavallo, "Health, Hygiene and Beauty," in Marta Ajmar-Wollheim and Flora Dennis (eds), *At Home in Renaissance Italy* (London, 2006), pp. 174–87, esp. p. 175.
195. ASV, Archivio Boncompagni Ludovisi, 899 (3 August 1684).
196. Ibid. (20 April 1685).
197. Ibid. (31 May 1686).
198. For further analysis of the gender differences in healthy eating and healthy practices, see Cavallo and Storey, *Healthy Living*, pp. 209, 218, 239.
199. On the physicians in the Borghese household, see ASV, Archivio Borghese, 3972, "Rolli della famiglia: 1682–1683" (January 1682). The importance of the quality of the physician appears throughout the correspondence. See ASV, Archivio Boncompagni Ludovisi, 900, 104v (1 September 1688). The presence of physicians is discussed in Sandra Cavallo and David Gentilcore's introduction to *Spaces, Objects and Identities in Early Modern Italian Medicine* (Oxford, 2008), p. 6.
200. Gigliola Fragnito has analyzed the categories of household employees in Roman households of cardinals. See her "La trattatistica cinque e seicentesca sulla corte cardinalizia," *Annali dell'Istituto Storico Italo-Germanico in Trento* 18 (1991): 135–85. On surgeons and physicians, pp. 143, 147.
201. ASV, Archivio Borghese, 122.
202. Scipione Mercurio, *De gli errori popolari d'Italia* (Verona, 1645), p. 214. Quoted in David Gentilcore, *Healers and Healing*, p. 59.
203. Midwifery was the last medical profession allowed to women; midwives were restricted from "administering internal medicines, letting blood or using surgical instruments of any sort, however useful these might have been." Gentilcore notes that this was unlikely to have been the practical reality, given that their practice continued to treat women's health issues of various kinds. See *Healers and Healing*, p. 84.
204. Pomata, "Practicing between Earth and Heaven," pp. 121–3, 125.

205. ASV, Archivio Boncompagni Ludovisi, 899 (12 July 1685); ASV, Archivio Boncompagni Ludovisi, 900, 101v (1 September 1688); 79r–79v (18 October 1688).
206. ASV, Archivio Boncompagni Ludovisi, 899 (12 July 1687); ASV, Archivio Boncompagni Ludovisi, 900, 122v (5 May 1688). On the concept of complexion, see Sandra Cavallo, "Health, Beauty and Hygiene," p. 178. For a summary of the early modern discourse on complexion, and the decline in its significance over time, see Cavallo and Storey, *Healthy Living*, p. 32.
207. ASV, Archivio Boncompagni Ludovisi, 900, 48v (5 March 1689); 46r (12 March 1689); 55v (2 April 1689).
208. ASV, Archivio Boncompagni Ludovisi, 899 (18 May 1685; 24 May 1685).
209. Ibid. (19 October 1685). The physicians consulted in Rome disagreed with the course of action recommended by Ippolita's physician in Sora.
210. On Eleonora's recourse to physicians' consultations in Rome, for the problems facing Ugo and the recommendation that Ippolita follow their advice, see ibid. (18 May 1685; 24 May 1685; 9 June 1685; 13 October 1685).
211. On all things in their "just measure," see ibid. (3 January 1686; 7 September 1686). Elsewhere she combines the idea of the just measure with the importance of patience in ibid. (1 March 1686; 26 September 1686 [a letter from Eleonora to her brother]). For further insights on the relevance of "buona regola" and the problems of its omission, ibid. (24 March 1685 [miscatalogued in packet of letters "1687–1689"]; 1 June 1685; 3 January 1686; 7 September 1686; 10 October 1686); ASV, Archivio Boncompagni Ludovisi, 900, 64r (22 June 1685); 141r (20 January 1688).
212. ASV, Archivio Boncompagni Ludovisi, 899 (1 June 1685).
213. Ibid. (1 June 1685).
214. Ibid. (15 April 1685).
215. Ibid. (18 December 1685).
216. Ibid. (3 November 1685; 31 November 1685 [*sic*]).
217. Ibid. (28 November 1685).
218. Ibid. (28 June 1686; 3 July 1686; 6 July 1686; 12 July 1686; 30 July 1686; 26 September 1686 [letter to her brother Gregorio]).
219. Ibid. (5 October 1686).
220. Ibid. (30 March 1686; 6 June 1686; 10 October 1686).
221. Evelyn Lincoln, "Curating the Renaissance Body," *Word and Image* 17.1&2 (2001): 42–61. On addressing the fear of children, see p. 53.
222. Cavallo, *Artisans of the Body*, p. 43.
223. ASV, Archivio Boncompagni Ludovisi, 899 (10 March 1686; 6 June 1686; 21 August 1686).
224. Ibid. (28 July 1684; 11 August 1684; 27 July 1685).
225. Ibid. (6 June 1686; 13 August 1686; 1 March 1686).
226. Ibid. (27 April 1685; 8 May 1685; 31 May 1686; 9 June 1685).
227. Ibid. (27 July 1685; 1 September 1685); ASV, Archivio Boncompagni Ludovisi, 900, 58v (28 June 1685).
228. On things neither men nor doctors understand, but that can be gained from women's experience, see ASV, Archivio Boncompagni Ludovisi, 899 (23 March 1686; 19 August 1686; 21 August 1686; 1 November 1686).
229. Ibid. (9 June 1685).

230. On "trifles" ("*bagatelle*"), see ASV, Archivio Boncompagni Ludovisi, 899 (23 March 1685; 19 August 1686; 21 August 1686; 1 November 1686). The historian Carlo Ginzburg has underscored the significance of minute observation as the foundation for the conjectural paradigm of knowledge, tracing its development from the practices of hunting to those of medicine and history – fields where observation and speculation intertwine. See Carlo Ginzburg, "Clues: Roots of an Evidential Paradigm," *Clues, Myths, and the Historical Method*, trans. John and Anne Tedeschi (Baltimore, 1986), pp. 96–125.
231. The Bologna decree of 1682 is translated and analyzed in Pomata, "Practicing Between Earth and Heaven," p. 120.
232. On the perspective of a "*vera madre*," and the experiences of Eleonora, see ASV, Archivio Boncompagni Ludovisi, 899 (3 January 1686; 23 March 1686; 5 October 1686).
233. Ibid. (17 August 1685).
234. Ibid. (12 July 1685; 14 June 1686). General doubts about the wisdom of purging children are expressed in ibid. (14 September 1685).
235. Ibid. (6 June 1686; 14 June 1686 [letter to her brother Gregorio]).
236. Ibid. (27 September 1684).
237. Ibid. (3 January 1686).
238. Ibid. (9 June 1685).
239. ASV, Archivio Boncompagni Ludovisi, 900, 58r (28 June 1685).
240. ASV, Archivio Boncompagni Ludovisi, 899 (13 October 1685). For another incident involving the deterioration of her son at the hands of a physician, see ibid. (17 August 1685).
241. Ibid. (27 June 1684; 3 June 1685).
242. Ibid. (27 June 1684; 24 May 1685; 8 September 1685). On avoiding pointless ingestion of medications see ibid. (1 September 1685).
243. Ibid. (1 June 1685; 6 June 1686; 16 June 1686).
244. Ibid. (8 September 1685; 27 September 1685; 23 May 1686).
245. Ibid. (19 October 1685).
246. Ibid. (23 May 1686). On the relationship between female noblewomen and their *donne* in the Spada-Veralli family, see Cavallo and Storey, *Healthy Living*, p. 58.
247. ASV, Archivio Boncompagni Ludovisi, 899 (19 October 1685). She pronounced her "lovable" in ibid. (27 September 1686 [a letter to her brother Gregorio]). She reiterated her praise to Ippolita in ibid. (7 September 1686; 20 September 1686; 10 October 1686).
248. Ibid. (2 August 1686). She sent this well-regarded midwife to deliver her own daughter; see ibid. (14 June 1686).
249. Fildes, *Breasts, Bottles, and Babies*, pp. 49, 162. Wet nurses in the Barberini family in the 1630s were paid approximately 6 scudi per month, according to Patricia Waddy, *Seventeenth-Century Palaces: Use and the Art of the Plan* (New York, 1990), p. 376, notes 11 and 12. Other expenses related to wet nursing are in BAV, Archivio Barberini, unarchived materials, "Giustificazioni di Taddeo Barberini (1630)," [31 May 1630] (expenses for her damask bedding); [4 April 1630] (for her shoes). These appear to be related to his child's wet nurse. Taddeo's records also refer to the "*figlia della mia balia*" [daughter of my wet nurse] whom he remembered with two annual payments. On the latter, see ibid. [5 June 1630] and BAV,

Computisteria, 187 "Giornale" (1629–30) [8 June 1630]. I thank Dr Luigi Cacciaglia of the Vatican Library for assistance with these sources.

250. The correspondence of Madame Roland, in France, who breastfed her daughter, underscores the role that a variety of servants in the household might attempt to play in the rearing of the child. George D. Sussman, *Selling Mothers' Milk: The Wet-Nursing Business in France, 1715–1914* (Urbana, 1982), pp. 83–4.

251. Caroline Castiglione, *Patrons and Adversaries: Nobles and Villagers in Italian Politics, 1640–1760* (New York, 2005), esp. pp. 147–80. For a general picture of the upsurge in legal activity in the Papal States, see Irene Fosi, *Papal Justice: Subjects and Courts in the Papal State, 1500–1750* (Washington, 2011).

252. On the readership according to gender of such texts, see Cavallo and Storey, *Healthy Living*, p. 33.

253. ASV, Archivio Boncompagni Ludovisi, 899 (27 June 1684; 8 July 1684).

254. Ibid. (6 September 1686).

255. On the potential negative impact of the medications taken by the wet nurse, see ibid. (1 June 1685).

256. Ibid. (20 April 1685). On the treatment of children by medicating the wet nurse, see Fildes, *Breasts, Bottles, and Babies*, p. 41; Fildes, *Wet Nursing*, p. 34.

257. ASV, Archivio Boncompagni Ludovisi, 899 (14 September 1685); ASV, Archivio Boncompagni Ludovisi, 900, 46r (12 March 1689).

258. ASV, Archivio Boncompagni Ludovisi, 899 (26 October 1685; 7 February 1687; 23 February 1687).

259. Ibid. (3 November 1685).

260. Ibid. (3 July 1686).

261. Ibid. (26 October 1685).

262. Ibid. (27 June 1684; 3 November 1685; 23 February 1686). Eleonora considers but does not seem convinced by the connection between milk and seizures, ibid. (20 April 1685; 21 April 1685; 28 April 1685; 11 May 1685).

263. Ibid. (26 October 1685).

264. Ibid. (26 October 1685; 18 December 1685).

265. In an undated letter, likely from the summer of 1686, Eleonora expressed regret over the decision of the physician Penna to withdraw the milk: ASV, Archivio Boncompagni Ludovisi, 900, 66v. For similar comments, see ASV, Archivio Boncompagni Ludovisi, 899 (18 December 1685; 30 March 1686; 5 April 1686; 6 September 1686).

266. ASV, Archivio Boncompagni Ludovisi, 899 (5 April 1686).

267. Ibid. (13 October 1685).

268. Ibid. (13 October 1685).

269. Ibid. (31 November 1685 [*sic*]; 10 March 1686).

270. Ibid. (6 September 1686).

271. Ibid. (30 March 1686).

272. Ibid. (18 December 1685).

273. Ibid. (5 April 1686; 16 June 1686).

274. Ibid. (3 May 1686).

275. Ibid. (9 May 1686).

276. Ibid. (28 June 1686; 6 July 1686).

277. Fildes chronicles the success of Van Helmont's views in converting some English aristocrats and members of the gentry to hand feeding. He popularized new (if unfounded) concerns about breast milk. Fildes, *Breasts, Bottles,*

and Babies, pp. 290–1. Skepticism against his recommended hand feeding re-emerged in the eighteenth century, when its contribution to infant mortality was eventually recognized. Ibid., p. 301. Van Helmont's medical views circulated widely in Europe. See Guido Giglioni, *Immaginazione e malattia: Saggio su Jan Baptiste van Helmont* (Milan, 2000).

278. ASV, Archivio Boncompagni Ludovisi, 899 (6 June 1686; 16 June 1686).
279. Ibid. (10 March 1686).
280. Ibid. (18 December 1685).
281. On the increasing recourse in the seventeenth century to broths (and the potential link to the rise in the increase of rickets) see Fildes, *Breasts, Bottles, and Babies*, pp. 214–15. Recent research advances the claim that the overuse of breast milk was the contributing cause for rickets among the Medici family of Florence. The evidence is speculative. See V. Giuffra et al., "Rickets in High Social Class of Renaissance Italy: The Medici Children," *International Journal of Osteoarcheology* (2013): 10.1002/oa.2324. I thank Hal Cook for this reference.
282. On ignoring Gregorio's reservations about the child's diet, see ASV, Archivio Boncompagni Ludovisi, 899 (27 July 1685; 3 July 1686; 24 August 1686). On ignoring everyone, if necessary, regarding Ugo's care, ibid. (3 July 1686). On disregarding Gregorio's opinions on Ippolita's maladies, ibid. (13 August 1686).
283. Ibid. (3 January 1686; 26 September 1686; 13 December 1686).
284. Ibid. (6 February 1686).
285. Ibid. (6 February 1686).
286. Ibid. (16 November 1687).
287. Ibid. (16 June 1686).
288. See Barry Schwartz, *The Paradox of Choice: Why Less is More* (New York, 2004), pp. 29–33.
289. ASV, Archivio Boncompagni Ludovisi, 899 (3 November 1685).
290. Ibid. (3 November 1685).
291. Ibid. (22 December 1686). On the child's memory of his mother's goodness to him, ibid. (10 January 1687).
292. Ibid. (18 January 1687; 25 January 1687).
293. The older mother admitted, "that you consider me cruel and little sympathetic to what has happened." See ibid. (7 February 1687).
294. Ibid. (10 January 1687).
295. Ibid. (22 December 1686; 18 January 1687).
296. Ibid. (22 December 1686).
297. Ibid. (10 January 1687).
298. Ibid. (18 January 1687).
299. Ibid. (7 February 1687).
300. Ibid. (25 January 1687).
301. Ibid. (10 January 1687; 18 January 1687; 25 January 1687; 1 March 1687; 16 May 1687).
302. Ibid. (22 December 1686; 1 January 1687).
303. ASV, Archivio Boncompagni Ludovisi, 900, 103r (1 September 1688).
304. ASV, Archivio Boncompagni Ludovisi, 899 (3 November 1685).
305. Ibid. (13 August 1686; 24 August 1686).
306. Ibid. (6 September 1687).
307. Luigi Fiorani, "Monache e Monasteri Romani nell'Età del Quietismo," *Ricerche per la storia religiosa di Roma* I (1977): 63–111, esp. pp. 102–6. For

more on religious controversies in the lives of Roman aristocratic women, see Chapter 4. I thank John Jeffries Martin for his insights on Eleonora's religious inclinations.

308. ASV, Archivio Boncompagni Ludovisi, 899 (6 September 1687).
309. Ibid. (6 September 1687).
310. Ibid. (11 November 1684).
311. Ibid. (28 April 1685).
312. Ibid. (3 June 1685).
313. Eleonora felt compelled to remind Ippolita that God would not return Ugo to her. See ASV, Archivio Boncompagni Ludovisi, 899 (18 January 1687). Criticisms of Ippolita's excessive worry over her other children were likely an indirect reference to the continued impact of Ugo's death. Ibid. (30 August 1687). Eleonora occasionally acknowledged that Ippolita's grief continued for years after the child's death. See ASV, Archivio Boncompagni Ludovisi, 900, 87r (10 December 1688). References to God's will and stories of other maternal loss seem to have been recounted as lessons for Ippolita. See ibid. (18 October 1688).
314. ASV, Archivio Boncompagni Ludovisi, 899 (14 June 1686). Lincoln emphasizes the presence of a person to calm the patient. See "Curating the Renaissance Body," p. 53.
315. ASV, Archivio Boncompagni Ludovisi, 899 (25 January 1687).
316. Ibid. (6 October 1684).
317. Ibid. (19 March 1686; 23 March 1686).
318. Ibid. (7 February 1687). I thank Renata Ago for her insights on this turn of phrase in the seventeenth-century context.
319. Ibid. (21 August 1686).
320. Ibid. (21 August 1686).
321. Ibid. (2 August 1688).
322. ASV, Archivio Boncompagni Ludovisi, 900, 147v (14 January 1688).
323. The problem of excessive love on the part of parents was a trope that appeared as early as the fifteenth century, in humanist and ecclesiastical writings. For a discussion of Renaissance precedents, see Patricia Fortini Brown, "Children and Education," in *At Home in Renaissance Italy*, ed. Marta Ajmar-Wollheim and Flora Dennis (London, 2006), pp. 136–43, esp. p. 143. The quote from Antoniano is cited in Bernardo Piciché, *Argisto Giuffredi: Gentiluomo borghese nel vicereame di Sicilia* (Rome, 2006), p 135, note 334. See Silvio Antoniano, *Educazione Christiana de' Figliuoli*, Libro Secondo, Verona, Capo XV, *Come il padre deve ammaestrare il figliuolo a pensare alla morte*, p. 111: "Questa troppa carnale tenerezza non si conviene a un petto cristiano."
324. ASV, Archivio Boncompagni Ludovisi, 899 (25 January 1687).
325. Ibid. (25 January 1687).

4 Ippolita's Wager: Letting Daughters Decide in the Early Eighteenth Century

1. Archivio Segreto Vaticana [hereafter ASV], Archivio Boncompagni Ludovisi, 787, fascicolo 1 (15 January 1698). I would like to thank Dr Gianni Venditti and Dr Beatrice Quaglieri for their assistance in the archives of the

Boncompagni Ludovisi archive of the Archivio Segreto Vaticano. I thank Naoko Shibusawa for her comments on familial conflict and the audiences at the following conferences for their queries on this case: New College of Florida Conference on Medieval and Renaissance Studies and Attending to Early Modern Women Conference.

2. See Chapter 3 for more on Eleonora Boncompagni Borghese (1642–95) and her role during Ippolita's early years of motherhood.
3. ASV, Archivio Boncompagni Ludovisi, 787, fascicolo 1 (15 January 1698).
4. Ibid.
5. ASV, Archivio Boncompagni Ludovisi, 899 (13 October 1684).
6. Ibid. (28 November 1685).
7. Ibid. (28 June 1686).
8. Ibid. (3 May 1686).
9. Ibid. (18 April 1686).
10. Ibid. (26 April 1686).
11. Ibid. (12 July 1686).
12. Ibid. (3 May 1686).
13. Ibid. (26 April 1686).
14. Ibid. (11 May 1686).
15. Ibid. (11 May 1686).
16. Ibid. (11 May 1686).
17. Ibid. (14 June 1686).
18. Ibid. (9 May 1686).
19. Ibid. (26 April 1686; 11 May 1686).
20. Ibid. (14 June 1686).
21. Ibid. (9 May 1686).
22. Ibid. (9 May 1686).
23. ASV, Archivio Boncompagni Ludovisi, 624, 230r.
24. On the illegitimate daughter, Marianna, see ASV, Archivio Boncompagni Ludovisi, 624, 443r.
25. C. Somasca, *I Boncompagni*, pp. 102–110, cited in Luigi Alonzi, *Famiglia, Patrimonio e Finanze Nobiliari: I Boncompagni (secoli XVI–XVIII)* (Rome, 2003), p. 266, note 10. See ibid., pp. 266–7. On their marriage arrangements, ASV, Archivio Boncompagni Ludovisi 619, 862r–905v.
26. Jutta Gisela Sperling, *Convents and the Body Politic in Late Renaissance Venice* (Chicago, 1999), pp. 26–9; see especially table 2 on page 28 for the summary of her findings.
27. Luigi Alonzi maintains that after the death of Gregorio, the four unmarried daughters "were initially opposed to varying degrees to their mother-guardian," but, in 1710, there was a shift and Ippolita, "won the girls' confidence." Alonzi, *Famiglia*, pp. 5, 293. Alonzi's evidence of the girls' opposition to Ippolita is not supported with specific references to the sources.
28. Alonzi, *Famiglia*, pp. 325, 330.
29. On her irrationality and eccentricity, see Alonzi, *Famiglia*, pp. 292, 318. On whether she was more eccentric than her daughter, Maria Eleonora, p. 324. On her frustrations and those of the women of her class, p. 292. On her surprising decision to marry all four daughters, p. 294.
30. Ibid., p. 287.
31. Ibid., pp. 292, 293–4.

32. Ibid., pp. 291, 319.
33. Francesco's maladies are discussed in Eleonora Boncompagni Borghese's correspondence to Ippolita in the 1680s. See Chapter 3.
34. For details of Cardinal Giacomo's trajectory through the church's hierarchy, see *The Hierarchy of the Catholic Church*. http://www.catholic-hierarchy.org/bishop/bboncog.html (accessed November 10, 2009). A slightly different account of his trajectory to the priesthood is offered by Luciano Meluzzi, *I vescovi e gli arcivescovi di Bologna* (Bologna, 1975), pp. 460–7.
35. *The Hierarchy of the Catholic Church*. http://www.catholic-hierarchy.org/bishop/bboncog.html. (accessed November 10, 2009).
36. ASV, Archivio Boncompagni Ludovisi, 787, fascicolo 1 (18 March 1690).
37. Ibid. (18 March 1690).
38. C. Somasca, *I Boncompagni*, pp. 77, 99, cited in Alonzi, *Famiglia*, p. 306.
39. Renata Ago, *Carriere e clientele nella Roma barocca* (Rome: Laterza, 1990), pp. 67–71; Marina d'Amelia, "Becoming a Mother in the Seventeenth Century: The Experience of a Roman Noblewoman," in *Time, Space, and Women's Lives in Early Modern Europe*, ed. Anne Jacobson Schutte, Thomas Kuehn, and Silvana Seidel Menchi (Kirksville, MO, 2001), pp. 223–44.
40. ASV, Archivio Boncompagni Ludovisi, busta 402 and busta 403 contain a few letters from Cardinal Giacomo to Ippolita. He wished that he could walk again with her in Rome and stated his desire to serve her as much as he could. See ASV, Archivio Boncompagni Ludovisi, 402, 581r, 615r.
41. According to Alonzi, the Ludovisi family experienced higher mortality among their male offspring than the Boncompagni (about 50 percent versus 20 percent). See *Famiglia*, pp. 263–4.
42. ASV, Archivio Boncompagni Ludovisi, 787, fascicolo 1 (23 January 1700); (undated letter fragment, ?late June 1707); (28 December 1707).
43. Ibid. (1 June 1707; 31 October 1708; 9 February 1709; 1 June 1709). In a letter of 16 July 1707, she mentions that she wanted "to live and die under his protection."
44. Ibid. (24 April 1707; 11 May 1707; undated letter fragment, ?late June 1707).
45. Ibid. (28 September 1707).
46. Ibid. (16 July 1707).
47. Ibid. (11 December 1699).
48. Ibid. (8 January 1700).
49. Ibid. (8 January 1707).
50. Ibid. (12 September 1709; 14 September 1709; 28 September 1709).
51. Ibid. (24 April 1710).
52. Ibid. (22 March 1710; 5 April 1710).
53. Ibid. (23 July 1707; 12 September 1714).
54. Ibid. (24 February 1714).
55. Ibid. (4 June 1701).
56. Ibid. (4 June 1701; 18 June 1701).
57. Ibid. (7 January 1709; 2 January 1711).
58. Ibid. (27 November 1706; 15 June 1707; 23 July 1707).
59. Ibid. (10 January 1711).
60. Ibid. (23 January 1711).
61. Ibid. (10 January 1711).
62. Ibid. (21 March 1711).

63. Ago, *Carriere e clientele*, pp. 67–71.
64. Biblioteca Apostolica Vaticana [hereafter BAV], Fondo Boncompagni Ludovisi, E 110, E 111, and E 112. Greetings from the kings of France and Spain are in E 111, 12r; 20r. Similar correspondence continues in volumes E 113 through E 118.
65. ASV, Archivio Boncompagni Ludovisi, 787, fascicolo 1 (30 April 1712).
66. Ippolita was not Cardinal Giacomo's only source on the Roman scene. His correspondents included the Abbé Baglioni, who described Roman events, family births, and illnesses to the cardinal. See BAV, Fondo Boncompagni Ludovisi, E 119.
67. She likely refers to Sebastiano Bonaventura, who had ties to the exiled King James III and his wife Clementina Sobieski. See "A Jacobite Gazetteer – Lazio: Montefiascone," http://www.jacobite.ca/gazetteer/Lazio/Montefiascone. htm (accessed March 8, 2011); "A Jacobite Gazetteer – Rome: Cappella della Madonna dell'Archetto," http://www.jacobite.ca/gazetteer/Rome/ CappellaMadonnaArchetto.htm (accessed March 8, 2011).

    References to Ippolita's friends include: ASV, Archivio Boncompagni Ludovisi, 787, fascicolo 1 (31 October 1708; 28 September 1709; 10 December 1709; 30 June 1714; 26 January 1709; 20 March 1709; 24 August 1709; 12 August 1711; 4 August 1714). Alonzi notes the longstanding connection between Ippolita and the Acquaviva family: Ippolita's older sister Lavinia – who died at the age of 23 after the birth of her first child – was the wife of Gian Girolamo Acquaviva. See Alonzi, *Famiglia*, p. 310.
68. C. Somasca, *I Boncompagni*, p. 94, cited in Alonzi, *Famiglia*, p. 273, note 17. On her Madrid sojourn, see ibid., pp. 277–8. A vast collection of letters from heads of state and members of court across Europe to the Boncompagni Ludovisi are in the archives of the Archivio Digitale Boncompagni Ludovisi, Villa Aurora (Rome). I thank Princess Rita Boncompagni Ludovisi and Prince Niccolò Boncompagni Ludovisi for access to their family archives. I thank Corey Brennan for sharing with me his knowledge of those sources.
69. On her walks, see ASV, Archivio Boncompagni Ludovisi, 787, fascicolo 1 (20 March 1709; 10 August 1709; 16 November 1709).
70. Ibid. (26 January 1709; 9 February 1709).
71. On the Roman court, see ibid. (3 April 1709; 12 April 1710; 6 February 1712). She provided indirect reporting of papal conversations, through reports from Monsignor Bonaventura. See ibid. (4 September 1709). On the appointment of cardinals to the papal legations, ibid. (14 September 1709; 28 September 1709).
72. Ibid. (8 December 1708). For the hermit comment, ibid. (26 January 1709).
73. Ibid. (16 July 1707).
74. Ibid. (9 February 1709).
75. BAV, Fondo Boncompagni Ludovisi, E 122.
76. On his vestments, ASV, Archivio Boncompagni Ludovisi, 787, fascicolo 1 (18 March 1690). On the tapestries for his church, ibid. (28 September 1709). On the invitation to host him in Rome, ibid. (7 April 1691).
77. On her stated lack of skill, so reminiscent of Anna Colonna's modesty about her abilities vis-à-vis her husband, see ibid. (10 January 1699). On her requests to serve him, see ibid. (10 June 1690; 14 March 1691; 7 April 1691; 10 January 1699; 27 June 1699; 19 December 1699; 5 February 1701; undated fragment, probably from 1707; 16 November 1709).

78. Ibid. (27 February 1700).
79. Ibid. (19 December 1699). On her interventions with Roman clerics, see ibid. (30 September 1713).
80. On the Roman aristocratic family project as a "team sport," see Renata Ago, "Giochi di squadra: Uomini e donne nelle famiglie nobili del xvii secolo," in *Signori, patrizi, cavalieri in Italia centro-meriodionale nell'età moderna*, ed. Maria Antonietta Visceglia (Rome: Laterza, 1992), pp. 256–64, especially pp. 260–3.
81. ASV, Archivio Boncompagni Ludovisi, 787, fascicolo 1 (28 September 1707; 14 November 1708).
82. Ibid. (undated fragment, probably late June 1707; 28 December 1707).
83. On the cold in Bologna, see ibid. (16 January 1709; 5 February 1710; 22 September 1717). On the dangers of the wind (23 January 1711). On the holiday cold weather (26 December 1708; 25 December 1709; 2 January 1711). On the drafty churches (10 January 1711). On his remote parishes (30 September 1713; 18 November 1713).
84. Ibid. (24 April 1707; 12 October 1709; 30 August 1710; 4 October 1710; 23 September 1711). For more on the health benefits of walking and its social practices, see Sandra Cavallo and Tessa Storey, *Healthy Living in Late Renaissance Italy* (Oxford, 2013), pp. 153–4, 172–7.
85. ASV, Archivio Boncompagni Ludovisi, 787, fascicolo 1 (26 January 1709). Concerns over the impact to health of the Lenten diet were widespread in the late seventeenth century. See Cavallo and Storey, *Healthy Living*, pp. 210, 215–18, 271.
86. On her more serious maladies, see ASV, Archivio Boncompagni Ludovisi, 787, fascicolo 1 (4 October 1710; 24 March 1714), "should have been," ibid. (15 June 1707); "blacker than crow" (29 May 1709).
87. For her "rotundity," see ibid. (4 October 1710; 8 October 1712; 29 May 1709); "so comfortable," see ibid. (30 September 1713).
88. Ibid. (23 October 1709; 2 November 1709; 16 November 1709; 21 December 1709; 2 August 1710; 23 September 1711; 21 March 1711; 8 October 1712; 10 August 1712; 21 October 1713; 18 November 1713).
89. Ibid. (20 March 1709; 4 October 1710; 14 February 1714). On baths (3 May 1710; 8 October 1712; 15 October 1712).
90. On his encouragement, see ibid. (10 August 1709). On his love of the Bologna theater scene and comparisons to Rome, ibid. (1 March 1710; 29 March 1710; 6 February 1712).
91. Ibid. (7 April 1691).
92. Ibid. (14 May 1695; 15 February 1710).
93. Ibid. (15 January 1698; 10 January 1699; 27 June 1699; 16 January 1706; ?28 February 1706; 24 December 1707).
94. Ibid. (?28 February 1706).
95. Ibid. (27 November 1706; 31 October 1707; 28 December 1708; 10 November 1708; 10 June 1709; 29 January 1710; 1 March 1710).
96. Ibid. (2 July 1707; 23 November 1707). On their walks together, ibid. (14 July 1709; 7 January 1710).
97. Ibid. (1 June 1707; 23 July 1707); "all that was left to [her]," (2 July 1707).
98. The gifts are in ibid. (24 December 1707; 29 May 1709; 6 January 1714; 10 January 1699; 10 August 1712).
99. Ibid. (15 February 1710; 1 March 1710).

100. Ibid. (31 October 1707; 10 November 1708; 8 December 1708; 29 January 1710).
101. Ibid. (22 September 1717).
102. Documents in the Archivio Boncompagni Ludovisi typically give his death date as February 1, 1707. See ASV, Archivio Boncompagni Ludovisi, 624, 502v. The family tree in the recently published inventory to the archive gives his death date as January 1, 1707. See Gianni Venditti and Beatrice Quaglieri, *Archivio Boncompagni Ludovisi*, vol. 5: *Indici e alberi genealogici. Collectanea Archivi Vaticani* (Vatican City, 2008).
103. See the account of Gregorio's *auditore*, Ricciardelli, in ASV, Archivio Boncompagni Ludovisi, 624, 653r (19 May 1707). On the difficulties of the family, see Alonzi, *Famiglia*, p. 269.
104. Ippolita's father, Niccolò, left a detailed will specifying the greater dowry for his eldest girl, Olimpia, who *"per il molto amore,"* was allocated a dowry of 100,000 scudi. He also designated specific amounts for the younger girls, Lavinia and Ippolita, each of whom was to receive a dowry of 40,000 scudi, *"per grazia speciale."* See ASV, Archivio Boncompagni Ludovisi, 293, fascicolo 33, esp. 430v.
105. ASV, Archivio Boncompagni Ludovisi, 293, fascicolo 37, 600r–600v. For the account of her passing by her confessor, including her desire to die "without leaving lawsuits," ibid., 612r–612v.
106. On Gregorio's dying without a will, see ASV, Archivio Boncompagni Ludovisi, 624, 233r. On the entangled financial accounts of Ippolita and Gregorio, see ibid., 746r–754v.
107. Ibid., 404r.
108. Gregorio's *auditore*, Ricciardelli, testified that he urged Gregorio to specify more clearly in a will both the fate of his inheritance and the assets of his wife. See ibid., 653r–654v (19 May 1707).
109. Alonzi, *Famiglia*, pp. 281–3.
110. ASV, Archivio Boncompagni Ludovisi, 624, 234r.
111. For more on the *auditore*, see "The Making of the *Mater Litigans* in Rome" in the Introduction to this volume.
112. ASV, Archivio Boncompagni Ludovisi, 624, 234r–234v. For further details on the legal reasoning of the Boncompagni side, see Archivio Boncompagni Ludovisi, 1206.
113. ASV, Archivio Boncompagni Ludovisi, 624, 234v–235r.
114. Ibid., 235r–235v.
115. Ibid., 235r–235v.
116. Ibid., 236r.
117. Ibid., 237r–237v. According to Alonzi, Ippolita's success in arranging the marriages of Teresa and Giulia "changed the terms of the debate." Alonzi, *Famiglia*, p. 284.
118. ASV, Archivio Boncompagni Ludovisi, 624, 9r.
119. Alonzi, *Famiglia*, pp. 298–9. The Neapolitan tribunal was the Sacro Regio Consiglio.
120. ASV, Archivio Boncompagni Ludovisi, 624, 12v–13r.
121. Ibid., 197v. On the familial connections that might have aided Ippolita to marry her last two daughters, see Alonzi, *Famiglia*, pp. 307–10.
122. Alonzi, *Famiglia*, pp. 285, 306.

123. ASV, Archivio Boncompagni Ludovisi, 624, 237v–250r.
124. Ibid., 617r–623r.
125. "saintly soul" from ASV, Archivio Boncompagni Ludovisi, 787, fascicolo 1 (undated letter fragment [possibly early June 1707]); "satire" (24 April 1707).
126. Ibid. (24 April 1707).
127. Ibid. (24 April 1707). The drawing up of the inventory would have been Antonio's responsibility. See Alonzi, *Famiglia*, pp. 281–2.
128. ASV, Archivio Boncompagni Ludovisi, 787, fascicolo 1 (24 April 1707).
129. Ibid.
130. Ibid.
131. On the shared management of Boncompagni properties by Giacomo, Gregorio, and Antonio, see Alonzi, *Famiglia*, p. 271. Letters among the three brothers underscore their method of combining resources and contacts from the three geographic areas to advance the Boncompagni interests. See ASV, Archivio Boncompagni Ludovisi, 785.
132. See ASV, Archivio Boncompagni Ludovisi, 785 (2 May 1689; marked "letter 223").
133. ASV, Archivio Boncompagni Ludovisi, 897, letters of 1705–10.
134. ASV, Archivio Boncompagni Ludovisi, 787, fascicolo 1 (24 April1707).
135. Ibid. (undated letter fragment, probably late June 1707): "*l'ha permesso Iddio per suo giusto giudizio.*"
136. Ibid. (28 September 1707).
137. For more on the particularities of this aspect of the settlement, see Alonzi, *Famiglia*, pp. 285–90.
138. Ibid., pp. 289–90. On Ippolita's claims about her dowry, see ASV, Archivio Boncompagni Ludovisi, 624, 411v.
139. ASV, Archivio Boncompagni Ludovisi, 624, 493r.
140. Alonzi, *Famiglia*, p. 287.
141. On Ippolita being named guardian, see ASV, Archivio Boncompagni Ludovisi, 581, fascicolo 14 (28 September 1707). Certainly, 1707 was a tense year – both a procurator for Ippolita's daughters and Antonio lay claim to the Boncompagni fiefs. Cf. ASV, Archivio Boncompagni Ludovisi, 581, fascicolo 15 (15 March 1707, the daughters' claims to the Boncompagni holdings) and ASV, Archivio Boncompagni Ludovosi, 581, fascicolo 16 (1 May 1707), which contain Antonio's claims to the same territories.
    Alonzi's narrative of Ippolita's advocacy for her daughters differs from mine in several respects. Especially important in his narration is the claim that Ippolita did not, from the beginning of her widowhood, advocate for her daughters. She began to do so only later, somewhere around 1710. He provides no explanation for this shift, which is the primary goal of this chapter. However, in contrast to what Alonzi concludes, there is strong evidence in the epistolary record for Ippolita's advocacy for her daughters' dowries from the first year of her widowhood, but her in-laws discouraged her active pursuit of this goal. Alonzi posits a conflict between Ippolita and her fifth daughter, Anna Maria, but this seems farfetched, especially in the years immediately following Gregorio's death (pp. 285, 291). Anna Maria was at that time only 11 years old and she resided in the Tor de' Specchi convent in Rome. It is possible that Alonzi confused Gregorio's illegitimate

daughter, Marianna, with Anna Maria, because Anna Maria (the legitimate daughter) is also listed as Marianna in some sources. See ASV, Archivio Boncompagni Ludovisi, 624, 428r, in which the illegitimate daughter evidently asked for the liquidation of the entire Boncompagni landed patrimony. Sources for Alonzi's claims are confusing. See *Famiglia*, pp. 284–5, note 28.

142. ASV, Archivio Boncompagni Ludovisi, 624, 426r.

143. Ibid., 489v–490r.

144. For Ippolita's struggles with her brother's tenant, see ASV, Archivio Boncompagni Ludovisi, 379, fascicolo 24; 59; 68.

145. Piombino had been awarded to Ippolita's father, Niccolò, but the fief remained entangled in the precarious politics of the early eighteenth century. The property passed briefly to Ippolita's sister, Olimpia, and was inherited by Ippolita at Olimpia's death in 1700. She and Gregorio co-ruled the territory in the early eighteenth century. See Alonzi, *Famiglia*, pp. 256–8, 329.

146. Venosa represents an interesting case study in women's attempts to beat back the claims of creditors in order to save a fief from alienation. See ASV, Archivio Boncompagni Ludovisi, 273, fascicolo 59 (especially 908r–908v); fascicoli 63; 65; 66; ASV, Archivio Boncompagni Ludovisi, 274, fascicolo 57; fascicolo 58 (681r–684v); fascicolo 59 (686r–688v).

147. Alonzi argues that Antonio wanted to use allodial lands and properties to restore the Boncompagni entailed holdings. By contrast, it was in the interest of the unmarried daughters (and Ippolita) to keep as much wealth as possible out of entail, so that it could be allocated for their dowries, although Ippolita would claim entailed lands for them as well. See Alonzi, *Famiglia*, pp. 285–6.

148. Archivio Boncompagni Ludovisi, 624, 230r.

149. Ibid.

150. Ibid., 231v. Giacomo reaffirmed the holdings in the Regno when he passed the primogeniture to his second son, Gregorio, at the death of his first-born son, Ugo.

151. Ibid., 232r.

152. Ibid., 233r–233v.

153. ASV, Archivio Boncompagni Ludovisi, 47, fascicolo 8, 48r–48v (23 January 1715). The language echoes the declaration by the Regio Consiglio of Naples, which had found in Antonio's favor in 1711. Alonzi provides a lengthy transcript of the dispatch of Charles VI, possibly from ASV, Archivio Boncompagni Ludovisi, 327. See Alonzi, *Famiglia*, pp. 295–6.

154. ASV, Archivio Boncompagni Ludovisi, 47, fascicolo 8, 47v.

155. ASV, Archivio Boncompagni Ludovisi, 624, 406r.

156. ASV, Archivio Boncompagni Ludovisi, 787, fascicolo 1 (3 April 1709; 14 July 1709).

157. On the dissipation of the Ludovisi family fortune by Ippolita's older brother, see Alonzi, *Famiglia*, p. 328. Giovanni Battista's infant son died the same year as he did (1699). See the detailed genealogical information in Venditti and Quaglieri, *Archivio Boncompagni Ludovisi*, vol. 5.

158. On Ippolita's struggle against the debts against Piombino, see Alonzi, *Famiglia*, pp. 328–9.

159. Benedetta Borello, *Trame sovrapposte: La socialità aristocratica e le reti di relazioni femminili a Roma (XVII–XVIII secolo)* (Naples, 2003).
160. ASV, Archivio Boncompagni Ludovisi, 787, fascicolo 1 (21 September 1709).
161. Ibid. (undated letter fragment, probably from early June 1707).
162. Ibid. (undated letter fragment, probably from late June 1707).
163. Ibid. (26 December 1708).
164. Ibid. (undated letter fragment, probably late June 1707).
165. Alonzi, *Famiglia*, pp. 258–63.
166. Ibid., pp. 272–3. On Gregorio's commitment to Spanish rule, see BAV, Fondo Boncompagni Ludovisi, F 44.
167. Alonzi claims that Ippolita's connections to Madrid undermined Antonio's ability to appeal to Vienna, placing Antonio in a position that was "humiliating and difficult to accept" – that he had to abandon the Spanish loyalties of his family. This conclusion misses the larger reality that southern Italy was ceded to the Austrians in the Treaty of Utrecht, making it impossible for Antonio, if he wished to hold his territories in the south, to ignore the authority of Vienna. This, as much as Ippolita's activities, must have motivated Antonio. See Alonzi, *Famiglia*, pp. 296–7, 299. It certainly must have been the case that the international dimensions of the struggle allowed Antonio and Ippolita to play the European powers against each other. See Alonzi, *Famiglia*, p. 298.
168. ASV, Archivio Boncompagni Ludovisi, 787, fascicolo 1 (16 July 1707).
169. Ibid. (undated letter fragment, probably early June 1707).
170. Ibid. (undated letter fragment, probably from late June 1707).
171. On Riccardelli (the *"torbido cervello"*), see ibid. (28 September 1707). On Viscardi's relationship to her husband, see ibid. (10 December 1707; 28 December 1707). Riccardelli had evidently been the *auditore* of her husband, so he was no stranger to the family. Riccardelli's worries about Ippolita did not convince Gregorio to make out a will. See Riccardelli's post facto account of his conversations with Gregorio, in ASV, Archivio Boncompagni Ludovisi, 624, 653r (19 May 1707).
172. ASV, Archivio Boncompagni Ludovisi, 624, 693r; 698r (26 January 1711; 14 February 1711).
173. ASV, Archivio Boncompagni Ludovisi, 788, letter from Antonio to Cardinal Giacomo (29 June 1711). In this letter Antonio is similarly bitter toward Ippolita and her demands for the girls' dowries, claiming that "they were ordered to marry," an odd claim not substantiated in other sources.
174. Alonzi, *Famiglia*, p. 273.
175. ASV, Archivio Boncompagni Ludovisi, 787, fascicolo 1 (3 August 1707; 9 February 1709).
176. Ibid. (11 May 1707).
177. Ibid. (21 September 1709).
178. Ibid. (19 October 1707; 9 October 1709).
179. Ibid. (11 May 1707; undated letter fragment, probably from late June 1707; 4 September 1709).
180. Alonzi also briefly acknowledges the religious dimension of the conflict, but he does so by situating the rebellious Ippolita in opposition to "post-Tridentine" or "Baroque" standards of female behavior. The religious dimensions of the conflict call for a more nuanced approach to the religious

sensibilities of the late seventeenth century. The spiritual dimension of Ippolita's upbringing and worldview cannot be ignored. Robert Aleksander Maryks has offered the most intelligible treatment of the importance of probabilism to the religious culture of the seventeenth century. See *Saint Cicero and the Jesuits: The Influence of the Liberal Arts on the Adoption of Moral Probabilism* (Burlington, VT, 2008). As Maryks observes, probabilism is a vastly understudied phenomenon and the wider impact of probabilism on European culture has yet to be fully examined (p. 147). Its publishing highpoint was from 1600 to 1630 but its influence extended far into the seventeenth century (p. 105).

181. Maryks notes that the critical feature of probabilism was not the recognition that there were many opinions on an issue, but rather that "in giving the *penitents* the consoling and liberating possibility of following in good conscience an opinion that is less 'safe' (exposed to a risk of material sin) and/or less plausible, even though it might contradict the advice of their confessors. The significance is moral and personal rather than strictly academic ... Probabilism changed the nature of the relationship between the penitent and the confessor, who had now to absolve not because he could back his decision with the opinion of safe authority, but because the penitent could claim a probable opinion." Ibid., p. 8. Regarding the difference between moral and speculative certainty, see ibid., pp. 132–3, 138–9.

182. "gran scrupolo di coscienza" in ASV, Archivio Boncompagni Ludovisi, 787, fascicolo 1 (23 November 1709).

183. See Maryks, *Saint Cicero*, pp. 8, 47, 98, 101, 105.

184. Ibid., pp. 67, 114.

185. Ibid., pp. 8, 17–18, 31, 45, 76, 113, 122.

186. Ibid., pp. 3, 7, 47, 78, 98, 100–1, 105. Cicero extended the utility of the use of probable opinions to the construction of a successful oration and the Jesuits followed his guidelines in teaching cases of conscience. See ibid., pp. 100–1.

187. Ibid., pp. 8, 114.

188. See ibid., pp. 67–8 and John O'Malley, *The First Jesuits* (Cambridge, MA, 1995), pp. 145, 147.

189. For more on the complex seventeenth-century history of probabilism, see Maryks, *Saint Cicero*, pp. 5, 70–1, 140–4. Among the Jesuits who rejected probabilism and returned to the medieval ethics of tutiorism was Cardinal Bellarmine, who investigated the scientist Galileo for heresy in the early seventeenth century. Galileo, Robert Maryks has argued, was likely influenced by probabilism: on Bellarmine, p. 143. On Galileo, p. 147. On their encounter, p. 70.

190. Maryks, *Saint Cicero*, p. 117. Maryks notes that *"deponere conscientiam"* was the practice of medieval tutiorism, the system of ethical practice initially embraced by the Jesuits, including Ignatius Loyola. Tutiorism never entirely disappeared, and had a variety of adherents across confessional lines in the sixteenth and seventeenth centuries. Ibid., pp. 70–1.

191. Maryks, *Saint Cicero*, pp. 8, 113.

192. Ibid., pp. 115, 132.

193. Ibid., p. 122. Paolo Segneri, a defender of probabilism in the late seventeenth century, carefully demarcated the conditions of such rebellion, namely emphasizing that "wickedness in high places" should be confronted

by the faithful. Segneri, *The Manna of the Soul: Meditations for Every Day of the Year*, 2 vols, 2nd edition (London, 1892), vol. 1, p. 353. Only moral superiors have to be obeyed and the goal of the true Christian was to die in the service of justice, if necessary. Segneri, *Manna of the Soul*, vol. 2, pp. 29, 218. On the more conservative aspects of some Jesuits' political thought, see Harro Höpfl, *Jesuit Political Thought: The Society of Jesus and the State*, c. *1540–1630* (New York, 2004), esp. pp. 51–2.

194. On the intriguing Jesuit perspective on familial authority residing equally in mothers and fathers, see Höpfl, *Jesuit Political Thought*, pp. 197–9.

195. ASV, Archivio Boncompagni Ludovisi, 787, fascicolo 1 (24 April 1707).

196. Ibid. (3 August 1707).

197. Ibid. (16 July 1707; 3 August 1707; 28 December 1707; 9 February 1709). In the controversy over her matrimony, Teresa is also referred to as "*la povera figliola innocente*," ibid. (7 November 1709).

198. Ibid. (14 November 1708; 8 December 1708). The letters of thanks and holiday wishes from the four girls echoed her sentiments. See ASV, Archivio Boncompagni Ludovisi, 786.

199. For the use of plaques to remind hospital residents to remember the intentions of their benefactors, see Matthew Sneider, "Charity and Property – The Patrimonies of Bolognese Hospitals" (PhD diss., Brown University, 2004) and Matthew Sneider, "Charity and Property: The Wealth of *opere pie* in Early Modern Bologna," in *Povertà e innovazioni istituzionali in Italia dal Medioevo ad oggi*, ed. Vera Zamagni (Bologna, 2000), p. 134.

200. ASV, Archivio Boncompagni Ludovisi, 787, fascicolo 1 (3 August 1707).

201. Ibid. (21 September 1709).

202. Ibid. (3 August 1707; 21 September 1709).

203. Alonzi, *Famiglia*, p. 270.

204. "*Le nostre comuni famiglie*," in ASV, Archivio Boncompagni Ludovisi, 787, fascicolo 1 (10 Nov 1709).

205. Alonzi, *Famiglia*, pp. 266–70.

206. ASV, Archivio Boncompagni Ludovisi, 787, fascicolo 1 (28 September 1707).

207. Ibid. (14 November 1708). Ippolita makes the case through an emphasis on Teresa's lack of vocation, but she clearly holds that the same standard should be applied to the situation of the other girls.

208. Thomas Kuehn's analysis of the Orsini inheritance practices of this kind in the fifteenth and sixteenth centuries offers a detailed look at how this worked (with some glitches) for one Roman family. See his "*Fideicommissum* and Family: The Orsini di Bracciano," *Viator* 39.2 (2008): 323–42.

209. Maura Piccialuti, *L'immortalità dei beni: Fidecommessi e primogeniture a Roma nei secoli xvii e xvii* (Rome, 1999), p. 248.

210. ASV, Archivio Boncompagni Ludovisi, 787, fascicolo 1 (24 April 1707).

211. Ibid. (10 December 1707). Gregorio's sister, Suor Maria Gerolama, a nun in a Neapolitan convent, claimed in a letter to Cardinal Giacomo that – as rumor had it – Ippolita was horrified by Giulia's good reaction to the Roman convent. See ASV, Archivio Boncompagni Ludovisi, 897, 223r (20 January ?1709). Considering the extreme financial difficulty of marrying all of the girls, it seems unlikely that Ippolita would have been opposed to the genuine inclination of one of her daughters toward the religious life. As

their guardian, she could have prevented them from the common practice of living with aunts (for a time) in convents. She did not.

212. Though a member of the Holy Congregation of the Council, Cardinal Giacomo never participated in their deliberations, although he actively recommended one woman in his bishopric who sought release from her religious vows. See Anne Jacobson Schutte, *By Force and Fear: Taking and Breaking Monastic Vows in Early Modern Europe* (Ithaca, NY, 2011), pp. 108, 209–10. Cardinal Giacomo's duties as bishop may have limited his trips to Rome to participate in the Congregation's deliberations, although Schutte does not note this as a possible explanation for his absence.

213. Archivio Boncompagni Ludovisi, 787, fascicolo 1 (24 February 1701).
214. Ibid. (5 February 1710).
215. Ibid. (10 November 1708).
216. Ibid. (10 November 1708).
217. Ibid. (3 April 1709).
218. See Chapter 3 of this volume.
219. I thank Professor Renata Ago for her insights on this term as a figure of speech.
220. ASV, Archivio Boncompagni Ludovisi, 787, fascicolo 1 (3 April 1709).
221. Ibid. (3 April 1709; 2 July 1707).
222. Christiane Klapisch-Zuber analyzed the conflicting family loyalties that Renaissance mothers experienced. See *Women, Family, and Ritual in Renaissance Italy* (Chicago, 1987), pp. 117–31. Giulia Calvi traced the juridical implications of these paradoxes, and the way in which seventeenth-century widows questioned the view that their children should be placed with their patrilinear kin. See *Il Contratto morale: Madri e figli nella Toscana moderna* (Rome, 1994), especially pp. 28–32.
223. ASV, Archivio Boncompagni Ludovisi, 787, fascicolo 1 (23 November 1709).
224. Ibid. (14 November 1708; 8 December 1708).
225. Paolo Segneri, "On Parental Obligation," in *Twelve Sermons*, trans. James Ford (London, 1859), pp. 254–75; Jennifer D. Selwyn, *A Paradise Inhabited by Devils: The Jesuits' Civilizing Mission in Early Modern Naples* (Vermont, 2004), p. 177; Elisa Novi Chavarria, "Ideologia e compartamenti familiari nei Predicatori Italiani tra cinque e settecento: tematiche e modelli," *Rivista Storica Italiana* 100.3 (1988): 679–723.
226. Ezio Bolis, *L'Uomo tra Peccato, Grazia e Libertà nell'Opera di Paolo Segneri sj (1624–1694)* (Rome, 1996), p. 81.
227. Ibid., p. 81.
228. Luigi Fiorani, "Monache e Monasteri Romani nell'Età del Quietismo," *Ricerche per la storia religiosa di Roma* I (1977): 63–111.
229. For more on the impact of the teaching of Molinos upon Eleonora Boncompagni Borghese's life, see Chapter 3.
230. On quietism in the Roman convents, see Fiorani, "Monache e Monasteri," and Bolis, *L'Uomo*, p. 87. On the high ranking prelates, see ibid., p. 81.
231. Bolis, *L'Uomo*, pp. 81–2.
232. This is the first and second proposition of Michele de Molinos's *Dux spiritualis* (Rome, 1675).
233. Bolis, *L'Uomo*, p. 86, note 143.
234. Ibid., p. 83.

235. Ibid., p. 83.
236. Ibid., pp. 34–5.
237. On the arc of Molinos's influence in three decades of preaching, see ibid., pp. 26–8.
238. *La Manna dell'anima. Ovvero esercizio facile insieme e fruttuoso per chi desidera in qualche modo d'attendere all'orazione. Per tutti i giorni dell'anno.* The work was first published in four volumes in the 1670s and early 1680s: *Primo Trimestre* (Bologna, 1673); *Secondo Trimestre* (Bologna, 1675); *Terzo Trimestre* (Firenze, 1679); *Quattro Trimestre* (Milano, 1680). See Bolis, *L'Uomo*, p. 233.
239. Bolis notes the widespread and enduring relevance of Segneri's writings, which were an inspiration as late as the early 1940s to the future pope, John XXIII. See Bolis, *L'Uomo*, p. 4, note 8. Since Bolis did not construct the publishing history of *Manna of the Soul*, I used WorldCat in order to formulate some idea of its success in print between 1673 and 1730. An edition by the printer Poletti in Venice, 1711, identified the text as its "nona impressione," which if correct, indicates that there were nine editions by 1711. I was able to track 14 different editions of the sermons *Il Quaresimale* between 1679 and 1730. There were 21 editions *Manna of the Soul* in the same time period.
240. ASV, Archivio Boncompagni Ludovisi, 787, fascicolo 1 (26 December 1708).
241. She noted in a letter of June 1709 that she had heard the rumors of interest in Teresa on the part of the Barberini family, but that she had intentionally ignored them, claiming that Teresa was not of the age to be married. As a result Cardinal Barberini had approached one of Cardinal Giacomo's sisters in the convent. Ibid. (10 June 1709).
242. Ibid. (14 July 1709).
243. Ibid. (7 November 1709; 23 November 1709).
244. Ibid. (14 July 1709). Ippolita distanced herself early in the struggle from the fate of her husband's illegitimate daughter, Marianna, noting that four daughters were all the weight that she could carry. See Archivio Boncompagni Ludovisi, 624, 443r.
245. ASV, Archivio Boncompagni Ludovisi, 787, fascicolo 1 (14 July 1709).
246. Ibid. (21 September 1709).
247. Ibid. (21 September 1709).
248. Ibid. (21 September 1709).
249. Ibid. (14 July 1709).
250. Ibid. (3 August 1707). On God alone knowing the sentiment of her heart, see ibid. (24 April 1707).
251. On the emergence of the heart as the center of human morality, see John Jeffries Martin, *Myths of Renaissance Individualism* (Basingstoke, 2004), pp. 104–5.
252. Segneri, *Twelve Sermons*, p. 79. The duty to family, for instance, is located "not in the statute, but in the heart;" ibid., p. 258.
253. ASV, Archivio Boncompagni Ludovisi, 787, fascicolo 1 (undated letter fragment, probably from early June 1707).
254. Segneri underscored that any labor done well is sanctifying. A valiant woman who could spin well, he observed, did "enough to make her a saint." *Manna of the Soul*, vol. 1, p. 184.
255. ASV, Archivio Boncompagni Ludovisi, 787, fascicolo 1 (21 September 1709).

256. Ibid. (undated letter fragment, probably from early June 1707).

257. Ibid. (21 September 1698).

258. Ibid. (2 July 1707).

259. See Chapter 3 of this volume.

260. Segneri, *Manna of the Soul*, vol. 1, p. 111.

261. "Guerra intestinale invisibile dal Cielo," in Mattia Naldi, *Regole per la cura del contagio* (Rome, 1656), p. 2, cited in Sheila C. Barker, "Plague Art in Early Modern Rome: Divine Directives and Temporal Remedies," in *Hope and Healing: Painting in Italy in a Time of Plague, 1500–1800*, ed. Gauvin Alexander Bailey, Pamela M. Jones, Franco Mormando, and Thomas W. Worcester (Worcester, MA, 2005), p. 51.

262. This broadly held idea had multiple religious, literary, and artistic manifestations in the seventeenth century. Art historians have emphasized the confluence of God's wrath and mercy in paintings related to the plague. See Franco Mormando, "Introduction: Response to the Plague in Early Modern Italy: What the Primary Sources, Printed and Painted, Reveal," in *Hope and Healing*, pp. 1–44. If one considers the imagery around the plague, seventeenth-century depictions in Rome tended to stress God's mercy and the necessity of human care for the afflicted mattered much more than the damnation of those upon whom the plague was inflicted. See Barker, "Plague Art in Early Modern Rome," pp. 45–64.

263. Segneri argued that such a scenario might be avoided by ceasing to be a sinner. See *Manna of the Soul*, vol. 1, p. 72.

264. ASV, Archivio Boncompagni Ludovisi, 787, fascicolo 1 (7 August 1707). Segneri lauded the value of patience in the face of adversity and in human spirituality more generally. *Manna of the Soul*, vol. 1, pp. 49–52, 59, 111, 114, 139.

265. ASV, Archivio Boncompagni Ludovisi, 787, fascicolo 1 (21 September 1709).

266. Ibid. (21 September 1709).

267. Ibid. (21 September 1709). It is ambiguous as to whether she is referring to the presence in the household of so many daughters (six) or to the fate of her girls to have to wait yet longer to know their fate – whether they would have dowries sufficient to marry or not.

268. Ibid. (21 September 1709).

269. Ibid. (23 November 1709).

270. Ibid. (23 November 1709). Segneri likewise put great emphasis on the necessity of working toward the perfection of oneself, or the centrality of "perform[ing] those actions that are proper to the community, to the state in which God has placed thee ... They are the duties of thy state." *Manna of the Soul*, vol. 2, p. 184.

271. ASV, Archivio Boncompagni Ludovisi, 787, fascicolo 1 (15 June 1707).

272. Ibid. (1 June 1709). Segneri legitimated the struggle for justice as one of the highest Christian virtues, which like charity, necessitated that the Christian "fall in love" with it, or contemplate its beauty. On the beauty of justice, see *Manna of the Soul*, vol. 2, pp. 546–7. On being "in love with charity," see ibid., vol. 1, p. 52.

273. Segneri, *Manna of the Soul*, vol. 2, p. 218. He cites Ecclesiastes 4:33.

274. ASV, Archivio Boncompagni Ludovisi, 624, 692r (26 January 1711); 696r (28 November 1711); 698r (14 February 1711).

275. Alonzi, *Famiglia*, pp. 320–1. Alonzi notes that this came to light after Ippolita's death in 1733, but since she openly made promises on the Ludovisi patrimony in order to marry off her remaining daughters, it is likely that she mentioned it in her negotiations.

276. The expression is Visceglia's. See *Il Bisogno di eternità: i comportamenti aristocratici a Napoli in età moderna* (Naples, 1988). Alonzi argues that Ippolita's choice fits most closely with the pattern identified by Visceglia. About half the female testators Visceglia studied in Naples recognized the priorities of primogeniture in the same way as their male counterparts. These women demonstrated a preference for their first-born male grandchild. See Alonzi's comparison with the Naples data, *Famiglia*, pp. 319–20. I argue that Ippolita recognizes her grandson in a particular way, without neglecting her daughters' needs for dowries, even if it diminished her grandson's later potential inheritance.

277. On her will and the postponement of Gaetano's inheritance to the future as a sign of Ippolita's "indecision and distress," see Alonzi, *Famiglia*, p. 319. I believe that she was trying to balance the interests of her offspring, as I outline above.

278. ASV, Archivio Boncompagni Ludovisi, 401, 666r (undated letter, Ippolita to Maria Eleonora); 673v (14 May 1724, Maria Eleonora to Ippolita); 675r (31 May 1724, Maria Eleonora to Ippolita).

279. On Gaetano's time with Ippolita in Rome and his indecisiveness on his future, see ibid., 663r–664r (26 November 1717); 695r–696v (1 August 1724).

280. Ibid., 697r (15 August 1724).

281. Ibid., 666v (Ippolita to Eleonora, undated letter).

282. Alonzi notes that the promissory note on future income from Piombino was not sustained by the Spanish monarchy. In 1739, Maria Eleonora was absolved by the Supremo Consiglio of Castile from having to pay 100,000 scudi on the income of Piombino as part of the dowry settlement of her sisters. On the decision, see Alonzi, *Famiglia*, pp. 325, 329. On the larger story of Piombino, including its legal status as potentially passing to either males or females, see ibid., pp. 323–8.

283. Gaetano's complaints about his familial situation were numerous. To save money his parents sent Gaetano to Bologna, and his uncle Cardinal Giacomo placed him in a seminary in Bologna, which he resented. See Alonzi, *Famiglia*, p. 305. Gaetano also resented his mother Maria Eleonora's attention to his siblings, especially his younger brother, even though he was given a privileged place in the family inheritance patterns. On the resentful behavior of Gaetano toward his younger brother, see ibid., pp. 311–13, 317. Alonzi grudgingly acknowledges Ippolita's role in bringing siblings closer to parity. He notes the similarities between Ippolita's and Maria Eleonora's attention to their children beyond the firstborn. In contrast to his more positive view of Maria Eleonora, however, Alonzi considers Ippolita "eccentric" and a "rebel" against the patrilinear system; ibid., p. 318. She was certainly the latter.

284. On the two reports with diverging advice for Antonio, see Alonzi, *Famiglia*, pp. 299–304. On Antonio's failure in the reports, see ibid., p. 300. Alonzi charges Antonio with being "timid and pessimistic in the administration of the inherited patrimony" (p. 315). The negotiations regarding the girls'

dowries were confusing from the beginning (p. 291). The reluctance of the Boncompagni men (Cardinal Giacomo and Antonio) contrasted sharply with the behavior of fathers (and some mothers) whose cruelties toward their children are documented in the cases of forced monarchization studied by Schutte, *By Force and Fear*.

285. Alonzi, *Famiglia*, p. 302.
286. Ibid., p. 302. "Professori Causidici" is an expression from the more conciliatory text.
287. Alonzi argues that this newer danger was in contrast to the emphasis in the sixteenth century on debts as the danger to families. Ibid., pp. 303–4. On the proliferation of legal challenges to primogeniture in Rome, see Piccialuti, *L'immortalità dei beni*, p. 248.
288. Alonzi, *Famiglia*, p. 291.

5 Extravagant Pretensions: The Triumph of Maternal Love in the World of Rome

1. Biblioteca Apostolica Vaticana [hereafter BAV], Archivio Barberini, Indice IV, 1572, 14r (22 December 1725); 278r–278v (21 September 1726).
2. Ibid., 258v (8 September 1725). I thank Dennis McEnnerney for his thoughts on resistance and history and the audience at the American Society for Eighteenth-Century Studies panel at the American Historical Association Conference.
3. Between 1714 and 1735, the Austrian Habsburgs ruled the Kingdom of Naples, where Charles VI referred to himself as the "King of Spain." See Ernst Wangermann, *The Austrian Achievement 1700–1800* (London, 1973), p. 12.
4. See Giulia Calvi, *Il contratto morale: madri e figli nella Toscana moderna* (Rome, 1994), for similar arguments in Tuscany.
5. For a brief overview of interpretations and significance of the painting, see *Art in Rome in the Eighteenth Century*, ed. Edgar Peters Bowron and Joseph J. Rishel (Philadelphia, 2000), pp. 384–5, plate 233.
6. Renata Ago, *Carriere e Clientele nella Roma barocca* (Rome, 1990), and idem, "Giochi di squadra: uomini e donne nelle famiglie nobili del XVII secolo," in *Signori, patrizi, cavalieri in Italia centro-meridionale nell'età moderna*, ed. Maria Antonietta Visceglia (Rome, 1992), pp. 256–64.
7. On female letter writing, see "The Making of the *Mater Litigans* in Rome," in the Introduction to this volume.
8. Marina D'Amelia, "Becoming a Mother in the Seventeenth Century: The Experience of a Roman Noblewoman," in *Time, Space, and Women's Lives in Early Modern Europe*, ed. Anne Jacobson Schutte, Thomas Kuehn, and Silvana Seidel Menchi (Kirksville, MO, 2001), pp. 225–6.
9. See BAV, Archivio Barberini, Indice II, 2256.
10. BAV, Archivio Barberini, Indice II, 1329, 7r.
11. Ibid., 34r–35v (18 November 1722): Accord between Cardinal Francesco and Teresa.
12. Ibid.; see also ibid., 7r–7v.
13. Ibid., 33r (18 November 1722): Letter from mediator to Cardinal Francesco.
14. Calvi, *Il contratto morale*, pp. 92–105.

15. BAV, Archivio Barberini, Indice II, 1329, 33r (18 November 1722): Letter from mediator to Cardinal Francesco.
16. Ibid.
17. Ibid., 7r–7v: Petition by Cardinal Francesco.
18. For more on this conflict, see Chapter 2 of this volume.
19. BAV, Archivio Barberini, Indice II, 1329, 28v: Petition by Cardinal Francesco.
20. Ibid., 8v: Petition by Cardinal Francesco.
21. Hanns Gross, *Rome in the Age of Enlightenment* (Cambridge, 1990), p. 54; BAV, Archivio Barberini, Indice II, 1329, 8r: Petition by Cardinal Francesco.
22. BAV, Archivio Barberini, Indice II, 1329, 8v: Petition by Cardinal Francesco.
23. Ludwig Von Pastor, *The History of the Popes*, trans. Dom Ernest Graf, O.S.B., (London, 1957), vol. 34, pp. 12, 101, 118, 129.
24. BAV, Archivio Barberini, Indice II, 1329, 9r: Petition by Cardinal Francesco. For a draft of the proposal in Francesco's hand, see ibid., 92r (6 September 1725, Palazzo alle Quattro fontane).
25. Ibid., 9v: Petition by Cardinal Francesco.
26. BAV, Archivio Barberini, Indice IV, 1572, 129r (3 August 1726): Letter from Cardinal Francesco to Carlo Borromeo.
27. BAV, Archivio Barberini, Indice II, 1237, and BAV, Indice II, 1246, on Francesco's negotiations.
28. BAV, Archivio Barberini, Indice IV, 1572, 45r–53r.
29. Ibid., 54r–55r (March 1726): Letter from Cardinal Franceso to Carlo Borromeo.
30. Ibid., 69r–69v (13 April 1726): Letter from Cardinal Francesco to Carlo Giacomo Cattaneo.
31. On Federico's excessive attention to his clothing, see ibid., 102r–102v (11 May 1726): Letter from Cardinal Francesco to Camilla. On his threat to withdraw to a hermitage, see ibid., 101r. On his excessive spending, see ibid., 124r–126v (13 July 1726): Letter from Cardinal Francesco to Carlo Borromeo.
32. Ibid., 82r–83v (3 May 1726): Letter from Cattaneo to Cardinal Francesco.
33. Ibid., 113r (16 May 1726): Letter from Cardinal Francesco to Camilla.
34. On his other negotiations, see (13 April 1726): Letter from Cardinal Francesco to Cattaneo; ibid., 196r–207r (September 1726): Letter from Cardinal Francesco to the Principessa Carbognano; ibid., 306v (5 October 1726): Letter from Teresa Boncompagni to Carlo Borromeo.
35. BAV, Archivio Barberini, Indice II, 1329, 8v: Petition by Cardinal Francesco. On the close ties between the Barberini family and the Convento dell' Incarnazione, see Luigi Cacciaglia, "*L'archivio del Monastero dell'Incarnazione detto 'le Barberine' alla Biblioteca Vaticana,*" in *Vite consacrate: gli archivi delle organizzazioni religiose femminili*, Atti del Convegno, Ravenna 28 sett. 2006, *Atti e memorie della deputazione di storia patria per l'Emilia e la Romagna 2007*.
36. BAV, Archivio Barberini, Indice II, 1329, 97r (19 September 1725): Petition by Cardinal Francesco.
37. Anna Colonna to Carlo Barberini (20 March 1646), in Pio Pecchiai, *I Barberini* (Rome, 1959), pp. 184–5. On Anna Colonna's mothering, see Chapter 1 of this volume.
38. BAV, Archivio Barberini, Indice IV, 1572, 23r–24v (1 February 1726): Cardinal Francesco to Monsignore Mario Mellini Auditore. On help from *auditore* Francesco Parensi to Cardinal Francesco, see ibid., 275r–276r.

39. Ibid., 358r–396r (15 November 1726): Letter from Camilla Barberini to Cardinal Francesco, describing the Rials family visit to the Borromeo family. On communications from Rials, forwarded to Cardinal Francesco, see ibid., 37r–38r (6 March 1726), 269r–270v (21 August 1726), and 353r (30 October 1726).
40. BAV, Archivio Barberini, Indice II, 1329, 319r–319v. The letter lacks a signature, but reports sympathetically of the valiant but unsuccessful attempts to negotiate a solution by Cardinal Cienfuegos, an official of the Holy Roman Emperor residing in Rome.
41. "Extravagant pretension" is in ibid., 118r–118v (29 December 1726): Letter from Cardinal Francesco to the Secretary of State, Marchese di Rials. See ibid., 398r–399v, for what appears to be a draft of a similar letter from Cardinal Francesco to the Holy Roman Emperor.
42. Ibid., 110v–111r (16 May 1726): Letter from Cardinal Francesco to Camilla Borromeo.
43. Ibid., 31r (6 February 1726): Letter from Cardinal Francesco to Cardinal Cienfuegos.
44. Ibid., 231r (1 March 1727): Letter from Cardinal Francesco to Camilla.
45. See Chapter 4 of this volume.
46. BAV, Archivio Barberini, Indice IV, 1572, 37r–38r (20 March 1726): Letter from Marchese Rials to Carlo Borromeo.
47. BAV, Archivio Barberini, Indice II, 1329, 1r (22 November 1725): Procurator Domenico Correale, on behalf of Teresa.
48. BAV, Archivio Barberini, Indice IV, 1572, 86r–92v: A version of Francesco's will that threatens to disinherit Cornelia if she did not marry Federico Borromeo.
49. Ibid., 21v (19 January 1726): Cardinal Francesco to the Rota.
50. Ibid., 227r: Response of Teresa to Francesco. Internal evidence suggests the document was written in 1725, although it is difficult to say with certainty.
51. Calvi, *Il contratto morale*, pp. 27–8.
52. BAV, Archivio Barberini, Indice IV, 1572, 227v: Response of Teresa to Francesco.
53. Ibid., 227v.
54. Ibid., 227v.
55. Ibid., 227v.
56. Ibid., 299r: Summary by Francesco; see also ibid., 340r (19 October 1726): Letter from Cardinal Cienfuegos to Carlo Borromeo.
57. Ibid., 14v (22 December 1725): Letter from Cardinal Cienfuegos.
58. Ibid., 306v (5 October 1726): Letter from Teresa to Carlo Borromeo in which she accused Cardinal Francesco of sacrificing Cornelia to his own interests.
59. Ibid., 306r.
60. Ibid., 398r–399v: Letter from Cardinal Francesco to the Holy Roman Emperor; a version of the letter was also sent to the Secretary of State, Marchese di Rials, in Vienna. See BAV, Archivio Barberini, Indice II, 1329, 118r–118v (29 December 1726).
61. BAV, Archivio Barberini, Indice II, 1329, 13v: Petition by Cardinal Francesco.
62. Caroline Castiglione, "The Politics of Mercy: Village Petitions and a Noblewoman's Justice in the Roman Countryside in the Eighteenth Century," in *Empowering Interactions: Political Cultures and the Emergence of the*

State in Europe, 14th–19th centuries, ed. Wim Blockmans, André Holenstein, and Jon Mathieu, (Aldershot, UK, 2009), pp. 79–90.

63. BAV, Archivio Barberini, Indice IV, 1572, 25r–26v (2 February 1726): Letter from Cardinal Francesco to Cardinal Cienfuegos.
64. BAV, Archivio Barberini, Indice II, 1329, 9v: Petition by Cardinal Francesco.
65. BAV, Archivio Barberini, Indice IV, 1572, 194r (30 September 1726): Letter from Cardinal Francesco to Camilla. According to this letter, Cornelia was particularly attached to one Paolino (sometimes also called Paoluccio) Borghese. This individual is not easy to identify in the Borghese genealogy. Cardinal Francesco evidently had a spy among the visitors to the Borghese villa at Frascati, who reported to the cardinal that Cornelia spent all her time with Paoluccio, calling to him to return to her whenever he tried to depart her company.
66. Ibid., 194r.
67. Ibid., 194r.
68. Ibid., 14r–14v (22 December 1725): Letter from Cardinal Cienfuegos to (Carlo Borromeo?).
69. Ibid., 14v.
70. Benedetta Borello, *Trame sovrapposte: la socialità aristocratica e le reti di relazioni femminili a Roma* (Naples, 2003), pp. 157–94.
71. On Cardinal Coscia, see von Pastor, *History of the Popes,* vol. 34, pp. 124–5, 127–8, 131–4. On Cardinal Coscia's supposed assistance to Teresa, see BAV, Archivio Barberini, Indice II, 1329, 21r–22r: Petition by Cardinal Francesco; and BAV, Archivio Barberini, Indice IV, 1572, 193r; 388r.
72. BAV, Archivio Barberini, Indice IV, 1572, 354r–354v. The letter is a fragment, but internal evidence suggests that it must be a response by Teresa to the letter Carlo Borromeo had sent to her. His letter was dated 19 October 1726.
73. BAV, Archivio Barberini, Indice 1329, 119r (29 December 1726): Letter from Cardinal Francesco to Marchese di Rials.
74. BAV, Archivio Barberini, Indice IV, 1572, 319r–319v (18 October 1726): Letter from Cardinal Cienfuegos to Marchese Rials.
75. Ibid., 305v (5 October 1726): Letter from Teresa to Carlo Borromeo.
76. Ibid., 306r.
77. Ibid., 306v.
78. Ibid., 307r.
79. Ibid., 307r.
80. Ibid., 307v.
81. Ibid., 307v.
82. Ibid., 309r (19 October 1726): Carlo Borromeo to Teresa Boncompagni.
83. Ibid., 310r.
84. Ibid., 311v.
85. Ibid., 310v.
86. Ibid., 379r–379v (11 December 1726): Carlo Borromeo to 276 (code number for Cardinal Cienfuegos).
87. BAV, Archivio Barberini, Indice II, 1329, 13v: Petition by Cardinal Francesco. Francesco seems to have used the term *"conversazioni"* to describe the informal gatherings at which were discussed the latest achievements in science, religious history, and archeology. See Gross, *Rome in the Age of Enlightenment,* 247, 267–9.
88. BAV, Archivio Barberini, Indice II, 1329, 13v–14r: Petition by Cardinal Francesco.
89. Ibid., 15r.

90. Ibid., 15v –16r. The new Secretary of State, Cardinal Niccolò Maria Lercari, was on Cardinal Francesco's side. Lercari conveyed to the pope how intently the Austrian monarch Charles VI wanted Cornelia confined to a convent.
91. Ibid., 17r.
92. Ibid., 18r.
93. Ibid., 18r.
94. Ibid., 19v–20r.
95. Ibid., 21r–22r.
96. Ibid., 22v–24v.
97. Ibid., 230r–231r (1 March 1727): Letter from Cardinal Francesco to Camilla Borromeo.
98. Ibid., 26v–28r: Petition by Cardinal Francesco. One must assume that Francesco meant Cardinal Alessandro Albani, with whom Francesco corresponded in this period. See ibid., 191r–191v (letter of 24 February 1727) and ibid., 232r–233r (letter of 3 March 1727).
99. Ibid., 27r–28r.
100. Ibid., 28v.
101. Ibid., 28v.
102. Ibid., 29r.
103. Ibid., 29r.
104. Ibid., 29v.
105. Von Pastor, *History of the Popes*, vol. 34, pp. 124–5; 127–8; 131–4. On how Cardinal Coscia damaged Benedict XIII's efforts at reform, see ibid., pp. 297–9.
106. Ibid., pp. 116, 159–60. Benedict could not abide beards or neckties either, but perruques were the primary enemy of clerical decorum for him. On his attempt to reform the clergy in other ways, see ibid., p. 158. On the wig-inspired papal insomnia in 1727, see ibid., p. 174.
107. BAV, Archivio Barberini, Indice II, 1329, 29v: Petition by Cardinal Francesco.
108. On the pope's refusal to use the usual papal apartments and his commissioning of a simple structure for sleeping in the papal gardens, see Von Pastor, *History of the Popes*, vol. 34, pp. 114 –15. On his love for Benevento, ibid., pp. 169–74.
109. BAV, Archivio Barberini, Indice II, 1329, 1r (22 November 1725): Procurator Domenico Correale, on behalf of Teresa.
110. Ibid., 180r (23 February 1727): Decree from Papal *auditore*.
111. Ibid., 284r–285v (Undated letter, in a child's hand, to "my Excellent Uncle," signed "your most humble servant, Cornelia Costanza Barberini").
112. Federica Ambrosini, "Toward a Social History of Women in Venice," in *Venice Reconsidered*, ed. John Martin and Dennis Romano (Baltimore, 2000), esp. pp. 435–6.
113. See Chapter 2 of this volume.
114. On Lercari's assistance to Francesco, see note 90. Von Pastor calls Lercari "a man of moderate ability, but utterly dependent on Coscia." Von Pastor, *History of the Popes*, vol. 34, p. 130.
115. This was the problem, for those who wished to reform the clergy. See Gross, *Rome in the Age of Enlightenment*, esp. pp. 271–2, on the failure of reform.
116. BAV, Archivio Barberini, Indice II, 1329, 174r (22 February 1726): Letter from Cardinal Francesco to Camilla Borromeo.
117. Ibid., 288r–289r (Letter of 18 May 1728).

118. See Chapter 2 of this volume.

119. BAV, Archivio Barberini, Indice II, 1329, 115v (29 December 1726): Letter from Francesco to Marchese di Rials.

120. Ibid., 118r–118v.

121. On the catalog of fear expected in the family, from reverential to grave, see Joanne M. Ferraro, *Marriage Wars in Late Renaissance Venice* (Oxford, 2001), pp. 41–2. For more on the theological dimensions of the concepts, see Anne Jacobson Schutte, *By Force and Fear: Taking and Breaking Monastic Vows in Early Modern Europe* (Ithaca, NY, 2011), pp. 144–6.

122. BAV, Archivio Barberini, Indice II, 1329, 110r (18 September 1726).

123. Ibid., 178r (23 February 1727): Statement by Francesco. Cardinal Francesco continued the pattern of whisking Cornelia away, even taking her surreptitiously from the convent for her impending nuptials the subsequent year. See Maria Giulia Barberini, "La *galleria dei ritratti* nel mezzanino di palazzo Barberini. Una strategia di famiglia," in *I Barberini e la Cultura Europea del Seicento*, ed. Lorenza Mochi Onori, Sebastian Schütze, and Francesco Solinas (Rome, 2007), pp. 605–18, esp. p. 614.

124. On the extermination/insanity defense of the Cardinal, see the second nearly unsuccessful encounter with the pope in his private chambers in BAV, Archivio Barberini, Indice II, 1329, 29r: Petition by Cardinal Francesco.

125. Ibid., 230r–231r (1 March 1727): Letter from Francesco to Camilla Borromeo. Francesco and his correspondents in Milan wrote part of their letters in code. The ciphers to Francesco Barberini codes have not all survived. I thank the archivist Dr. Carlo Antonio Pisoni for his guidance in the Borromeo Archive, especially in its collections of ciphers. See Archivio Borromeo (Isola Bella) Culto (hereafter ABIB) Cardinali, A-B, cartella no. 4834; and ABIB, Fondo Famiglia Borromeo, Borromeo Cifra, cartella no. 16.

126. BAV, Archivio Barberini, Indice II, 1329, 117v (29 December 1726): Letter from Francesco to Marchese di Rials.

127. Ibid., 230r–231r (1 March 1727): Letter from Francesco to Camilla Borromeo; ibid., 131r–131v (10 February 1727).

128. Ibid., 230r–231r (1 March 1727): Letter from Francesco to Camilla Borromeo.

129. Ibid., 26r–26v: Petition by Cardinal Francesco.

130. On the language of absolutism and France in the eighteenth century, see Jeffrey Merrick, "Fathers and Kings: Patriarchalism and Absolutism in Eighteenth-Century French Politics," *Studies on Voltaire and the Eighteenth Century* 308 (1993): 281–303.

131. BAV, Archivio Barberini, Indice II, 1329, 176r–177v (23 February 1727): Letter of Olimpia Giustiniani to Benedict XIII.

132. Ibid., 21v: Petition by Cardinal Francesco.

133. Ibid., 139v: Romana Tutelae de Barberinis, Restrictus Facti, & Juris, Pro ... Cardinali Francisco Barberino, item number 7.

134. Ibid., 239r (2 March 1727): Petition of Teresa Boncompagni.

135. See Chapter 2 of this volume.

136. Jürgen Habermas's classic is still of interest: *The Structural Transformation of the Public Sphere*, trans. Thomas Burger with Frederick Lawrence (Cambridge, 1991). However, its separation of reason and emotion in eighteenth-century culture is highly problematic. See John L. Brooke, "Reason and Passion

in the Public Sphere: Habermas and the Cultural Historians," *Journal of Interdiciplinary History* 29.1 (Summer 1998): 43–67.
137. On Jansenism, see Gross, *Rome in the Age of Enlightenment*, pp. 271–2, 276, 280.
138. Here I follow Wayne Te Brake's definition of early modern politics, "an ongoing bargaining process between those who claim governmental authority ... and those over whom that authority is said to extend." See *Shaping History: Ordinary People in European Politics, 1500–1700* (Berkeley, 1998), p. 6.
139. Raymond Grew, "Finding Social Capital: The French Revolution in Italy," *Journal of Interdisciplinary History* 29 (1999): 407–33, esp. pp. 413–14.
140. Gross, *Rome in the Age of Enlightenment*, p. 48. His precise numbers are 1,200 lawyers in a city of 166,000.
141. On Giulio Cesare's attitudes, see Caroline Castiglione, "Adversarial Literacy: How Peasant Politics Influenced Noble Governing of the Roman Countryside during the Early Modern Period," *American Historical Review* 109 (2004): 783–804.
142. Calvi, *Il contratto morale*, esp. pp. x, 29–32, 70, 82, 112–18, 158–61.
143. See Chapter 2 of this volume.
144. Lynn Hunt, "The Paradoxical Origins of Human Rights," in *Human Rights and Revolutions*, ed. Jeffrey N. Wasserstrom, Lynn Hunt, and Marilyn B. Young (Lanham, MD, 2000), pp. 3–17. On emotion and the law, see António Manuel Hespanha,"Early Modern Law and the Anthropological Imagination," in *Early Modern History and the Social Sciences*, ed. John Marino (Kirksville, MO, 2002), pp. 191–204, esp. pp. 195–7.
145. BAV, Archivio Barberini, Indice IV, 1572, 251r (18 September 1726): Petition of Cardinal Francesco to the Pope.
146. BAV, Archivio Barberini, Indice II, 1329 (23 February 1727): Letter of Olimpia Giustiniani to Pope Benedict XIII.
147. Ibid., 231r (1 March 1727): Letter from Cardinal Francesco to Camilla.
148. Martha C. Nussbaum, *Upheavals of Thought: The Intelligence of Emotions* (Cambridge, 2001), pp. 3–4.
149. Hunt, "The Paradoxical Origins of Human Rights."
150. See Barberini, "La Galleria dei Ritratti," pp. 614–15, for more on Cornelia's rejection of the division of the patrimony as stipulated by Cardinal Francesco.

Conclusion

1. On the significance of agnatic ties for women, see Thomas Kuehn, *Law, Family, and Women: Toward a Legal Anthropology of Renaissance Italy* (Chicago, 1991), esp. "Some Ambiguities in Female Inheritance Ideology in the Renaissance," pp. 238–57; "Daughters, Mothers, Wives, and Widows: Women as Legal Persons," in *Time, Space, and Women's Lives in Early Modern Europe*, ed. Anne J. Schutte, Thomas Kuehn, and Silvana Seidel Menchi (Kirksville, MO, 2001), pp. 97–115.
2. Archivio Segreto Vaticano [hereafter ASV], Archivio Boncompagni Ludovisi, busta 899 (19 September 1685).
3. The expression is by Christiane Klapisch-Zuber, who extended it even to women's status in their fathers' households. See *Women, Family, and Ritual in Renaissance Italy*, trans. Lydia G. Cochrane (Chicago, 1985), p. 118.

4. Giulia Calvi, *Il contratto morale: madri e figli nella Toscana moderna* (Bari, 1994), pp. 23–4, 77–9, 130–4.
5. Calvi, *Il contratto morale*, pp. 28–30.
6. Ibid., p. 115.
7. Ibid., pp. 148–9.
8. Arcangela Tarabotti, *Paternal Tyranny*, ed. and trans. Letizia Panizza (Chicago, 2004), pp. 49–51, 58–60.
9. Tarabotti, *Paternal Tyranny*, pp. 65, 77.
10. Ibid., pp. 61, 68–9, 112, 141–3.
11. Tiziana Plebani documents the paramount importance of the "just and loving father," in Goldoni. See "Un Secolo di sentimenti: Amori e conflitti generazionali nella Venezia del Settecento" (PhD diss., Università Ca' Foscari Venezia, 2008), esp. pp. 73–4, 239–41.
12. Renata Ago, *Carriere e clientele nella Roma barocca* (Bari, 1990), p. 71.
13. Rome presents an intriguing case of clerical masculinity about which we need to know more. Laurie Nussdorfer has advanced this important line of inquiry: "Masculine Hierarchies in Roman Ecclesiastical Households," forthcoming, *European Review of History* (2016); "Men at Home in Baroque Rome," *I Tatti Studies in the Italian Renaissance* 17.1 (Spring 2014): 103–29; "Priestly Rulers, Male Subjects: Swords and Courts in Papal Rome," in *Violent Masculinities: Male Aggression in Early Texts and Culture*, ed. Jennifer Feather and Catherine E. Thomas (Basingstoke, 2013), pp. 109–28.
14. On lawsuits, see Maura Piccialuti, *L'Immortalità dei beni: Fedecommessi e primogeniture a Roma nei secoli xvii e xviii* (Roma, 1999), esp. p. 258.
15. Judith Butler, *Gender Trouble* (New York, 1999), pp. 198–9.
16. For a sixteenth-century point of comparison, see Edward Muir, "The Double Binds of Manly Revenge in Renaissance Italy," in *Gender Rhetorics: Postures of Dominance and Submission in Human History*, ed. Richard C. Trexler (Binghamton, NY, 1994), pp. 65–82.
17. Arlette Farge, "Protestors Plain to See," in *A History of Women in the West: Renaissance and Enlightenment Paradoxes*, ed. Natalie Zemon Davis and Arlette Farge (Cambridge, 1993), pp. 489–505.
18. Cesare Beccaria, *On Crimes and Punishments and Other Writings*, ed. Richard Bellamy, trans. Richard Davies with Virginia Cox and Richard Bellamy (Cambridge, 1995), p. 61.
19. Maggie Günsberg argues that Goldoni's position on the family is essentially conservative. See "Artful Women: Morality and Materialism in Goldoni," in *Gender and the Italian Stage* (Cambridge, 1997), pp. 88–120. Tiziana Plebani offers a more perceptive reading of Goldoni in the context of archival materials. She underscores the shock for contemporaries when faced with rebellion against paternal authority, and the controversial celebration of love as the basis for family life. See "Un Secolo di sentimenti," pp. 59–60, 73–4, 78.
20. Biblioteca Apostolica Vaticana [hereafter BAV], Archivio Barberini, Indice II, 1329, 118r–118v (29 December 1726).
21. BAV, Archivio Barberini, Indice II, 1329, 29r: Petition by Cardinal Francesco Barberini.
22. Irene Polverini Fosi, *Papal Justice: Subjects and Courts in the Papal State, 1500–1750*, trans. Thomas V. Cohen (Washington, 2011), pp. 224–36.
23. Fosi, *Papal Justice*, p. 231.

24. John A. Marino was the first to analyze systematically the way the early modern state acted as a broker between competing interests. See *Pastoral Economics in the Kingdom of Naples* (Baltimore, MD, 1998).
25. Barbara McClung Hallman, *Italian Cardinals, Reform, and the Church as Property* (Berkeley, 1985), p. 162.
26. Lawrence Stone, *The Family, Sex and Marriage in England, 1500–1800* (New York, 1977); Philippe Ariès, *L'enfant et la vie familiale sous l'Ancien Régime* (originally published in Paris in 1960; English translation, 1962). For a further discussion of the works and the subsequent historiography, see the Introduction to this volume, note 80.
27. Martha C. Nussbaum, *Upheavals of Thought: The Intelligence of Emotions* (Cambridge: Cambridge University Press, 2001), pp. 3–4.
28. John Bossy, "Postscript," in *Disputes and Settlements: Law and Human Relations in the West*, ed. John Bossy (Cambridge, 1984), pp. 287–93 (291).
29. Franco Venturi, "Cesare Beccaria and Legal Reform," in *Italy and the Enlightenment: Studies in a Cosmopolitan Century*, ed. with an Introduction by Stuart Woolf, trans. Susan Corsi (London, 1972), pp. 154–64; John H. Langbein, *Torture and the Law of Proof: Europe and England in the Ancien Régime* (Chicago, 2006). Langbein acknowledges legal change but attributes it to the work of magistrates.
30. On the network of female letter writers important to the success of bourgeois families, see David Sabean, *Property, Production, and Family in Neckarhausen, 1700–1870* (Cambridge, 1990).

Bibliography

Archives Consulted and Their Abbreviations

ABIB Archivio Borromeo (Isola Bella)
AC   Archivio Capitolino (Rome)
ADBL Archivio Digitale Boncompagni Ludovisi, Villa Aurora (Rome)
ADP   Archivio Doria Pamphilj (Rome)
ASR   Archivio di Stato (Rome)
ASV   Archivio Segreto Vaticano (Vatican City)
BAV   Biblioteca Apostolica Vaticana (Vatican City)
OFP   Orsini Family Papers, Collection 902, Special Collections, Charles E. Young Research Library (University of California, Los Angeles)

Printed Sources

Abu-Lughod, Lila. "Writing Against Culture." In *Recapturing Anthropology: Working in the Present*, ed. Richard G. Fox, pp. 137–162. Santa Fe, 1991.

Adami, Antonio. *Il Novitiato del Maestro di Casa*. Rome, 1636.

Ago, Renata. "Burocrazia, 'nazioni' e parentele nella Roma del settecento." *Quaderni Storici* 23 (1988): 73–98.

Ago, Renata. *Carriere e clientele nella Roma barocca*. Rome, 1990.

Ago, Renata. "Ecclesiastical Careers and the Destiny of Cadets." *Continuity and Change* 7 (1992): 271–82.

Ago, Renata. "The Family in Rome: Structure and Relationships." In *Rome, Amsterdam: Two Growing Cities in Seventeenth-Century Europe*, ed. Peter van Kessel and Elisja Schulte et al., pp. 85–91. Amsterdam, 1997.

Ago, Renata. "Giochi di squadra: Uomini e donne nelle famiglie nobili del xvii secolo." In *Signori, patrizi, cavalieri in Italia centro-meriodionale nell'età moderna*, ed. Maria Antonietta Visceglia, pp. 256–64. Bari, 1992.

Ago, Renata. "Una Giustizia personalizzata: I Tribunali civili di Roma nel XVII secolo." *Quaderni Storici* 34.2 (1999): 390–412.

Ago, Renata. *Il Gusto delle Cose*. Rome, 2006.

Ago, Renata. "Maria Spada Veralli, la buona moglie." In *Barocco al femminile*, ed. Giulia Calvi, pp. 51–70. Bari, 1992.

Ago, Renata. "Ruoli familiari e statuto giuridico." *Quaderni Storici* 88 (1995): 111–33.

Ago, Renata. "Le Stanze di Olimpia. La principessa Giustiniani Barberini e il linguaggio delle cose." In *I linguaggi del potere nell'età barocca*, vol. 2: *Donne e sfera pubblica*, ed. Francesca Cantù, pp. 171–95. Rome, 2009.

Ago, Renata. "Universel/particulier: femmes et droits de propriété." *Clio* 7 (1998): 101–16.

Ago, Renata. "Young People in the Age of Absolutism: Paternal Authority and Freedom of Choice in Seventeenth-Century Italy." In *A History of Young People in the West*, vol. 1: *Ancient and Medieval Rites of Passage*, ed. Giovanni Levi and Jean-Claude Schmitt and trans. Camille Naish, pp. 283–322. Cambridge, MA, 1997.

Ago, Renata, Maura Palazzi, and Gianna Pomata, eds. "Costruire la Parentela." Special issue of *Quaderni Storici* 86 (1994).

Ajmar-Wollheim, Marta and Flora Dennis, eds. *At Home in Renaissance Italy*. London, 2006.

Albala, Ken. *Eating Right in the Renaissance*. Berkeley, 2002.

Alonzi, Luigi. *Famiglia, Patrimonio e Finanze Nobiliari: I Boncompagni (secoli XVI–XVIII)*. Rome, 2003.

Amayden, Teodoro. *A New Relation of Rome as to the Government of the City; the Noble Families Thereof ... Taken out of one of the Choicest Cabinets of Rome; and English'd by Gio. Torriano, and Italian, and Professor of the Italian Tongue*. London, 1664.

Ambrosini, Federica. "Between Heresy and Free Thought, between the Mediterranean and the North: Heterodox Women in Seventeenth-Century Women." In *Mediterranean Urban Culture, 1400–1700*, pp. 83–94. Exeter, 2000.

Ambrosini, Federica. "Toward a Social History of Women in Venice." In *Venice Reconsidered*, ed. John Martin and Dennis Romano, pp. 420–53. Baltimore, 2000.

Amussen, Susan. *An Ordered Society: Class and Gender in Early Modern England*. London, 1988.

Amussen, Susan and Adele Seeff, eds. *Attending to Early Modern Women*. Cranbury, NJ, 1998.

Andretta, Elisa. *Roma medica: anatomie d'un système médical au XVIe siècle*. Rome, 2011.

Andretta, S. "Francesco Colonna." In *Dizionario degli Italiani* 6: 303–4. Rome, 1964.

Angiolini, F. "Le base economiche del potere aristocratico nell'Italia centrosetten-trionale tra XVI e XVIII secolo." *Società e storia* 1 (1978): 317–31.

"Anna Colonna Barberini." *The Art Quarterly* 9.3 (1946): 270–3.

Appadurai, Arjun, ed. *The Social Life of Things: Commodities in Cultural Perspective*. Cambridge, 1986.

Arcangelo, Alessandro. *Recreation in the Renaissance: Attitudes toward Leisure and Past Times in European Culture 1425–1675*. Basingstoke, 2003.

Ariès, Philippe. *Centuries of Childhood: A Social History of Family Life*, trans. Robert Baldick. New York, 1962.

Astarita, Tommaso. *The Continuity of Feudal Power: The Caracciolo di Briena in Spanish Naples*. Cambridge, 1992.

Baernstein, P. Renée. "Sposa, figlia, sorella e vecchia madre: Invecchiare donna in età moderna, tra demografia e cultura." *Storia delle donne* 2 (2006): 1–19.

Barbagli, Marzio. *Sotto lo Stesso Tetto: Mutamenti della famiglia in Italia dal XV al XX secolo*. Bologna, 1984.

Barberini, Maria Giulia. "La *galleria dei ritratti* nel mezzanino di palazzo Barberini. Una strategia di famiglia." In *I Barberini e la Cultura Europea del Seicento*, ed. Lorenza Mochi Onori, Sebastian Schütze, and Francesco Solinas, pp. 605–18. Rome, 2007.

Barker, Sheila C. "Plague Art in Early Modern Rome: Divine Directives and Temporal Remedies." In *Hope and Healing: Painting in Italy in a Time of Plague, 1500–1800*, ed. Gauvin Alexander Bailey, Pamela M. Jones, Franco Mormando, and Thomas W. Worcester, pp. 45–64. Worcester, MA, 2005.

Bastress-Dukehart, Erica. "Negotiating for Agnes' Womb." In *Contested Spaces of Nobility in Early Modern Europe*, ed. Matthew P. Romaniello and Charles Lipp, pp. 41–59, Burlington, VT, 2011.

Beccaria, Cesare. *On Crimes and Punishments and Other Writings*, ed. Richard Bellamy, trans. Richard Davies with Virginia Cox and Richard Bellamy. Cambridge, 1995.

Bell, Rudolph M. *How to Do It: Guides to Good Living for Renaissance Italians*. Chicago, 1999.

Benadusi, Giovanna. "The Gender Politics of Vittoria della Rovere." In *Medici Women: The Making of a Dynasty in Gran Ducal Tuscany*, ed. Giovanna Benadusi and Judith Brown. Toronto: Centre for Reformation and Renaissance Studies, forthcoming.

Benadusi, Giovanna. "Investing the Riches of the Poor: Servant Women and Their Last Wills." *American Historical Review* 109.3 (2004): 805–26.

Beneš, Mirka. "Villa Pamphilj 1630–1670: Family, Gardens and Land in Papal Rome." PhD dissertation, Yale University, 1989.

Bolis, Ezio. *L'Uomo tra Peccato, Grazia e Libertà nell'Opera di Paolo Segneri sj (1624–1694)*. Rome, 1996.

Borello, Benedetta. "Parlare e tacere di potere. La conversazione epistolare tra fratelli aristocratici (secoli XVII–XVIII)." In *I linguaggi del potere nell'età barocca*, vol. 2: *Donne e sfera pubblica*, ed. Francesca Cantù, pp. 143–69. Rome, 2009.

Borello, Benedetta. *Trame sovrapposte: La socialità aristocratica e le reti di relazioni femminili a Roma (XVII–XVIII)*. Naples, 2003.

Bossy, John, ed. *Disputes and Settlements: Law and Human Relations in the West*. Cambridge, 1984.

Bowron, Edgar Peters and Joseph J. Rishel, eds. *Art in Rome in the Eighteenth Century*. Philadelphia, 2000.

Boydston, Jeanne. "Gender as a Question of Historical Analysis." *Gender and History* 20.3 (2008): 558–83.

Brooke, John L. "Reason and Passion in the Public Sphere: Habermas and the Cultural Historians." *Journal of Interdisciplinary History* 29.1 (1998): 43–67.

Brown, Judith C. and Robert C. Davis, *Gender and Society in Renaissance Italy*. London, 1998.

Brown, Patricia Fortini, "Children and Education." In *At Home in Renaissance Italy*, ed. Marta Ajmar-Wollheim and Flora Dennis, pp. 136–43. London, 2006.

Bryson, Frederick Robertson. *The Point of Honor in Sixteenth-Century Italy: An Aspect of the Life of the Gentleman*. New York, 1935.

Burke, Peter. *The Fabrication of Louis XIV*. New Haven, CT, 1992.

Burke, Peter. "Representations of the Self from Petrarch to Descartes." In *Rewriting the Self: Histories from the Renaissance to the Present*, ed. Roy Porter, pp. 17–28. London, 1997.

Burke, Peter. "Varieties of Performance in Seventeenth-Century Italy." In *Performativity and Performance in Baroque Rome*, ed. Peter Gillgren and Mårten Snickare, pp. 15–23. Burlington, VT, 2012.

Butler, Judith. *Gender Trouble*, 2nd edition. New York, 1990.

Bynum, Caroline Walker. *Holy Feast and Holy Fast*. Berkeley, 1987.

Cabré, Montserrat. "Keeping Beauty Secrets in Early Modern Iberia." In *Secrets and Knowledge in Medicine and Science, 1500–1800*, ed. Elaine Leong and Alisha Rankin, pp. 167–90. Burlington, VT, 2011.

Cabré, Montserrat. "Women or Healers?: Household Practices and the Categories of Health Care in Late Medieval Iberia." *Bulletin of the History of Medicine* 82.1 (2008): 18–51.

Cabrera, Miguel A. "Language, Experience, and Identity: Joan W. Scott's Theoretical Challenge to Historical Studies." In *The Question of Gender: Joan W. Scott's Critical Feminism*, ed. Judith Butler and Elizabeth Weed, pp. 31–49. Bloomington, IN, 2011.

Cacciaglia, Luigi. "L'archivio del Monastero dell'Incarnazione detto 'le Barberine' alla Biblioteca Vaticana." In *Vite consacrate: gli archivi delle organizzazioni religiose femminili*, Atti del Convegno, Ravenna 28 sett. 2006, *Atti e memorie della deputazione di storia patria per l'Emilia e la Romagna 2007*.

Caffiero, Marina, "Sovrane nella Roma dei papi. Cerimoniali femminili, ruoli politici e modelli religiosi." In *I linguaggi del potere nell'età barocca*, vol. 2: *Donne e sfera pubblica*, ed. Francesca Cantù, pp. 97–123. Rome, 2009.

Caffiero, Marina and Manola Ida Venzo, eds. *Scritture di donne: La memoria restiutita*. Rome, 2007.

Calvi, Giulia. *Il Contratto morale: Madri e figli nella Toscana moderna*. Bari, 1994.

Calvi, Giulia. "'Cruel' and 'Nurturing' Mothers: The Construction of Motherhood in Tuscany (1500–1800)." *L'Homme* 17.1 (2006): 75–92.

Calvi, Giulia. "Maddalena Nerli and Cosimo Tornabuoni: A Couple's Narrative of Family History in Early Modern Florence." *Renaissance Quarterly* 45.2 (1992): 312–39.

Calvi, Giulia. "Reconstructing the Family: Widowhood and Remarriage in Tuscany in the Early Modern Period." In *Marriage in Italy, 1300–1650*, ed. Trevor Dean and K. J. P. Lowe, pp. 275–96. Cambridge, 1991.

Calvi, Giulia. "Sans espoir d'hériter: Les mères, les enfants, et l'État en Toscane, XVIe–XVIIe siècles." *CLIO: Histoire, Femmes, et Sociétés* 21 (2005): 43–68.

Caravale, Mario and Alberto Caracciolo. *Lo Stato pontificio da Martino V a Pio IX*. Turin, 1978.

Castiglione, Caroline. "Accounting for Affection: Battles between Aristocratic Mothers and Sons in Eighteenth-Century Rome." *Journal of Family History* 25 (2000): 405–31.

Castiglione, Caroline. "Adversarial Literacy: How Peasant Politics Influenced Noble Governing of the Roman Countryside during the Early Modern Period." *American Historical Review* 109 (2004): 783–804.

Castiglione, Caroline. "Mothers and Children." In *The Renaissance World*, ed. John Jeffries Martin, pp. 381–97. New York, 2007.

Castiglione, Caroline. *Patrons and Adversaries: Nobles and Villagers in Italian Politics, 1640–1760*. New York: Oxford University Press, 2005.

Castiglione, Caroline. "Peasants at the Palace: Wet Nurses and Aristocratic Mothers in Early Modern Rome." In *Medieval and Renaissance Lactations – Images, Rhetorics, Practices*, ed. Jutta Sperling, pp. 79–99. Burlington, VT, 2013.

Castiglione, Caroline. "The Politics of Mercy: Village Petitions and a Noblewoman's Justice in the Roman Countryside in the Eighteenth Century." In *Empowering Interactions: Political Cultures and the Emergence of the State in Europe, 14th–19th Centuries*, ed. Wim Blockmans, André Holenstein, and Jon Mathieu, pp. 79–90. Aldershot, 2009.

Castiglione, Caroline. "To Trust is Good but Not to Trust is Better: An Aristocratic Woman in Search of Social Capital in Seventeenth-Century Rome." In *Sociability and Its Discontents: Civil Society, Social Capital, and Their Alternatives in Late Medieval and Early Modern Europe*, ed. Nicholas A. Eckstein and Nicholas Terpstra, pp. 149–70. Turnhout, 2009.

Castiglione, Caroline. "When a Woman 'Takes' Charge: Marie-Anne de la Trémoille (1642?–1722) and the End of the Patrimony of the Dukes of Bracciano." *Viator* 39.2 (2008): 363–79.

Cavallo, Sandra. *Artisans of the Body in Early Modern Italy*. Manchester, 2007.

Cavallo, Sandra. "Health, Hygiene and Beauty." In *At Home in Renaissance Italy*, ed. Marta Ajmar-Wollheim and Flora Dennis, pp. 174–87. London, 2006.

Cavallo, Sandra. "Proprietà o possesso? Composizione e controllo dei beni delle donne a Torino (1650–1710)." In *Le Ricchezze delle donne: Diritti patrimoniali e poteri familiari in Italia (XIII–XIX secc.)*, ed. Giulia Calvi and Isabelle Chabot, pp. 187–207. Turin, 1998.

Cavallo, Sandra. "Secrets to Healthy Living: The Revival of the Preventive Paradigm in Late Renaissance Italy." In *Secrets and Knowledge in Medicine and Science, 1500–1800*, ed. Elaine Leong and Alisha Rankin, pp. 191–212. Burlington, VT, 2011.

Cavallo, Sandra and Simona Cerutti. "Female Honor and the Social Control of Reproduction in Piedmont between 1600 and 1800." In *Sex and Gender in Historical Perspective*, ed. Edward Muir and Guido Ruggiero, pp. 73–109. Baltimore, 1990. Cavallo, Sandra and David Gentilcore, eds. *Spaces, Objects and Identities in Early Modern Italian Medicine*. Oxford, 2008.

Cavallo, Sandra and Tessa Storey. *Healthy Living in Late Renaissance Italy*. Oxford, 2013.

Celletti, Vincenzo. *Gli Orsini di Bracciano*. Rome, 1963.

Cermakian, Marianne. "La Princesse des Ursins: Sa Vie et Ses Lettres." PhD dissertation, University of Paris, 1969.

Chabot, Isabelle. "Seconde nozze e identità materna nella Firenze del tardo Medioevo." In *Tempi e spazi di vita femminile tra medioevo ed età moderna*, ed. Silvana Seidel Menchi, Anne Jacobson Schutte, and Thomas Kuehn, pp. 493–523. Bologna, 1999.

Chartier, Roger, ed. *A History of Private Life: the Passions of the Renaissance*. Cambridge, 1989.

Chavarria, Elisa Novi. "Ideologia e comportamenti familiari nei Predicatori Italiani tra cinque e settecento: tematiche e modelli." *Rivista Storica Italiana* 100.3 (1988): 679–723.

Chojnacka, Monica. *Working Women of Early Modern Venice*. Baltimore, 2001.

Chojnacki, Stanley. "'The Most Serious Duty': Motherhood, Gender, and Patrician Culture in Renaissance Venice." *Journal of Family History* 17.4 (1992): 371–95.

Chojnacki, Stanley. *Women and Men in Renaissance Venice: Twelve Essays on Patrician Society*. Baltimore, 2000.

Christiansen, Ann and Barbara Sebek. "The Traffic in/by Women: Placing Women in Real and Symbolic Economies." In *Attending to Early Modern Women*, ed. Susan Amussen and Adele Seefe, pp. 105–7. Newark, 1998.

Cipolla, Carlo. "The Medical Profession in Galileo's Tuscany." In *Public Health and the Medical Profession in the Renaissance*, pp. 67–124. Cambridge, 1976.

Cohen, Elizabeth S. "Miscarriages of Apothecary Justice: Un-Separate Spaces of Work and Family in Early Modern Rome." In *Spaces, Objects and Identities in*

Early Modern Italian Medicine, ed. Sandra Cavallo and David Gentilcore, pp. 8–32. Oxford, 2008.

Cohen, Elizabeth S. "The Trials of Artemisia Gentileschi: A Rape as History." *Sixteenth-Century Journal* 31.1 (2000): 47–75.

Cohen, Elizabeth S. and Thomas Cohen. *Daily Life in Renaissance Italy*. Westport, CT, 2001.

Cohn, Samuel. *Women in the Streets*. Baltimore, 1996.

Colonna, Prospero. *I Colonna*. Rome, 1927.

Constance, Jordan. "The Household and the State: Transformations in the Representation of an Analogy from Aristotle to James I." *Modern Language Quarterly* 54 (1993): 307–26.

Cook, Harold J. *The Decline of the Old Medical Regime in Stuart London*. Ithaca, NY, 1986.

Cortese, Isabella. *I Secreti della Signora Isabella Cortese ne' Quali si Contengono cose minerali, medecinali, arteficiose & alchimiche ...(Venice, 1584)*. With an introduction by Chicca Gagliardo. Milan, 1995.

Cowan, A. F. "Love, Honour and the *Avogaria de Comun* in Early Modern Venice." *Archivio Veneto* 144 (1995): 5–19.

Cowan, A. F. *The Urban Patriciate, Lübeck and Venice, 1580–1700*. Cologne, 1986.

Cox, Virginia. *Women's Writing in Italy: 1400–1650*. Baltimore, 2008.

Crabb, Ann. "How to Influence Your Children: Persuasion and Form in Alessandra Macigni Strozzi's Letters to Her Sons." In *Women's Letters Across Europe, 1400–1700: Form and Persuasion*, ed. Jane Couchman and Ann Crabb, pp. 21–41. Burlington, VT, 2005.

Crabb, Ann. "'If I Could Write': Margherita Datini and Letter Writing, 1385–1410." *Renaissance Quarterly* 60 (2007): 1170–206.

Crabb, Ann and Jane Couchman, eds. *Women's Letters Across Europe, 1400–1700: Form and Persuasion*. Burlington, VT, 2005.

Crouzet-Pavan, Elisabeth. "Les faux-semblants d'une histoire des relations affectives: L'exemple italien." In *The Household in Late Medieval Cities: Italy and Northwestern Europe Compared*, ed. Myriam Carlier and Tim Soens, pp. 147–63. Leuven, 2000.

Cunningham, Hugh. *Children and Childhood in Western Society since 1500*, 2nd edition. Harlowe, 2005.

D'Amelia, Marina. "Becoming a Mother in the Seventeenth Century: The Experience of a Roman Noblewoman." In *Time, Space, and Women's Lives in Early Modern Europe*, ed. Anne Jacobson Schutte, Thomas Kuehn, and Silvana Seidel Menchi, pp. 223–44. Kirksville, MO, 2001.

D'Amelia, Marina. "Nepotismo al femminile. Il caso di Olimpia Maidalchini Pamphilj." In *La Nobiltà romana in età moderna*, ed. Maria Antonietta Visceglia, pp. 353–99. Rome, 2001.

D'Amelia, Marina. "La nuova Agrippina. Olimpia Maidalchini Pamphilj e la tirannia femminile nell'immaginario politico del Seicento." In *I linguaggi del potere nell'età barocca*, vol. 2: *Donne e sfera pubblica*, ed. Francesca Cantù, pp. 45–95. Rome, 2009.

D'Amelia, Marina. "La Presenza delle madri nell'Italia medievale e moderna." In *Storia della Maternità*, pp. 3–52. Rome, 1997.

D'Amelia, Marina. "Lo scambio epistolare tra Cinque e Seicento: scene di vita quotidiana e aspirazioni segrete." In *Per Lettera: La scrittura epistolare femminile tra archivio e tipografia secoli XV–XVII*, ed. Gabriella Zarri, pp. 79–110. Rome, 1999.

Davis, J. C. *A Venetian Family and Its Fortune 1500–1900: The Donà and the Conservation of Their Wealth.* Philadelphia, 1975.

Davis, Natalie Zemon. "Boundaries and the Sense of Self in Sixteenth-Century France." In *Reconstructing Individualism: Autonomy, Individuality, and the Self in Western Thought*, ed. Thomas C. Heller, Morton Sosna, and David E. Wellbery, pp. 53–63. Stanford, 1986.

Davis, Natalie Zemon. *Fiction in the Archives.* Stanford, 1987.

Davis, Natalie Zemon. *Women on the Margins.* Cambridge, MA, 1995.

Davis, Natalie Zemon and and Arlette Farge, eds. *A History of Women: Renaissance and Enlightenment Paradoxes.* Cambridge, MA, 1993.

Dean, Trevor and K. J. P. Lowe, eds. *Marriage in Italy, 1300–1650.* Cambridge, 1991.

Del Re, Niccolò. *La Curia Romana. Lineamenti storico-giurici.* 3rd edition. Rome, 1970.

Delumeau, Jean. *Vie économique et sociale de Rome dans la seconde moitié du XVIe siècle.* 2 vols. Paris, 1957–59.

deMause, Lloyd, ed. *History of Childhood.* London, 1974.

De Renzi, Silvia. "A Career in Manuscripts: Genres and Purposes of a Physician's Writing in Rome, 1600–1630." *Italian Studies* 66.2 (2011): 234–48.

De Renzi, Silvia. "Medical Competence, Anatomy and the Polity in Seventeenth-Century Rome." In *Spaces, Objects and Identities in Early Modern Italian Medicine*, ed. Sandra Cavallo and David Gentilcore, pp. 79–95. Oxford, 2008.

De Renzi, Silvia. "Tales from Cardinals' Deathbeds: Medical Hierarchy, Courtly Etiquette and Authority in the Counter Reformation." In *Être médecin à la cour: Italie, France et Espagne, XIII–XVIII siècles*, ed. Elisa Andretta and Marilyn Nicoud, pp. 235–58. Florence, 2013.

Dewald, Jonathan. *Aristocratic Experience and the Origins of Modern Culture, France, 1570–1715.* Berkeley and Los Angeles, 1993.

Dewald, Jonathan. *The European Nobility: 1400–1800.* Cambridge, 1996.

Diefendorf, Barbara B. "Give Us Back Our Children: Patriarchal Authority and Parental Consent to Religious Vocations in Early Counter-Reformation France." *Journal of Modern History* 68 (1996): 265–307.

Doise, Willem. "Social Representations in Personal Identity." In *Social Identity: International Perspectives*, ed. Stephen Worchel, J. Francisco Morales, Darío Pàez, and Jean-Claude Deschamps, pp. 14–23. London, 1998.

Donati, Claudio. *L'idea di nobiltà in Italia, secoli XIV–XVIII.* Bari, 1988.

Donato, Maria Pia and Kraye, Jill, eds. *Conflicting Duties: Science, Medicine and Religion in Rome, 1550–1770.* London, 2003.

Doniger, Wendy. *The Implied Spider.* New York, 1999.

Dooley, Brendan. *Morandi's Last Prophecy and the End of Renaissance Politics* Princeton, 2002.

Dunn, Marilyn. "Piety and Patronage in Seicento Rome: Two Noblewomen and Their Convents." *Art Bulletin* 74.4 (1994): 644–64.

Dunn, Marilyn. "Spiritual Philanthropists: Women as Convent Patrons in Seicento Rome." In *Women and Art in Early Modern Europe: Patrons, Collectors, and Connoisseurs*, ed. Cynthia Lawrence, pp. 154–88. State College, PA, 1997.

Dursteler, Eric R. *Renegade Women: Gender, Identity, and Boundaries in the Early Modern Mediterranean.* Baltimore, 2011.

Eamon, William. "How to Read a Book of Secrets." In *Secrets and Knowledge in Medicine and Science, 1500–1800*, ed. Elaine Leong and Alisha Rankin, pp. 23–46. Burlington, VT, 2011.

Eamon, William. *The Professor of Secrets*. Washington, 2010.
Ehrlich, Tracy L. "... dall'Agricoltura venne la Nobiltà ...": The Rural Landscape of the Villa Mondragone near Frascati." In *Villas and Gardens in Early Modern Italy and France*, ed. Mirka Beneš and Dianne Harris, pp. 114–37. Cambridge, 2001.
Ehrlich, Tracy L. *Landscape and Identity in Early Modern Rome: Villa Culture at Frascati in the Borghese Era*. Cambridge, 2002.
Eisenach, Emlyn. *Husbands, Wives, and Concubines*. Kirksville, MO, 2004.
Ellington, Donna Spivey. *From Sacred Body to Angelic Soul: Understanding Mary in Late Medieval and Early Modern Europe*. Washington, DC, 2001.
Esposito, Anna. "Men and Women in Roman Confraternities." In *The Politics of Ritual Kinship: Confraternities and Social Order in Early Modern Italy*, pp. 82–97. Cambridge, 1999.
Farge, Arlette. "Protestors Plain to See." In *A History of Women in the West: Renaissance and Enlightenment Paradoxes*, ed. Natalie Zemon Davis and Arlette Farge, pp. 489–505. Cambridge, 1993.
Farr, James. *Hands of Honor, Artisans and their World in Dijon, 1550–1650*. Ithaca, NY, 1988.
Farr, James. "Honor, Law, and Custom in Renaissance Europe." In *A Companion to the Worlds of the Renaissance*, ed. Guido Ruggiero, pp. 124–38. London, 2002.
Feci, Simona. *Pesci fuor d'acqua: donne a Roma in età moderna, diritti e patrimoni*. Rome, 2004.
Feci, Simona and Maria Antonietta Visceglia, "Tra due famiglie: Anna Colonna Barberini "prefettessa" di Roma." In *I linguaggi del potere nell'età barocca*, vol. 2: *Donne e sfera pubblica*, ed. Francesca Cantù, pp. 257–327. Rome, 2009.
Ferraro, Joanne M. *Marriage Wars in Late Renaissance Venice*. New York, 2001.
Ferraro, Richard. "The Nobility of Rome, 1560–1700: A Study of Its Composition, Wealth, and Investments." PhD dissertation, University of Wisconsin-Madison, 1994.
Fildes, Valerie. *Breasts, Bottles, and Babies: A History of Infant Feeding*. Edinburgh, 1986.
Fildes, Valerie. *Wet Nursing: A History from Antiquity to the Present*. Oxford, 1988.
Findlen, Paula, Wendy Wassyng Roworth, and Catherine Sama, eds. *Italy's Eighteenth Century: Gender and Culture in the Age of the Grand Tour*. Stanford, 2009.
Fiorani, Luigi. "Monache e monasteri Romani nell'Età del Quietismo." *Ricerche per la storia religiosa di Roma* I (1977): 63–111.
Flandrin, Jean-Louis. *Families in Former Times: Kinship, Household and Sexuality in Early Modern France*. Cambridge, 1979.
Fonte, Moderata. *The Worth of Women*, ed. and trans. Virginia Cox. Chicago, 1997.
Fosi, Irene. *All'ombra dei Barberini. Fedeltà e servizio nella Roma barocca*. Rome, 1997.
Fosi, Irene. "'Molto Illustre et Amattissimo figlio': Lettere di Laura Marsili a Fabio Chigi (1629–39)." *Dimensioni e Problemi della Ricerca Storica* 2 (2004): 207–29.
Fosi, Irene. *Papal Justice: Subjects and Courts in the Papal State, 1500–1750*, trans. Thomas V. Cohen. Washington, 2011.
Fosi, Irene. "Sovranità, patronage, e giustizia: suppliche e lettere alla corte romana nel primo Seicento." In *La Corte di Roma tra Cinque e Seicento 'teatro' della politica europea*, ed. Maria Antonietta Visceglia, pp. 207–41. Rome, 1998.

Fosi, Irene and Maria Antonietta Visceglia. "Marriage and Politics at the Papal Court in the Sixteenth and Seventeenth Centuries." In *Marriage in Italy, 1300–1650*, ed. Trevor Dean and K. J. P. Lowe, pp. 197–224. Cambridge, 1991.

Fragnito, Gigliola. "La trattatistica cinque e seicentesca sulla corte cardinalizia." *Annali dell'Istituto Storico Italo-Germanico in Trento* 18 (1991): 135–85.

Frigerio, Bartolomeo. *L'Economo Prudente*. Rome, 1629.

Furet, François and Jacques Ozouf. *Lire et Écrire: L'alphabétisation des français de Calvin à Jules Ferry*. 2 vols. Paris, 1977.

Gallucci, Margaret A. *Benvenuto Cellini: Sexuality, Masculinity, and Artistic Identity in Renaissance Italy*. Basingstoke, 2003.

Gentilcore, David. *Healers and Healing in Early Modern Italy*. Manchester and New York, 1998.

Gentilcore, David. "The Organisation of Medical Practice in Malpighi's Italy." In *Marcello Malpighi: Anatomist and Physician*, ed. Domenico Bertoloni Meli, pp. 75–110. Florence, 1997.

Gigli, Giacinto. *Diario Romano (1608–1670)*, ed. Giuseppe Ricciotti. Rome, 1958.

Gillgren, Peter and Mårten Snickare, eds. *Performativity and Performance in Baroque Rome*. Burlington, VT, 2012.

Ginzburg, Carlo. *The Cheese and the Worms*, trans. John and Anne Tedeschi. Baltimore, 1980.

Ginzburg, Carlo. "Clues: Roots of an Evidential Paradigm." *Clues, Myths, and the Historical Method*, trans. John and Anne Tedeschi, pp. 96–125. Baltimore, 1986.

Ginzburg, Carlo. "The Inquisitor as Anthropologist." in *Clues, Myths, and the Historical Method*, trans. John and Anne Tedeschi, pp. 156–64. Baltimore, 1989.

Ginzburg, Carlo. "Microstoria: Due or tre cose che so di lei." *Quaderni storici* 86.2 (1994): 511–39.

Giuffra, V. et al., "Rickets in a High Social Class of Renaissance Italy: The Medici Children." *International Journal of Osteoarcheology* (2013): 10.1002/oa.2324.

Green, Monica. "Women's Medical Practice and Health Care in Medieval Europe." *Signs* 14.2 (1989): 434–73.

Greenblatt, Stephen J. *Renaissance Self-Fashioning: From More to Shakespeare*. Chicago, 1980.

Grendi, Edoardo. "Ripensare la microstoria?" *Quaderni storici* 86.2 (1994): 539–49.

Grew, Raymond. "Finding Social Capital: The French Revolution in Italy." *Journal of Interdisciplinary History* 29.3 (1999): 407–33.

Grieco, Sara Matthews. "Breastfeeding, Wet Nursing and Infant Mortality in Europe (1400–1800)." In *Historical Perspectives on Breastfeeding*, pp. 15–62. Florence, 1991.

Grieco, Sara Matthews. "Persuasive Pictures: Didactic Prints and the Construction of the Social Identity of Women in Sixteenth-Century Italy." In *Women in Italian Renaissance Culture and Society*, ed. Letizia Panizza, pp. 285–314. London: 2000.

Grieco, Sara Matthews and Sabrina Brevaglieri. *Monaca, Moglie, Serva, Cortigiana: Vita e immagine delle donne tra Rinascimento e Controriforma*. Florence, 2001.

Groppi, Angela. "La Malinconia di Lucrezia Barberini D'Este." In *I linguaggi del potere nell'età barocca*, vol. 2: *Donne e sfera pubblica*, ed. Francesca Cantù, pp. 197–227. Rome, 2009.

Groppi, Angela. "La Sindrome Malinconica di Lucrezia Barberini D'Este." *Quaderni Storici*: 129.3 (2008): 725–49.

Gross, Hanns. *Rome in the Age of Enlightenment*. Cambridge, 1990.

Grubb, James. *Provincial Families of the Renaissance: Private and Public Life in the Veneto*. Baltimore, 1996.

Guarini, Elena Fasano. "The Prince, the Judges and the Law: Cosimo I and Sexual Violence, 1558." In *Crime, Society and the Law in Renaissance Italy*, ed. Trevor Dean and K. J. P. Lowe, pp. 121–41. Cambridge, 1994.

Guglielmi, F. "Anna Colonna Barberini e il Monastero di Regina Coeli." *Bollettino Alma Roma* 32.3–4 (1991): 51–69.

Günsberg, Maggie. "Artful Women: Morality and Materialism in Goldoni." In *Gender and the Italian Stage*, pp. 88–120. Cambridge, 1997.

Habermas, Jürgen. *The Structural Transformation of the Public Sphere*, trans. Thomas Burger with Frederick Lawrence. Cambridge, 1991.

Hacke, Daniela. *Women, Sex, and Marriage in Early Modern Venice*. Aldershot, 2004.

Hallman, Barbara McClung. *Italian Cardinals, Reform, and the Church as Property*. Berkeley, 1985.

Hanley, Sarah. "Engendering the State: Family Formation and State Building in Early Modern France." *French Historical Studies* 16 (1989): 4–27.

Hanley, Sarah. "Identity Politics and Rulership in France: Female Political Place and the Fraudulent Salic Law in Christine de Pizan and Jean de Montreuil." In *Changing Identities in Early Modern France*, ed. Michael Wolf, pp. 78–94. Durham, NC, 1997.

Hanley, Sarah. "Social Sites of Political Practice in France: Lawsuits, Civil Rights, and the Separation of Powers in Domestic and State Government, 1500–1800." *American Historical Review* 102: (1997): 7–52.

Hardwick, Julie. *The Practice of Patriarchy: Gender and the Politics of Household Authority in Early Modern France*. University Park, PA, 1998.

Hareven, Tamara. "The History of the Family and the Complexity of Social Change." *American Historical Review* 96 (1991): 95–124.

Hespanha, Antonio Manuel. "Early Modern Law and the Anthropological Imagination of Old European Culture." In *Early Modern History and the Social Sciences*, ed. John Marino, pp. 191–204. Kirksville, MO, 2002.

Hibbard, Howard. "Palazzo Borghese Studies I: The Garden and Its Fountains." *The Burlington Magazine* 100.663 (1958): 205–15.

Hirschman, Albert O. *The Passions and the Interests*. Princeton, 1977.

Höpfl, Harro. *Jesuit Political Thought: The Society of Jesus and the State, c. 1450–1630*. New York, 2004.

Houston, R. A. *Literacy in Early Modern Europe: Culture and Education 1500–1800*, 2nd edition. New York, 2002.

Hudon, William V. "Religion and Society in Early Modern Italy – Old Questions, New Insights." *American Historical Review* 101 (1996): 783–804.

Hufton, Olwen. *The Prospect Before Her*. New York, 1996.

Hughes, Diane Owen. "Representing the Family: Portraits and Purposes in Early Modern Italy." In *Art and History: Images and Their Meaning*, ed. Robert I. Rotberg and Theodore K. Rabb, pp. 7–38. Cambridge, 1986.

Hunt, Lynn. "The Paradoxical Origins of Human Rights." In *Human Rights and Revolutions*, ed. Jeffrey N. Wasserstrom, Lynn Hunt, and Marilyn B. Young, pp. 3–17. Lanham, MD, 2000.

Hurtubise, Pierre. *Une Famille témoin Les Salviati*. Vatican City, 1985.

Hyde, Elizabeth. "Use and Reception." In *A Cultural History of Gardens in the Renaissance, 1400–1650*, 99–125. London, 2013.

Israel, J. *Radical Enlightenment: Philosophy and the Making of Modernity, 1650–1750*. Oxford, 2001.

Jenner, Mark S. R. and Patrick Wallis. "The Medical Marketplace." In *Medicine and the Market in England and Its Colonies, c. 1450–1850*, pp. 1–23. Basingstoke, 2007.

Kandare, Camilla. "CorpoReality: Queen Christina of Sweden and the Embodiment of Sovereignty." In *Performativity and Performance in Baroque Rome*, ed. Peter Gillgren and Mårten Snickare, pp. 47–63. Burlington, VT, 2012.

Kelly, Veronica and Dorothea von Mücke, eds. *Body and Text in the Eighteenth Century*. Stanford, 1994.

Kertzer, David and Marzio Barbagli, eds. *Family Life in Early Modern Times, 1500–1789*, vol. 1: *The History of the European Family*. New Haven, 2002.

Kertzer, David and Richard P. Saller, eds. *The Family in Renaissance Italy: From Antiquity to Present*. New Haven, 1991.

Klapisch-Zuber, Christiane. *Women, Family and Ritual in Renaissance Italy*, trans. Lydia G. Cochrane. Chicago, 1995.

Konstan, David. "Not Quite Emotions: Sentiments That Did Not Make the Grade." In *Affektive Dinge: Objektberührungen in Wissenschaft und Kunst*, ed. Natascha Adamowsky, Robert Felfe, Marco Formisano, Georg Toepfer, and Kirsten Wagner, pp. 113–26. Göttingen, 2011.

Kuehn, Thomas. "Daughters, Mothers, Wives, and Widows: Women as Legal Persons." In *Time, Space, and Women's Lives in Early Modern Europe*, ed. Anne J. Schutte, Thomas Kuehn, and Silvana Seidel Menchi, pp. 97–115. Kirksville, MO, 2001.

Kuehn, Thomas. "*Fideicommissum* and Family: The Orsini di Bracciano." *Viator* 39.2 (2008): 323–41.

Kuehn, Thomas. *Law, Family, and Women: Toward a Legal Anthropology of Renaissance Italy*. Chicago, 1991.

Kuehn, Thomas. "Person and Gender in the Laws." In *Gender and Society in Renaissance Italy*, ed. Judith C. Brown and Robert C. Davis, pp. 87–106. New York, 1998.

Kuehn, Thomas. "Reading Microhistory: The Example of Giovanni and Lusanna." *Journal of Modern History* 61.3 (1989): 512–34.

La Marca, Nicola. *La Nobiltà romana e i suoi strumenti di perpetuazione del potere*. Rome, 2000.

Landes, Joan. *Women and the Public Sphere in the Age of the French Revolution*. Ithaca, NY, 1988.

Langbein, John H. *Torture and the Law of Proof: Europe and England in the Ancien Régime*. Chicago, 2006.

La Rocca, Chiara. "Interessi famigliari e libero consenso nella Livorno del Settecento." In *Matrimoni in dubbio: unioni controverse e nozze clandestine in Italia dal XIV al XVIII secolo*, ed. Silvana Seidel Menchi and Diego Quaglioni, pp. 529–49. Bologna, 2001.

Laslett, Peter and Richard Wall, eds. *Household and Family in Past Time*. Cambridge, 1972.

Laven, Mary. *Virgins of Venice: Broken Vows and Cloistered Lives in the Renaissance Convent*. New York, 2003.

Leone, Stephanie. *The Palazzo Pamphilj in the Piazza Navona: Constructing Identity in Early Modern Rome.* London, 2008.

Leong, Elaine and Alisha Rankin. "Secrets and Knowledge." In *Secrets and Knowledge in Medicine and Science, 1500–1800,* ed. Elaine Leong and Alisha Rankin, pp. 1–20. Burlington, VT, 2011.

Liberati, Francesco. *Il Perfetto Maestro di Casa.* Rome, 1658, 1665, 1668.

Lincoln, Evelyn. "Curating the Renaissance Body." *Word and Image* 17.1&2 (2001): 42–61.

Lindemann, Mary. "Gender Tales: Multiple Identities of Maiden Heinrich, Hamburg 1700." In *Gender in Early Modern German History,* ed. Ulinka Rublack, pp. 131–51. Cambridge, 2002.

Litchfield, R. Burr. *Emergence of a Bureaucracy: the Florentine Patricians, 1530–1790.* Princeton, 1986.

Lodispoto, Giuseppe Sacchi. "Anna Colonna Barberini ed il suo monumento nel monastero di Regina Coeli." *Strenna dei romanisti* 43 (1982): 460–78.

Lombardi, Daniela. "Famiglie di antico regime." In *Innesti: Donne e genere nella storia sociale,* ed. Giulia Calvi, pp. 200–21. Rome, 2004.

Lombardi, Daniela. "Intervention by Church and State in Marriage Disputes in Sixteenth- and Seventeenth-Century Florence." In *Crime, Society and the Law in Renaissance Italy,* ed. Trevor Dean and K. J. P. Lowe, pp. 142–56. Cambridge, 1994.

Lynch, Katerine A. "The Family and the History of Public Life." *Journal of Interdisciplinary History* 24.4 (1994): 665–84.

Mahler, Guendalina Ajello. "The Orsini Family Papers at the University of California, Los Angeles: Property Administration, Political Strategy, and Architectural Legacy." *Viator* 39.2 (2008): 297–321.

Marchetti, Elisabetta. "Le Lettere di Teresa di Gesù: Prime traduzioni ed edizioni italiane." In *Per Lettera: La scrittura epistolare femminile tra archivio e tipografia secoli XV–XVII,* ed. Gabriella Zarri, pp. 263–84. Rome, 1999.

Marino, John A. *Pastoral Economics in the Kingdom of Naples.* Baltimore, 1998.

Marino, John and Thomas Kuehn. *A Renaissance of Conflicts: Visions and Revisions of Law and Society in Italy and Spain.* Toronto, 2004.

Martin, John Jeffries. *Myths of Renaissance Individualism.* Basingstoke, 2004.

Maryks, Robert Aleksander. *Saint Cicero and the Jesuits: The Influence of the Liberal Arts on the Adoption of Moral Probabilism.* Burlington, VT, 2008.

Matthews-Grieco, Sara. "Breastfeeding, Wet Nursing and Infant Mortality in Europe (1400–1800)." In *Historical Perspectives on Breastfeeding,* pp. 15–62. Florence, 1991.

Maza, Sarah C. *Private Lives and Public Affairs: The Causes Celebres of Prerevolutionary France.* Berkeley, 1993.

Maza, Sarah C. "Stories in History: Cultural Narratives in Recent Work in European History." *American Historical Review* 101.5 (1996): 1493–515.

McGough, Laura. "Women, Private Property, and the Limitations of State Authority in Early Modern Venice." *Journal of Women's History* 14.3 (2002): 32–52.

Medick, Hans and David Warren Sabean. "Interest and Emotion in Family and Kinship Studies: A Critique of Social History and Anthropology." In *Interest and Emotion: Essays on the Study of Family and Kinship,* pp. 9–27. Cambridge, 1984.

Meluzzi, Luciano. *I vescovi e gli arcivescovi di Bologna.* Bologna, 1975.

Menchi, Seidel. "The Girl and the Hourglass: Periodization of Women's Lives in Western Preindustrial Societies." In *Time, Space, and Women's Lives in Early Modern Europe*, ed. Anne Jacobson Schutte, Thomas Kuehn, and Silvana Seidel Menchi, pp. 41–74. Kirksville, MO, 2001.

Merola, A. "Francesco Barberini." In *Dizionario Biografico degli Italiani*, vol. 6: 164–5. Rome, 1964.

Merrick, Jeffrey. "The Cardinal and the Queen: Sexual and Political Disorders in the Mazarinades." *French Historical Studies* 18 (1994): 667–99.

Merrick, Jeffrey. "Fathers and Kings: Patriarchalism and Absolutism in Eighteenth-Century French Politics." *Studies on Voltaire and the Eighteenth Century* 308 (1993): 281–303.

Merrick, Jeffrey. "Impotence in Court and at Court." *Studies in Eighteenth-Century Culture* 25 (1996): 187–202.

Messbarger, Rebecca. "Reforming the Female Class: Il Caffè's 'Defense of Women.'" *Eighteenth-Century Studies* 32.3 (1999): 355–69.

Miller, Naomi J. and Naomi Yavneh, eds. *Maternal Measures: Figuring Caregiving in the Early Modern Period*. Burlington, VT, 2000.

Mirrer, Louise, ed. *Upon My Husband's Death: Widows in the Literature and Histories of Medieval Europe*. Michigan, 1992.

Miskimin, Harry A. "Widows Not So Merry: Women and the Courts in Late Medieval France." In *Upon My Husband's Death: Widows in the Literature and Histories of Medieval Europe*, ed. Louise Mirrer, 207–219. Ann Arbor, MI, 1992.

Moch, Leslie Page, Nancy Folbre, Daniel Scott Smith, Laurel L. Cornell, and Louise A. Tilly. "Family Strategy: A Dialogue." *Historical Methods* 20 (1987): 113–25.

Mormando, Franco. "Introduction: Response to the Plague in Early Modern Italy: What the Primary Sources, Printed and Painted, Reveal." In *Hope and Healing: Painting in Italy in a Time of Plague, 1500–1800*, ed. Gauvin Alexander Bailey, Pamela M. Jones, Franco Mormando, and Thomas W. Worcester, pp. 1–44. Worcester, MA, 2005.

Muir, Edward. "The Double Binds of Manly Revenge in Renaissance Italy." In *Gender Rhetorics: Postures of Dominance and Submission in Human History*, ed. Richard C. Trexler, pp. 65–82. Binghamton, NY, 1994.

Muir, Edward. "Observing Trifles." In *Microhistory and the Lost Peoples of Europe*, ed. Edward Muir and Guido Ruggiero, pp. vii–xviii. Baltimore, 1991.

Muir, Edward. "The Sources of Civil Society in Italy." *Journal of Interdisciplinary History* 29.3 (1999): 379–406.

Muir, Edward and Guido Ruggiero, eds. *Sex and Gender in Historical Perspective*. Baltimore, 1990.

Murata, Margaret. *Operas for the Papal Court, 1631–1668*. Ann Arbor, MI, 1981.

Murphy, Caroline P. "Il Ciclo della vita femminile: Norme comportamentali e pratiche di vita." In *Monaca, moglie, serva, cortigiana: Vita e imagine delle donne tra Rinascimento e Controriforma*, ed. Sara F. Matthews-Grieco with the assistance of Sabrina Brevaglieri, pp. 14–47. Florence, 2001.

Murphy, Caroline P. *The Pope's Daughter*. Oxford, 2005.

Musacchio, Jacqueline M. "Conception and Birth." In *At Home in Renaissance Italy*, ed. Marta Ajmar-Wollheim and Flora Dennis, pp. 124–35. London, 2006.

Nader, Helen. *Power and Gender in Renaissance Spain: Eight Women of the Mendoza Family, 1450–1650*. Urbana, 2004.

Newman, Louise M. "Critical Theory and the History of Women: What's at Stake in Deconstructing Women's History." *Journal of Women's History* 2.3 (1991): 58–68.

Nubola, Cecilia. "Supplications between Politics and Justice: The Northern and Central Italian States in the Early Modern Age." In *Petitions in Social History*, ed. Lex Heerma van Voss, pp. 35–56. Cambridge, 2002.

Nussbaum, Martha. *Upheavals of Thought: The Intelligence of Emotions.* Cambridge, 2001.

Nussdorfer, Laurie. *Brokers of Public Trust: Notaries in Early Modern Rome.* Baltimore, 2009.

Nussdorfer, Laurie. *Civic Politics in the Rome of Urban VIII.* Princeton, 1992.

Nussdorfer, Laurie. "Men at Home in Baroque Rome." *I Tatti Studies in the Italian Renaissance* 17.1 (Spring 2014): 103–29.

Nussdorfer, Laurie. "Priestly Rulers, Male Subjects: Swords and Courts in Papal Rome." In *Violent Masculinities: Male Aggression in Early Texts and Culture*, ed. Jennifer Feather and Catherine E. Thomas, pp. 109–28. Basingstoke, 2013.

Offen, Karen, Ruth Roach Pierson, and Jane Rendall, eds. *Writing Women's History: International Perspectives.* Bloomington, 1991.

Olin, Martin. "Diplomatic Performances and the Applied Arts in Seventeenth-Century Europe." In *Performativity and Performance in Baroque Rome*, ed. Peter Gillgren and Peter Mårten Snickare, pp. 25–45. Burlington, VT, 2012.

O'Malley, John. *The First* Jesuits. Cambridge, MA, 1995.

Orland, Barbara. "Enlightened Milk: Reshaping a Bodily Substance into a Chemical Object." In *Materials and Expertise in Early Modern Europe: Between Market and Laboratory*, ed. Ursula Klein and E. C. Spary, pp. 163–97. Chicago, 2010.

Ostovich, Helen and Elizabeth Sauer, eds., assisted by Melissa Smith. "Mothers' Legacies and Medical Manuals." In *Reading Early Modern Women: An Anthology of Texts in Manuscript and Print, 1550 –1700*, pp. 97–101. New York, 2004.

Palmer, Richard. "Medicine at the Papal Court in the Sixteenth Century." In *Medicine at the Courts of Europe, 1500–1837*, ed. Vivian Nutton, pp. 49–78. London, 1990.

Panizza, Letizia and Sharon Wood, eds. *A History of Women's Writing in Italy.* Cambridge, 2001.

Park, Katherine. *Doctors and Medicine in Early Renaissance Florence.* Princeton, 1985.

Park, Katherine. *Secrets of Women: Gender, Generation, and the Origins of Human Dissection.* New York, 2010.

Partner, Peter. *The Pope's Men: The Papal Civil Service in the Renaissance.* Oxford, 1990.

Paschini, Pio. *I Colonna.* Rome, 1945.

Patrizi, Adreana. *Palestrina nel Settecento.* Cava, 1987.

Pecchiai, Pio. *I Barberini.* Rome, 1959.

Perry, Mary Elizabeth. *Gender and Disorder in Early Modern Seville.* Princeton, 1990.

Petrucci, Armando. *Scrivere lettere: una storia plurimillenaria.* Rome, 2008.

Piccialuti, Maura. *L'immortalità dei beni: Fedecommessi e primogeniture a Roma nei secoli xvii e xviii.* Rome, 1999.

Piciché, Bernardo. "La Letteratura del disagio: gli avvertimenti cristiani." In *Argisto Giuffredi: Gentiluomo borghese nel vicereame di Sicilia*, pp. 59–143. Rome, 2006.

Pietrangeli, Carlo. *Palazzo Braschi.* Rome, 1958.

Pitt-Rivers, Julian. "Honour and Social Status." In *Honour and Shame: The Values of Mediterranean Society*, ed. J. G. Peristiany, pp. 19–77. Chicago, 1966.

Plebani, Tiziana. "Un Secolo di sentimenti: Amori e conflitti generazionali nella Venezia del Settecento." PhD dissertation, Università Ca' Foscari Venezia, 2008.

Pollock, Linda A. "Anger and the Negotiation of Relationships in Early Modern England." *The Historical Journal* 47.3 (2004): 567–90.

Pollock, Linda A. "Parent–Child Relations." In *Family Life in Early Modern Times, 1500–1789*, vol. 1: *The History of the European Family*, ed. David I. Kertzer and Marzio Barbagli, pp. 191–220. New Haven, 2001.

Pollock, Linda A. "Rethinking Patriarchy and the Family in Seventeenth Century England." *Journal of Family History* 23 (1998): 3–27.

Pomata, Gianna. *Contracting a Cure: Patients, Healers, and the Law in Early Modern Bologna*, trans. with the assistance of Rosemarie Foy and Anna Taraboletti-Segre. Baltimore, 1998.

Pomata, Gianna. "Family and Gender." In *Early Modern Italy*, ed. John A. Marino, pp. 69–86. Oxford, 2002.

Pomata, Gianna. "Practicing between Earth and Heaven: Women Healers in Seventeenth-Century Bologna." *Dynamis: Acta Hispanica ad Medicinae Scientiarumque Historiam Illustrandam* 19 (1999): 119–43.

Porter, Roy. "The Patient's View: Doing Medical History From Below." *Theory and Society* 14.2 (1985): 175–98.

Povolo, Claudio. *L'Intrigo dell'Onore: Poteri e Istituzoni nella Repubblica di Venezia tra Cinque e Seicento*. Verona, 1997.

Prodi, Paolo. *The Papal Prince: One Body and Two Souls: The Papal Monarchy in Early Modern Europe*, trans. Susan Haskins. Cambridge, 1987.

Prosperi, Adriano. "Spiritual Letters." In *Women and Faith: Catholic Religious Life in Italy from Late Antiquity to the Present*, ed. Lucetta Scaraffia and Gabriella Zarri, pp. 113–28. Cambridge, MA, 1999.

Putnam, Robert D. with Roberto Leonardi and Raffaella Y. Nanetti. *Making Democracy Work: Civic Traditions in Modern Italy*. Princeton, 1993.

Ray, Meredith K. *Writing Gender in Women's Letter Collections of the Italian Renaissance*. Toronto, 2009.

Reinhard, Wolfgang. *Papstfinanz und Nepotismus unter Paul V (1605–1621). Studien und Quellen zur Struktur und zu quantitativen Aspekten des päpstlichen Herrschafssystem*. 2 vols. Stuttgart, 1974.

Reinhardt, Volker. *Kardinal Scipione Borghese 1605–1633: Vermögen, Finanzen und Sozialer Aufsteig*. Tübingen, 1984.

Revel, Jacques. "Microanalisi e costruzione del sociale." *Quaderni storici* 86.2 (1994): 549–75.

Rietbergen, Peter. *Power and Religion in Baroque Rome: Barberini Cultural Politics*. Leiden, 2006.

Romaniello, Matthew P. and Charles Lipp, eds. *Contested Spaces of Nobility in Early Modern Europe*. Burlington, VT, 2011.

Romano, Dennis. *Housecraft and Statecraft*. Baltimore, 1996.

Roper, Lyndal. *The Holy Household: Women and Morals in Reformation Discourse in Early Modern Germany*. Cambridge, 1984.

Rosenthal, Elaine G. "The Position of Women in Renaissance Florence: Neither Autonomy nor Subjection." In *Florence and Italy: Renaissance Studies in Honour of Nicolai Rubinstein*, ed. Peter Denley and Caroline Elam, pp. 369–81. London, 1988.

Rosenwein, Barbara H. "Worrying about Emotions in History." *American Historical Review* 107.3 (2002): 821–45.

Ross, James Bruce. "The Middle-Class Child in Urban Italy, Fourteenth to Early Sixteenth Century." In *The History of Childhood*, ed. Lloyd De Mause, pp. 183–228. London, 1974.

Ross, Sarah Gwyneth. *The Birth of Feminism: Women as Intellect in Renaissance Italy and England*. Cambridge, MA, 2009.

Rossi, Emete. "La fuga del Cardinale Antonio Barberini." *Archivio della Società Romana di Storia Patria* 59 (1936): 303–27.

Rossi-Doria, Anna. *A che punto è la storia delle donne in Italia?* Rome, 2003.

Ruberg, Willemijn. "The Letter as Medicine: Health and Illness in Dutch Daily Correspondence 1770–1850." *Social History of Medicine* 23.3 (2010): 492–508.

Rublack, Ulinka. "Pregnancy, Childbirth and the Female Body in Early Modern Germany." *Past and Present* 150 (1996): 84–110.

Ruggiero, Maria Grazia Pastura. *Le Reverenda Camera Apostolica e i suoi archvi secoli XV–XVIII*. Rome, 1984.

Sabean, David. *Property, Production, and Family in Neckarhausen, 1700–1870*. Cambridge, 1990.

Sama, Catherine. "Liberty, Equality, Frivolity! An Italian Critique of Fashion Periodicals." *Eighteenth-Century Studies* 37.3 (2004): 389–414.

Scanlan, Suzanne. "Doorways to the Demonic and the Divine: Visions of Santa Francesca Romana and the Frescoes of Tor De' Specchi." PhD dissertation. Brown University, 2010.

Scanzani, Barbara. "Camilla e Costanza Barberini: lettere a Urbano VIII." In *Scritture di donne: La memoria restituita*, ed. Marina Caffiero and Manola Ida Venzo, pp. 167–83. Rome, 2004.

Schneider, Jane. "Trousseau as Treasure: Some Contradictions of Late Nineteenth-Century Change in Sicily." In *Beyond the Myths of Culture: Essays in Cultural Materialism*, ed. Eric B. Ross, pp. 323–56. New York, 1985.

Schutte, Anne Jacobson. *By Force and Fear: Taking and Breaking Monastic Vows in Early Modern Europe*. Ithaca, NY, 2011.

Schwartz, Barry. *The Paradox of Choice: Why Less is More*. New York, 2004.

Scott, James C. *Domination and the Arts of Resistance: Hidden Transcripts*. New Haven, 1990.

Scott, Joan Wallach. *Gender and the Politics of History*, 2nd edition. New York, 1999.

Scott, John Beldon. *Images of Nepotism: The Painted Ceilings of Palazzo Barberini*. Princeton, 1991.

Segneri, Paolo. "On Parental Obligation." In *Twelve Sermons*, trans. James Ford. London, 1859.

Segneri, Paolo. *La Manna dell'anima. Ovvero esercizio facile insieme e fruttuoso per chi desidera in qualche modo d'attendere all'orazione. Per tutti i giorni dell'anno.* 4 vols. Bologna, 1673, 1675; Florence, 1679; Milan, 1680.

Segneri, Paolo. *The Manna of the Soul: Meditations for Every Day of the Year*. 2 vols. 2nd edition. London, 1892.

Selwyn, Jennifer D. *A Paradise Inhabited by Devils: The Jesuits' Civilizing Mission in Early Modern Naples*. Burlington, VT, 2004.

Serio, Alessandro. *Una Gloriosa sconfitta: I Colonna tra papato e impero nella prima età*. Rome, 2008.

Signorotto, Gianvittorio and Maria Antonietta Visceglia. *Court and Politics in Papal Rome, 1492–1700.* Cambridge, 2002.

Siraisi, Nancy. *"Historiae,* Natural History, Roman Antiquity, and Some Roman Physicians." In *Historia: Empiricism and Erudition in Early Modern Europe,* ed. Gianna Pomata and Nancy Siraisi, pp. 325–54. Cambridge, 2005.

Smith, Lisa. "The Relative Duties of a Man: Domestic Medicine in England and France, circa 1685–1740." *Journal of Family History* 31.3 (2006): 237–56.

Sneider, Matthew. "Charity and Property – The Patrimonies of Bolognese Hospitals." PhD dissertation, Brown University, 2004.

Sneider, Matthew. "Charity and Property: The Wealth of *opere pie* in Early Modern Bologna." In *Povertà e innovazioni istituzionali in Italia dal Medioevo ad oggi,* ed. Vera Zamagni. Bologna, 2000.

Sperling, Jutta Gisela. *Convents and the Body Politic in Renaissance Venice.* Chicago, 1999.

Sperling, Jutta Gisela, ed. *Medieval and Renaissance Lactations: Images, Rhetorics, Practices.* Burlington, 2013.

Staves, Susan. *Married Women's Separate Property.* Boston, 1990.

Stewart, Frank Henderson. *Honor.* Chicago, 1994.

Stinger, Charles L. *The Renaissance in Rome.* Bloomington, 1985.

Stone, Lawrence. *The Crisis of the Aristocracy, 1558–1641.* London, 1965.

Stone, Lawrence. *The Family, Sex and Marriage in England, 1500–1800.* New York, 1977.

Storey, Tessa. *Carnal Commerce in Counter-Reformation Rome.* Cambridge, 2008.

Storey, Tessa. "Face Waters, Oils, Love Magic and Poison: Making and Selling Secrets in Early Modern Rome." In *Secrets and Knowledge in Medicine and Science, 1500–1800,* ed. Elaine Leong and Alisha Rankin, pp. 143–63. Burlington, VT, 2011.

Strocchia, Sharon T. "Taken into Custody: Girls and Convent Guardianship in Renaissance Florence." *Renaissance Studies* 17.2 (2003): 177–99.

Sussman, George D. *Selling Mothers' Milk: The Wet-Nursing Business in France, 1715–1914.* Urbana, 1982.

Tarabotti, Arcangela. *Paternal Tyranny,* trans. and ed. Letizia Panizza. Chicago, 2004.

Te Brake, W. *Shaping History: Ordinary People in European Politics, 1500–1700.* Berkeley, 1998.

Terpstra, Nicholas. *Abandoned Children of the Italian Renaissance: Orphan Care in Florence and Bologna.* Baltimore, 2005.

Terpstra, Nicholas. "Mothers, Sisters, and Daughters: Girls and Conservatory Guardianship in Late Renaissance Florence." *Renaissance Studies* 17.2 (2003): 201–29.

Thornton, Arland. *Reading History Sideways: The Fallacy and Enduring Impact of the Developmental Paradigm on Family Life.* Chicago, 2005.

Tilly, Louise A. "Women's History and Family History: Fruitful Collaboration or Missed Connection?" *Journal of Family History* 12 (1987): 303–15.

Tosi, Mario. *La società romana dalla feudalità al patriziato (1816–1853).* Rome, 1968.

Urban, Marsha. *Seventeenth-Century Mother's Advice Books.* Gordonsville, VA, 2006.

Valone, Carolyn. "The Art of Hearing: Sermons and Images in the Chapel of Lucrezia della Rovere." *Sixteenth Century Journal* 31.3 (2000): 753–77.

Valone, Carolyn. "Mothers and Sons: Two Paintings for San Bonaventura in Early Modern Rome." *Renaissance Quarterly* 53.1 (2000): 108–32.

Valone, Carolyn. "Piety and Patronage: Women and the Early Jesuits." In *Creative Women in Medieval and Early Modern Italy*, ed. E. Ann Matter and John Coakley, pp. 157–84. Philadelphia, 1994.

Valone, Carolyn. "Spiritual Philanthropists: Women as Convent Patrons in Seicento Rome." In *Women and Art in Early Modern Europe: Patrons, Collectors, and Connoisseurs*, ed. Cynthia Lawrence, pp. 154–88. State College, PA, 1997.

Valone, Carolyn. "Women on the Quirinal Hill: Patronage in Rome, 1560–1630." *The Art Bulletin* 76.1 (1994): 129–46.

Venditti, Gianni with Beatrice Quaglieri. *Archivio Boncompagni Ludovisi. Collectanea Archivi Vaticani*. 5 vols. Vatican City, 2008.

Venturi, Franco. "Cesare Beccaria and Legal Reform." In *Italy and the Enlightenment: Studies in a Cosmopolitan Century*, ed. with an Introduction by Stuart Woolf, trans. Susan Corsi, pp. 154–64. London, 1972.

Visceglia, Maria Antonietta. *Il Bisogno di eternità: i comportamenti aristocratici a Napoli in età moderna*. Naples, 1988.

Visceglia, Maria Antonietta. "La nobiltà romana: dibattito storiografico e ricerche in corso." In *La Nobiltà romana in età moderna: Profili istituzionali e pratiche sociali*. Rome, 2001.

Visceglia, Maria Antonietta, ed. *Signori, patrizi, cavalieri in Italia centro-meridionale nell'età moderna*. Rome, 1992.

Visconti, Pietro Ercole. *Città e famiglie nobili e celebri dello stato Pontificio: Dizionario Storico*. Rome, 1847.

Völkel, Markus. *Römische Kardinalshaushalte des 17.Jahrhunderts: Borghese-Barberini-Chigi*. Tübingen, 1993.

von Pastor, Ludwig. *The History of the Popes from the Close of the Middle Ages*, trans. Ernest Graf et al. 40 vols. London, 1891–1953.

Waddy, Patricia. *Seventeenth-Century Roman Palaces: Use and the Art of the Plan*. Cambridge, 1990.

Walker, Garthine. "Domestic Relations in Early Modern England." *History Workshop Journal* 41 (1996): 281–5.

Walker, Stefanie and Frederick Hammond, eds. *Life and the Arts in the Baroque Palaces of Rome*. New Haven, 1999.

Wangermann, Ernst. *The Austrian Achievement 1700–1800*. London, 1973.

Wiesner, Merry E. *Women and Gender in Early Modern Europe*, 2nd edition. Cambridge, 2000.

Winnicott, Donald. *Holding and Interpretation: Fragment of an Analysis*. New York, 1986.

Zarri, Gabriella, ed. *Per Lettera: La scrittura epistolare femminile tra archivio e tipografia secoli XV–XVII*. Rome, 1999.

Index

Note: dates of birth are given for individuals with the same name; illustrations are indexed by artist; notes are indexed for key terms by scholars; spellings of rural territories are given in early modern form; women are listed with their patrilinear family; "n" after a page reference indicates a note on that page.